D0919930

Scholar's Guide to Intelligence Literature:

Bibliography of the Russell J. Bowen Collection

Scholar's Guide to Intelligence Literature:

Bibliography of the Russell J. Bowen Collection

in the
Joseph Mark Lauinger Memorial Library
Georgetown University

Edited by
Marjorie W. Cline, Carla E. Christiansen,
and
Judith M. Fontaine

Published for
The National Intelligence Study Center

UNIVERSITY PUBLICATIONS OF AMERICA, INC.
Frederick, Maryland

Library of Congress Catalog Card Number: 83-080922
ISBN: 0-89093-540-8.

TABLE OF CONTENTS

FIRST PART

INTELLIGENCE ORGANIZATIONS AND ACTIVITIES

SECOND PART

INTELLIGENCE RELATED TOPICS

INDEX

INTRODUCTION
TO THE BOWEN COLLECTION

I am often asked how I came to assemble the somewhat eclectic collection of publications represented in this bibliography and have been at some pains to come up with a suitable response. The best answer, I believe, is that it grew naturally as a reflection of some of the many professional interests that I have pursued in a series of mini-careers related in one way or another to national security and international affairs. Over the past forty years, in my alter egos of army reserve officer and engineering consultant, I have been associated with such diverse areas as chemical and psychological warfare, information control, special weapons development, arms control inspection, strategic area analysis, foreign technology assessment, and technology transfer, to name a few.

Strange as it may seem, there is a thread of continuity in all of this. It is my long-held view of the essential incompatibility of creativity and organization, coupled with my early awareness of a close relationship between information and profitable action in any goal-directed endeavor. In a general sense, the collection is a reflection of my abiding interest in the vulnerability of large, bureaucratic institutions to the actions of small numbers of highly qualified people, suitably trained, equipped, and motivated. Secrecy, deception, and surprise are, of course, important adjunct features of such action.

What started out as a collection of books relating to military intelligence came to include many volumes on state security, in particular, the secret police depredations of Nazi Germany and Soviet Russia. Later, I began to add writings on a variety of covert activities, such as paramilitary operations, psychological warfare, and secret weapons programs. Some ten years ago, when the collection had grown to about 2,000 titles, I decided to expand my holdings with the thought of creating a data base for writing on these and related subjects during my retirement years. In the meantime, I became aware of the need of Georgetown University for a collection such as mine to support its many teaching and research activities in the fields of foreign affairs and national security. I have made the collection available to Georgetown on a loan basis, with the intention of eventually transferring control entirely to the university.

It is my earnest hope that the collection will help students and scholars to achieve an appreciation of the increasing importance of the intelligence function as societies become ever more complex and bureaucratic. I hope, also, that users of the collection will issue publications which will serve to inform the general public of the essential nature of intelligence and intelligence-related activities as indispensable to maintaining stability in any organized society. Without accurate and timely information, for example, human endeavors stand little chance of success in the face of a determined opposition that makes full use of all intelligence functions.

Lastly, I wish to acknowledge the support and cooperation of a number of persons who have assumed the care and maintenance of the collection at the Joseph Mark Lauinger Memorial Library of Georgetown University. They are Joseph E. Jeffs, University Librarian; G. Martin Barringer, Special Collections Librarian; and Herbert H. Fockler, Special Assistant to the Librarian, who has played the role of catalyst and expediter in all phases of my association with the university. Nor should I fail to acknowledge the inspiration of George C. Constantinides in first calling to my attention Georgetown's need for such a collection. My final words of thanks are due to Ray S. Cline, President of the National Intelligence Study Center, for promoting the concept of this scholar's guide, and to Walter Pforzheimer, dean of intelligence literature collectors, for his constant encouragement and support.

Russell J. Bowen
Colonel, AUS (Ret.)
Arlington, Virginia
March 1983

ACKNOWLEDGEMENTS

A note of appreciation is due to the book dealers of the Western World, particularly those with establishments located along the East Coast of the United States, between Virginia and Maine, without whose entrepreneurial efforts my collection would not have been possible. Further thanks are due to the many individuals who have made voluntary contributions of intelligence-related materials to the Bowen Collection. Their names are listed here, both in grateful recognition of the gifts themselves and in the hope that others will be prompted to come forward in the future with items which may be of interest to scholars of Intelligence.

Capt. Richard W. Bates, USN (Ret.)
Mr. I. D'Arcy Brent
Mr. William W. Buchanan
Ms. Marjorie W. Cline
Dr. Ray S. Cline
Mr. Martin G. Cramer
Prof. Stevan Dedijer
Ms. M. Christine Flowers
Mr. Herbert H. Fockler
Lt. Col. Carl S. Leaver, USAF (Ret.)
Mr. Owen A. Lock
Mr. John Moscato

LCDR Prescott W. Palmer, USN (Ret.)
Mr. Hayden Peake
Dr. Walter Pforzheimer
Dr. Vittorfranco S. Pisano
Dr. I. Ralph Rostron
Mr. Edward F. Sayle
Col. Eugene J. Suto, AUS (Ret.)
Dr. Eugene P. Tadie
Mr. Thomas F. Troy
Ms. Joy W. Viola
Ms. Mary E. Walsh
Ms. Mary M. Young

Russell J. Bowen

FOREWORD

The National Intelligence Study Center (NISC) proudly presents this unique bibliographical guide to facilitate scholars' use of the remarkable special collection of books on intelligence now in the Joseph Mark Lauinger Memorial Library of Georgetown University.

Colonel Russell J. Bowen, the career military officer and bibliophile who put together this private library on the literature of intelligence, wanted to make his books available in an academic community to enrich research and responsible writing on the subject of intelligence and intelligence-related fields. I am much indebted to him for placing the Bowen Collection at Georgetown. For several years, since my retirement from the post of Director of Intelligence and Research at the U.S. Department of State, I have been teaching a pioneer seminar on "Strategic Intelligence and World Power." It is my experience that this special library collection will make it much easier to interest students and faculty members alike in the study of intelligence as a part of the political process and international relations. Accordingly, NISC adopted as its major project for 1981, 1982, and the first quarter of 1983 the cataloguing of some 5,000 titles in the Bowen Collection—now more than 6,000 volumes—and the preparation of this *Scholar's Guide to Intelligence Literature: Bibliography of the Russell J. Bowen Collection.*

The First Part of the Guide covers intelligence organizations and activities. It classifies publications in nine categories according to subject matter under standard terms which the professional intelligence officer uses in describing the key components of the whole intelligence process whereby evidence is collected, analyzed, and provided to policymakers.

Section I contains treatments of various national intelligence establishments.

Section II includes titles pertaining to the *Collection of Information*, a rich category with many case histories of clandestine operations dating from the sixteenth century through the period after World War II. It shows clearly how human effort in espionage supplements the knowledge accumulated from technical means of which the most important are satellite photography and cryptanalysis. When nations conceal within their borders facts that may threaten U.S. security or disturb stability in other parts of the world, collecting the needed data by whatever methods feasible is the first order of business of intelligence agencies.

All of this evidence is examined and reported to government policymakers by research analysts, as is discussed in Section III. Studies on Pearl Harbor indicate that the scholarly function of *Research and Analysis* is crucially important to understanding the fundamental character of foreign countries and their leaders' plans.

Counterintelligence, in Section IV, deals with dangers by hostile secret agents and political police, especially Soviet and Nazi, and techniques employed by the United

States and its friends to negate their efforts or eliminate them altogether. It, too, has extensive coverage.

Covert Action presents political or paramilitary programs conducted abroad by a nation intending to conceal its sponsorship and deny attribution. The books within this category, in Section V, concentrate on the well-known American attempts to support foreign governments or leaders, as in Chile, Cuba, Iran, and Vietnam, friendly to the United States and needing help to maintain political stability.

Subversion, on the other hand, in Section VI, covers Communist and Nazi secret political penetrations throughout the world. These are in a sense historical covert actions hostile to the United States and aimed at bringing target nations within their political control.

Section VII, *Intelligence Support*, lists titles describing administrative and technical support required for the conduct of intelligence activities.

Legal and Moral Considerations and *Criticisms and Exposés*, Sections VIII and IX, cover the problems, restrictions, or limitations of intelligence activities in a free society.

The Second Part, under thirteen diverse intelligence-related topics, lists books and articles dealing with events or subjects that contain illuminating material relevant to one or more of the intelligence functions that are described in the First Part. All of this subject matter is pertinent to an understanding of the new profession, discipline, and academic field—the study of intelligence. The titles reflect world conditions in which intelligence agencies operate. Some of the prime topics are assassinations, international crime (including smuggling and narcotics trade), escape and evasion, political dissent, psychological warfare, and unconventional warfare. The activities of terrorists, guerrillas, mercenaries, and revolutionary movements without foreign sponsorship are included. In addition, the Second Part contains histories of most of the conventional wars and warfare dating, in general, from the American Revolution to the present day.

Marjorie Wilson Cline, an Army G-2 officer during World War II and also a professional librarian, editor, and writer, volunteered her services for this monumental undertaking of preparing the *Scholar's Guide* on behalf of NISC. She has been ably assisted for many months in the final painstaking task of checking and classifying the books and articles by a young researcher with ten years of intelligence experience, Carla E. Christiansen. A third volunteer, Judith M. Fontaine, who also spent almost ten years in the field of intelligence analysis, participated extensively in the work of identifying subject classifications and, in particular, in preparing the index. I am extremely grateful to all three for their heroic work in making the valuable resource accessible for students and researchers interested in different aspects of intelligence activities and related topics.

In the earlier phase of this project, Elizabeth Longley Lacy, a twenty-five-year career intelligence officer in the U.S. Departments of Army and Defense, contributed a great deal to the project. On a part-time basis, three Georgetown University graduate students—Lori Michele Ragosa, J. Casey Hammond, and David Weincek—spent one summer on library research, giving a substantial boost to the volunteers. The whole effort benefited enormously at all times from the enthusiastic backing of the NISC Advisory Board and Board of Directors, as well as of Colonel Bowen himself.

The study of intelligence is a new field of research and much work must be done if future generations are to learn how to avoid some of the mistakes and build upon some of the many achievements of the American intelligence organizations chronicled in the books listed in this bibliography. If this *Scholar's Guide* helps to open the way to better comprehension of what intelligence is and the critical role it plays in our open society, the efforts of NISC in publishing this volume will be eminently worthwhile.

Ray S. Cline, President
National Intelligence Study Center
March 1983

FIRST PART

INTELLIGENCE ORGANIZATIONS AND ACTIVITIES

I. NATIONAL INTELLIGENCE ESTABLISHMENTS

General

Alexandrov, Victor. *O.S.1.services secrets de Staline contre Hitler.* Paris: Editions Planète, 1968, 331 p. (paperback).

Andrew, Christopher. "Whitehall, Washington and the Intelligence Services." *International Affairs,* July 1977, pp. 390-404.

Barker, Elisabeth. *Churchill and Eden at War.* New York: St. Martin's Press, 1978, 346 p.

Blackstock, Paul W. *The Secret Road to World War Two: Soviet Versus Western Intelligence, 1921-1939.* Chicago: Quadrangle Books, 1969, 384 p.

Bryant, Arthur, Sir. *Triumph in the West: A History of the War Years Based on the Diaries of Field Marshal Lord Alanbrooke, Chief of the Imperial General Staff.* Garden City, N.Y.: Doubleday, 1959, 438 p.

Caroz, Yaakov. *The Arab Secret Service[s].* London: Transworld Publishers, 1978, 440 p. (paperback).

Deacon, Richard, *pseud.* (McCormick, Donald). *The Chinese Secret Service.* New York: Taplinger, 1974, 523 p.

Deacon, Richard, *pseud.* (McCormick, Donald). *The Silent War: A History of Western Naval Intelligence.* Newton Abbot, England: David and Charles; New York: Hippocrene Books, 1978, 288 p.

De Gramont, Sanche, *pseud.* (Morgan, Ted). *The Secret War: The Story of International Espionage Since World War II.* New York: Putnam, 1962, 515 p.

De Vosjoli, P.L. Thyraud. *Lamia.* Boston: Little, Brown, 1970, 344 p.

Doris, Charles. *Secret Memoirs of Napoleon: By One Who Never Quitted Him for Fifteen Years.* London: J. Gowans and Son, 1896, 367 p.

Dvornik, Francis. *Origins of Intelligence Services: The Ancient Near East, Persia, Greece, Rome, Byzantium, the Arab Muslim Empires, the Mongol Empire, China, Moscovy.* New Brunswick, N.J.: Rutgers University Press, 1974, 334 p.

Farago, Ladislas. *Burn After Reading: The Espionage History of World War II.* New York: MacFadden-Bartell, 1963, 239 p. (paperback).

Farago, Ladislas. *Spymaster.* New York: Paperback Library, Inc., 1962, 284 p. (paperback edition of *War of Wits: The Anatomy of Espionage and Intelligence.* New York: Funk and Wagnalls, 1954, 379 p.).

Felstead, Sidney Theodore. *Intelligence: An Indictment of a Colossal Failure.* London: Hutchinson, 1941, 253 p.

Fitz Gibbon, Constantine. *Secret Intelligence in the Twentieth Century.* New York: Stein and Day, 1976, 350 p.

Froment, A. *L'espionnage militaire et le service des renseignements en France et à l'étranger.* Paris: F. Juven, Editeur, 1897, 316 p.

Garder, Michel. *La Guerre secrète des services spéciaux français, 1935-1945.* Paris: Plon, 1967, 524 p.

Gauché, General. *Le Deuxième Bureau au Travail (1935-1940).* Paris: Amiot-Dumont, 1953, 239 p. (paperback).

Grant, Hamil. *Spies and Secret Service: The Story of Espionage, its Main Systems and Chief Exponents.* New York: Frederick A. Stokes. 1915, 320 p.

Hahn, James Emanuel. *The Intelligence Service Within the Canadian Corps, 1914-1918.* Toronto: Macmillan of Canada, 1930, 263 p.

Hall, Richard. *The Secret State: Australia's Spy Industry.* Stanmore: Cassell, Australia, 1978, 252 p.

Haswell, Chetwynd John Drake. *Spies and Spymasters: A Concise History of Intelligence.* London: Thames and Hudson, 1977, 176 p.

Ind, Allison. *A Short History of Espionage.* New York: D. McKay, 1963, 337 p.

Irving, Clifford and **Burkholz, Herbert.** *Spy: The Story of Modern Espionage.* New York: Macmillan, 1969, 206 p.

Karadeniz, Engin. *"Establishment of Internal Security Undersecretariat Reported."* Washington: U.S. Joint Publications Research Service, no. 073296, April 24, 1979, p. 63. (translation from *Cumhuriyet* (Istanbul), March 14, 1979, p. 1).

Kimche, Jon. *General Guisans Zweifrontenkrieg.* Frankfurt/M; Berlin: Verlag Ullstein GmbH., 1962, 231 p.

Kimche, Jon. *Spying for Peace: General Guisan and Swiss Neutrality.* New York: Roy Publishers, 1961, 168 p.

Klembovskii, V. *Die Militärspionage im Frieden und im Kriege.* Translated from the Russian by Freiherr von Tettau. Ann Arbor, Mich.: University Microfilms, 1974, 79 p. (original: Hannover, Helwingsche Verlagsbuchhandlung, 1894).

Klembovsky, General. "Military Espionage in Austria." *Journal of the Royal United Service Institution,* v. LXVII (February–November 1922), pp. 500-502 (summary of his article in the *Historical Military Review* (Moscow), no. 4, 1920).

Kreibich, Karel, ed. *Spione und Verschwörer.* Prague: 1937, 60 p.

Kremer, J.v. *Le livre noir de l'espionnage: Les dessous de la guerre de l'ombre.* Paris: Editions Fleuve Noir, 1955, 222 p.

Kurz, Hans Rudolf. *Nachrichtenzentrum Schweiz. Die Schweiz im Nachrichtendienst des Zweiten Weltkriegs.* Frauenfeld, Stuttgart: Huber, 1972, 131 p.

Landau, Henry. *Secrets of the White Lady.* New York: Putnam, 1935, 314 p.

Lasswell, Harold Dwight and **Lerner, Daniel,** eds. *World Revolutionary Elites: Studies in Coercive Ideological Movements.* Cambridge: M.I.T. Press, 1966, 478 p.

Lettow-Vorbeck, Paul Emil von, ed. *Die Weltkriegsspionage: Authentische Enthüllungen über Entstehung, Art, Arbeit, Technik, Schliche, Handlungen, Wirkungen und Geheimnisse der Spionage vor, während und nach dem Kriege auf Grund amtlichen Materials aus Kriegs-, Militär-, Gerichts- und Reichsarchiven, vom Leben und Sterben, von den Taten und Abenteuern der bedeutendsten Agenten bei Freund und Feind.* Munich: J. Moser, 1931, 688 p.

Mohammed Reza Pahlavi, Shah of Iran. *Answer to History.* Translated by Michael Joseph Ltd. New York: Stein and Day, 1980, 204 p.

Moravec, Frantisek. *Master of Spies: The Memoirs of General Frantisek Moravec.* Garden City, N.Y.: Doubleday, 1975, 240 p.

Paillole, Paul. *Services spéciaux: 1935-1945.* Paris: R. Laffont, 1975, 565 p. (paperback).

Paine, Lauran. *Double Jeopardy.* London: R. Hale, 1978, 191 p.

Pardera, Sergio. "A Year and a Half Since Enactment of Reorganization—Why are the Secret Services Still at the Point of Departure?" Washington: U.S. Joint Publications Research Service, no. 073254, April 18, 1979. (translation from *L'Unita* (Rome), March 8, 1979, p. 2).

Phillips, Alan. *The Living Legend: The Story of the Royal Canadian Mounted Police.* Boston: Little, Brown, 1957, 328 p.

Phillips, David Atlee. "Castro's Spies Are No Longer Teenagers." *Retired Officer,* January 18, 1982, pp. 16-18.

Ribeiro, Goncalves. "Prominent Figures on Creation of Intelligence Service." Washington: U.S. Joint Publications Research Service, [Report] pp. 120-126. (translation from the Portuguese of statements by internal administration minister Goncalves Ribeiro, Almeida e Costa, and Magalhaes Mota as reported in the *Diario de Noticias* (Lisbon), May 12, 1979, p. 33).

Rowan, Richard Wilmer. *Spy and Counter-spy: The Development of Modern Espionage.* New York: Viking Press, 1928, 322 p.

Rowan, Richard Wilmer. *Terror in our Time: The Secret Service of Surprise Attack.* New York; Toronto: Longmans, Green, 1941, 438 p.

Rowan, Richard Wilmer with **Deindorfer, Robert G.** *Secret Service: Thirty-three Centuries of Espionage.* [New and rev. ed.] New York: Hawthorn Books, 786 p. (original edition, 1937).

Sawatsky, John. *Men in the Shadows: The RCMP Security Service.* Toronto: Doubleday Canada, 1980, 302 p.

Schramm, Wilhelm, *Ritter von. Der Geheimdienst in Europa 1937-1945.* Munich; Vienna: Langen Müller, 1974, 406 p.

Scoville, Herbert, Jr. "Is Espionage Necessary for our Security?" *Foreign Affairs,* v. 54, no. 3 (April 1976), pp. 482-495.

Seth, Ronald. *Secret Servants: A History of Japanese Espionage.* New York: Farrar, Straus and Cudahy, 1957, 278 p.

Stead, Philip John. *Second Bureau.* London: Evans Bros., 1959, 212 p.

Strong, Kenneth. *Men of Intelligence: A Study of the Roles and Decisions of Chiefs of Intelligence from World War I to the Present Day.* London: Cassell, 1970, 183 p.

Sun Tzŭ. *The Art of War: The Oldest Military Treatise in the World.* Translated from the Chinese by Lionel Giles. Harrisburg, Pa.: The Military Service Publishing Company, 1944, 99 p.

Sweeney, Walter Campbell. *Military Intelligence, a New Weapon in War.* New York: Frederick A. Stokes, 1924, 259 p.

Thompson, James Westfall and **Padover, Saul K.** *Secret Diplomacy: Espionage and Cryptography, 1500-1815.* New York: F. Ungar Pub. Co., 1963, 290 p.

Vivés, Juan. *Les maîtres de Cuba.* Paris: R. Laffont, 1981, 391 p. (paperback).

Vögeli, Robert. *Spionage in der Gegenwart.* Kreuzlinger, Neptun-Verlag, 1969, 97 p. (Schriftenreihe der Aktion für freie Demokratie, v. 1).

Whiting, Charles. *The Battle for Twelveland: An Account of Anglo-American Intelligence Operations Within Nazi Germany, 1939-1945.* London: Cooper, 1975, 240 p.

Whiting, Charles. *The War in the Shadows.* New York: Ballantine Books, 1973, 268 p.

Wise, David and **Ross, Thomas B.** *The Espionage Establishment.* New York: Random House, 1967, 308 p.

Germany, including Nazi Germany

Abshagen, Karl Heinz. *Canaris.* Translated by Alan Houghton Brodrick. London: Hutchinson, 1956, 264 p.

Allied Forces. Supreme Headquarters. *The German Intelligence Service.* London: Supreme Headquarters, Allied Expeditionary Forces, Counterintelligence War Room, April 1945. 30 p.

Bartz, Karl. *The Downfall of the German Secret Service.* [Translated from the German by Edward Fitzgerald]. London: Kimber, 1956, 202 p.

Brissaud, André. *Canaris: The Biography of Admiral Canaris, Chief of German Military Intelligence in the Second World War.* Translated [from the French] and edited by Ian Colvin. New York: Grosset and Dunlap, 1974, 347 p.

Brissaud, André. *The Nazi Secret Service.* Translated from the French by Milton Waldman. New York: Norton, 1974, 320 p.

Buchheit, Gert. *Der deutsche Geheimdienst: Geschichte der militärischen Abwehr.* Munich: List, 1966, 494 p.

Buchheit, Gert. *Spionage in zwei Weltkriegen: Schachspiel mit Menschen.* Landshut: Verlag Politisches Archiv, 1975, 352 p.

Busch, Moritz. *Bismarck: Some Secret Pages of his History: Being a Diary Kept by Dr. Moritz Busch During Twenty-five Years' Official and Private Intercourse with the Great Chancellor.* New York: Macmillan; London: Macmillan, 1898, 2v.

Butler, Rupert. *The Black Angels: A History of the Waffen-SS.* New York: St. Martin's Press, 1979, 276 p.

Charisius, Albrecht and **Mader, Julius.** *Nicht länger geheim: Entwicklung, System und Arbeitsweise des imperialistischen deutschen Geheimdienstes.* Berlin: Deutscher Militärverlag, 1969, 631 p.

Colvin, Ian Goodhope. *Chief of Intelligence.* London: Gollancz, 1951, 223 p.

Cookridge, E.H. *pseud.* (Spiro, Edward). *Gehlen: Spy of the Century.* New York: Random House, 1971, 402 p.

Crankshaw, Edward. *Gestapo, Instrument of Tyranny.* New York: Viking Press, 1956, 275 p.

Delarue, Jacques. *Gestapo: A History of Horror.* Translated from the French by Mervyn Savill. New York: Morrow, 1964, 384 p.

Erasmus, Johannes. *Der geheime Nachrichtendienst.* Göttingen: Musterschmidt, 1952, 89 p.

Farago, Ladislas. *The Game of the Foxes: The Untold Story of German Espionage in the United States and Great Britain During World War II.* New York: D. McKay, 1971, 696 p.

Felstead, Sidney Theodore. *Germany and her Spies: A Story of the Intrigues of the Nazis.* London: Hutchinson, 1940, 232 p.

Frischauer, Willi. *Berlin Betrayal.* New York: Belmont Publications, 1958, 221 p. (paperback of *The Man Who Came Back: The Story of Otto John.* London: Muller, 1958, 276 p.).

Gehlen, Reinhard. *Der Dienst: Erinnerungen 1942-1971.* Mainz: v. Hase and Koehler, 1971, 424 p.

Gehlen, Reinhard. *The Service: The Memoirs of General Reinhard Gehlen.* Translated by David Irving. New York: World Pub., 1972, 386 p.

The German Spy System from Within by Ex-Intelligence Officer. London; New York [etc.]: Hodder and Stoughton, 1915, 195 p.

Giles, Otto Charles Felix William. *The Gestapo.* Oxford: Clarendon Press, 1940, 32 p.

Graber, S.G. *History of the SS.* New York: D. McKay, 1978, 244 p.

Höhne, Heinz. *Canaris.* Translated from the German by J. Maxwell Brownjohn. Garden City, N.Y.: Doubleday, 1979, 703 p.

Höhne, Heinz. *The Order of the Death's Head: The Story of Hitler's S.S.* Translated from the German by Richard Barry. New York: Ballantine Books, 1971, 786 p. (paperback).

John, Otto. *Twice Through the Lines: The Autobiography of Otto John.* Translated from the German by Richard Barry. New York: Harper and Row, 1972, 340 p.

Kahn, David. *Hitler's Spies: German Military Intelligence in World War II.* New York: Macmillan, 1978, 671 p.

Koehler, Hansjürgen. *Inside the Gestapo: Hitler's Shadow Over the World.* London: Pallas Publishing Co., 1940, 287 p.

Mader, Julius, *Der Banditenschatz: Ein dokumentarbericht über den geheimen Goldschatz Hitlerdeutschlands.* Berlin: Verlag der Nation, 1973, 311 p.

Manvell, Roger advised by **Fraenkel, Heinrich.** *Gestapo: S.S. and Gestapo, Rule by Terror.* New York: Ballantine Books, 1969, 160 p.

Mollo, Andrew. *A Pictorial History of the S.S., 1923-1945.* New York: Stein and Day, 1976, 192 p.

Nicolai, Walter. *The German Secret Service.* Translated, with an additional chapter, by George Renwick. London: S. Paul and Co., 1924, 298 p.

Nicolai, Walter. *Secret Powers: German Military Intelligence in the First War.* A "new translation" by an unidentified British officer. [post 1924], 113 p. (typescript).

Nollau, Günther. *Das Amt: 50 Jahre Zeuge d. Geschichte.* Munich: Bertelsmann, 1978, 303 p.

Persico, Joseph E. *Piercing the Reich: The Penetration of Nazi Germany by American Secret Agents During World War II.* New York: Viking Press, 1979, 376 p.

Radziwill, Catherine, *Princess* (Kolb-Danvin, Catherine). *Germany under Three Emperors.* New York: Funk and Wagnalls, 1917, 379 p.

Reifer, Arnold. *Design for Terror: An Analysis of the Organization and Function of the Oppressive Government Systems in Soviet Russia and Nazi Germany.* New York: Exposition Press, 1962, 82 p.

Schellenberg, Walter. *Hitler's Secret Service.* New York: Pyramid Books, 1958, 222 p. (paperback edition of *The Schellenberg Memoirs.* Edited and translated by Louis Hagen. London: A. Deutsch, 1956, 479 p.; original title: *The Labyrinth*).

Stieber, Wilhelm. *The Chancellor's Spy: The Revelations of the Chief of Bismarck's Secret Service.* Translated from the German by Jan Van Heurch. New York: Grove Press and Random House, 1979, 224 p.

Stieber, Wilhelm. *Denkwürdigkeiten des geheimen Regierungsrathes Dr. Stieber aus seinen hinterlassenen papieren.* Edited by Dr. Leopold Auerbach. Berlin: Verlag von Julius Engelmann, 1884, 310 p.

Whiting, Charles. *Gehlen: Master Spy of the Century.* New York: Ballantine Books, 1972, 275 p. (paperback).

Wykes, Alan. *SS Leibstandarte.* New York: Ballantine Books, 1974, 160 p.

Zolling, Hermann and **Höhne, Heinz.** *The General Was a Spy: The Truth About General Gehlen and his Spy Ring.* New York: Coward, McCann and Geoghegan, 1972, 347 p.

Israel

Bar-Zohar, Michel. *Spies in the Promised Land: Iser Harel and the Israeli Secret Service.* Translated from the French by Monroe Stearns. Boston: Houghton Mifflin, 1972, 292 p.

"Crisis in Israeli Intelligence Services Discussed," unsigned article originally published in *Israel and Palestine* entitled "The Israeli Intelligence Crisis." Washington: U.S. Joint Publications Research Service, Document no. 8127, CSO 4805, n.d., 9 p.

Deacon, Richard, *pseud.* (McCormick, Donald). *The Israeli Secret Service.* London: Hamilton, 1977, 318 p.

Derogy, Jacques and **Carmel, Hesi.** *The Untold History of Israel.* New York: Grove Press and Random House, 1979, 346 p.

Eisenberg, Dennis; Dan, Uri; *et al. The Mossad Inside Stories: Israel's Secret Intelligence Service.* New York: Paddington Press, 1978, 272 p.

Eytan, Steve. *Das Auge Davids: Israels Geheimdienst in Aktion.* Translated from the French by Ingrid Kollpacher. Vienna-Munich-Zürich: Verlag Fritz Molden, 1971, 224 p. (translation of *L'Oeil de Tel-Aviv.* Paris: Editions Publications Premières).

Korneev, L. "Voennaia razvedka Izrailia." *Voennyi Vestnik* (Moscow), no. 5 (May 1978), pp. 115–117.

Piekalkiewicz, Janusz. *Israels langer Arm: Geschichte d. israel Geheimdienste u. Kommandounternehmen.* Frankfurt/M: Goverts, 1975, 407 p.

Piekalkiewicz, Janusz. *Les Services Secrets d'Israël.* Paris: Pensée Moderne, 1977, 320 p.

Steven, Stewart. *The Spymasters of Israel.* New York: Macmillan, 1980, 329 p.

USSR/Russia

Abramowitsch, R. *Die politischen Gefangenen in der Sowjet-Union.* Berlin: J.H.W. Dietz Nachf. GmbH, 1930, 52 p.

Agabekov, Grigorii Sergeevich. *OGPU, the Russian Secret Terror.* Translated from the French by Henry W. Bunn. New York: Brentano's, 1931, 277 p.

Barron, John. *KGB: The Secret Work of Soviet Secret Agents.* New York: Reader's Digest Press and Dutton, 1974, 462 p.

Belikov, Il'ia Grigor'evich; Boiko, Ivan Kuz'mich; *et al. Imeni Dzerzhinskogo: Boevoi put' ordena Lenina Krasnoznam. Divisii im. F.E. Dzerzhinskogo.* Moscow: Voenizdat, 1976, 206 p.

Blackstock, Paul W. *The Secret Road to World War Two: Soviet Versus Western Intelligence, 1921–1939.* Chicago: Quadrangle Books, 1969, 384 p.

Canada, Royal Commission to Investigate Disclosures of Secret and Confidential Information to Unauthorized Persons. *The Report of the Royal Commission Appointed Under Order in Council P.C. 411 of February 5, 1946 ... Honourable Mr. Justice Robert Taschereau, Honourable Mr. Justice R.L. Kellock, Commissioners ...* Ottawa: E. Cloutier, printer, 1946, 733 p.

Colton, Timothy J. *Commissars, Commanders and Civilian Authority: The Structure of Soviet Military Politics.* Cambridge, Mass.: Harvard University Press, 1979, 365 p. (Russian Research Center studies; 79).

Cookridge, E.H., *pseud.* (Spiro, Edward). *The Net That Covers the World.* New York: Holt, 1955, 264 p.

Cookridge, E.H., *pseud.* (Spiro, Edward). *Soviet Spy Net.* London: F. Muller, 1955, 264 p.

Deacon, Richard, *pseud.* (McCormick, Donald). *A History of the Russian Secret Service.* New York: Taplinger, 1972, 568 p.

Deriabin, Petr Sergeevich and **Gibney, Frank.** *The Secret World.* Garden City, N.Y.: Doubleday, 1959, 334 p.

Dzerzhinskii, Feliks Édmundovich. *Feliks Édmundovich Dzerzhinskii. Zhizn' i Deiatel'nost' v fotogr. i dokumentakh.* Compiled by S.I. Elkina and I.M. Mishakova. Moscow: Politizdat, 1972, 95 p.

Dzerzhinskii, Feliks Édmundovich. *Isbrannye proizvedeniia ...* [Compiled by] In-t Marksizma-Leninizma pri TSK KPSS. Moscow: Politizdat, 3d ed., 1977, 2 v.

Ebon, Martin. *Malenkov, Stalin's Successor.* New York: McGraw-Hill, 1953, 284 p.

Fomin, Fedor Timofeevich. *Memoirs of an Old Chekist.* Washington: U.S. Joint Publications Research Service, no. 55688, April 12, 1972, 172 p. (translation of *Zapiski starogo chekista,* Moscow: Polit. Lit-ry, 1964).

Gerson, Lennard D. *The Secret Police in Lenin's Russia.* Philadelphia: Temple University Press, 1976, 332 p.

Gerson, Lennard D. *The Shield and the Sword: Felix Dzerzhinskii and the Establishment of the Soviet Secret Police.* Ann Arbor, Mich.: University Microfilms, 1976, 211 p. (Ph.D. thesis, George Washington University, Washington, 1973).

Godson, Roy, ed. *Counterintelligence.* Washington: National Strategy Information Center, 1980, 339 p. (Intelligence Requirements for the 1980s; no. 3).

Graham, Stephen. *Ivan the Terrible: Life of Ivan IV of Russia.* New Haven: Yale University Press, 1933, 335 p.

Gul', Roman Borisovich. *Les maîtres de la Tchéka: Histoire de la terreur en U.R.S.S., 1917-1938.* Translated from the Russian by the author. Paris: Editions de France, 1938, 244 p.

Hingley, Ronald. *The Russian Secret Police: Muscovite, Imperial Russian, and Soviet Political Security Operations.* New York: Simon and Schuster, 1970, 313 p.

Khromov, Semen Spiridonovich. *F.É. Dzerzhinskii na khoziaistvennom fronte, 1921-1926.* Moscow: Mysl', 1977, 340 p.

Korol'kov, IUrii Mikhailovich. *Feliks—znachit schastlivyi ...: Povest' o Felikse Dzerzhinskom.* Moscow: Politizdat, 1974, 461 p.

Koslow, Jules. *Ivan the Terrible.* New York: Hill and Wang, 1961, 271 p.

Krivitsky, Walter G. *In Stalin's Secret Service: An Exposé of Russia's Secret Policies by the Former Chief of the Soviet Intelligence in Western Europe.* New York: Harper, 2d ed., 1939, 273 p. (U.S. edition of *I Was Stalin's Agent,* London: H. Hamilton).

Krylov, S.; Artuzov, A.; et al. *Collection of Articles on Soviet Intelligence and Security Operations.* Translated from the Russian by U.S. Joint Publications Research Service. Springfield, Va.: U.S. Department of Commerce, National Technical Information Service, 1972, 229 p. (JPRS no. 55623, April 4, 1972).

Leggett, George. *The Cheka: Lenin's Political Police.* Oxford and New York: Oxford University Press, 1981, 514 p.

Lewytzkyj, Borys. *The Uses of Terror: The Soviet Secret Police, 1917-1970.* Translated by H.A. Piehler. New York: Coward, McCann and Geoghegan, [1972], 349 p. (translation of *Die rote Inquisition*).

Longeran, Thomas C. "CHEKA." *Infantry Journal,* v. XXXIII, no. 2 (August 1928), pp. 182-192.

Monas, Sidney. *The Third Section: Police and Society in Russia Under Nicholas I.* Cambridge, Mass.: Harvard University Press, 1961, 354 p. (Russian Research Center studies, 42).

MChK—iz istorii Moskovskoi Chrezvychainoi komissii: 1918-1921: sbornik dokumentov. Compiled by A.S. Velidov, I.E. Polikarenko et al. Moscow: Mosk. Rabochii, 1978, 319 p.

Myagkov, Aleksei. *Inside the KGB: An Exposé by an Officer of the Third Directorate.* Richmond, Surrey [England]: Foreign Affairs Publishing, 1977, 131 p.

Os'machka, Teodosii. *Red Assassins: A Factual Story Revealing How the Ukraine Lost its Freedom.* Minneapolis: T.S. Denison, 1959, 375 p.

Pincher, Chapman. *Their Trade is Treachery.* London: Sidgwick and Jackson, 1981, 240 p.

Pistrak, Lazar. *The Grand Tactician: Khrushchev's Rise to Power.* New York: Praeger, 1961, 296 p. (Praeger Publications in Russian History and World Communism, no. 87).

Popov, Georgii Konstantinovich. *Tscheka, der Staat im Staate; Erlebnisse und Erfahrungen mit der Russischen Ausserordentlichen Kommission.* Frankfurt am Main: Frankfurter Societäts-Druckerei, 1925, 306 p.

Reifer, Arnold. *Design for Terror: An Analysis of the Organization and Function of the Oppressive Government Systems in Soviet Russia and Nazi Germany.* New York: Exposition Press, 1962, 82 p.

Rusten, Paul. *Communist Training and Indoctrination.* [n.p.]: Center for Historic Documentation, January 1968, 74 p. (typescript).

Schild und Flamme. Erzählgn. u. Berichte aus d. Arbeit d. Tscheka. [Berlin]: Militärverl. d. DDR, 1974, 478 p. (translation of selections from Chekisty).

Seth, Ronald. *The Executioners: The Story of SMERSH.* New York: Hawthorn Books, 1967, 199 p.

Sinevirskii, Nikolai. *Smersh.* Edited by Kermit and Milt Hill; translated by Constantin W. Boldyreff. New York: Holt, 1950, 253 p.

Spravochnik tsentral'nykh i mestnykh uchrezhdenii R.S.F.S.R.: Partinykh organizatsii i professional'nykh soiuzov. Moscow: Spravochnogo Otdela V.TS.I.K., 2d ed., 1920, 25 p.

Squire, Peter Stansfield. *The Third Department: The Establishment and Practices of the Political Police in the Russia of Nicholas I.* London: Cambridge University Press, 1968, 272 p.

Tishkov, Arsenii Vasil'evich. *Dzerzhinskii.* Moscow: Mol. Gvardiia, 1974, 382 p. (Zhizn' zamechatel'nykh liudei: Seriia Biografii; no. 9 (541)).

Vaitkunas, Prantsishkus Stepanovich. *Feliks Ėdmundovich Dzerzhinskii.* Moscow: Mysl', 1977, 104 p. (Partiinye publitsisty).

Vaitkunas, Prantsishkus Stepanovich. *Feliksas Dzerzinskis.* Vilnius: Mintis, 1977, 51 p.

Vasil'ev, Aleksiei Tikhonovich. *The Ochrana: the Russian Secret Police, by A.T. Vassilyev, the Last Chief of Police Under the Tsar.* Edited by René Fülöp-Miller. Philadelphia and London: Lippincott, 1930, 305 p.

Waliszewski, Kazimierz. *Ivan the Terrible.* Translated from the French by Lady Mary Loyd. Philadelphia: Lippincott, 1904, 431 p.

Whaley, Barton. *Soviet Clandestine Communication Nets: Notes for a History of the Structure of the Intelligence Services of the USSR.* Cambridge, Mass.: M.I.T., 1969, 199 p. (manuscript).

Wittlin, Tadeusz. *Commissar: The Life and Death of Lavrenty Pavlovich Beria.* New York: Macmillan, 1972, 566 p.

Wolin, Simon and **Slusser, Robert M.,** eds. *The Soviet Secret Police.* New York: Praeger, 1957, 408 p. (Studies of the Research Program on the U.S.S.R., no. 14).

Zubov, Nikolai Ivanovich. *F.Ė. Dzerzhinskii: Biografiia.* Moscow: Polit. Lit-ry, 2d ed., 1965, 364 p.

Zubov, Nikolai Ivanovich. *F.Ė. Dzerzhinskii: A Biography.* Moscow: Polit. Lit-ry, 1971, 423 p.

United Kingdom

Andrew, Christopher. "The British Secret Service and Anglo-Soviet Relations in the 1920s. Part I: From the Trade Negotiations to the Zinoviev Letter." *Historical Journal,* 20, no. 3 (1977), pp. 673–706.

Andrew, Christopher. "The Mobilization of British Intelligence for the Two World Wars." [draft paper for the International Security Studies Program, The Wilson Center, Washington, D.C.], 1979, 28 p.

Aubrey, Crispin. *Who's Watching You? Britain's Security Services and the Official Secrets Act.* Harmondsworth, Middlesex, [England]: Penguin Books, 1981, 294 p. (paperback).

Deesly, Patrick. *Very Special Admiral: The Life of Admiral J.H. Godfrey.* London: Hamilton, 1980, 345 p.

British Policy Towards Wartime Resistance in Yugoslavia and Greece. Edited by Phyllis Auty and Richard Clogg. New York: Harper and Row, 1975, 308 p.

Bunyan, Tony. *The Political Police in Britain.* New York: St. Martin's Press, 1976, 320 p.

Cherniak, Efim Borisovich. *Sekretnaia diplomatiia Velikobritanii: iz istorii tainoi voiny.* Moscow: Mezhdunar. Otnosheniia, 1975, 371 p.

Cockerill, A.W. *Sir Percy Sillitoe.* London: W.H. Allen, 1975, 223 p.

Cockerill, George Kynaston, Sir. *What Fools We Were.* London, New York [etc.]: Hutchinson, 1944, 175 p.

Cookridge, E.H., pseud. (Spiro, Edward). *Set Europe Ablaze.* New York: Crowell, 1967, 410 p.

Deacon, Richard, pseud. (McCormick, Donald). *A History of the British Secret Service.* New York: Taplinger Pub., 1970, 440 p.

Everitt, Nicholas. *British Secret Service During the Great War.* London: Hutchinson, 1920, 320 p.

Fitch, Herbert Trevor. *Traitors Within: The Story of the Special Branch, New Scotland Yard.* Garden City, N.Y.: Doubleday, Doran, 1933, 305 p.

Foot, Michael Richard Daniel. "Britain—Intelligence Services." *Economist,* March 14, 1980, pp. 51–58.

Foot, Michael Richard Daniel. *SOE in France: An Account of the Work of the British Special Operations Executive in France, 1940–1944.* London: H.M. Stationery Off., 1966 [2d impression, with amendments, 1968], 550 p.

Foot, Michael Richard Daniel. "Was SOE Any Good?" *Journal of Contemporary History,* v. 16, no. 1 (January 1981), pp. 167–181.

Foot, Michael Richard Daniel and **Langley, J.M.** *MI 9: Escape and Evasion, 1939–1945.* London: The Bodley Head, Ltd., 1979, 365 p.

Foot, Michael Richard Daniel and **Langley, J.M.** *MI 9: Escape and Evasion, 1939–1945.* Boston: Little, Brown, 1980, 351 p.

Fraser, Antonia (Pakenham), Lady. *Mary, Queen of Scots.* New York: Delacorte Press, 1970, 613 p.

Fuller, Jean Overton. *The German Penetration of SOE: France 1941-1944.* London: Kimber, 1975, 192 p.

[Guy, Henry]. *Moneys Received and Paid for Secret Services of Charles II. and James II. from 30th March, 1679, to 25th December, 1688.* Edited from a manuscript in the possession of William Selby Lowndes, Esq., by John Yonge Akerman. London: Printed for the Camden Society, 1851, 240 p.

[Guy, Henry]. *Moneys Received and Paid for Secret Services of Charles II. and James II. from 30th March, 1679, to 25th December, 1688.* Edited from a manuscript in the possession of William Selby Lowndes, Esq., by John Yonge Akerman. New York: Johnson Reprint Corp., 1968, 240 p.

Harrison, Richard. *The C.I.D. and the F.B.I.* London: F. Muller, 1956, 196 p.

Haswell, Chetwynd John Drake. *British Military Intelligence.* London: Weidenfeld and Nicolson, 1973, 262 p.

Hinsley, Francis Harry with **Thomas, E.E.** et al. *British Intelligence in the Second World War: Its Influence on Strategy and Operations.* London: H.M. Stationery Off., 1979-1981, 2v.

Hobman, Daisy Lucie. *Cromwell's Master Spy: A Study of John Thurloe.* London: Chapman and Hall, 1961, 186 p.

Hyde, Harford Montgomery. *Room 3603: The Story of the British Intelligence Center in New York During World War II.* New York: Farrar, Straus, 1963, 257 p.

Jones, Reginald Victor. *Most Secret War.* London: Hamilton, 1978, 556 p.

Landau, Henry. *Spreading the Spy Net: The Story of a British Spy Director.* London: Jarrolds, Ltd., 1938, 284 p.

McLachlan, Donald. *Room 39: A Study in Naval Intelligence.* New York: Atheneum, 1968, 438 p.

Masterman, John Cecil, Sir. *The Double-Cross System in the War of 1939 to 1945.* New Haven: Yale University Press, 1972, 203 p.

Mattingly, Garrett. *The Armada.* Boston: Houghton Mifflin, 1959, 443 p.

Paine, Lauran. *Britain's Intelligence Service.* London: Hale, 1979, 188 p.

Parritt, B.A.H. *The Intelligencers: The Story of British Military Intelligence up to 1914.* Headquarters Third Division, Bulford, Wiltshire: [post 1957]. (typescript).

Read, Conyers. *Mr. Secretary Walsingham and the Policy of Queen Elizabeth.* Oxford: The Clarendon Press, 1925, 3v.

Seid, Alfred. *Der Englische Geheimdienst.* Berlin: Junker and Dünnhaupt, 1940, 44 p.

Stafford, David. *Britain and European Resistance, 1940-1945: A Survey of the Special Operations Executive, with Documents.* London: Macmillan; Toronto: University of Toronto Press, 1980, 295 p.

Stevenson, William. *A Man Called Intrepid: The Secret War.* New York: Harcourt, Brace, Jovanovich, 1976, 486 p.

Strong, Kenneth. *Intelligence at the Top: The Recollections of an Intelligence Officer.* London: Cassell, 1968, 271 p.

Trenowden, Ian. *Operations Most Secret: SOE: The Malayan Theatre.* London: Kimber, 1978, 231 p.

United States
General

Allison, Graham and **Szanton, Peter.** Remaking Foreign Policy: The Organizational Connection. New York: Basic Books, 1976, 238 p.

Alsop, Stewart. *The Center: The Anatomy of Power in Washington.* London: Hodder and Stoughton, 1968, 365 p.

Ambrose, Stephen E. with **Immerman, Richard H.** *Ike's Spies: Eisenhower and the Espionage Establishment.* Garden City, N.Y.: Doubleday, 1981, 368 p.

Betts, Richard K. *Soldiers, Statesmen, and Cold War Crises.* Cambridge: Harvard University Press, 1977, 292 p.

Boston Study Group. *The Price of Defense: A New Strategy for Military Spending.* New York: Times Books, 1979, 359 p.

Brown, Seyom. *The Crises of Power: An Interpretation of United States Foreign Policy During the Kissinger Years.* New York: Columbia University Press, 1979, 170 p.

Cline, Ray S. "Policy Without Intelligence." *Foreign Policy,* no. 17 (Winter 1974-75), pp. 121-135.

Dallek, Robert. *Franklin D. Roosevelt and American Foreign Policy, 1932-1945.* New York: Oxford University Press, 1979, 657 p.

De Santis, Hugh. *The Diplomacy of Silence: The American Foreign Service, the Soviet Union, and the Cold War, 1933-1947.* Chicago: University of Chicago Press, 1980, 270 p.

Divine, Robert A. *Eisenhower and the Cold War.* New York: Oxford University Press, 1981, 181 p. (paperback).

Documents. Edited by Christy Macy and Susan Kaplan; compiled under the sponsorship of the Center for National Security Studies. Middlesex, Eng.; New York: Penguin Books, 1980, 400 p.

Donner, Frank J. *The Age of Surveillance: The Aims and Methods of America's Political Intelligence System.* New York: Knopf and Random House, 1980, 554 p.

Donovan, Robert J. *Conflict and Crisis: The Presidency of Harry S. Truman, 1945-1948.* New York: Norton, 1977, 473 p.

Dulles, Eleanor Lansing. *Eleanor Lansing Dulles, Chances of a Lifetime: A Memoir.* Englewood Cliffs, N.J.: Prentice-Hall, 1980, 390 p.

Forrestal, James. *The Forrestal Diaries.* Edited by Walter Millis with the collaboration of E.S. Duffield. New York: Viking Press, 1951, 581 p.

Gephardt, Thomas. "There's No Survival Without Intelligence." *Enquirer* (Cincinnati), February 3, 1980. (editorial).

Godson, Roy, ed. *Elements of Intelligence.* Washington: National Strategy Information Center, 1979, 129 p. (Intelligence Requirements for the 1980s; no. 1).

Goldwater, Barry Morris. *With no Apologies: The Personal and Political Memoirs of United States Senator Barry M. Goldwater.* New York: Morrow, 1979, 320 p.

Graham, Daniel Orrin. *U.S. Intelligence at the Crossroads.* Washington: United States Strategic Institute, 1976, 17 p.

Hedley, John Hollister. *Harry S. Truman, the 'Little' Man from Missouri.* Woodbury, N.Y.: Barron's, 1979, 353 p.

Hilsman, Roger. *Strategic Intelligence and National Decisions.* Glencoe, Ill.: Free Press, 1956, 187 p.

Hoxie, Ralph Gordon. *Command Decision and the Presidency: A Study in National Security Policy and Organization.* New York: Reader's Digest Press and Crowell, 1977, 505 p.

Jeffreys-Jones, Rhodri. *American Espionage: From Secret Service to CIA.* New York: Free Press, 1977, 276 p.

Jordan, Amos A. and **Taylor, William Jr.** *American National Security: Policy and Process.* Baltimore: Johns Hopkins University Press, 1981, 604 p.

Julien, Claude. *L'Empire américain.* Paris: B. Grasset, 1968, 419 p.

Kent, Sherman. *Strategic Intelligence for American World Policy.* Princeton: Princeton University Press, 1949, 226 p.

Kent, Sherman. *Strategic Intelligence for American World Policy.* Hamden, Conn.: Archon Books, 1965, 226 p.

King, Nicholas. *George Bush: A Biography.* New York: Dodd, Mead, 1980, 146 p.

Kirkpatrick, Lyman B., Jr. *The U.S. Intelligence Community: Foreign Policy and Domestic Activities.* New York: Hill and Wang, 1973, 212 p.

Lay, Tracy Hollingsworth. *The Foreign Service of the United States.* New York: Prentice-Hall, 1925, 438 p.

MacCloskey, Monro. *The American Intelligence Community.* New York: Rosen Press, 1967, 190 p.

McLellan, David S. *Dean Acheson: The State Department Years.* New York: Dodd, Mead, 1976, 466 p.

Medved, Michael. *The Shadow Presidents: The Secret History of the Chief Executives and their Top Aides.* New York: Times Books, 1979, 401 p.

Meyer, Cord. *Facing Reality: From World Federalism to the CIA.* New York: Harper and Row, 1980, 433 p.

Morgenstern, Oskar. *The Question of National Defense.* New York: Random House, 1959, 306 p.

Mosley, Leonard. *Dulles: A Biography of Eleanor, Allen and John Foster Dulles and their Family Network.* New York: Dial Press, 1978, 530 p.

National Security Council Structure: [Statement by the President of the United States, January 12, 1982]. Washington: The White House, Office of the Press Secretary, 7 p. (press release).

Pinkerton, Roy H. "The Role of Intelligence in Policymaking." *Military Review,* July 1966, pp. 40-51.

Posvar, Wesley W. "National Security Policy: The Realm of Obscurity." *Orbis,* v. IX, no. 3 (Fall 1965), pp. 694–713.

Program on Information Resources Policy. *Incidental Paper: Seminar on Command, Control, Communications and Intelligence.* Guest presentations, Spring 1980, by William E. Colby, B.R. Inman, William Odom . . . *et al.* Cambridge, Mass.: Harvard University, Program on Information Resources Policy, 1980, 183 p.

Ransom, Harry Howe. "Being Intelligent About Secret Intelligence Agencies." *American Political Science Review,* v. 74, Spring 1980, pp. 141-148.

Ransom, Harry Howe. *Can American Democracy Survive Cold War?* Garden City, N.Y.: Doubleday (Anchor Books), 1964, 262 p. (paperback).

Raskin, Marcus G. *The Politics of National Security.* New Brunswick, N.J.: Transaction Books, 1979, 211 p.

The Role of American Intelligence Organizations. Edited by George Wittman. New York: H.W. Wilson, 1976, 160 p.

Rositzke, Harry August. "America's Secret Operations: A Perspective." *Foreign Affairs,* v. 53, no. 2 (January 1975), pp. 334–351.

Schlesinger, Arthur Meier, Jr. *The Imperial Presidency.* Boston: Houghton Mifflin, 1973, 505 p.

Schlesinger, Arthur Meier, Jr. *Robert Kennedy and his Times.* Boston: Houghton Mifflin, 1978, 1066 p.

Scoville, Herbert, Jr. "Is Espionage Necessary for our Security?" *Foreign Affairs,* v. 54, no. 3, (April 1976), pp. 482-495.

Smoot, Dan. *The Invisible Government.* Belmont, Mass.: Western Islands, 1977, 240 p. (paperback).

Szanton, Peter and **Allison, Graham.** "Intelligence: Seizing the Opportunity," *Foreign Policy,* no. 22 (Spring 1976), pp. 183–214.

Truman, Margaret. *Harry S. Truman.* New York: Pocket Books, 1974, 660 p. (paperback).

Twining, Nathan Farragut. *Neither Liberty nor Safety: A Hard Look at U.S. Military Policy and Strategy.* New York: Holt, Rinehart and Winston, 1966, 320 p.

U.S. Commission on Organization of the Executive Branch of the Government (1953-1955). *Intelligence Activities; a Report to the Congress.* Washington: U.S. GPO, 1955, 76 p.

U.S. Commission on the Organization of the Government for the Conduct of Foreign Policy. *Commission on the Organization of the Government for the Conduct of Foreign Policy: [Report].* Washington: U.S. GPO, 1975, 278 p.

U.S. Congress, Senate, Committee on Government Operations. *The National Security Council; Jackson Subcommittee Papers on Policy-making at the Presidential Level.* Edited by Henry M. Jackson. New York: Praeger, 1965, 311 p.

U.S. Congress, Senate, Select Committee to Study Governmental Operations with Respect to Intelligence Activities. *Final Report . . . Book VI. Supplementary Reports on Intelligence Activities.* April 23, 1976, 94th Congress, 2d session. Washington: U.S. GPO, 1976, 378 p.

U.S. Counter Intelligence Corps School, Baltimore. *History and Mission of the Counter Intelligence Corps in World War II: Special Text.* Baltimore: CIC School, Counter Intelligence Corps Center, 1951, 83 p.

U.S. Industrial College of the Armed Forces. *Economic Intelligence and Economic Warfare.* Washington: Industrial College of the Armed Forces, 1954, 72 p. (Emergency Management of the National Economy, v. XV).

Walters, Vernon A. *Silent Missions.* Garden City, N.Y.: Doubleday, 1978, 654 p.

Weil, Martin. *A Pretty Good Club: The Founding Fathers of the U.S. Foreign Service.* New York: Norton, 1978, 313 p.

Weyl, Nathaniel. *The Battle Against Disloyalty.* New York: Crowell, 1951, 378 p.

Wise, David; Ransom, Harry Howe *et al.* "Espionage: USA." *Society,* v. 12, no. 3 (March/April 1975), entire issue.

Wriston, Henry Merritt. *Executive Agents in American Foreign Relations.* Gloucester, Mass.: Peter Smith, 1967, 874 p.

Yoshpe, Harry Beller and **Falk, Stanley L.** *Organization for National Security.* Washington: Industrial College of the Armed Forces, 1963, 190 p.

FBI and Secret Service

Baker, La Fayette Charles. *History of the United States Secret Service.* Philadelphia: King and Baird, 1868, 704 p.

Baker, La Fayette Charles. *Secret Service.* Washington: The National Tribune, 1898, 398 p. (paperback).

Collins, Frederick Lewis. *The FBI in Peace and War.* New York: Putnam, 1943, 297 p.

Cook, Fred J. *The FBI Nobody Knows.* New York: Macmillan, 1964, 436 p.

Demaris, Ovid. *The Director: an Oral Biography.* New York: Harper's Magazine Press, 1975, 405 p.

De Toledano, Ralph. *J. Edgar Hoover: The Man in his Time.* New York: Manor Books, 1974, 384 p.

Felt, W. Mark. *The FBI Pyramid from the Inside.* New York: Putnam, 1979, 351 p.

Floherty, John Joseph. *Inside the F.B.I.* Philadelphia: Lippincott, 1943, 191 p.

Floherty, John Joseph. *Our F.B.I.: An Inside Story.* Philadelphia: Lippincott, 1951, 155 p.

Harrison, Richard. *The C.I.D. and the F.B.I.* London: F. Muller, 1956, 196 p.

Kuhn, Ferdinand. *The Story of the Secret Service.* New York: Random House, 1957, 174 p. (juvenile literature).

Lowenthal, Max. *The Federal Bureau of Investigation.* New York: Sloane, 1950, 559 p.

Mogelever, Jacob. *Death to Traitors: The Story of General Lafayette C. Baker, Lincoln's Forgotten Secret Service Chief.* Garden City, N.Y.: Doubleday, 1960, 429 p.

Nash, Jay Robert. *Citizen Hoover: A Critical Study of the Life and Times of J. Edgar Hoover and his FBI.* Chicago: Nelson-Hall, 1972, 298 p.

Neal, Harry Edward. *The Story of the Secret Service.* New York: Grosset and Dunlap, 1971, 123 p.

Ollestad, Norman. *Inside the F.B.I.* New York: L. Stuart, 1967, 319 p.

Overstreet, Harry Allen and **Overstreet, Bonaro.** *The FBI in our Open Society.* New York: Norton, 1969, 400 p.

Reynolds, Quentin James. *The F.B.I.* New York: Random House, 1954, 180 p.

Rowan, Richard Wilmer. *The Story of Secret Service.* New York: The Literary Guild of America, 1937, 732 p.

Sullivan, William C. with **Brown, Bill.** *The Bureau: My Thirty Years in Hoover's FBI.* New York: Norton, 1979, 286 p.

Tully, Andrew. *Inside the FBI: From the Files of the Federal Bureau of Investigation and Independent Sources.* New York: McGraw-Hill, 1980, 288 p.

Ungar, Sanford J. *FBI.* Boston: Little, Brown, 1976, 682 p.

U.S. National Archives. *Preliminary Inventory of the Records of the United States Secret Service.* Compiled by Lyle J. Holverstott. Washington: 1949, 16 p. (typescript).

U.S. Secret Service. *The United States Secret Service; What it is, What it does.* Washington: U.S. GPO, 1956, 30 p.

Whitehead, Don. *Le F.B.I.* Paris: Morgan, 1957, 452 p.

Whitehead, Don. *The FBI Story: A Report to the People.* New York: Random House, 1956, 368 p.

Wright, Richard O., ed. *Whose FBI?* LaSalle, Ill.: Open Court, 1974, 405 p.

Military Organizations

Dorwart, Jeffery M. *The Office of Naval Intelligence: The Birth of America's First Intelligence Agency, 1865-1918.* Annapolis, Md.: Naval Institute Press, 1979. 173 p.

Green, James Robert. *The First Sixty Years of the Office of Naval Intelligence.* Ann Arbor, Mich.: Xerox University Microfilms, 1975, 138 p.

McChristian, Joseph A. *The Role of Military Intelligence, 1965-1967.* Washington: Department of the Army, U.S. GPO, 1974, 182 p.

The Origin and Development of the Army Security Agency, 1917-1947. Laguna Hills, Calif.: Aegean Park Press, 1978, 51 p.

Powe, Marc B. "American Military Intelligence Comes of Age: A Sketch of a Man and His Times." *Military Review,* December 1975, pp. 17-30.

Smith, Truman. *Air Intelligence Activities: Office of the Military Attaché, American Embassy, Berlin, Germany, August 1935—April 1939 (with Special Reference to the Services of Colonel Charles A. Lindbergh, Air Corps Res.).* n.p., 1954-1956, 163 p. (typescript).

U.S. Army Intelligence Center and School, Fort Huachuca, Arizona. *The Evolution of American Military Intelligence* by Marc B. Powe and Edward E. Wilson. Fort Huachuca, Ariz.: U.S. Army Intelligence Center and School, May 1973, 123 p.

U.S. Naval War College. *The Service of Information and Security,* by W.S. Pye. Newport, R.I.: 1916, 309 p.

Van Deman, R.H. *Early History of Military Intelligence.* United States Army, 1950, 133 p.

Zumwalt, Elmo R. *On Watch: A Memoir.* New York: Quadrangle/New York Times Book Co., 1976, 568 p.

OSS and CIA

Alsop, Stewart and **Braden, Thomas.** *Sub Rosa: The O.-S.-S. and American Espionage.* New York: Reynal and Hitchcock, 1946, 237 p.

Aron, Raymond. *The Imperial Republic: The United States and the World, 1945-1973.* Translated from the French by Frank Jellinek. Englewood Cliffs, N.J.: Prentice-Hall, 1974, 339 p.

Casey, William J. *The Clandestine War in Europe (1942-1945):* [remarks on receipt of the William J. Donovan Award at dinner of Veterans of Office of Strategic Services]. December 5, 1974, 19 p.

Cline, Ray S. *The CIA under Reagan, Bush and Casey.* Washington: Acropolis Books, 1981, 351 p.

Cline, Ray S. *Secrets, Spies, and Scholars: Blueprint of the Essential CIA.* Washington: Acropolis Books, 1976, 294 p.

Colby, William Egan and **Forbath, Peter.** *Honorable Men: My Life in the CIA.* New York: Simon and Schuster, 1978, 493 p.

Colby, William E. "Intelligence in the 1980s." *Information Society,* v. 1, no. 1 (1981), p. 53+.

Colby, William E. and **Mondale, Walter F.** "Reorganizing the CIA: Who and How." *Foreign Policy,* no. 23 (Summer 1976), pp. 53-63.

Cooper, Chester L. "The CIA and Decision-Making." *Foreign Affairs,* January 1972, pp. 223-236.

Dulles, Allen Welsh. *The Craft of Intelligence.* New York: New American Library, 1965, 256 p.

Edwards, Robert and **Dunne, Kenneth.** *A Study of a Master Spy.* London: Housmans, 1961, 79 p. (Allen Dulles).

Ford, Corey and **MacBain, Alastair.** *Cloak and Dagger: The Secret Story of OSS.* New York: Random House, 1946, 216 p.

Hymoff, Edward. *The OSS in World War II.* New York: Ballantine Books, 1972, 405 p. (paperback).

Jeffers, Harry Paul. *The CIA: A Close Look at the Central Intelligence Agency.* New York: Lion Press, 1970, 159 p.

Joesten, Joachim. *De Amerikaanse Geheime Dienst.* Utrecht/Antwerp: Prisma-Boeken, 1962, 192 p. (paperback edition of *C.I.A. Wie der amerikanische Geheimdienst arbeitet.* Munich: Isar Verlag, 1958, 190 p.).

Kirkpatrick, Lyman B., Jr. *The Real CIA.* New York: Macmillan, 1968, 312 p.

Langer, William Leonard. *In and Out of the Ivory Tower: The Autobiography of William L. Langer.* New York: N. Watson Academic Publications, 1977, 268 p.

Lowther, William. "The S.O.B. of the C.I.A." *Macleans,* March 6, 1978, pp. 46-50. (Stansfield Turner).

Martin, David C. *Wilderness of Mirrors.* New York: Harper and Row, 1980, 236 p.

Murphy, Charles V.J. "Uncloaking the CIA." *Fortune,* June 1975, p. 88.

Paine, Lauran. *The CIA at Work.* London: R. Hale, 1977, 192 p.

Patti, Archimedes L.A. *Why Viet Nam? Prelude to America's Albatross.* Berkeley: University of California Press, 1980, 612 p.

Persico, Joseph E. *Piercing the Reich: The Penetration of Nazi Germany by American Secret Agents During World War II.* New York: Viking Press, 1979, 376 p.

Powers, Thomas. *The Man Who Kept the Secrets: Richard Helms and the CIA.* New York: Knopf, 1979, 393 p.

Ransom, Harry Howe. *Central Intelligence and National Security.* Cambridge: Harvard University Press, 1959, 287 p.

Ransom, Harry Howe. *The Intelligence Establishment.* Cambridge: Harvard University Press, 1970, 309 p.

Salisbury, Harrison E. "The Gentlemen Killers of the CIA." *Penthouse,* May 1975, p. 47+.

The Secret War Report of the OSS. Edited with an introduction by Anthony Cave Brown. New York: Berkley Pub. Corp., 1976, 572 p. (paperback).

Smith, Richard Harris. *OSS: The Secret History of America's First Central Intelligence Agency.* Berkeley: University of California Press, 1972, 458 p.

Smith, Thomas Bell. *The Essential CIA.* 1975, 204 p.

Troy, Thomas F. *Donovan and the CIA: A History of the Establishment of the Central Intelligence Agency.* Langley, Virginia: Central Intelligence Agency, Center for the Study of Intelligence, 1981, 589 p. (paperback) (later published commercially: Frederick, Maryland: Aletheia Books, University Publications of America, Inc., 1981, 589 p.).

U.S. Central Intelligence Agency. *Central Intelligence Agency Fact Book.* Washington: Central Intelligence Agency, 1980, 30 p.

U.S. Central Intelligence Agency. *Presidents of the United States on Intelligence.* Issued by the Office of Training. Washington: Central Intelligence Agency, April 1975, 33 p.

U.S. War Department Strategic Services Unit, History Project. *War Report of the OSS (Office of Strategic Services).* Prepared by History Project, Strategic Services Unit, Office of the Assistant Secretary of War, War Department. New York: Walker, 1976, 261 p.

U.S. War Department Strategic Services Unit, History Project. *War Report of the OSS (Office of Strategic Services), v. II: the Overseas Targets.* Prepared by History Project, Strategic Services Unit, Office of the Assistant Secretary of War, War Department. New York: Walker; and Washington: Carrollton Press, 1976, 460 p.

Warner, Edwin. "Strengthening the CIA." *Time,* April 30, 1979, pp. 95-96.

II. COLLECTION OF INFORMATION

Clandestine Operations

Espionage

General

Altavilla, Enrico. *The Art of Spying.* Englewood Cliffs, N.J.: Prentice-Hall, 1967, 199 p.

Barton, George. *The World's Greatest Military Spies and Secret Service Agents.* Boston: Page, 1918, 322 p.

Benjamin, Robert Spiers, ed. *Eye Witness: By Members of the Overseas Press Club of America.* New York: Alliance Book Corp., 1940, 306 p.

Bergh, Hendrik van. *ABC der Spione: Eine illustrierte Geschichte der Spionage in der Bundesrepublik Deutschland seit 1945.* Pfaffenhofen a.d. Ilm: Ilmgau Verlag, 1965, 424 p.

Bergier, Jacques. *Secret Armies: The Growth of Corporate and Industrial Espionage.* Translated from the French by Harold J. Salemson. Indianapolis: Bobbs-Merrill, 1975, 268 p. (translation of the author's three separate works originally published under titles *L'espionnage industriel, L'espionnage scientifique,* and *L'espionnage stratégique*).

Bergier, Jacques and **Delaban, Jean-Philippe.** *L'espionnage stratégique.* Paris: Hachette, 1973, 189 p. (paperback).

Berndorff, Hans Rudolf. *Diplomatische Unterwelt.* Stuttgart: Dieck, 1930, 309 p. (English translation of pp. 69–106).

Blum, Richard H. *Deceivers and Deceived: Observations on Confidence Men and Their Victims, Informants and Their Quarry, Political and Industrial Spies and Ordinary Citizens.* Springfield, Ill.: Thomas, 1972, 328 p. (a publication of the Institute of Public Policy Analysis, Stanford University).

Boveri, Margret. *Treason in the Twentieth Century.* Translated by Jonathan Steinberg. New York: Putnam, 1963, 370 p.

Bryan, George Sands. *The Spy in America.* Philadelphia: Lippincott, 1943, 256 p.

Buchheit, Gert. *Secrets des services secrets: [Missions, méthodes, expériences].* Translated by François Ponthier. Paris: B. Arthaud, 1974, 354 p. (paperback).

Chistiakov, Nikolai Fedorovich and **Smol'nikov, V.E.** *Taina ne tol'ko v seifakh.* Moscow: Voenizdat, 1968, 104 p.

Comisso, Giovanni, ed. *Les agents secrets de Venise au XVIIIe Siècle (1705–1797): Documents choisis .... * Translated from the Italian by Lucien Leluc. Paris: B. Grasset, 1944, 260 p.

Cookridge, E.H., pseud. (Spiro, Edward). *Orient Express: The Life and Times of the World's Most Famous Train.* New York: Harper and Row, 1978, 288 p. (paperback).

Cookridge, E.H., pseud. (Spiro, Edward). *Sisters of Delilah: Stories of Famous Women Spies.* London: Oldbourne, 1959, 224 p.

Cookridge, E.H., pseud. (Spiro, Edward). *Spy Trade.* New York: Walker, 1972, 288 p.

Copeland, Miles. *Without Cloak or Dagger: The Truth About the New Espionage.* New York: Simon and Schuster, 1974, 351 p.

Dan, Ben. *The Secret War.* Translated from the French by Jacqueline Kahanoff. New York: Sabra Books, n.d., 243 p. (original: *Poker d'espions à Tel-Aviv et au Caire,* Paris: Fayard, 1970).

De Gramont, Sanche, pseud. (Morgan, Ted). *The Secret War: The Story of International Espionage Since World War II.* New York: Putnam, 1962, 515 p.

Deindorfer, Robert, ed. *The Spies: Great True Stories of Espionage.* Greenwich, Conn.: Fawcett, 1949, 204 p. (paperback).

Deindorfer, Robert, *ed. True Spy Stories.* Greenwich, Conn.: Fawcett, 1961, 192 p. (paperback).

Draeger, Donn F. *Ninjutsu: The Art of Invisibility: Japan's Feudal-Age Espionage Methods.* Phoenix: Phoenix Books; Tokyo: Lotus Press, 1980, 118 p.

Dudney, Robert. "America: World's No. 1 Spy Target." *U.S. News and World Report,* December 10, 1979, pp. 36-40.

Dulles, Allen Welsh, *comp. Great True Spy Stories.* New York: Harper and Row, 1968, 393 p.

Ecke, Heinz, *comp. Four Spies Speak.* London: Hamilton, 1933, 242 p. (translated from the German).

Edwardes, Michael. *Playing the Great Game: A Victorian Cold War.* London: Hamilton, 1975, 167 p.

Epstein, Samuel and **Williams, Beryl.** *The Real Book About Spies.* Garden City, N.Y.: Garden City Books, 1953, 192 p.

Espionnage, no. 9 (March 1971). Paris: Editions OPTA, 127 p.

Espionnage Actualité, no. 11 (May 1971). Paris: Editions OPTA, 127 p.

Felix, Christopher, *pseud. A Short Course in the Secret War.* New York: Dutton, 1963, 314 p.

Finlay, Winifred and **Hancock, Gillian.** *Spies and Secret Agents.* London: Kaye and Ward, 1977, 128 p.

Fonroy, J.H. *La bataille des services secrets.* Paris: Editions du Milieu du Monde, 1958, 284 p.

Franklin, Charles, *pseud.* (Usher, Frank Hugh). *The Great Spies.* New York: Hart, 1967, 272 p.

Frewin, Leslie Ronald, *comp. The Spy Trade: An Anthology of International Espionage in Fact and Fiction.* London: Leslie Frewin, 1966, 248 p.

Gelb, Norman. *Enemy in the Shadows: The World of Spies and Spying.* New York: Hippocrene Books, 1976, 157 p.

The German Army From Within; by a British Officer Who Has Served in It. New York: Doran, 1914, 192 p.

Gheysens, Roger. *Les espions: Un panorama de l'espionnage de notre temps.* Paris: Elsevier Séquoia, 1973, 315 p.

Gibson, Walter Brown, *ed. The Fine Art of Spying.* New York: Grosset and Dunlap, 1967, 243 p. (paperback)

Godechot, Jacques Léon. *The Counterrevolution: Doctrine and Action, 1789-1804.* Translated from the French by Salvator Attanasio. London: Routledge and K. Paul, 1972, 405 p. (original: *La contre-révolution*).

Gollomb, Joseph. *Armies of Spies.* New York: Macmillan, 1939, 213 p.

Gollomb, Joseph. *Spies* New York: Macmillan, 1928, 389 p.

Hagen, Louis Edmund. *The Secret War for Europe: A Dossier of Espionage.* London. Macdonald, 1968, 287 p

Hefter, Joseph and **Elting, John R.** "Mexican Spy Company, 1846-1848." *Military Collector and Historian,* v. XXI, no. 2 (Summer 1969), pp. 48-50.

Hinchley, Vernon. *Spies Who Never Were.* New York: Dodd, Mead, 1965, 211 p.

Hinchley, Vernon. *Spy Mysteries Unveiled.* New York: Dodd, Mead, 1964, 254 p.

Hoehling, Adolph A. *Women Who Spied.* New York: Dodd, Mead, 1967, 204 p.

Hutton, Joseph Bernard. *Women in Espionage.* New York: Macmillan, 1972, 192 p. (reprint of *Women Spies,* 1971).

Ind, Allison. *A Short History of Espionage.* New York: D. McKay, 1963, 337 p.

Innes, Brian. *The Book of Spies: 4000 Years of Cloak and Dagger.* New York: Grosset and Dunlap, 1966, 96 p.

Irving, Clifford and **Burkholz, Herbert.** *Spy: The Story of Modern Espionage.* New York: Macmillan, 1969, 206 p.

Irwin, William Henry and **Johnson, Thomas M.** *What You Should Know About Spies and Saboteurs.* New York: Norton, 1943, 227 p.

Joesten, Joachim. *They Call It Intelligence: Spies and Spy Techniques Since World War II.* London, New York: Abelard-Schuman, 1963, 314 p.

Kreibich, Karel, *ed. Spione und Verschwörer.* Prague, 1937, 60 p.

Kremer, J.v. *Le livre noir de l'espionnage: les dessous de la guerre de l'ombre.* Paris: Editions Fleuve Noir, 1955, 222 p.

Lanier, Henry Wysham. *Secret Life of a Secret Agent: The Strange Training and Adventures of a Man Whose Work Was Melodrama.* Philadelphia: Lippincott, 1938, 306 p.

Lanoir, Paul. *The German Spy System in France.* Translated from the French of Paul Lanoir by an English officer. London: Mills and Boon, 1910, 264 p.

Liston, Robert A. *The Dangerous World of Spies and Spying.* New York: Platt and Munk, 1967, 274 p.

Lotz, Wolfgang. *A Handbook for Spies.* New York: Harper and Row, 1980, 146 p.

Lüdecke, Winfried. *The Secrets of Espionage: Tales of the Secret Service.* Philadelphia: Lippincott, 1929, 250 p. (U.S. edition of *Behind the Scenes of Espionage,* London: Harrap).

McCormick, Donald. *The Master Book of Spies: The World of Espionage, Master Spies, Tortures, Interrogations, Spy Equipment, Escapes, Codes and How You Can Become a Spy.* New York: F. Watts, 1974, 190 p.

McKay, Randle and **Gerrard, R.J.** *The "Intelligence" Game of Secret Service Cases and Problems.* New York: McBride, 1935, 217 p.

Maclean, Fitzroy. *Take Nine Spies.* London: Weidenfeld and Nicolson, 1978, 341 p.

Makin, William James. *Brigade of Spies.* New York: Dutton, 1938, 284 p.

The Man From Uncle: A.B.C. of Espionage. London: Souvenir Press and New English Library, 1966, 126 p.

Murphy, Brian Michael. *The Business of Spying.* London: Dolphin, 1973, 208 p.

Newman, Bernard. *Epics of Espionage.* New York: Philosophical Library, 1951, 270 p.

Newman, Bernard. *The World of Espionage.* New York: British Book Centre, 1962, 254 p.

Nolen, Barbara, ed. *Spies, Spies, Spies.* New York: F. Watts, 1965, 250 p.

Pastor Petit, Domingo. *L'Espionnage.* Translated from the Spanish by Paul Werrie. Paris: René Julliard, 1973, 351 p. (original: *Anatomía del espionaje.* Barcelona: Plaza and Janés, 1970).

Perles, Alfred, ed. *Great True Spy Adventures.* London: Arco, 1957, 210 p.

Ray, Oscar, *pseud.* (Farkas, Aladar). *Espions et espionnage.* Paris: Gallimard, 1936, 268 p.

Rowan, Richard Wilmer. *Secret Agents Against America.* New York: Doubleday, Doran, 1939, 267 p.

Rowan, Richard Wilmer. *Spy and Counter-Spy: The Development of Modern Espionage.* New York: Viking Press, 1928, 322 p.

Rowan, Richard Wilmer. *The Spy Menace: An Exposure of International Espionage.* London: T. Butterworth, 1934, 284 p.

Rowan, Richard Wilmer and **Deindorfer, Robert G.** *Secret Service: Thirty-three Centuries of Espionage.* New York: Hawthorn Books, 1967, 786 p.

Scharnhorst, Gerd. *Spione in der Bundeswehr: Ein Dokumentar-Bericht.* Bayreuth: Hestia-Verlag, 1965, 296 p.

Seth, Ronald. *Anatomy of Spying.* New York: Dutton, 1963, 368 p.

Seth, Ronald. *The Art of Spying.* London: P. Owen, 1957, 183 p.

Seth, Ronald. *Secret Servants: A History of Japanese Espionage.* New York: Farrar, Straus and Cudahy, 1957, 278 p.

Seth, Ronald. *Some of My Favorite Spies.* Philadelphia: Chilton, 1968, 189 p.

Seth, Ronald. *Spies at Work: A History of Espionage.* London: P. Owen, 1954, 234 p.

Tadmor, Joshua. *The Silent Warriors.* Translated from the Hebrew by Raphael Rothstein. New York: Macmillan, 1969, 189 p.

TSvigun, Semen Kuz'mich. *Tainyi front: O podryvnoi deiatel'nosti imperializma protiv SSSR i bditel'nosti sov. liudei.* Moscow: Politizdat, 1973, 399 p.

TSybov, Sergei Ivanovich and **Chistiakov, Nikolai Fedorovich.** *Front of the Secret War.*

TSybov, Sergei Ivanovich and **Chistiakov, Nikolai Fedorovich.** *Front Tainoi Voiny.* Moscow: Voen. Izd-vo, 1968, 158 p.

"Vigilant." *Secrets of Modern Spying.* London: J. Hamilton, 1932, 299 p.

Viktorov, Boris Alekseevich. *Shpiony pod maskoi turistov.* Ann Arbor, Mich.: University Microfilms, 1976, 53 p. (original published by Voen. Izd-vo, Moscow, 1963).

Vögeli, Robert. *Spionage in der Gegenwart.* Kreuzlingen: Neptun-Verlag, 1969, 97 p. (Schriftenreihe der Aktion für Freie Demokratie, v. 1).

Votinov, A. *IAponskii shpionazh v russko-iaponskuiu voiny 1904–1905 gg.* Moscow: Voen. Izd-vo Narkomata oborony Soiuza SSSR, 1939, 71 p.

Wade, Alexander Gawthrop. *Spies To-day.* London: S. Paul, 1939, 288 p.

Wighton, Charles. *The World's Greatest Spies: True-Life Dramas of Outstanding Secret Agents.* New York: Taplinger, 1962, 319 p.

Wilkinson, Burke, comp. *Cry Spy! True Stories of 20th Century Spies and Spy Catchers.* Englewood Cliffs, N.J.: Bradbury Press, 1969, 271 p.

Fiction and Collections of Spy Stories

Agabekov, Grigorii Sergeevich. *Die Tscheka bei der Arbeit.* Translated by A. Chanoch. Stuttgart: Union Deutsche Verlagsgesellschaft, 1932, 297 p. (paperback).

Cassidy, John. *A Station in the Delta: A Novel.* New York: Scribner, 1979, 380 p.

Clark, Ronald William. *Great Moments in Espionage.* London: Phoenix House; New York: Roy Publishers, 1963, 126 p.

Deming, Richard. *American Spies: Real Life Stories of Undercover Agents in Our History.* Racine, Wis.: Whitman, 1960, 210 p.

Duke, Madelaine. *Top Secret Mission.* New York: Criterion Books, 1955, 208 p.

Farrington, Robert. *Tudor Agent.* New York: St. Martin's Press, 1974, 278 p.

Fifty Amazing Secret Service Dramas. London: Odhams, n.d., 704 p.

Gerteis, Walter. *Detektivi u. Zivotu i Romanima.* Zagreb: Novinarsko Izdavacko Poduzese, 1961, 172 p. (translation of *Detektive, ihre Geschichte im Leben und in der Literatur.* Munich: Heimeran, 1953, 187 p.).

Gofman, Genrikh Borisovich. *Chernyi general; Dvoe nad okeanom: Povesti.* Moscow: Sov. Pisatel', 1977, 413 p.

Graves, Armgaard Karl, pseud. *The Secrets of the Hohenzollerns.* New York: McBride, Nast, 1915, 251 p.

Greene, Graham. *The Quiet American.* New York: Viking Press, 1956, 249 p.

Greshing, Robert. *Forever and Ever Mamewaka.* New York: Vantage Press, 1975, 76 p.

Healey, Tim. *Spies.* London: Macdonald Educational, 1978, 61 p.

Hollander, John. *Reflections on Espionage: The Question of Cupcake.* New York: Atheneum, 1976, 76 p.

Howe, George Locke. *Call It Treason, a Novel.* New York: Viking Press, 1949, 344 p.

Jenkins, Alan C., comp. *Spy! An Anthology of Espionage Stories.* London: Blackie, 1969, 415 p.

Komroff, Manuel. *True Adventures of Spies.* Boston: Little, Brown, 1954, 220 p.

Korshunov, Evgenii Anatol'evich. *I pridet bol'shoi dozhd' . . .: Operatsiia Zolotoi Lev: Povest'.* Moscow: Mol. Gvardiia, 1974, 238 p.

Lebedev, Mikhail Mikhailovich. *Treason—for my Daily Bread.* Edited by W.G. Stanton. Saint Peter Port, Guernsey: Vallancey, 1977, 407 p.

McKenna, Marthe (Cnokaert). *Hunt the Spy.* London: Jarrolds, 1939, 255 p.

Maggio, Joe. *Company Man: A Novel.* New York: Putnam, 1972, 222 p.

Moore, Robin. *The Country Team: A Novel.* New York: Crown, 1967, 408 p.

Schurmacher, Emile Carlos. *Our Secret War Against Red China.* New York: Paperback Library, 1962, 176 p.

Singer, Kurt D. *The Men in the Trojan Horse.* Boston: Beacon Press, 1953, 258 p.

Singer, Kurt D. *More Spy Stories, Including "Mona Lisa's Last Smile."* London: W.H. Allen, 1955, 222 p.

Singer, Kurt D. *Spies and Traitors: A Short History of Espionage.* London: W.H. Allen, 1953, 222 p.

Singer, Kurt D. *Spies Over Asia.* London: W.H. Allen, 1956, 223 p.

Singer, Kurt D. *Spy Omnibus.* London: W.H. Allen, 1959, 344 p.

Singer, Kurt D. *Spy Omnibus.* Minneapolis: Denison, 1962, 443 p.

Singer, Kurt D. *Women Spies.* Toronto, Winnipeg: Harlequin, 1953, 158 p. (paperback).

Singer, Kurt D. *The World's Greatest Women Spies.* London: W.H. Allen, 1951, 199 p.

Singer, Kurt D., ed. The Secret Agent's Badge of Courage by Ernest Hemingway [and Eight Other Stories]. New York: Belmont, 1961, 158 p. (reprinted from The World's Greatest Spy Stories).

Singer, Kurt D., ed. Spies Who Changed History. New York: Ace Books, 1960, 320 p. (paperback).

Singer, Kurt D., ed. Three Thousand Years of Espionage: An Anthology of the World's Greatest Spy Stories. New York: Prentice-Hall, 1948, 384 p.

Singer, Kurt D., ed. The Traitor by W. Somerset Maugham [and Seven Other Spy Stories]. New York: Belmont, 1961, 158 p. (reprinted from The World's Greatest Spy Stories).

Singer, Kurt D. and **Sherrod, Jane.** Spies for Democracy. Minneapolis: Denison, 1960, 272 p.

Spy and Mystery Stories. Edited by Kenneth Allen. London: Octopus Books, 1978, 399 p.

Spy in Black Lace. Edited by Noah Sarlat. New York: Lancer Books, 1964, 144 p. (paperback).

Sweetman, David. Spies and Spying. Hove, East Sussex [England]: Wayland Publishers, 1978, 96 p.

Tevekelian, Vartkes Arutiunovich. Mr. Kochek's Advertising Agency. Washington: U.S. Joint Publications Research Service, no. 55530, March 24, 1972, 340 p. (translation of Reklamnoe Biuro Gospodina Kocheka: Zhivaia legenda: Roman, Moscow: Sov. Pisatel', 1967).

Vange, Norman. A Spy in Damascus. London: Sampson Low, Marston, 1950, 248 p.

Weeden, George Dewey. I Rode the Rods Through Naval Intelligence. New York: Vantage Press, 1954, 342 p.

Widder, Arthur. Adventures in Black: [The Inside Story of Undercover Agents, Espionage, and Counterespionage Activities—From the Civil War to the Present]. New York: Harper and Row, 1962, 180 p.

Soviet/Communist

Australia, Royal Commission on Espionage. Report. Sydney: A.H. Pettifer, Govt. Printer for New South Wales, 1955, 483 p.

Bailey, Geoffrey, pseud. The Conspirators. New York: Harper, 1960, 306 p.

Blackstock, Paul S. The Secret Road to World War Two: Soviet Versus Western Intelligence, 1921-1939. Chicago: Quadrangle Books, 1969, 384 p.

Bulloch, John and **Miller, Henry.** Spy Ring: The Full Story of the Naval Secrets Case. London: Secker and Warburg, 1961, 224 p.

Carpozi, George. Red Spies in the U.S. New Rochelle, N.Y.: Arlington House, 1973, 251 p.

Carpozi, George. Red Spies in Washington. New York: Trident Press, 1968, 252 p.

Carran, Edward. The Soviet Spy Web. London: Ampersand, 1961, 86 p. (paperback).

Dallin, David J. Soviet Espionage. New Haven: Yale University Press, 1955, 558 p.

De Toledano, Ralph. The Greatest Plot in History. New York: Duell, Sloan and Pierce, 1963, 306 p.

Handleman, Howard. "The Soviet KGB in America." Air Force, June 1979, pp. 57-60.

Heilbrunn, Otto. The Soviet Secret Services. London: Allen and Unwin, 1956, 216 p.

Hirsch, Richard. The Soviet Spies: The Story of Russian Espionage in North America. London: N. Kaye, 1947, 164 p.

Huss, Pierre John and **Carpozi, George, Jr.** Red Spies in the UN. New York: Coward-McCann, 1965, 287 p.

Hutton, Joseph Bernard. School for Spies: The ABC of How Russia's Secret Service Operates. New York: Coward-McCann, 1962, 222 p.

Hutton, Joseph Bernard. Struggle in the Dark: How Russian and Other Iron Curtain Spies Operate. London: Harrap, 1969, 208 p.

Hyde, Harford Montgomery. The Atom Bomb Spies. New York: Atheneum, 1980, 339 p.

Lewis, David. "The Assault on NATO: How Russian Agents Nearly Put NATO to Bed." Penthouse, February 1976, p. 45+.

Lucas, Norman. The Great Spy Ring. London: Barker, 1966, 284 p.

Newman, Bernard. The Red Spider Web: The Story of Russian Spying in Canada. London: Latimer House, 1947, 254 p.

Newman, Bernard. Soviet Atomic Spies. London: R. Hale, 1952, 239 p.

[Newman, Joseph]. Famous Soviet Spies: The Kremlin's Secret Weapon. Washington: Books by U.S. News and World Report, 1973, 223 p.

Noel-Baker, Francis Edward. *The Spy Web.* New York: Vanguard Press, 1955, 242 p.

Orlov, Alexander. *Handbook of Intelligence and Guerrilla Warfare.* Ann Arbor: University of Michigan Press, 1963, 187 p.

Seth, Ronald. *Unmasked! The Story of Soviet Espionage.* New York: Hawthorn Books, 1965, 306 p. (U.S. edition of *Forty Years of Soviet Spying*).

Skousen, Willard Cleon. *The Naked Communist.* Salt Lake City: Ensign, 1960, 343 p.

Steele, Alexander. *How to Spy on the U.S.* New Rochelle, N.Y.: Arlington House, 1974, 185 p.

Szulc, Tad. "The KGB in Washington." *Washington Post Magazine,* March 2, 1980, p. 12+.

Tietjen, Arthur. *Soviet Spy Ring.* New York: Coward-McCann, 1961, 190 p.

U.S. Congress, House, Committee on Un-American Activities. *The Shameful Years: Thirty Years of Soviet Espionage in the United States.* Washington: U.S. GPO, 1951, 70 p. (House report no. 1229).

U.S. Congress, Joint Committee on Atomic Energy. *Soviet Atomic Espionage.* Washington: U.S. GPO, 1951, 222 p. (82d Congress, 1st Session).

U.S. Congress, Senate, Committee on the Judiciary, Subcommittee to Investigate the Administration of the Internal Security Act and Other Internal Security Laws. *Scope of Soviet Activity in the United States. Hearing ... 84th Congress, 2d Session.* Washington: U.S. GPO, 1956, pts. 1-42. (hearings held February 8, 1956—November 29, 1957).

Voitsekhovskii, Sergei L'vovich. *Trest: Vospominaniia i dokumenty.* London, Ont.: Zaria, 1974, 192 p.

Weyl, Nathaniel. *The Battle Against Disloyalty.* New York: Crowell, 1951, 378 p.

White, John Baker. *The Soviet Spy System.* London: Falcon Press, 1948, 133 p.

United Kingdom/United States

Army Times, Washington, D.C. *Modern American Secret Agents,* by the editors of the *Army Times.* New York: Dodd, Mead, 1966, 143 p.

Bakeless, John Edwin. *Christopher Marlow.* New York: Haskell House, 1975, 357 p.

Bulloch, John. *Akin to Treason.* London, Barker, 1966, 188 p.

Daniloff, Nicholas. "How We Spy on the Russians." *Washington Post Magazine,* December 9, 1979, p. 24+.

Daniloff, Ruth. "Defectors: Spy Satellites Can't See Through Metal or Tell Us What's Inside the Russian Mind." *Washington Post Magazine,* December 9, 1979, p. 36+.

Great Britain, Central Office for Information. *Their Trade is Treachery:* [security manual]. Prepared for Her Majesty's Government by the Central Office for Information, 1962, 59 p.

Hutton, Joseph Bernard. *Commander Crabb is Alive.* New York: Universal Publishing and Distributing Corp., 192 p. (paperback).

Hutton, Joseph Bernard. *Frogman Spy, the Incredible Case of Commander Crabb.* New York: McDowell, Obolensky, 1960, 180 p.

Pincher, Chapman. *Inside Story: A Documentary of the Pursuit of Power.* New York: Stein and Day, 1979, 400 p.

Prebble, John. *Glencoe: The Story of the Massacre.* New York: Holt, Rinehart and Winston, 1966, 336 p.

Pugh, Marshall. *Frogman: Commander Crabb's Story.* New York: Scribner, 165 p.

Rositzke, Harry August. *The CIA's Secret Operations: Espionage, Counterespionage, and Covert Action.* New York: Reader's Digest Press, 1977, 286 p.

Ward, Stephen George Peregrine. *Wellington's Headquarters: A Study of the Administrative Problems in the Peninsula, 1809-1814.* London: Oxford University Press, 1957, 219 p.

Weyl, Nathaniel. *Treason: The Story of Disloyalty and Betrayal in American History.* Washington: Public Affairs Press, 1950, 491 p.

Whitehouse, Arthur George Joseph. *Espionage and Counterespionage: Adventures in Military Intelligence.* Garden City, N.Y.: Doubleday, 1964, 298 p.

American Revolution

Bakeless, John Edwin. "General Washington's Spy System." *Manuscripts,* v. XII, no. 2 (Spring 1960), pp. 28-37.

Bakeless, John Edwin. *General Washington's Spy System: An Address by John Bakeless. A Report by*

Francis S. Ronalds. A Report by the Board of Trustees of the Washington Association of New Jersey. Morristown, N.J., February 23, 1959; 40 p.

Bakeless, John Edwin. *Turncoats, Traitors, and Heroes.* Philadelphia: Lippincott, 1959, 406 p.

Bemis, Samuel Flagg. "British Secret Service and the French-American Alliance." *American Historical Review,* v. XXIX (April 1924), pp. 474-495.

Bemis, Samuel Flagg. "Secret Intelligence, 1777: Two Documents." *Huntington Library Quarterly,* v. XXIV, no. 3 (May 1961), pp. 233-248.

Booth, Sally Smith. *The Women of '76.* New York: Hastings House, 1976, 329 p.

[Bunce, Oliver Bell]. *The Romance of the Revolution: Being True Stories of the Adventures, Romantic Incidents, Hairbreadth Escapes, and Heroic Exploits of the Days of '76....* Philadelphia: Porter and Coates, 1870, 444 p.

Clark, John. "Letters From Major John Clark, Jr., to Gen. Washington Written During the Occupation of Philadelphia by the British Army." *Bulletin of the Historical Society of Pennsylvania,* v. I (1845-1847), pp. 1-36.

De Pauw, Linda Grant. *Four Traditions: Women of New York During the American Revolution.* Albany: New York State American Revolution Bicentennial Commission, 1974, 39 p.

Engle, Paul. *Women in the American Revolution.* Chicago: Follett, 1976, 299 p.

Ford, Corey. *A Peculiar Service.* Boston: Little, Brown, 1965, 358 p.

[Marks, Mary A.M. (Hoppus)]. *A Great Treason, A Story of the War of Independence.* New York: Macmillan, 1883, 595 p.

Mathews, Hazel C. *Frontier Spies: The British Secret Service, Northern Department, During the Revolutionary War.* Fort Myers, Fla.: Ace Press, 1971, 288 p.

Pennypacker, Morton. *General Washington's Spies on Long Island and in New York.* Brooklyn: Long Island Historical Society, 1939, v. 1; East Hampton, N.Y.: Pennypacker Long Island Collection, East Hampton Free Library, 1948, v. 2.

Rigg, Robert B. "Of Spies and Specie." *Military Review,* August 1962, pp. 13-21.

U.S. Central Intelligence Agency. *Intelligence in the War of Independence.* Washington: Central Intelligence Agency, 1976, 40 p.

Wise, William. *The Spy and General Washington.* New York: Dutton, 1965, 87 p.

Young, Philip. *Revolutionary Ladies.* New York: Knopf and Random House, 1977, 225 p.

American Civil War

Bakeless, John Edwin. *Spies of the Confederacy.* Philadelphia: Lippincott, 1970, 456 p.

Bakeless, Katherine (Little) and **Bakeless, John.** *Confederate Spy Stories.* Philadelphia: Lippincott, 1973, 159 p.

Baker, La Fayette Charles. *Daring Exploits of Scouts and Spies: A Graphic History of Rich and Exciting Experiences, Perilous Adventures, Hairbreadth Escapes, and Valuable Services Rendered by the National Secret Service Bureau of the United States, Including the Origin and Organization of the Department of Detective Police.* Chicago: Thompson and Thomas, 1894, 398 p.

Baker, La Fayette Charles. *The United States Secret Service in the Late War, Comprising the Author's Introduction to the Leading Men at Washington....* Philadelphia: J.E. Potter, 1874, 398 p. (published in 1894 under the title: *Spies, Traitors and Conspirators of the Late Civil War*).

Beymer, William Gilmore. *On Hazardous Service: Scouts and Spies of the North and South.* New York and London: Harper, 1912, 286 p.

Bulloch, James Dunwody. *The Secret Service of the Confederate States in Europe: or, How the Confederate Cruisers were Equipped.* New York: T. Yoseloff, 1959, 2 v.

Catton, Bruce. *The Centennial History of the Civil War. Volume 1: The Coming Fury.* New York: Doubleday, 1961, 563 p.

Fitch, John. *Annals of the Army of the Cumberland: Comprising Biographies, Descriptions of Departments, Accounts of Expeditions, Skirmishes, and Battles ... and Official Reports of the Battle of Stone River.* Philadelphia: Lippincott, 1863, 671 p.

Foreman, Allan. "A Bit of Secret Service History." *Magazine of American History,* v. XII, no. 4 (October 1884), pp. 323-331.

Gaddy, David W. "Gray Cloaks and Daggers." *Civil War Times Illustrated,* July 1975, pp. 20-27.

Greene, Charles S. *Thrilling Stories of the Great Rebellion: Comprising Heroic Adventures and Hair-Breadth Escapes of Soldiers, Scouts, Spies, and Refugees; Daring Exploits of Smugglers, Guerrillas, Desperadoes, and Others; Tales of Loyal and Disloyal Women; Stories of the Negro. . . .* Philadelphia: J.E. Potter, 1864, 384 p.

Hazelton, Joseph Powers, *pseud.* (Brocket, Linus Pierpont). *Scouts, Spies, and Heroes of the Great Civil War. . . .* Jersey City: Star Publishing Co., 1982, 512 p.

"Intelligence and Security." *Civil War History,* v. 10, no. 4 (December 1964), pp. 341–459.

Kane, Harnett Thomas. *Spies for the Blue and Gray.* New York: Ace Books, 1954, 221 p.

Miller, Francis Trevelyan, ed. *The Photographic History of the Civil War . . . 1861–65. Volume 8: Soldier Life, Secret Service.* New York: Castle Books, 1957, 383 p.

Mogelever, Jacob. *Death to Traitors: The Story of General Lafayette C. Baker, Lincoln's Forgotten Secret Service Chief.* Garden City, N.Y.: Doubleday, 1960, 429 p.

Pittenger, William. *Capturing a Locomotive: A History of Secret Service in the Late War.* Washington: The National Tribune, 1885, 354 p.

Richardson, Albert Deane. *The Secret Service: The Field, the Dungeon, and the Escape.* Hartford, Conn.: American Publishing, 1865, 512 p.

Stern, Philip Van Doren. *Secret Missions of the Civil War: First-Hand Accounts by Men and Women Who Risked Their Lives in Underground Activities for the North and the South. . . .* Chicago: Rand McNally, 1959, 320 p.

World War I

Adam, George Jefferys. *Treason and Tragedy: An Account of French War Trials.* London: J. Cape, 1929, 253 p.

Aston, George Grey, Sir. *Secret Service.* New York: Cosmopolitan Book, 1930, 348 p.

Barton, George. *Celebrated Spies and Famous Mysteries of the Great War.* Boston: Page, 1919, 345 p.

Barton, George. *More Real Spies.* New York: Universal, 1966, 123 p. (paperback edition based on *Celebrated Spies. . . .*).

Barton, George. *Real Spies.* New York: Universal, 1965, 124 p. (paperback edition based on *Celebrated Spies. . . .*).

Beaufort, J.M. de. *Behind the German Veil: A Record of a Journalistic War Pilgrimage.* London: Hutchinson, 1917, 367 p.

Berndorff, Hans Rudolf. *Espionage!* Translated by Bernard Miall. New York: D. Appleton, 1930, 267 p.

Boucard, Robert. *Revelations from the Secret Service.* Translated by Raglan Somerset. London: Hutchinson, n.d., 173 p. (original: *Les dessous des archives secrètes d'un espionnage à l'autre,* Paris: Editions de France, 1929).

Boucard, Robert. *The Secret Services of Europe.* Translated by Ronald Leslie-Melville. London: S. Paul, 1940, 260 p.

Busch, Tristan, *pseud.* (Schuetz, Arthur). *Entlarvter geheimdienst, secretinismus.* Zürich: Pegasus Verlag, 1946, 478 p.

Cooper, Courtney Ryley. *The Eagle's Eye: A True Story of the Imperial German Government's Spies and Intrigues in America from Facts Furnished by William J. Flynn, Recently Retired Chief of the U.S. Secret Service, Novelized by Courtney Ryley Cooper.* New York: Prospect Press, 1918, 377 p.

Deeds of Heroism and Bravery: the Book of Heroes and Personal Daring. Edited by Elwyn A. Barron. New York: Harper, 1920, 402 p.

Everitt, Nicholas. *British Secret Service During the Great War.* London: Hutchinson, 1920, 320 p.

Felger, Friedrich, ed. *Was Wir vom Weltkrieg nicht wissen,* im Auftrage der Weltkriegsbücherei herausgegeben. Berlin and Leipzig: W. Andermann, 1929, 640 p.

Felstead, Sidney Theodore, comp. *German Spies at Bay, Being an Actual Record of the German Espionage in Great Britain During the Years 1914–1918.* New York: Brentano's, 288 p.

Gowenlock, Thomas Russell with **Murchie, Guy, Jr.** *Soldiers of Darkness.* Garden City, N.Y.: Doubleday, Doran, 1937, 286 p.

Gross, Felix. *I Knew Those Spies.* London: Hurst and Blackett, 1940, 255 p.

Grote, Hans Henning, *Freiherr,* ed. *Vorsicht! Feind hört mit! Eine Geschichte der Weltkriegs und Nachkriegsspionage.* Berlin: Neufeld and Henius, 1930, 339 p.

Hahn, James Emanuel. *The Intelligence Service Within the Canadian Corps, 1914-1918.* Toronto: Macmillan, 1930, 263 p.

Hoy, Hugh Cleland. *40 O.B.: Or, How the War Was Won.* London: Hutchinson, 1932, 287 p.

Johnson, Thomas Marvin. *Our Secret War: True American Spy Stories, 1917-1919.* Indianapolis: Bobbs-Merrill, 1929, 340 p.

Jones, John Price. *America Entangled: The Secret Plotting of German Spies in the United States and the Inside Story of the Sinking of the Lusitania.* New York: A.C. Laut, 1917, 224 p. (U.S. edition of *The German Spy in America,* London: Hutchinson).

Jones, John Price and **Hollister, Paul Merrick.** *The German Secret Service in America.* Boston: Small, Maynard, 1918, 340 p.

Lake, Harold. *Campaigning in the Balkans.* New York: McBride, 1918, 229 p.

Landau, Henry. *All's Fair: The Story of the British Secret Service Behind the German Lines.* New York: Putnam, 1934, 329 p.

Landau, Henry. *The Enemy Within: The Inside Story of German Sabotage in America.* New York: Putnam, 1937, 323 p.

Landau, Henry. *Secrets of the White Lady.* New York: Putnam, 1935, 314 p.

Landau, Henry. *Spreading the Spy Net: The Story of a British Spy Director.* London: Jarrolds, 1938, 284 p.

Le Queux, William. *German Spies in England: An Exposure.* London: S. Paul, 1915, 224 p.

Lettow-Vorbeck, Paul Emil von, ed. *Die Weltkriegsspionage: Authentische Enthüllungen über Entstehung, Art, Arbeit, Technik, Schliche, Handlungen, Wirkungen und Geheimnisse der Spionage vor, während und nach dem Kriege auf Grund amtlichen Materials aus Kriegs-, Militär-, Gerichts- und Reichsarchiven, vom Leben und Sterben, von den Taten und Abenteuern der bedeutendsten Agenten bei Freund und Feind.* Munich: J. Moser, 1931, 688 p.

McKenna, Marthe (Cnokaert). *Spies I Knew.* New York: McBride, 1934, 236 p.

Maugham, William Somerset. *Ashenden: Or, the British Agent.* New York: New Avon Library, 1943, 190 p. (fiction).

Newman, Bernard. *Secret Servant.* London: V. Gollancz, 1935, 287 p. (fiction).

My Secret Service: Vienna, Sophia, Constantinople, Nish, Belgrade, Asia Minor, etc., by the Man Who Dined With the Kaiser. New York: Doran, 1916, 235 p.

Nicolai, Walter. *The German Secret Service.* Translated by George Renwick. London: S. Paul, 1924, 298 p.

Nicolai, Walter. *Nachrichtendienst, Presse und Volksstimmung im Weltkrieg.* Berlin: E.S. Mittler, 1920, 226 p.

Nicolai, Walter. *Secret Powers: German Military Intelligence in the First War.* A "new translation" by an unidentified British officer. [post-1924], 113 p.

Oliver, Frederick Scott. *Ordeal by Battle.* London: Macmillan, 1915, 437 p.

Pierrefue, Jean de. *C.Q.G. Secteur 1.* Paris: G. Cres, 1922, 2 v.

Rawlinson, Alfred. *Adventures in the Near East, 1918-1922.* London: Andrew Melrose Ltd., 1924, 375 p.

Reilly, Henry Joseph. *Why Preparedness: The Observations of an American Army Officer in Europe, 1914-1915.* Chicago: Daughaday, 1916, 401 p.

Rowan, Richard Wilmer, ed. *Modern Spies Tell Their Stories: Personal Narratives of Many Exploits in Secret Service.* New York: R.M. McBride, 1934, 482 p.

Russell, Charles Edmund. *True Adventures of the Secret Service.* New York: A.L. Burt Co., n.d., 316 p.

Seeliger, Emil, comp. *Spione und Verräter: Die Maulwürfe des Völkerringens.* Berlin: Verlag für kultur-politik, 1930, 270 p.

Selection from Papers found in the Possession of Captain von Papen, late German Military Attaché at Washington, Falmouth, January 2 and 3, 1916. London: H.M. Stationery Office, Harrison and Sons, Printers, 1916, 35 p.

Silber, Jules Crawford. *The Invisible Weapons.* London: Hutchinson, 1932, 288 p.

Skaggs, William Henry. *German Conspiracies in America, From an American Point of View, by an American.* London: T.F. Unwin, 1915, 332 p.

Sperry, Earl Evelyn assisted by **West, Willis M.** *German Plots and Intrigues in the United States During the Period of our Neutrality.* Washington: Committee on Public Information, 1918, 64 p.

Thomson, Basil Home, Sir. *The Allied Secret Service in Greece.* London: Hutchinson, 1931, 288 p.

Thwaites, Norman Graham. *Velvet and Vinegar.* London: Grayson and Grayson, 1932, 283 p.

Tunney, Thomas Joseph. *Throttled! The Defection of the German and Anarchist Bomb Plotters . . .* as told to Paul Merrick Hollister. Boston: Small, Maynard, 1919, 277 p.

Tuohy, Ferdinand. *The Secret Corps: A Tale of "Intelligence" on all Fronts.* London: J. Murray, 1920, 289 p.

U.S. Army. A.E.F., 1917-1920. General Staff, G-2. *Instructions for Regimental Intelligence Service.* Paris: General Staff, American Expeditionary Forces, October 21, 1918, 35 p.

U.S. Army. A.E.F., 1917-1920. General Staff, G-2. *Intelligence and its Relation to the Air Service.* Issued by the Second Section, General Staff, American Expeditionary Forces, June 1, 1918. Paris: General Headquarters A.E.F., 1918, 15 p.

U.S. Army. A.E.F., 1917-1920. General Staff, G-2. *Notes on Branch Intelligence.* Issued by Second Section, General Staff, American Expeditionary Forces, November 1, 1918. n.p.: Printed at the Base Printing Plant, 29th Engineers, U.S. Army, 1919, 31 p.

U.S. Army. A.E.F., 1917-1920. General Staff, G-2. *Regulations for the Intelligence Section of the General Staff.* Paris: General Staff, American Expeditionary Forces, August 31, 1917, 48 p.

U.S. Army. A.E.F., 1917-1920. General Staff, G-2. *Two Lectures on Intelligence* by Colonel Vivian, British Army, and Major Williams, U.S. Army. Nancy, France: Second Section, General Staff, G.H.Q., American Expeditionary Forces, April 15, 1918, 34 p.

U.S. Army. 2d Division. Historical Section, Army War College. *General Orders: Intelligence Reports, 1918.* Washington: November 28, 1928, v. 9.

Woodhall, Edwin Thomas. *Spies of the Great War: Adventures with the Allied Secret Service.* London: J. Long, 1932, 251 p.

World War II

General

Bergier, Jacques. *Secret Weapons-Secret Agents.* London: Hurst and Blackett, 1956, 184 p.

Bryant, Arthur, Sir. *Triumph in the West: A History of the War Years Based on the Diaries of Field-Marshal Lord Alanbrooke, Chief of the Imperial General Staff.* Garden City, N.Y.: Doubleday, 1959, 438 p.

Cave Brown, Anthony. *Bodyguard of Lies.* New York: Harper and Row, 1975, 947 p.

Cruikshank, Charles Greig. *Deception in World War II.* Oxford; New York: Oxford University Press, 1979, 248 p.

Deacon, Richard, *pseud.* (McCormick, Donald); **West, Nigel.** *et al. Spy!* London: British Broadcasting Corporation, 1980, 190 p.

De Vosjoli, P.L. Thyraud. *Lamia.* Boston: Little, Brown, 1970, 344 p.

Downes, Donald C. *The Scarlet Thread: Adventures in Wartime Espionage.* London: D. Verschoyle, 1953, 207 p.

Farago, Ladislas. *Burn After Reading: The Espionage History of World War II.* New York: Macfadden-Bartell, 1963, 239 p.

Farago, Ladislas. *Spymaster.* New York: Paperback Library, 1962, 284 p. (paperback edition of *War of Wits: The Anatomy of Espionage and Intelligence.* New York: Funk and Wagnalls, 1954, 379 p).

Foot, Michael Richard Daniel. *Resistance: European Resistance to Nazism, 1940-1945.* New York: McGraw-Hill, 1977, 346 p.

Foot, Michael Richard Daniel. *Six Faces of Courage.* London: Eyre Methuen, 1978, 134 p.

Frogner, Carsten. *Die unsichtbare Front.* Zürich: Europa Verlag, 1944, 201 p.

Garder, Michel. *La Guerre secrète des services spéciaux français, 1935-1945.* Paris: Plon, 1967, 524 p.

Haswell, Chetwynd John Drake. *D-Day: Intelligence and Deception.* New York: Times Books, 1979, 208 p.

Howarth, David Armine. *The Sledge Patrol.* London: Collins, 1957, 254 p.

Kimche, Jon. *General Guisans Zweifrontenkrieg.* Frankfurt/M; Berlin: Verlag Ullstein, 1962, 231 p.

Kimche, Jon. *Spying for Peace: General Guisan and Swiss Neutrality.* New York: Roy Publishers, 1961, 168 p.

Kurz, Hans Rudolf. *Nachrichtenzentrum Schweiz. Die Schweiz im Nachrichtendienst des Zweiten Welt-kriegs.* Frauenfeld, Stuttgart: Huber, 1972, 131 p.

Musnik, Henry. *Service secret: souvenirs et documents d'agents de renseignements.* Paris: Editions "La France au Combat," 1945, 61 p.

Olsen, Oluf Reed. *Two Eggs on My Plate.* Translated from the Norwegian by F.H. Lyon. Chicago: Rand McNally, 1953, 365 p. (original: *Vi kommer igjen and Contact*).

Paillole, Paul. *Services spéciaux: 1935–1945.* Paris: R. Laffont, 1975, 565 p.

Piekalkiewicz, Janusz. *Spione, Agenten, Soldaten: Geheime Kommandos im 2. Weltkrieg.* Based on the TV documentary. Edited by Margret M. Laufenberg. Munich: Südwest Verlag, 1969, 528 p.

Prange, Gordon William. *At Dawn We Slept: The Untold Story of Pearl Harbor.* New York: McGraw-Hill, 1981, 873 p.

The Reader's Digest. *Secrets and Spies: Behind-the-Scenes Stories of World War II.* Pleasantville, N.Y.: Reader's Digest, 1964, 576 p.

The Reader's Digest. *Secrets and Stories of the War: A Selection of the Articles and Book Condensations in Which the Reader's Digest Recorded the Second World War.* London: Reader's Digest, 1963, 2 v.

Rowan, Richard Wilmer. *Terror in our Time: The Secret Service of Surprise Attack.* New York; Toronto: Longmans, Green, 1941, 438 p.

Schramm, Wilhelm, *Ritter von. Der Geheimdienst in Europa 1937–1945.* Munich; Vienna: Langen Müller, 1974, 406 p.

Schurmacher, Emile Carlos. *Assignment X: Top Secret.* New York: Paperback Library, 1965, 283 p.

Singer, Kurt D. *Duel for the Northland: The War of Enemy Agents in Scandinavia.* London: R. Hale, 1945, 192 p.

Singer, Kurt D. *Spies and Traitors of World War II.* New York: Prentice-Hall, 1945, 295 p.

Singer, Kurt D. *Spy Stories from Asia.* New York: W. Funk, 1955, 336 p.

Stead, Philip John. *Second Bureau.* London: Evans Bros., 1959, 212 p.

Tompkins, Peter. *Italy Betrayed.* New York: Simon and Schuster, 1966, 352 p.

Tompkins, Peter. *The Murder of Admiral Darlan, a Study in Conspiracy.* New York: Simon and Schuster, 1965, 287 p.

Whiting, Charles. *The Battle for Twelveland: An Account of Anglo-American Intelligence Operations Within Nazi Germany, 1939–1945.* London: Cooper, 1975, 240 p.

Whiting, Charles. *The War in the Shadows.* New York: Ballantine Books, 1973, 268 p.

Woytak, Richard A. *On the Border of War and Peace: Polish Intelligence and Diplomacy in 1937–1939 and the Origins of the Ultra Secret.* Boulder, Colo.: East European Quarterly; New York: Columbia University Press, 1979, 141 p.

Axis

Bellamy, Francis Rufus. *Blood Money: The Story of U.S. Treasury Secret Agents.* New York: Dutton, 1947, 257 p.

Buchheit, Gert. *Spionage in zwei Weltkriegen: Schachspiel mit Menschen.* Landshut: Verlag Politisches Archiv, 1975, 352 p.

Carlson, John Roy, *pseud.* (Derounian, Arthur). *Under Cover: My Four Years in the Nazi Underworld of America—the amazing revelation of how Axis agents and our enemies within are now plotting to destroy the United States.* New York: Dutton, 1943, 544 p.

Carter, Carolle J. *The Shamrock and the Swastika: German Espionage in Ireland in World War II.* Palo Alto, Calif.: Pacific Books, 1977, 287 p.

Dasch, George John. *Eight Spies Against America.* New York: R.M. McBride, 1959, 241 p.

Farago, Ladislas. *The Game of the Foxes: The Untold Story of German Espionage in the United States and Great Britain During World War II.* New York: D. McKay, 1971, 696 p.

Felstead, Sidney Theodore. *Intelligence: An Indictment of a Colossal Failure.* London: Hutchinson, 1941, 253 p.

Havas, Laslo. *Assassinat au sommet: Téhéran, 1943.* Paris: Arthaud, 1968, 335 p.

Havas, Laslo. *Hitler's Plot to Kill the Big Three.* Translated from the Hungarian by Kathleen Szasz. Revised edition with additional material translated by Jean Ure. New York: Cowles Book, 1967, 280 p.

Hoettl, Wilhelm. *Hitler's Paper Weapon.* Translated from the German by Basil Creighton. London: R. Hart-Davis, 1955, 187 p.

Hynd, Alan. *Betrayal from the East: The Inside Story of Japanese Spies in America.* New York: R.M. McBride, 1943. 287 p.

Hynd, Alan. *Passport to Treason: The Inside Story of Spies in America.* New York: R.M. McBride, 1943, 306 p.

Jowitt, William Allen. *Some Were Spies.* London: Hodder and Stoughton, 1954, 223 p.

Kahn, David. *Hitler's Spies: German Military Intelligence in World War II.* New York: Macmillan, 1978, 671 p.

Mader, Julius. *Der Banditenschatz; Ein Dokumentarbericht über den geheimen Goldschatz Hitlerdeutschlands.* Berlin: Verlag der Nation, 1973, 311 p.

Mader, Julius. *Les Généraux Espions d'Hitler Déposent.* Paris: Librairie Hachette, 1973, 271 p. (paperback) (French edition of *Hitlers Spionagegenerale sagen aus: Ein Documentarbericht über Aufbau, Struktur und Operationen des OKW Geheimdienstamtes Ausland. Abwehr mit einer Chronologie seiner Einsätze von 1933 bis 1944.* Berlin: Verlag der Nation, 1970, 475 p.).

Mader, Julius. *Hitlers Spionagegenerale sagen aus: Ein Documentarbericht über Aufbau, Struktur und Operationen des OKW Geheimdienstamtes Ausland. Abwehr mit einer Chronologie seiner Einsätze von 1933 bis 1944.* Berlin: Verlag der Nation, 1970, 475 p.

Mosley, Leonard. *The Druid.* New York: Atheneum, 1981, 240 p.

Newman, Bernard. *German Secret Service at Work.* New York: R.M. McBride, 1940, 264 p.

Nikitinskii, I. *Gitlerovskii shpionazh.* Moscow: Ogiz, Gospolitizdat, 1943, 39 p.

Pirie, Anthony. *Operation Bernard.* New York: Morrow, 1962, 303 p.

Rachlis, Eugene. *They Came to Kill: The Story of Eight Nazi Saboteurs in America.* New York: Random House, 1961, 306 p.

Rittlinger, Herbert. *Geheimdienst mit beschränkter Haftung: Bericht vom Bosporus.* Stuttgart: Deutsche Verlags-Anstalt, 1973, 339 p.

Sayers, Michael and **Kahn, Albert E.** *Sabotage! The Secret War Against America.* New York and London: Harper, 1942, 266 p.

Stephan, Enno. *Spies in Ireland.* Translated from the German by Arthur Davidson. Harrisburg: Stackpole, 1965, 311 p.

Thompson, Carlos. *The Assassination of Winston Churchill.* Gerrards Cross: Smythe, 1969, 461 p.

U.S. War Dept., Strategic Bombing Survey. Japanese Intelligence Section, G-2. *Japanese Military and Naval Intelligence Division: Survey, November 1, 1945 through February 1, 1946.* Washington: U.S. GPO, April 1946, 124 p.

Whaley, Barton. *Codeword BARBAROSSA.* Cambridge: M.I.T. Press, 1973, 376 p.

USSR

Berezniak, Evgenii Stepanovich. *Parol' "Dum spiro ...": Rasskaz razvedchika.* Translated from the Ukrainian. Kiev: Politizdat Ukrainy, 1979, 321 p. (fiction).

Blackstock, Paul W. *The Secret Road to World War Two: Soviet Versus Western Intelligence, 1921-1939.* Chicago: Quadrangle Books, 1969, 384 p.

Bogdanov, A.A. et al. *V poedinke s abverom: Dokum. Ocherk o Chekistakh Leningr. Fronta, 1941-1945.* Leningrad: Leninizdat, 1974, 318 p.

Bogomolov, Vladimir Osipovich. *V avguste sorok chetvertogo: Roman.* Moscow: Mol. Gvardiia, 1974, 430 p.

Dewitt, Kurt. *The Role of the Partisans in Soviet Intelligence.* Maxwell Air Force Base, Ala.: Air Research and Development Command, Human Resources Research Institute, 1954, 52 p. (War Documentation Project "Alexander"; Research Study no. 6, v. 1).

Dol'd-Mikhailnik, IUrii Petrovich. *I odin v pole voin.* Translated from the Ukrainian. Kiev: Radanskii Pis'mennik, 1965, 749 p. (fiction).

Flicke, Wilhelm F. *Agenten funken nach Moskau: Funkspionagegruppe "Rote Drei."* In freier Bearbeitung den Tatsachen nacherzählt. Wels [Austria]: Verlag Welsermühl, 1957, 472 p.

Flicke, Wilhelm F. *Spionagegruppe Rote Kapelle.* In freier Bearbeitung den Tatsachen nacherzählt. Wels [Austria]: Verlag Welsermühl, 1958, 418 p.

Foote, Alexander. *Handbook for Spies.* London: Museum Press, 1949, 223 p.

Front bez linii fronta. Compiled by M. Lavrik. Kuibyshev: Agentstva Pechati Novosti, 1965, 256 p.

Front bez linii fronta: Sbornik vospominanii. Compiled by I.E. Polikarpenko. Moscow: Mosk. Rabochii, 1975, 464 p.

Geroi nezrimogo fronta: Sbornik. Compiled by S.D. Ivanov. Uzhgorod: Karpaty, 1978, 229 p.

Gruzdev, Konstantin Aleksandrovich. *V gody surovykh ispytanii.* Minsk: Belarus', 1976, 189 p.

Höhne, Heinz. *Codeword: Direktor; the Story of the Red Orchestra.* Translated from the German by Richard Barry. New York: Coward, McCann and Geoghegan, 1971, 310 p. (original: *Kennwort: Direktor*).

Koroteev, Nikolai Ivanovich. *TSiklon nad Sarydzhaz: Prikliuchencheskie povesti.* Moscow: Molodaia Gvardiia, 1976, 206 p. (fiction).

Kozhevnikov, Vadim Mikhailovich. *Shield and Sword.* Washington: U.S. Joint Publications Research Service, 19 May 1972, 4 v. (JPRS series nos. 56046-1 through 56046-4; translation of *Shchit i mech: roman,* Moscow: Sovetskii pisatel', 1966).

Kubatkin, P. *Podryvnaia rabota fashistskoi razvedki na leningradskom fronte.* Leningrad: Gospolitizdat, 1944, 35 p.

Kubatkin, P. *Razoblachat' proiski fashistskoi razvedki.* Moscow: Gospolitizdat, 1942, 19 p.

Kulakov, Aleksandr Stepanovich. *Ognëm i bronei.* Moscow: DOSAAF, 1978, 128 p. (fiction).

Leonov, Nikolai Ivanovich and **Kostrov, IU.V.** *Operatsiia "Viking."* Moscow: Sovetskaia Rossiia, 1974, 381 p.

Na linii ognia. Edited by I.K. IAkovleva. Moscow: IUrid. Lit., 1976, 344 p.

Nasibov, Aleksandr Ashotovich. *Tainik na El'be.* Moscow: Trudrezervizdat, 1959, 433 p. (fiction).

Operatsiia prodolzhaetsia: Povesti. Compiled by I.V. Chebushev. Moscow: Voenizdat, 1970, 512 p. (fiction).

The Rote Kapelle: The CIA's History of Soviet Intelligence and Espionage Networks in Western Europe, 1936-1945. Washington: University Publications of America, 1979, 390 p.

Semenov, IUlian Semenovich. *Tainaia voina Maksima Maksimovicha Isaeva.* Moscow: Sov. Rossiia, 1974, 624 p.

Vasilev, Arkadii Nikolaevich. *One O'clock in the Afternoon, Your Excellency.* Washington: U.S. Joint Publications Research Service, May 1972, 2 v. (JPRS series nos. 56096-1 and 56096-2; translation of *V chas dnia, Vashe prevoskhoditel'stvo: roman,* Moscow: Khudozh. Lit-ra, 1975).

Vasilevich, Ivan. *I snova cherez front.* ... Moscow: DOSAAF, 1977, 160 p. (fiction).

United Kingdom

Barker, Elisabeth. *Churchill and Eden at War.* New York: St. Martin's Press, 1978, 346 p.

British Policy Towards Wartime Resistance in Yugoslavia and Greece. Edited by Phyllis Auty and Richard Clogg. New York: Harper and Row, 1975, 308 p.

Buckmaster, Maurice J. *Specially Employed: The Story of British Aid to French Patriots of the Resistance.* London: Batchworth Press, 1952, 200 p.

Buckmaster, Maurice J. *They Fought Alone: The Story of British Agents in France.* New York: Norton, 1958, 255 p.

Colvin, Ian Goodhope. *The Unknown Courier.* With a note on the situation confronting the Axis in the Mediterranean in the spring of 1943 by Field-Marshal Kesselring. London: Kimber, 1953, 208 p.

Cookridge, E.H., *pseud.* (Spiro, Edward). *They Came From the Sky.* New York: Crowell, 1967, 257 p.

Cookridge, E.H., *pseud.* (Spiro, Edward). *Set Europe Ablaze.* New York: Crowell, 1967, 410 p.

Cowburn, Benjamin. *No Cloak, No Dagger.* London: Jarrolds, 1960, 192 p.

The Diary of a Staff Officer (Air Intelligence Liaison Officer) at Advanced Headquarters, North B.A.F.F. 1940. London: Methuen, 1941, 79 p.

Drummond, John Dorman. *But for These Men: How Eleven Commandos Saved Western Civilization.* New York: Award Books, 1965, 219 p.

Foot, Michael Richard Daniel. *SOE in France: An Account of the Work of the British Special Operations Executive in France, 1940-1944.* London: H.M. Stationery Off., 1966 (2d impression, with amendments, 1968), 550 p.

Fuller, Jean Overton. *Double Webs: Light on the Secret Agents' War in France.* London: Putnam, 1958, 256 p.

Gallagher, Thomas Michael. *Assault in Norway: Sabotaging the Nazi Nuclear Bomb.* New York: Harcourt, Brace, Jovanovich, 1975, 234 p.

Ganier-Raymond, Philippe. *The Tangled Web.* Translated from the French by Len Ortzen. London: Barker, 1968, 203 p.

Ganier-Raymond, Philippe. *The Tangled Web.* Translated from the French by Len Ortzen. New York: Paperback Library, 1972, 222 p.

Gubbins, Colin. "Resistance Movements in the War." *Journal of the Royal United Service Institution,* v. XCIII (February—November 1948), pp. 210-223.

Haukelid, Knut Anders. *Attack on Telemark.* New York: Ballantine Books, 1974, 160 p. (paperback edition of *Skis Against the Atom).*

Hinsley, Francis Harry with **Thomas, E.E.** *et al. British Intelligence in the Second World War: Its Influence on Strategy and Operations.* London: H.M. Stationery Off., 1979-1981, 2 v.

Howarth, Patrick. *Special Operations.* London: Routledge and Paul, 1955, 239 p.

James, Meyrich Edward Clifton. *The Counterfeit General Montgomery.* New York: Avon, n.d., 142 p. (paperback edition of *I Was Monty's Double.* London; New York: Rider, 1954, 192 p.).

Johnson, Stowers. *Agents Extraordinary.* London: Hale, 1975, 192 p.

Leasor, James. *The Unknown Warrior.* London: Heinemann, 1980, 263 p.

McLachlan, Donald. *Room 39: A Study in Naval Intelligence.* New York: Atheneum, 1968, 438 p.

Montagu, Ewen. *The Man Who Never Was.* New York: Avon, 1953, 128 p. (paperback).

Nicholas, Elizabeth. *Death Be Not Proud.* London: Cresset Press, 1958, 294 p.

Peis, Günter. *The Mirror of Deception: How Britain Turned the Nazi Spy Machine Against Itself.* Translated by William Steedman. New York: Pocket Books, 1980, 252 p. (paperback).

Pinto, Oreste. *Friend or Foe?* New York: Popular Library, 1954, 176 p. (paperback).

Sootland, A P *The London Cage.* London: Evans Bros., 1957, 203 p.

Seth, Ronald. *A Spy Has No Friends.* New York: Ballantine Books, 1972, 216 p. (paperback).

Stafford, David. *Britain and European Resistance, 1940-1945: A Survey of the Special Operations Executive, with Documents.* London: Macmillan; Toronto: University of Toronto Press, 1980, 295 p.

Stevenson, William. *A Man Called Intrepid: The Secret War.* New York: Harcourt, Brace, Jovanovich, 1976, 486 p.

Strong, Kenneth. *Intelligence at the Top: The Recollections of an Intelligence Officer.* London: Cassell, 1968, 271 p.

Tickell, Jerrard. *Moon Squadron.* London: A. Wingate, 1956, 204 p.

Tickell, Jerrard. *Moon Squadron.* Garden City, N.Y.: Doubleday, 1958, 204 p.

Trenowden, Ian. *Operations Most Secret: SOE: The Malayan Theatre.* London: Kimber, 1978, 231 p.

Wheeler, Mark C. *Britain and the War for Yugoslavia, 1940-1943.* Boulder: East European Monographs; New York: Columbia University Press, 1980, 351 p.

White, John Baker. *The Big Lie.* New York: Crowell, 1955, 235 p.

United States

Alcorn, Robert Hayden. *No Banners, No Bands: More Tales of the OSS.* New York: D. McKay, 1965, 275 p.

Alcorn, Robert Hayden. *No Bugles for Spies: Tales of the OSS.* New York: D. McKay, 1962, 209 p.

Alcorn, Robert Hayden. *Spies of the OSS.* London: Robert Hale, 1973, 192 p.

Ambrose, Stephen E. "Eisenhower and the Intelligence Community in World War II." *Journal of Contemporary History,* v. 16, no. 1 (January 1981), pp 153-166 p.

Ambrose, Stephen E. with **Immerman, Richard H.** *Ike's Spies: Eisenhower and the Espionage Establishment.* Garden City, N.Y.: Doubleday, 1981, 368 p.

Andersen, Hartvig. *The Dark City: Being an Account of the Adventures of a Secret Agent in Berlin.* London: Cresset Press, 1954, 254 p.

Booth, Waller B. *Mission Marcel-Proust: The Story of an Unusual OSS Undertaking.* Philadelphia: Dorrance, 1972, 168 p.

Campbell, Rodney. *The Luciano Project: The Secret Wartime Collaboration of the Mafia and the U.S. Navy.* New York: McGraw-Hill, 1977, 299 p.

Galang, Ricardo C. *Secret Mission to the Philippines.* Manila: University Pub., 1948, 234 p.

Gosset, Renée Pierre. *Conspiracy in Algiers, 1942–1943.* Translated from the French by Nancy Hecksher. New York: The Nation, 1945, 248 p.

Harrington, Joseph Daniel. *Yankee Samurai: The Secret Role of Nisei in America's Pacific Victory.* Detroit: Pettigrew Enterprises, 1979, 383 p.

Hernandez, Al. *Bahála na, Come What May: The Story of Mission ISRM (I Shall Return MacArthur) an Army-Navy Intelligence Mission in the Pacific, as told to Dixon Earle.* Berkeley, Calif.: Howell-North, 1961, 315 p.

Holmes, Wilfred Jay. *Double-edged Secrets: U.S. Naval Intelligence Operations in the Pacific During World War II.* Annapolis: Naval Institute Press, 1979, 231 p.

Howarth, David Armine. *The Sledge Patrol.* London: Collins, 1957, 254 p.

Ind, Allison. *Allied Intelligence Bureau: Our Secret Weapon in the War Against Japan.* New York: McKay, 1958, 305 p.

Infantry Journal, v. 59, July-December 1946, including index to v. 58 and 59, January-December 1946. Washington: Infantry Journal Press.

Intelligence Bulletin. Washington: U.S. War Dept., Military Intelligence Division. v. 1, nos. 10, 11, and 12; v. 2, nos. 1, 2, and 3; v. 3, no. 7: 1943-1945.

Koch, Oscar W. with **Hays, Robert G.** *G-2: Intelligence for Patton.* Philadelphia: Whitmore Pub., 1971, 167 p.

Kramer, Paul. "Nelson Rockefeller and British Security Coordination." *Journal of Contemporary History,* v. 16, January 1981, pp. 73–88.

Larson, James C. *Operations of the Fourth (French) Operational Group Office of Strategic Services, in France, August 17 to September 20, 1944 (Operation Lindsay, Southern France Campaign): Monograph Written While a Member of the Advanced Infantry Officers Class No. 1.* Fort Benning, Ga.: The Ground General School, October 1949, 11 p.

MacCloskey, Monro. *Secret Air Missions.* New York: R. Rosen Press, 1966, 159 p.

Smith, Bradley F. and **Agarossi, Elena.** *Operation Sunrise: The Secret Surrender.* New York: Basic Books, 1979, 234 p.

Smith, Nicol and **Clark, Blake.** *Into Siam, Underground Kingdom.* Indianapolis: Bobbs-Merrill, 1945, 315 p.

Smyth, Howard McGaw. *Secrets of the Fascist Era: How Uncle Sam Obtained Some of the Top-Level Documents of Mussolini's Period.* Carbondale: Southern Illinois University Press, 1975, 305 p.

U.S. Army Forces, Pacific Theater, Office of the Chief Engineer. *Engineers of the Southwest Pacific, 1941–1945. Volume III: Engineer Intelligence.* Washington: U.S. GPO, 1950, 467 p.

Industrial Espionage and Economic Warfare

Barlay, Stephen. *The Secrets Business.* New York: Crowell, 1974, 344 p. (first published under title *Double Cross*).

Barlay, Stephen. *Double Cross: Encounters With Industrial Spies.* London: Hamilton, 1973, 279 p.

Bellamy, Francis Rufus. *Blood Money, the Story of U.S. Treasury Secret Agents.* New York: Dutton, 1947, 257 p.

Bergier, Jacques. *Promyshlennyi shpionazh.* Translated from the French by M.A. Terterova. Moscow: Mezhdunarodnye Otnosheniia, 1972, 175 p. (original: *L'espionnage industriel,* Hachette, 1969).

Bergier, Jacques. *Secret Armies: The Growth of Corporate and Industrial Espionage.* Translated from the French by Harold J. Salemson. Indianapolis: Bobbs-Merrill, 1975, 268 p. (translation of the author's three separate works originally published under titles: *L'espionnage industriel, L'espionnage scientifique,* and *L'espionnage stratégique*).

Bowen, Walter Scott and **Neal, Harry Edward.** *The United States Secret Service.* Philadelphia: Chilton, 1960, 205 p.

Calkins, Clinch. *Spy Overhead, the Story of Industrial Espionage.* New York: Harcourt, Brace, 1937, 363 p.

Costello, John and **Hughes, Terry.** *The Concorde Conspiracy.* New York: Scribner, 1976, 302 p.

Davenport, Elaine; Eddy, Paul; *et al. The Plumbat Affair.* Philadelphia: Lippincott, 1978, 192 p.

Engberg, Edward. *The Spy in the Corporate Structure and the Right to Privacy.* Cleveland: World, 1967, 274 p.

Eisenberg, Dennis; Landau, Eli; *et al. Operation Uranium Ship.* New York: New American Library, 1978, 196 p. (paperback).

Greene, Richard M. *Business Intelligence and Espionage.* Homewood, Ill.: Dow Jones-Irwin, 1966, 312 p.

Hoettl, Wilhelm. *Hitler's Paper Weapon.* Translated from the German by Basil Creighton. London: R. Hart-Davis, 1955, 187 p.

Hougan, Jim. "The Plot to Wreck the Golden Greek: Prelude to Watergate." *Playboy,* September 1978, pp. 1-8.

Hougan, Jim. *Spooks: The Haunting of America: The Private Use of Secret Agents.* New York: Morrow, 1978, 478 p.

Howard, Sidney Coe with **Dunn, Robert.** *The Labor Spy.* New York: Republic, 1924, 200 p. (paperback).

Huberman, Leo. *The Labor Spy Racket.* New York: Modern Age Books, 1937, 195 p.

Hungarian Peoples' Republic, Ministry of Home Affairs. *Report of the Hungarian Ministry of Home Affairs on the MAORT Sabotage.* Budapest: Miklos Nagy and Atheneum, 1948, 61 p.

Hutton, Joseph Bernard. *The Traitor Trade.* New York: I. Obolensky, 1963, 223 p.

Mader, Julius. *Der Banditenschatz: ein Dokumentarbericht über den geheimen Goldschatz Hitlerdeutschlands.* Berlin: Verlag der Nation, 1973, 311 p.

Martin, James Stewart. *All Honorable Men.* Boston: Little, Brown, 1950, 326 p.

Mead, Shepherd. *How to Succeed at Business Spying by Trying: A Novel About Industrial Espionage.* New York: Simon and Schuster, 1968, 255 p.

Pirie, Anthony. *Operation Bernhard.* New York: Morrow, 1962, 303 p.

Smith, Paul Ignatius Slee. *Industrial Intelligence and Espionage.* London: Business Books, 1970, 172 p.

Sweeny, T.H. "The Value of Financial Intelligence." *Journal of the Royal United Service Institution,* v. XCIII (February-November 1948), pp. 444-451.

U.S. Industrial College of the Armed Forces. *Economic Intelligence and Economic Warfare.* Washington: Industrial College of the Armed Forces, 1954, 72 p. (Emergency Management of the National Economy, v. XV).

Wilensky, Harold L. *Organizational Intelligence: Knowledge and Policy in Government and Industry.* New York: Basic Books, 1967, 226 p.

Wu, Yuan-li. *Economic Warfare.* New York: Prentice-Hall, 1952, 403 p.

Observation and Reconnaissance

Applegate, Rex. *Scouting and Patrolling: Ground Reconnaissance Principles and Training.* Boulder, Colo.: Paladin Press, 1980, 117 p.

Armstrong, Nevill Alexander Drummond. *Fieldcraft, Sniping and Intelligence.* Boulder, Colo.: Paladin Press, 1975, 223 p.

"Battlefield Reconnaissance: A Study by the School of Musketry, Fort Sill." *Infantry Journal,* v. XIII, no. 5 (February 1917), pp. 474-490.

Bonatz, Heinz. *Die deutsche Marine-Funkaufklärung 1914-1945.* Darmstadt: Wehr und Wissen Verlagsgesellschaft, 1970, 174 p. (Beiträge zur Wehrforschung, v. 20/21).

Brown, R. Shepard. *Stringfellow of the Fourth.* New York: Crown, 1960, 307 p. (Frank Stringfellow).

Burnham, Frederick Russell. *Scouting on Two Continents.* Edited and arranged by Mary Nixon Everett. Garden City, N.Y.: Garden City, 1926, 370 p.

Clemens, Martin. "A Coastwatcher's Diary." Edited by Stephen W. Sears. *American Heritage,* v. XVII, no. 2 (February 1966), pp. 104-110.

Downs, Edward C. *Four Years a Scout and Spy. "General Bunker," One of Lieut. General Grant's Most Daring and Successful Scouts. Being a Narrative of the Thrilling Adventures, Narrow Escapes, Nobel Daring, and Amusing Incidents in the Experience of Corporal Ruggles During Four Years' Service as a Scout and Spy for the Federal Army; Embracing his Services for Twelve of the Most Distinguished Generals in the U.S. Army.* Zanesville, Ohio: H. Dunne, 1866, 404 p.

Drannan, William F. *Capt. W.F. Drannan, Chief of Scouts, as Pilot to Emigrant and Government Trains, Across the Plains of the Wild West of Fifty Years Ago. As Told by Himself.* ... Chicago: Rhodes and McClure, 1910, 407 p.

Feldt, Eric Augustus. *The Coastwatchers.* New York: Ballantine Books, [post 1946], 240 p.

Furse, George Armand. *Information in War: Its Acquisition and Transmission.* London: W. Clowes, 1895, 324 p.

Grant, Robert McQueen. *U-Boat Intelligence, 1914-1918.* Hamden, Conn.: Archon Books, 1969, 192 p.

Great Britain, War Office, General Staff. *Scouting and Patrolling.* Edited at Army War College. [Washington: U.S. GPO, 1918,], 56 p. (reprint from an official British document; U.S. War Department, Office of the Adjutant General, document no. 772).

Henderson, David. *The Art of Reconnaissance.* London: J. Murray, 1914, 197 p.

Heymont, Irving. *Combat Intelligence in Modern Warfare.* Harrisburg, Pa.: Military Service Division, Stackpole, 1960, 244 p.

Horton, Dick Crofton. *Fire over the Islands: The Coast Watchers of the Solomons.* London: Cooper, 1975, 256 p.

Idriess, Ion Llewellyn. *The Scout.* Sydney; London: Angus and Robertson, 1943, 123 p. (The Australian Guerrilla, book VI).

Keay, John. *The Gilgit Game: The Explorers of the Western Himalayas, 1865-95.* Hamden, Conn.: Archon Books, 1979, 277 p.

Lord, Walter. *Lonely Vigil: Coastwatchers of the Solomons.* New York: Viking Press, 1977, 322 p.

Marshall, Francis Cutler and **Simonds, George S.** *A Military Primer, Including an Outline of the Duties and Responsibilities of the Military Profession and an Elementary Discussion of the Principles and Practice of the Service of Security and Information.* Columbus, Ohio: E.T. Miller, 1913, 195 p.

Nolan, Jeannette (Covert). *George Rogers Clark, Soldier and Hero, November 19, 1752—February 13, 1818.* New York: J. Messner, 1954, 190 p. (fiction).

Paterson, William. *Notes on Military Surveying and Reconnaissance.* London: Trübner, 1881, 142 p.

Simonian, Rair Georgievich, et al. *Razvedka v boevykh primerakh: Velikaia Otech. Voina 1941-1945 gg. i poslevoen. period.* Moscow: Voenizdat, 1972, 310 p.

Simonian, Rair Georgievich, et al. *Takticheskaia razvedka.* Moscow: Voenizdat, 1968, 276 p.

Simonian, Rair Georgievich and **Grishin, Sergei Vladimirovich.** *Razvedka v osobykh usloviakh.* Moscow: Voenizdat, 1975, 191 p.

Smith, Gaddis. *Britain's Clandestine Submarines, 1914-1915.* New Haven: Yale University Press, 1964, 155 p. (Yale historical publications; Wallace Notestein essays, 4).

Stevens, Phillip H. *Search out the Land: A History of American Military Scouts.* Chicago: Rand McNally, 1969, 192 p.

U.S. Army, Field Artillery School, Fort Sill, Okla. *Reconnaissance, Occupation and Organization of Position: Field Artillery.* Fort Sill: The Field Artillery School, 1936, 199 p.

U.S. Dept. of the Army. *Ranger Training and Ranger Operations.* Washington: n.p., 1962, 344 p. (FM21-50).

U.S. War Dept. *Basic Field Manual. Volume I: Chapter 9, Scouting and Patrolling, Dismounted.* Washington: U.S. GPO, 1939, 19 p.

U.S. War Dept. *Military Intelligence: Observation.* Washington: U.S. GPO, 1940, 44 p. (FM30-10).

Veshchunov, S.S. *Motostrelkovoe otdelenie v razvedke.* Edited by N.F. Chistiakov. Moscow: Voenizdat, 1977, 93 p.

Waldron, William Henry. *Scouting and Patrolling.* Washington: U.S. Infantry Association, 1916, 122 p.

Wetmore, Helen (Cody). *Last of the Great Scouts: The Life Story of Col. William F. Cody, "Buffalo Bill," as Told by His Sister.* Gloucester, Mass.: Peter Smith, n.d.; New York: International Book Publishing, 1900, 296 p.

Biographies and Case Histories
General

Abbott, Wilbur Cortez. *Colonel John Scott of Long Island, 1634 (?)-1696.* New Haven: Yale University Press, 1918, 93 p.

Alberts, Robert C. *The Most Extraordinary Adventures of Major Robert Stobo.* Boston: Houghton-Mifflin. 1965, 423 p.

Brook-Shepherd, Gordon. *Between Two Flags: The Life of Baron Sir Rudolf von Slatin Pasha, GCVO, KCMG, CB.* New York: Putnam, 1973, 366 p.

Davies, David William. *Elizabethans Errant: The Strange Fortunes of Sir Thomas Sherley and his Three Sons, as Well in the Dutch Wars as in Muscovy, Morocco, Persia, Spain, and the Indies.* Ithaca: Cornell University Press, 1967, 337 p.

Deacon, Richard, *pseud.* (McCormick, Donald). *John Dee: Scientist, Geographer, Astrologer and Secret Agent to Elizabeth I.* London: Muller, 1968, 309 p.

Dee, John. *The Private Diary of Dr. John Dee, and the Catalogue of his Library of Manuscripts, from the Original Manuscripts in the Ashmolean Museum at Oxford, and Trinity College Library, Cambridge.* Edited by James Orchard Halliwell. London: Printed for the Camden Society by J.B. Nichols, 1842, 102 p.

French, Peter J. *John Dee: The World of an Elizabethan Magus.* London: Routledge and K. Paul, 1972, 243 p.

Goreau, Angeline. *Reconstructing Aphra: A Social Biography of Aphra Behn.* New York: Dial Press, 1980, 339 p.

Griscelli de Vezzani, Jacques François. *Memoirs of the Baron de Rimini (Griscelli de Vezzani), Secret Agent of Napoleon III (1850-58), Cavour (1859-61), Antonelli (1861-62), Francis II (1862-64), the Emperor of Austria (1864-67).* 2d ed. London: Remington, 1888, 319 p.

Groma, Peter. *Der Kaiser der Spione.* Hamburg: Akros Verlag, 1900, 315 p. (Novel about Karl Schulmeister).

Hall, John, *Sir.* *General Pichegru's Treason.* London: Smith, Elder, 1915, 353 p.

Izon, John. *Sir Thomas Stucley, c. 1525-1578, Traitor Extraordinary.* London: A. Melrose, 1956, 240 p.

Lang, Andrew. *Pickle, the Spy: or, The Incognito of Prince Charles.* 3d ed. London: Longmans, Green, 1897, 344 p. (Alastair Ruadh Macdonell).

Le Carone, *pseud.* (Beach, Thomas Miller). *Twenty-five Years in the Secret Service: The Recollections of a Spy.* 5th ed. London: W. Heinemann, 1892, 311 p.

Marana, Giovanni Paolo. *Letters Writ by a Turkish Spy.* Selected and edited by Arthur J. Weitzman. New York: Columbia University Press, 1970, 233 p.

Muller, Paul. *L'Espionnage militaire sous Napoléon Ier.* Ann Arbor, Mich.: Xerox University Microfilms, 1974, 179 p. (original published in Paris by Berger-Levrault et Cie., Editeurs, 1896).

O Herir, Brendan. *Harmony from Discords: A Life of Sir John Denham.* Berkeley: University of California Press, 1968, 288 p.

Orczy, Emmuska. *A Spy of Napoleon.* New York: Putnam, 1934, 338 p.

Wade, Eileen Kirkpatrick. *The Chief: The Story of Robert Baden-Powell.* Rev. ed., London: Wolfe, 1975, 142 p.

William Harborne and the Trade with Turkey, 1578-1582: A Documentary Study of the First Anglo-Ottoman Relations. Compiled by S.A. Skilliter. Published for the British Academy, London: Oxford University Press, 1977, 291 p.

American Revolution

Alberts, Robert C. "The Fantastic Adventures of Captain Stobo." *American Heritage,* v. XIV, no. 5 (August 1963), pp. 65-77.

Alberts, Robert C. *The Golden Voyage: The Life and Times of William Bingham, 1752-1804.* Boston: Houghton Mifflin, 1969, 570 p.

Andrè, John. *Major Andrè's Journal.* New York: New York Times, 1968, 128 p.

Arnold, Isaac Newton. *The Life of Benedict Arnold: His Patriotism and His Treason.* Chicago: Jansen, McClurg, 1880, 444 p.

Barnum, H.L. *The Spy Unmasked: or, Memoirs of Enoch Crosby, alias Harvey Birch, the Hero of Mr. Cooper's Tale of the Neutral Ground: Being an Authentic Account of the Secret Services Which he Rendered His Country During the Revolutionary War. (Taken from his own lips, in short-hand.)* New York: J. and J. Harper, 1828, 206 p.

Brown, Charles Walter. *Nathan Hale, the Martyr Spy. An Incident of the Revolution.* Chicago: Gladiolus Bindery, 1899, 149 p.

Brown, Sanborn Conner. *Benjamin Thompson, Count Rumford.* Cambridge: M.I.T. Press, 1979, 361 p.

Clark, Barbara Louise. *E.B.: The Story of Elias Boudinot IV, his Family, his Friends, and his Country.* Philadelphia: Dorrance, 1977, 472 p.

Clark, Jane. "Metcalf Bowler as a British Spy." *Rhode Island Historical Society Collections,* v. XXIII, no. 4 (October 1930), pp. 101-117.

Crary, Catherine Snell. "The Tory and the Spy: The Double Life of James Rivington." *William and Mary Quarterly,* v. XVI, no. 1 (January 1959), pp. 61-72 p.

Darcy, Mary. "Parole Boston, Countersign St. Patrick." *Newsletter of the Revolutionary War Bicentennial Commission, Committee of Correspondence,* no. 8 (March 1968), and no. 9 (June 1968). (Hercules Mulligan, a secret agent for Washington).

Davis, Matthew L. *Memoirs of Aaron Burr: With Miscellaneous Selections from his Correspondence.* New York: Harper, 1836-1837, 2 v.

Dos Passos, John. "The Conspiracy and Trial of Aaron Burr." *American Heritage,* v. XVII, no. 2 (February 1966), p. 4.

Dudley, Albertus True. *A Spy of '76.* Boston: Lothrop, Lee and Shepard, 1933, 323 p. (fiction).

Ellis, George Edward. *Memoir of Sir Benjamin Thompson, Count Rumford, with Notices of his Daughter.* Published for the Academy of Arts and Sciences. Philadelphia: Claxton, Remsen, and Haffelfinger, 1871, 680 p.

Falkner, Leonard. "A Spy for Washington," *American Heritage,* v. VIII, no. 5 (August 1957), pp. 58-64. (John Honeyman).

Farnham, Thomas J. *A Child I Set Much By: A Life of Nathan Hale.* New Haven, Conn.: The New Haven Colony Historical Society, 1975, 54 p.

Fast, Howard Melvin. *Haym Salomon, Son of Liberty.* New York: J. Messner, 1941, 243 p.

Flexner, James Thomas. "Benedict Arnold: How the Traitor was Unmasked." *American Heritage,* v. XVIII, no. 6 (October 1967), p. 6.

Flexner, James Thomas. *The Traitor and the Spy: Benedict Arnold and John André.* New York: Harcourt, Brace, 1953, 431 p.

French, Allen. *General Gage's Informers: New Material Upon Lexington and Concord, Benjamin Thompson as Loyalist and the Treachery of Benjamin Church, Jr.: A Study.* New York: Greenwood Press, 1968, 1932, 207 p.

Fryer, Mary Beacock. *Loyalist Spy: The Experiences of Captain John Walden Meyers During the American Revolution.* Brockville, Ont.: Besancourt Publishers, 1974, 254 p.

Groh, Lynn. *The Culper Spy Ring.* Philadelphia: Westminster Press, 1969, 144 p. (Robert Townsend) (juvenile literature).

Hall, Charles Swain. *Benjamin Tallmadge, Revolutionary Soldier and American Businessman.* New York: Columbia University Press, 1943, 375 p.

Hart, Charles Spencer. *General Washington's Son of Israel and Other Forgotten Heroes of History.* Philadelphia: Lippincott, 1936, 229 p. (Haym Salomon).

Hickok, Laurens P. *A Sermon Preached at Litchfield, Conn., at the Funeral of Col. Benjamin Tallmadge, March 12, 1835.* New York: J.M. Elliot, 1835, 24 p. (photocopy).

Hill, George Canning. *The Life of Benedict Arnold.* New York: A.L. Burt, n.d., 295 p.

Howe, John. *A Journal Kept by Mr. John Howe, While he was Employed as a British Spy, During the Revolutionary War; Also, While he was Engaged in the Smuggling Business, During the Late War.* Concord, N.H.: L. Roby, 1827, 44 p.

Johnston, Henry Phelps. *Commemorative of Nathan Hale, Martyr-Spy of the Revolution.* New York: Press of "The Hub," 1887, 28 p.

Johnston, Henry Phelps. *Nathan Hale, 1776: Biography and Memorials.* Rev. and enl. ed. New Haven: Yale University Press, 1914, 296 p.

Koke, Richard J. *Accomplice in Treason: Joshua Hett Smith and the Arnold Conspiracy.* New York: New-York Historical Society, 1973, 325 p.

Lawson, John L. "The 'Remarkable Mystery' of James Rivington, 'Spy'." *Journalism Quarterly,* v. 35, no. 3 (Summer 1958), p. 317.

Lengyel, Cornel Adam. *I Benedict Arnold: The Anatomy of Treason.* Garden City, N.Y.: Doubleday, 1960, 237 p.

Lewis, Alfred Henry. *An American Patrician: or, The Story of Aaron Burr.* New York: D. Appleton and Company, 1908, 335 p.

Lomask, Milton. "Benedict Arnold: The Aftermath of Treason." *American Heritage,* v. XVIII, no. 6 (October 1967), p. 17+.

Lossing, Benson John. *The Two Spies: Nathan Hale and John André.* New York: D. Appleton and Company, 1904, 169 p.

Moody, James. *Lieutenant James Moody's Narrative of his Exertions and Sufferings.* New York: Arno Press, 1968, 57 p. (reprint of 1783 edition).

Moore, George Henry. *"Mr. Lee's Plan—March 29, 1777." The Treason of Charles Lee, Major General, Second in Command in the American Army of the Revolution.* New York: C. Scribner, 1860, 115 p.

Morpurgo, J.E. *Treason at West Point: The Arnold-André Conspiracy.* New York: Mason/Charter, 1975, 181 p.

Nathan, Adele (Gutman). *Gentleman Spy.* London: Sidgwick and Jackson, 1970, 175 p. (Major John André) (juvenile literature).

New York (City), Common Council. *Report of the Select Committee on Erecting a Monument, to the Memory of John Paulding, with an Address by the Mayor of the City of New York.* New York: W.A. Davis, 1827, 47 p.

O'Dea, Anna and **Pleasants, Samuel A.** "The Case of John Honeyman: Mute Evidence," *Proceedings of the New Jersey Historical Society,* v. 84, (July 1966), pp. 174-181.

Partridge, William Ordway. *Nathan Hale, the Ideal Patriot: A Study of Character.* New York: Funk and Wagnalls, 1902, 134 p.

Pennypacker, Morton. *The Two Spies, Nathan Hale and Robert Townsend.* Boston: Houghton Mifflin, 1930, 118 p

Russell, Charles Edward. *Haym Salomon and the Revolution.* New York: Cosmopolitan Book, 1930, 317 p.

Sargent, Winthop. *The Life and Career of Major John André, Adjutant-General of the British Army in America.* Boston: Ticknor and Fields, 1861, 471 p.

Sargent, Winthrop. *The Life and Career of Major John André, Adjutant-General of the British Army in America.* New ed. Edited by William Abbatt. New York: W. Abbatt, 1902, 543 p.

Scheer, George F. "The Sergeant Major's Strange Mission," *American Heritage,* v. VIII, no. 6 (October 1957), p. 26.

Seed, Geoffrey. "A British Spy in Philadelphia, 1775-1777." *Pennsylvania Magazine of History and Biography,* v. LXXXV, no. 1 (January 1961), pp. 3-37. (Gilbert Darkly).

Sellers, Charles Coleman. *Benedict Arnold, the Proud Warrior.* New York: Minton, Balch, 1930, 303 p.

Sellers, Charles Coleman. *Patience Wright, American Artist and Spy in George III's London.* Middleton, Conn.: Wesleyan University Press, 1976, 281 p.

Seth, Ronald. *The Spy in Silk Breeches: The Story of Montague Fox, 18th Century Admiralty Agent Extraordinary.* London: Frewin, 1968, 176 p.

Seymour, George Dudley. *Captain Nathan Hale, 1755-1776: Yale College, 1773; Major John Palsgrave Wyllys, 1754-1790; Yale College, 1773; Friends and Yale Classmates, Who Died in their Country's Service, One Hanged as a Spy by the British, the Other Killed in an Indian Ambuscade on the far Frontier. A Digressive History now Told with Many Antiquarian Excursions, Genealogical, Architectural, Social, and Controversial: With an Account of some Members of a Great Patrician Family, their Manorial Establishment in Hartford, their Custody for Generations of the Charter of King Charles the Second, and the Story of the Hiding Thereof.* New Haven: Privately printed for the author. [The Tuttle, Morehouse and Taylor Company], 1933, 296 p.

Seymour, George Dudley. *Documentary Life of Nathan Hale, Comprising all Available Official and Private Documents Bearing on the Life of the Patriot, Together with an Appendix, Showing the Background of his Life.* New Haven: Privately printed for the author, 1941, 627 p.

Sherwin, Oscar. *Benedict Arnold, Patriot and Traitor.* New York: The Century Co., 1931, 395 p.

Simms, Jeptha Root. *The American Spy, or Freedom's Early Sacrifice: A Tale of the Revolution, Founded upon Fact.* Albany: J. Munsell, 1846, 63 p. (fiction).

Smith, Joshua Hett. *An Authentic Narrative of the Causes Which led to the Death of Major André, Adjutant-General of His Majesty's Forces in North America. To which is added a monody on the death of Major André by Miss Seward.* New York: Evert Duyckinck, 1809, 214 p.

Sparrow, W.J. *Knight of the White Eagle, Sir Benjamin Thompson, Count Rumford of Woburn, Mass.* New York: Crowell, 1965, 302 p.

Stimson, Frederic Jesup. *My Story: Being the Memoirs of Benedict Arnold: Late Major-General in the Continental Army and Brigadier-General in that of His Britannic Majesty.* New York: C. Scribner's, 1917, 622 p. (fiction).

Stuart, Isaac William. *Life of Captain Nathan Hale, the Martyr-Spy of the American Revolution.* Hartford: F.A. Brown, 1856, 230 p.

Sullivan, Edward Dean. *Benedict Arnold, Military Racketeer.* New York: Vanguard Press, 1932, 306 p.

Tallmadge, Benjamin. *Memoir of Colonel Benjamin Tallmadge.* Edited by Henry Phelps Johnston. New York: The Gilliss Press, 1904, 167 p.

Tallmadge, Benjamin. *Memoir of Colonel Tallmadge.* New York: New York Times, 1967, 70 p.

Thayer, Simeon. *The Invasion of Canada in 1775: Including the Journal of Captain Simeon Thayer, Describing the Perils and Sufferings of the Army under Colonel Benedict Arnold, in its March Through the Wilderness to Quebec.* Providence, Rhode Island: Knowles, Anthony, 1867, 380 p.

Thompson, Ray. *Benedict Arnold in Philadelphia.* Fort Washington, Penn.: Bicentennial Press, 1975, 184 p.

Tillotson, Harry Stanton. *The Beloved Spy: The Life and Loves of Major John André.* Caldwell, Idaho: Caxton Printers, 1948, 199 p.

Van Doren, Carl Clinton. *Secret History of the American Revolution: An Account of the Conspiracies of Benedict Arnold and Numerous Others, Drawn from the Secret Service Papers of the British Headquarters in North America, now for the First Time Examined and Made Public.* New York: Viking Press, 1968, 534 p.

Varick, Richard. *The Varick Court of Inquiry to Investigate the Implication of Colonel Varick (Arnold's private secretary) in the Arnold Treason.* Edited by Albert Bushnell Hart. Boston: Bibliophile Society, 1907, 217 p.

Wallace, Willard Mosher. *Traitorous Hero: The Life and Fortunes of Benedict Arnold.* New York: Harper, 1954, 394 p.

Wandell, Samuel Henry and **Minnigerode, Meade.** *Aaron Burr: a Bibliography Compiled from Rare, and in Many Cases Unpublished Sources.* New York: Putnam, 1925, 2 v.

Watson, Elkanah. *Men and Times of the Revolution: or, Memoirs of Elkanah Watson, Including his Journals of Travels in Europe and America, from the Year 1777 to 1842, and his Correspondence with Public Men, and Reminiscences and Incidents of the American Revolution.* Edited by his son, Winslow C. Watson. 2d ed. New York: Dana and Company, 1857, pp. 136–141. (Patience Wright).

French Revolution

Blakeney, John, *pseud.* (Barstow, John Montagu Orczy). *The Life and Exploits of the Scarlet Pimpernel (Sir Percy Blakeney, bart.).* New York: I. Washburn, 1935, 306 p.

Coryn, Marjorie. *The Chevalier d'Eon, 1728–1810.* London: Thornton Butterworth, 1932, 253 p.

Gaillardet, Frédéric. *The Memoirs of Chevalier d'Eon.* Translated from the French by Antonia White. London: Blond, 1970, 314 p.

Hesdin, Raoul, *pseud.* (Fletcher, Charles Robert Leslie). *The Journal of a Spy in Paris During the Reign of Terror, January–July 1794.* New York: Harper, 1896, 204 p.

Lenotre, G. *pseud.* (Gosselin, Louis Léon Théodore). *Two Royalist Spies of the French Revolution.* Translated by Bernard Miall. New York: Henry Holt, 1924, 269 p. (Louis Fauche-Borel and Charles Frédéric Perlet).

Minnigerode, Meade. *Marie Antoinette's Henchman: The Career of Jean, Baron de Batz, in the French Revolution.* New York: Farrar and Rinehart, 1936, 317 p.

Mitchell, Harvey. *The Underground War Against Revolutionary France: The Missions of William Wickham, 1794–1800.* Oxford: Clarendon Press, 1965, 286 p.

Nixon, Edna. *Royal Spy, the Strange Case of the Chevalier d'Eon: Dressed as a Man He was none the less a Woman; Dressed as a Woman She was none the less a Man.* New York: Reynal, 1965, 260 p.

War of 1812

Henry, John. *Documents from Henry, the British Spy!!* Washington: 1812, 22 p.

Henry, John. *Facts Relative to John Henry and his Negociation.* [Washington? 1812?], 8 p.

Henry, John. *Message from the President of the U. States, Transmitting Copies of Certain Documents Obtained from a Secret Agent of the British Government, Employed in Fomenting Disaffection to the Constituted Authorities, and in Bringing About Resistance to the Laws; and Eventually, in Concert with a British Force, to Destroy the Union of the United States.* Washington City: R.C. Weightman, 1812, 50 p.

Henry, John. *Report of the Committee on Foreign Relations to whom was referred the message of the President of the United States ... Covering Copies of Certain Documents Communicated to him by John Henry, a Secret Agent of the British Government. Testimony to the Committee by Count Edward de Crillon, an Acquaintance of Mr. Henry.* Washington City: R.C. Weightman, 1812, 11 p.

Shreve, Royal Ornan. *The Finished Scoundrel. General James Wilkinson, Sometime Commander-in-Chief of the Army of the United States, who Made Intrigue a Trade and Treason a Profession.* Indianapolis: Bobbs-Merrill, 1933, 319 p.

American Civil War

Boyd, Belle. *Belle Boyd in Camp and Prison, Written by Herself.* A new edition prepared from new materials by Curtis Carroll Davis. South Brunswick, [N.J.]: T. Yoseloff, 1968, 448 p.

Brown, R. Shepard. *Stringfellow of the Fourth.* New York: Crown, 1960, 307 p. (Frank Stringfellow).

Brown, Spencer Kellogg. *Spencer Kellogg Brown, his Life in Kansas and his Death as a Spy, 1842-1863, as Disclosed in his Diary.* Edited by George Gardner Smith. New York: D. Appleton, 1903, 380 p.

Dannett, Sylvia, G.L. *She Rode with the Generals: The True and Incredible Story of Sarah Emma Seelye, Alias Franklin Thompson.* New York: T. Nelson, 1960, 326 p.

Downs, Edward C. *Four Years a Scout and Spy: "General Bunker," one of Lieut. General Grant's Most Daring and Successful Scouts. Being a Narrative of the Thrilling Adventures, Narrow Escapes, Noble Daring, and Amusing Incidents in the Experience of Corporal Ruggles During Four Years' Service as a Scout and Spy for the Federal Army; Embracing his Services for Twelve of the Most Distinguished Generals in the U.S. Army.* Zanesville, Ohio: H. Dunne, 1866, 404 p. (C. Lorain Ruggles).

Edmonds, S. Emma E., *pseud.* (Edmundson, Sarah Emma). *The Female Spy of the Union Army. The Thrilling Adventures, Experiences and Escapes of a Woman, as Nurse, Spy and Scout, in Hospitals, Camps and Battle-fields.* Boston: De Wolfe, Fiske, 1864, 384 p. (also issued under title: *Nurse and Spy in the Union Army;* and, *Unsexed; or, the Female Soldier).* (autobiography).

Hergesheimer, Joseph. *Swords and Roses.* New York: Knopf, 1929, 327 p. (Belle Boyd).

Horan, James David. *Confederate Agent: a Discovery in History.* New York: Crown, [1954], 326 p. (Thomas H. Hines).

Kerbey, Joseph Orton. *The Boy Spy: A Substantially True Record of Secret Service During the War of the Rebellion ... the Only Practical History of War Telegraphers in the Field ... Thrilling Scenes of Battles, Captures and Escapes.* Chicago: M.A. Donohue, 1887, 557 p. (autobiography).

Newcome, Louis A. *Lincoln's Boy Spy.* New York: Putnam, 1929, 197 p. (autobiography).

Pinkerton, Allan. *The Spy of the Rebellion: Being a True History of the Spy System of the United States Army During the Rebellion. Revealing Many Secrets of the War Hitherto not Made Public.* Compiled from official reports prepared for President Lincoln, General McClellan, and the Provost Marshal-General. New York: G.W. Carleton, 1883, 688 p. (autobiography).

Ross, Ishbel. *Rebel Rose: Life of Rose O'Neal Greenhow, Confederate Spy.* New York: Harper, 1954, 294 p.

Sigaud, Louis Adrien. *Belle Boyd, Confederate Spy.* Richmond, Va.: Dietz Press, 1944, 254 p.

Williams, Frances Leigh. *Matthew Fontaine Maury, Scientist of the Sea.* New Brunswick: Rutgers University Press, 1963, 720 p.

Young, Rosamond McPherson. *The Spy with Two Hats.* New York: D. McKay, 1966, 210 p. (fictionized biography of Timothy Webster).

Pre-World War I

Adler, Lory and **Dalby, Richard.** *The Dervish of Windsor Castle: The Life of Arminius Vambery.* London: Bachman and Turner, 1979, 512 p.

Asprey, Robert B. *The Panther's Feast.* New York: Putnam, 1959, 317 p. (Alfred Victory Redl).

Baden-Powell, Robert Stephenson Smyth Baden-Powell, *Baron. My Adventures as a Spy.* London: C.A. Pearson, 1915, 159 p.

Greener, William Oliver. *A Secret Agent in Port Arthur.* London: Archibald Constable, 1905, 316 p. (autobiography).

Monaghan, James. *Schoolboy, Cowboy, Mexican Spy.* Berkeley: University of California Press, 1977, 218 p.

Reynolds, Ernest Edwin. *Baden-Powell: A Biography of Lord Baden-Powell of Gilwell, O.M., G.C.M.G., G.C.V.O., K.C.B.* London: Oxford University Press, 1943, 283 p.

World War I

Bauermeister, Alexander ("Agricola"). *Spies Break Through: Memoirs of a German Secret Service Officer.* Translated and introduced by Hector C. Bywater. London: Constable, 1934, 184 p.

Bauermeister, Alexander ("Agricola"). *Spione durchbrechen die Front.* Berlin: Vorhut-Verlag Otto Schlegel, 1933, 181 p.

Binder, Heinrich. *Spionagezentrale Brüssel: Der Kampf der deutschen Armee mit der belgisch-englischen Spionage und der Meisterspionin Gabriele Petit; aus den Papieren der Geheim Agenten E.C. und M.A.* Hamburg: Hanseatische Verlagsanstalt, 1929, 178 p.

Bywater, Hector Charles and **Ferraby, Hubert Cecil.** *Intelligence service: Souvenirs du service secret de l'Amirauté britannique; traduit de l'anglais par le capitaine de corvette André Guieu.* Paris: Payot, 1932, 269 p. (paperback).

Bywater, Hector Charles and **Ferraby, Hubert Cecil.** *Strange Intelligence: Memoirs of Naval Secret Service.* London: Constable, 1931, 299 p.

Carl, Ernst. *One Against England: The Death of Lord Kitchener and the Plot Against the British Fleet.* New York: E.P. Dutton, 1935, 288 p.

Carrillo, E. Gomez. *Mata Hari: Das Geheimnis ihres Lebens und ihres Todes.* Leipzig: Verlag C. Weller, 1927, 199 p. (Margaretha Gertruida Zelle).

Cavell, Edith Louisa. *The Case of Miss Cavell, From the Unpublished Documents of the Trial: The Property of a Former Commissary of the German Government.* Edited by Ambroise Got. London: Hodder and Stoughton, 1920, 198 p.

Cook, Graeme. *Missions Most Secret.* Blandford, [Eng.]: Harwood-Smart, 1976, 185 p.

Coulson, Thomas. *Mata Hari: Courtesan and Spy.* New York: Harper, 1930, 312 p. (Margaretha Gertruida Zelle).

Desgranges, Pierre, pseud. (Crozier, Joseph) and **Belleval,** Marquis de. *In the Enemy's Country.* Translated from the French by Forrest Wilson. New York: Knopf, 1931, 235 p. (translation of *En mission chez l'ennemi*) *(Joseph Crozier).*

Durand, Paul. *Agents secrets: l'affaire Fauquenot-Birckel. Paris: Payot, 1937, 236 p.*

"East Seven," pseud. (Barton, Frederick John). *She is a Spy.* London: Queensway Press, [1934], 283 p. (Jeanne de Bossett, teacher of Mata Hari).

[Fitzgerald, Alice Louise Florence]. *The Edith Cavell Nurse from Massachusetts: A Record of One Year's Personal Service with the British Expeditionary Force in France, Boulogne—the Somme, 1916-1917, with an Account of the Imprisonment, Trial, and Death of Edith Cavell.* Boston: W.A. Butterfield, [1917], 95 p.

Gibson, William J. *Wild Career: My Crowded Years of Adventure in Russia and the Near East.* London: G.G. Harrap, [1935], 287 p.

Goltz, Horst von der. *My Adventures as a German Secret Service Agent.* New York: R. M. McBride, 1917, 288 p.

Great Britain, Foreign Office. *Correspondence with the United States Ambassador Respecting the Execution of Miss Cavell at Brussells.* London: H.M. Stationery Office, Harrison and Sons, 1915, 15 p.

Grey, Elizabeth, pseud. (Hogg, Beth Tootill) *Friend Within the Gates: The Story of Nurse Edith Cavell.* Boston: Houghton Mifflin, 1961, 194 p.

Groundsell, Frank. *The Lunatic Spy.* London: Jarrolds, 1935, 288 p.

Halsalle, Henry de. *Who Goes There? Being an Account of the Secret Service Adventures of "Ex-Intelligence" During the Great War of 1914-1918.* London: Hutchinson, [1927], 253 p.

Hemmert, Danielle and **Roudène, Alex.** *Mata-Hari, Eva Peron. [Paris]: Rombaldi, 1974, 300 p. (Margaretha Gertruida Zelle).*

Herrmann, Carl. *Geheimkrieg: Dokumente und Untersuchungen eines Polizeichefs an der Westfront.* Hamburg: Hanseatische verlagsanstalt, 1930, 214 p. (paperback).

Hill, George Alexander. *Go Spy the Land: Being the Adventure of I.K. 8 of the British Secret Service.* London: Cassell, 1932, 283 p.

Hoehling, Adolph A. *A Whisper of Eternity: The Mystery of Edith Cavell.* New York: T. Yoseloff, 1957, 191 p.

Holmes, Robert. *Walter Greenway, Spy and Hero: His Life Story.* Edinburgh: W. Blackwood, 1917, 295 p.

Holst, Bernhart Paul. *My Experience with Spies in the Great European War.* Boone, Iowa: Holst Publishing, 1916, 222 p.

Hubbard, Samuel T. *Memoirs of a Staff Officer, 1917-1919.* Bronxville, N.Y.: n.p., 299 p.

Jenssen, Carla, *Baroness. I Spy: The True Story of a Woman Secret Service Agent.* New York: Dodd, Mead, 1930, 282 p.

Judson, Helen. *Edith Cavell.* New York: Macmillan, 1941, 288 p.

Kaledin, Victor K. *K. 14-O.M. 66: Adventures of a Double Spy.* London: Hurst and Blackett, 1937, 252 p.

Kaledin, Victor K. *Underground Diplomacy: Adventures of a Private Spy.* London: Hurst and Blackett, 1938, 334 p.

Knyvett, R. Hugh. *"Over There" with the Australians.* New York: Scribner, 1918, 339 p. (Captain Knyvett was Anzac scout, intelligence officer, fifteenth Australian infantry.)

Lacaze, L. *Aventures d'un agent secret francais, 1914-1918.* Paris: Payot, 1934, 283 p.

Ladoux, Georges. *Les chasseurs d'espions.* Paris: Librairie des Champs-Elysée, 1932, 254 p. (Margaretha Gertruida Zelle.)

Ladoux, Georges. *Marthe Richard, the Skylark: The Foremost Woman Spy of France.* Edited with a biographical introduction and notes by Warrington Dawson. London: Cassell, 1932, 250 p.

Lawson, John Cuthbert. *Tales of Aegean Intrigue.* New York: Dutton, 1921, 271 p. (Lawson was naval intelligence officer.)

Lincoln, Ignatius Timothy Trebich. *Revelations of an International Spy.* New York: R.M. McBride, 1916, 323 p.

Lord, John. *Duty, Honor, Empire: The Life and Times of Colonel Richard Meinertzhagen.* New York: Random House, 1970, 412 p.

Lucieto, Charles. *On Special Missions.* Translated from the French. New York: R.M. McBride, 1927, 280 p.

"M." *My Experiences in the German Espionage: Why I Deserted the Kaiser's Secret Service and Came to America, after Perilous Journey from South Africa, Through England and Holland to Germany and out again, over Rotterdam and London, During the Great War.* New York: Henri Rogowski Linotype Co., 1916, 45 p.

McKenna, Marthe (Cnokaert). *I Was a Spy!* Foreword by Rt. Hon. Winston S. Churchill. Edited by E.E.P. Tisdall. New York: A.L. Burt, 1933, 288 p.

McKenna, Marthe (Cnokaert). *My Master Spy: A Narrative of War Time Secet Service.* London: Jarrolds, 1936, 287 p. (Clive Granville, "Agent 33").

McKenna, Marthe (Cnokaert). *A Spy Was Born.* London: Jarrolds, 1935, 255 p.

Mackenzie, Compton, *Sir. First Athenian Memories.* London: Cassell, 1931, 401 p. (second volume of author's war memoirs).

Mackenzie, Compton, *Sir. Gallipoli Memories.* London: Cassell, 1929, 405 p. (first volume of author's war memoirs).

Mackenzie, Compton, *Sir. Greek Memories.* London: Cassell, 1932, 587 p. (third volume of author's war memoirs).

Mashbir, Sidney Forrester. *I Was an American Spy.* New York: Vantage Press, 1953, 374 p.

Nedava, Joseph. *Trebitsch-Lincoln; das Lebendes Grossen Spions und Abenteurers.* Translated by Meir Faerber. Tel-Aviv: Union verlag, 1957, 305 p.

Newman, Bernard. *Inquest of Mata Hari.* London: R. Hale, 1956, 191 p. (Margaretha Gertruida Zelle).

Ostrovsky, Erika. *Eye of Dawn: The Rise and Fall of Mata Hari.* New York: Macmillan, 1978, 273 p. (Margaretha Gertruida Zelle).

Poretsky, Elisabeth K. *Our Own People: A Memoir of 'Ignace Reiss' and his Friends.* Ann Arbor: University of Michigan Press, 1970, 278 p.

Reilly, Sidney George. *Britain's Master Spy: The Adventures of Sidney Reilly; a Narrative Written by Himself.* Edited and completed by his Wife. New York: Harper, 1933, 296 p.

Rintelen, Franz von. *The Dark Invader: Wartime Reminiscences of a German Naval Intelligence Officer.* New York: Penguin Books, 1939, 189 p. (paperback).

Rintelen, Franz von. *The Return of the Dark Invader.* London: Peter Davies, 1935, 266 p.

Rogers, Cameron. *Gallant Ladies.* New York: Harcourt, Brace, 1928, 363 p. (Mata Hari).

Ryder, Rowland. *Edith Cavell.* New York: Stein and Day, 1975, 278 p.

Seth, Ronald. *The Spy Who Was Never Caught.* New York: Hawthorn, 1967, 240 p. (Jules Crawford Silber).

Smith, Janet Adam. *John Buchan, a Biography.* Boston: Little, Brown, 1965, 524 p.

Smythe, Donald. *Guerrilla Warrior: The Early Life of John J. Pershing.* New York: Scribner, 1973, 370 p.

Snowden, Nicholas (Soltész, Miklós). *Memoirs of a Spy: Adventures Along the Eastern Fronts.* New York: Scribner, 1934, 330 p.

Steinhauer, Gustav. *Steinhauer, The Kaiser's Master Spy: The Story as Told by Himself.* Edited by Sidney T. Felstead. London: John Lane, 1930, 356 p.

Templewood, Samuel John Gurney Hoare, *1st Viscount. The Fourth Seal: The End of a Russian Chapter.* London: W. Heinemann, 1930, 377 p.

Thurston, Ernest Temple. *Portrait of a Spy.* London: Putnam, 1928, 300 p. (novel about Margaretha Gertruida Zelle).

Waagenaar, Sam. *The Murder of Mata Hari.* London: A. Barker, 1964, 286 p. (Margaretha Gertruida Zelle).

Wertenbaker, Lael Tucker. *The Eye of the Lion: A Novel Based on the Life of Mata Hari.* Boston: Little, Brown, 1964, 379 p. (Margaretha Gertruida Zelle).

Wild, Max. *Secret Service on the Russian Front.* Translated by Anthony Haigh. London: G. Bles, 1932, 324 p. (translation of *In geheimen Auftrag an der Ostfront*) (autobiography).

Wittenberg, Ernest. "The Thrifty Spy on the Sixth Avenue El." *American Heritage,* v. XVII, no. 1 (December 1965), p. 60+. (Heinrich Friedrich Albert).

Wood, Eric Fisher. *The Note-book of an Intelligence Officer.* New York: Century, 1917, 346 p.

Zelle, Margaretha Gertruida. *The Diary of Mata Hari.* Translated, and with a preface, by Mark Alexander. North Hollywood, Calif.: Brandon House, 1967, 248 p.

Zimmer, George Francis. *K-7: Spies at War as Told to Burke Boyce.* New York: D. Appleton-Century, 1934, 312 p.

Russian Revolution

Agar, Augustus. *Baltic Episode: A Classic of Secret Service in Russian Waters.* London: Hodder and Stoughton, 1963, 255 p.

Agar, Augustus. *Footprints in the Sea.* London: Evans, 1959, 336 p. (autobiography).

Blair, Dorian and **Dand, C.H.** *Russian Hazard: The Adventures of a British Secret Service Agent in Russia.* London: R. Hale, 1937, 288 p.

Dukes, Paul, *Sir. Red Dusk and the Morrow: Adventures and Investigations in Red Russia.* Garden City, N.Y.: Doubleday, Page, 1922, 322 p.

Dukes, Paul, *Sir. The Story of "ST 25": Adventure and Romance in the Secret Intelligence Service in Red Russia.* London: Cassell, 1938, 379 p.

Hill, George Alexander. *Go Spy the Land, Being the Adventures of I.K. 8 of the British Secret Service.* London: Cassell, 1932, 283 p.

Lockhart, Robin N. Bruce. *Ace of Spies.* New York: Tower Publications, 1967, 220 p. (Sidney Reilly) (paperback).

Morgan, Ted. *Maugham.* New York: Simon and Schuster, 1980, 711 p. (Somerset Maugham).

Nikolaevskii, Boris Ivanovich. *Aseff, the Spy, Russian Terrorist and Police Stool.* Translated from the Russian by George Reavy. Garden City, N.Y.: Doubleday, Doran, 1934, 307 p. (Evno Fishelevich Azef).

Reilly, Sidney George. *Britain's Master Spy: The Adventures of Sidney Reilly; a Narrative Written by Himself.* Edited and completed by his Wife. New York: Harper and Brothers, 1933, 296 p.

Templewood, Samuel John Gurney Hoare, *1st viscount. The Fourth Seal: The End of a Russian Chapter.* London: W. Heinemann, 1930, 377 p.

Van Der Rhoer, Edward. *Master Spy: A True Story of Allied Espionage in Bolshevik Russia.* New York: Scribner, 1981, 260 p. (Sidney Reilly).

Pre-World War II

Budkevich, Sergei Leonidovich. *"Delo Zorge."* Moscow: Nauka, 1969, 231 p. (Richard Sorge).

Butenko, Theodor. *Revelations About Moscow.* Washington: U.S. Joint Publications Research Service, no. 5058, n.d., 48 p.

Deakin, Frederick William Dampier and **Storry, George Richard.** *The Case of Richard Sorge.* New York: Harper and Row, 1966, 373 p.

Dement'eva, Irina Aleksandrovna. *Comrade Sorge.* Washington: U.S. Joint Publications Research Service, no. 55492, 21 March 1972, 54 p. (translation of *Tovarishch Zorge: dokumenty, vospominaniia, inter'iu o podvige sovetskogo razvedchika.* Moscow: Sovetskaia Rossiia, 1965) (Richard Sorge).

Draper, Christopher. *The Mad Major.* Letchworth, Hertfordshire: Air Review, 1962, 231 p. (autobiography).

Dunn, Robert. *World Alive: A Personal Story.* New York: Crown, 1956, 480 p.

"E. 7." *I am a Spy.* London: L. Dickson, 1938, 303 p.

Ex-Legionnaire 1384, *pseud.* (Harvey, J.H.) with **Blackledge, W.J.** *With the Secret Service in Morocco.* London: Sampson Low: Marston, [192-?], 244 p.

Huxley-Blythe, Peter J. *The Man who was Uncle: The Biography of a Master Spy.* London: Barker, 1975, 186 p. (Nicholas Dulger-Sheikin).

Johnson, Chalmers A. *An Instance of Treason: Ozaki Hotsumi and the Sorge Spy Ring.* Stanford, Calif: Stanford University Press, 1964, 278 p. (Richard Sorge).

Kolesnikov, Mikhail Sergeevich. *Takim Byl Rikhard Zorge.* Moscow: Voen. Izd-vo, 1965, 220 p.

Kolesnikova, Mariia Vasil'evna and **Kolesnikov, Mikhail Sergeevich.** *Rikhard Zorge.* Moscow: Mol. Gvardiia, 2d ed., 1975, 314 p.

Korol'kov, IUrii Mikhailovich. *Kio ku mitsu!: sovershenno sekretno—pri opasnosti szhech'!* Moscow: Sovetskii Pisatel', 1972, 639 p.

Meissner, Hans Otto. *The Man with Three Faces.* Rinehart, 1955, 243 p. (Richard Sorge).

Nord, Pierre. *Et Staline décapita l'Armée rouge.* Paris: Librairie des Champs-Elysées, 1975, 250 p. (fiction).

Operator 1384, *pseud.* [Harvey, J.H.?] *The Devil's Diplomats.* London: Hutchinson, [1935], 286 p.

Poncins, Léon de. *Top Secret.* Chiré-en-Montreuil: Diffusion de la Pensée française, 1972, 289 p. (Richard Sorge).

U.S. Congress, Senate, Committee on the Judiciary, Subcommittee to Investigate the Administration of the Internal Security Act and Other Internal Security Laws. *The Legacy of Alexander Orlov.* 93d Congress, 1st Session. Washington: U.S. GPO, 1973, 150 p.

Vespa, Amleto. *Secret Agent of Japan.* Boston: Little, Brown, 1938, 301 p. (autobiography).

Volkov, Fedor Dmitrievich. *Podvig Rikharda Zorge.* Moscow: Znanie, 1976, 96 p.

Willoughby, Charles Andrew. *Shanghai Conspiracy: The Sorge Spy Ring, Moscow, Shanghai, Tokyo, San Francisco, New York.* New York: Dutton, 1952, 315 p. (Richard Sorge).

World War II
General

Bokun, Branko. *Spy in the Vatican, 1941–45.* New York: Praeger, 1973, 259 p.

Bondy, Ruth. *The Emissary: A Life of Enzo Sereni.* Translated from the Hebrew by Shlomo Katz. Boston: Little, Brown, 1977, 265 p.

Goldsmith, John. *Accidental Agent.* New York: Scribner, 1971, 192 p.

Listowel, Judith Márffy-Mantuano Hare, *Countess of.* Crusader in the Secret War. London: C. Johnson, 1952, 287 p.

Lovell, Stanley P. *Of Spies and Stratagems.* Englewood Cliffs, N.J.: Prentice-Hall, 1963, 191 p.

Michniewicz, Ladislas. *Opération Haïfa.* Adaptation de Jacques Helle. Tournai, Belgium: Casterman, 1969, 206 p. (Sanson Mikiciński) (paperback).

Rota, Virginia. *De journal d'une espionne.* Paris: Le Hameau, 1974, 234 p. (paperback).

S.K. *Agent in Italy.* Garden City, N.Y.: Doubleday, Doran, 1942, 331 p.

France

Boulle, Pierre. *My Own River Kwai.* Translated from the French by Xan Fielding. New York: Vanguard Press, 1967, 214 p. (translation of *Aux sources de la Rivière Kwai).*

Chailleux-Mathis, Roger. *Millionnaire pour la Gestapo: Souvenirs de l'Agent P 2 - 34050.* Paris: Editions Surmelin, 1972, 253 p (paperback).

Katona, Edita and **Macnaghten, Patrick.** *Code-name Marianne: An Autobiography* [of Edita Katona]. New York: D. McKay, 1976, 224 p.

Passy, Colonel, *pseud.* (Dewavrin, André). *Souvenirs. Volume 1: 2e Bureau Londres.* Monte-Carlo: R. Solar, 1947, 237 p. (paperback).

Remy, *pseud.* (Renault-Roulier, Gilbert). *Comment devenir agent secret.* Paris: A. Michel, 1963, 283 p. (paperback).

Remy, *pseud.* (Renault-Roulier, Gilbert). *Portrait of a Spy.* Translated by Lancelot C. Sheppard. New York: Roy Publishers, 1955, 224 p. (translation of *Profil d'un espion*) (Georges Henri Delfanne).

Serguéiew, Lily. *Secret Service Rendered.* Translated and expanded from the Fench manuscript by the author. London: Kimber, 1968, 223 p. (translation of *Seule face à l'Abwehr.* Paris: Arthème Fayard, 1966).

Germany, including Nazi Germany

Bazna, Elyesa in collaboration with **Nogly, Hans.** *I was Cicero.* Translated by Eric Mosbacher. New York: Harper and Row, 1962, 212 p.

Beus, Jacobus Gijsbertus de. *Tomorrow at Dawn!* New York: Norton, 1980, 191 p. (Gijsbert J. Sas, Hans Oster).

Bleicher, Hugo Ernst. *Colonel Henri's Story: The War Memoirs of Hugo Bleicher, former German Secret Agent.* Related to Erich Borchers. Edited by Ian Colvin. 2d ed. London: Kimber, 1962, 160 p. (translation of *Monsieur Jean: Die Geheimmission eines Deutschen*) (paperback).

Carré, Mathilde Bélard ("La Chatte"). *I was "The Cat": The Truth About the Most Remarkable Woman Spy Since Mata Hari—by Herself.* Translated by Mervyn Savill. New York: Lancer Books, 1969, 255 p. (Mathilde Carré associated with Hugo Ernst Bleicher).

Chailleux-Mathis, Roger. *Millionnaire pour la Gestapo: Souvenirs de l'Agent P 2 - 34050.* Paris: Editions Surmelin, 1972, 253 p. (paperback).

Eppler, John W. *Condor: l'espion de Rommel.* Paris: Laffont, 1974, 327 p. (autobiography).

Eppler, John W. *Geheimagent im Zweiten Weltkrieg: Zwischen Berlin, Kabul und Kairo.* Preussisch Oldendorf: K.W. Schütz, 1974, 374 p.

Eppler, John W. *Operation Condor: Rommel's Spy.* Translated from the French by S. Seago. London: Macdonald and Jane's, 1977, 250 p. (translation of *Condor: l'espion de Rommel*).

Gimpel, Erich. *Spy for Germany.* Translated by Eleanor Brockett. London: Hale, 1957, 238 p.

Laurens, Anne. *L'Affaire King Kong, 5e colonne aux Pays-Bas.* Paris: A. Michel, 1969, 224 p. (Christian Lindemans).

Laurens, Anne. *Betrayal at Arnhem.* New York: Award Books, 1975, 169 p. (translation of *L'Affaire King Kong, 5e colonne aux Pays-Bas*) (Christian Lindemans) (paperback).

Mosley, Leonard. *The Cat and the Mice.* London: A. Barker, 1958, 159 p. (John Eppler).

Mosley, Leonard. *Foxhole in Cairo.* New York: Belmont Productions, 1961, 141 p. (John Eppler) (paperback edition of *The Cat and the Mice*).

Moyzisch, L.C. *Operation Cicero.* With a Postscript by Franz von Papen. Translated by Constantine Fitzgibbon and Heinrich Fraenkel. London: Readers Union, 1952, 208 p.

Norden, Peter. *Espionnage sur L'Oreiller* (Salon Kitty-Berlin, 1940–1943). Paris: Les Presses de la Cité, 1971, 248 p. (German edition: *Salon-Kitty: Report e. geheimen Reichssache.* Wiesbaden: Limes Verlag, 1976, 336 p.).

O'Callaghan, Sean. *The Jackboot in Ireland.* New York: Roy Publishers, 1958, 157 p. (Hermann Görtz).

Paine, Lauran. *Mathilde Carré, Double Agent.* London: Hale, 1976, 192 p. (Mathilde Carré associated with Hugo Ernst Bleicher).

Popov, Dusko. *Spy/Counterspy: The Autobiography of Dusko Popov.* New York: Grosset and Dunlap, 1974, 339 p.

Putlitz, Wolfgang Gans, Edler Herr zu. *The Putlitz Dossier.* London: Wingate, 1957, 252 p.

Schulz-Holthus, Bernard. *Daybreak in Iran: A Story of the German Intelligence Service.* Translated by Mervyn Savill. London: Staples Press, 1954, 319 p. (autobiographical).

Ströbinger, Rudolf. *A-54: Spion mit drei Gesichtern.* Munich: List Verlag, 1965, 256 p.

Wighton, Charles and **Peis, Günter.** *Hitler's Spies and Saboteurs: Based on the German Secret Service War Diary of General Lahousen.* New York: Holt, 1958, 285 p. (Erwin Lahousen).

Wighton, Charles and **Peis, Günter.** *Hitler's Spies and Saboteurs: Based on the German Secret Service War Diary of General Lahousen.* New York: Award Books, 1958, 283 p. (Erwin Lahousen) (paperback).

Young, George Gordon. *The Cat with Two Faces.* New York: Coward-McCann, 1957, 223 p. (Mathilde Carré associated with Hugo Ernst Bleicher).

USSR

Accoce, Pierre and **Quet, Pierre.** *A Man Called Lucy: 1939–1945.* Translated by A.M. Sheridan Smith. New York: Coward-McCann, 1968, 192 p. (paperback).

Arsenijevic, Drago. *Genève appelle Moscou.* Paris: R. Laffont, 1969, 317 p. (paperback).

Fedotov, Mikhail Nikolaevich. *Razvedka vedet poisk.* Minsk: Belarus', 1976, 156 p. (Alexander Rado and Rudolf Roessler, alias "Lucie").

Gouzenko, Igor. *The Iron Curtain.* New York: Dutton, 1948, 279 p. (rewritten by A.W. O'Brien of Montreal) (Canadian edition under title: *This Was My Choice*).

Granovsky, Anatoli. *All Pity Choked: The Memoirs of a Soviet Secret Agent.* London: Kimber, 1955, 248 p.

Granovsky, Anatoli. *I was an NKVD Agent: A Top Soviet Spy Tells his Story.* New York: Devin-Adair, 1962, 343 p.

Khokhlov, Nikolai Evgen'evich. *In the Name of Conscience.* Translated by Emily Kingsbery. New York: D. McKay, 1959, 365 p.

Kozlova, Mariia Stepanovna. *Ukhozhu na zadanie: Zapiski razvedchitsy.* Minsk: Belarus', 1975, 174 p.

Markova, Galina Ivanovna. *Ofitser razvedki.* Moscow: Mosk. Rabochii, 1974, 136 p. (Aleksandr Borisovich Kazaev).

Perrault, Gilles. *The Red Orchestra.* Translated by Peter Wiles. New York: Simon and Schuster, 1969, 512 p. (Translation of *L'orchestre rouge*).

Radó, Sándor. *Code name Dora.* Translated from the authorized German edition by J.A. Underwood. London: Abelard, 1977, 298 p. (Translation of *Dóra jelenti*).

Radó, Sándor. *Dora Reporting.* Washington: JPRS L/3955, November 9, 1971, 39 p.

Read, Anthony and **Fisher, David.** *Operation Lucy: Most Secret Spy Ring of the Second World War.* London: Hodder and Stoughton, 1980, 254 p.

Sobolev, Aleksei Mikhailovich. *Razvedka boem: Zapiski voeskovogo Razvedchika.* Moscow: Mosk. Rabochii, 1975, 238 p.

Trepper, Léopold. *Le grand jeu.* Paris: A. Michel, 1975, 417 p.

Voloshin, Maksim Afanas'evich. *Razvedchiki Vsegda Vperedi.* Moscow: Voenizdat, 1977, 272 p.

United Kingdom

Arnold, Ralph. *A Very Quiet War.* New York: Macmillan, 1962, 176 p.

Barker, Ralph. *One Man's Jungle: A Biography of F. Spencer Chapman, DSO.* London: Chatto and Windus, 1975, 373 p.

Bleicher, Hugo Ernst. *Colonel Henri's Story: The War Memoirs of Hugo Bleicher, former German Secret Agent.* Related to Erich Borchers. Edited by Ian Colvin. 2d ed. London: Kimber, 1962, 160 p. (translation of *Monsieur Jean: Die Geheimmission eines Deutschen)* (paperback).

Bowen, John. *Undercover in the Jungle.* London: Kimber, 1978, 206 p.

Brome, Vincent. *The Spy.* New York: Pyramid Books, 1959, 192 p. (paperback edition of *The Way Back: The Story of Lieut.-Commander Pat O'Leary, G.C., D.S.O., R.N.* 2d ed. London: Cassell, 1957, 267 p.).

Butler, Ewan. *Amateur Agent.* New York: Norton, 1964, 240 p.

Chapman, Edward Arnold. *Free Agent: Being the Further Adventures of Eddie Chapman.* London: Wingate, 1955, 223 p.

Chapman, Edward Arnold. *Triple Cross.* New York: Popular Library, 1954, 208 p. (paperback edition of Owen, Frank: *The Eddie Chapman Story.* New York: J. Messner, 1954, 242 p.).

Chapman, Frederick Spencer. *The Jungle is Neutral.* London: Chatto and Windus, 1963, 378 p.

Churchill, Peter. *Duel of Wits.* London: Hodder and Stoughton, 1953, 319 p. (sequel to *Of Their Own Choice*) (Odette Marie Churchill).

Churchill, Peter. *Of Their Own Choice.* London: Hodder and Stoughton, 1952, 218 p.

Churchill, Peter. *The Spirit in the Cage.* London: Hodder and Stoughton, 1954, 251 p. (autobiographical) (also, Odette Marie Churchill).

Clarke, Dudley. *Seven Assignments.* London: J. Cape, 1948, 262 p.

Cook, Graeme. *Missions Most Secret.* Blandford, Eng.: Harwood-Smart, 1976, 185 p.

Cooper, Adolphe Richard. *The Adventures of a Secret Agent.* London: F. Muller, 1957, 255 p.

Darling, Donald. *Secret Sunday.* London: Kimber, 1975, 208 p.

Darling, Donald. *Sunday at Large: Assignments of a Secret Agent.* London: Kimber, 1977, 174 p.

Davidson, Basil. *Special Operations Europe: Scenes from the Anti-Nazi War.* London: Gollancz, 1980, 288 p.

Davidson-Houston, James Vivian. *Armed Pilgrimage.* London: Hale, 1949, 313 p.

Davies, Edmund Frank. *Illyrian Venture: The Story of the British Military Mission to Enemy-Occupied Albania, 1943–44.* London: Bodley Head, 1952, 246 p.

Delmer, Sefton. *The Counterfeit Spy.* New York: Harper and Row, 1971, 256 p.

Dormer, Hugh. *Hugh Dormer's Diaries.* Westminster, Maryland: The Newman Bookshop, 1948, 159 p.

Duke, Madelaine. *Slipstream: The Story of Anthony Duke.* London: Evans Bros., 1955, 243 p.

Dumais, Lucien A. and **Popham, Hugh.** *The Man Who Went Back.* London: Leo Cooper, 1975, 213 p. (French Canadian in SOE).

Evans, Jack. *Confessions of a Special Agent, as told to Ernest Dudley.* London: Hale, 1957, 192 p.

Farran, Roy Alexander. *Winged Dagger: Adventures on Special Service.* London: Collins, 1948, 384 p.

Franks, Norman L.R. *Double Mission: RAF Fighter Ace and SOE Agent, Manfred Czernin, DSO, MC, DFC.* London: Kimber, 1976, 192 p.

Fuller, Jean Overton. *Conversations with a Captor.* London: Fuller d'Arch Smith, 1973, 69 p. (poem about Noor Inayat Khan—"Madeleine") (paperback).

Fuller, Jean Overton. *No. 13, Bob.* Boston: Little, Brown, 1954, 240 p. (Noor Inayat Khan—"Madeleine"; John A.R. Starr).

Fuller, Jean Overton. *The Starr Affair.* London: Gollancz, 1954, 222 p. (John A.R. Starr; Noor Inayat Khan—"Madeleine").

Garby-Czerniawski, Roman. *The Big Network.* London: G. Ronald, 1961, 248 p.

Gribble, Leonard. *On Secret Service.* London: Burke Publishing, [before 1959], 192 p.

Hamilton, Alexander. *Wings of Night: The Secret Missions of Group Captain Charles Pickard.* London: Kimber, 1977, 206 p.

Hamilton-Hill, Donald. *SOE Assignment.* London: Kimber, 1973, 186 p.

Heslop, Richard. *Xavier: The Famous British Agent's Dramatic Account of his Work in the French Resistance.* London: Hart-Davis, 1970, 272 p.

Howarth, Patrick. *Undercover: The Men and Women of the Special Operations Executive.* London: Routledge and Kegan Paul, 1980, 248 p.

Johns, Philip. *Within Two Cloaks: Missions with SIS and SOE.* London: Kimber, 1979, 216 p.

Langelaan, George. *The Masks of War: From Dunkirk to D-Day—the Masquerades of a British Intelligence Agent.* Garden City, N.Y.: Doubleday, 1959, 284 p.

Le Chêne, Evelyn. *Watch for me by Moonlight: A British Agent with the French Resistance.* London: Eyre Methuen, 1973, 224 p (Robert Burdett).

Lincoln, John, *pseud.* (Cardif, Maurice). *Achilles and the Tortoise: An Eastern Aegean Exploit.* London: Heinemann, 1958, 256 p.

Lockhart, Robert Hamilton Bruce. *Comes the Reckoning.* London: Putnam, 1947, 384 p.

Marshall, Bruce. *The White Rabbit.* From the story told to the author by F.F.E. Yeo-Thomas. Garden City, N.Y.: Doubleday (Permabooks), 1954, 262 p. (paperback).

Martelli, George. *Agent Extraordinary: The Story of Michel Hollard, D.S.O., Croix de Guerre.* London: Collins, 1960, 285 p.

Martelli, George. *The Man Who Saved London: The Story of Michel Hollard, D.S.O., Croix de Guerre.* Garden City, N.Y.: Doubleday, 1961, 258 p.

Masson, Madeleine. *Christine: A Search for Christine Granville, G.M., O.B.E., Croix de Guerre.* London: Hamilton, 1975, 263 p.

Masterman, John Cecil, Sir. *On the Chariot Wheel: An Autobiography.* London: Oxford University Press, 1975, 384 p.

Millar, George Reid. *Road to Resistance: An Autobiography.* London: Bodley Head, 1979, 411 p.

Minney, Rubeigh James. *Carve Her Name With Pride.* London: G. Newnes, 1956, 187 p. (Violette Bushell Szabo).

Minshall, Merlin. *Guilt-Edged.* London: Bachman and Turner, 1975, 319 p.

Moss, William Stanley. *Ill Met by Moonlight.* London: Harrap, 1950, 192 p.

Moss, William Stanley. *A War of Shadows.* London: Boardman, 1952, 240 p. (sequel to author's *Ill Met by Moonlight*).

Muggeridge, Malcolm. *Chronicles of Wasted Time. Chronicle 2: The Infernal Grove.* New York: Morrow, 1974, 280 p.

Munthe, Malcolm. *Sweet is War.* London: Duckworth, 1954, 185 p.

Ogilvy, David. *Blood, Brains and Beer.* New York: Atheneum, 1978, 181 p.

Pitt, Roxane. *The Courage of Fear.* New York: Duell, Sloan and Pearce, 1957, 242 p.

Pitt, Roxane. *Operation Double Life: An Autobiograpy.* London: Bachman and Turner, 1975, 183 p.

Popov, Dusko. *Spy/Counterspy: The Autobiography of Dusko Popov.* New York: Grosset and Dunlap, 1974, 339 p.

Rake, Denis. *Rake's Progress.* London, Frewin, 1968, 271 p.

Reid, Miles. *Last on the List.* London: Leo Cooper, 1974, 228 p.

Sweet-Escott, Bickham. *Baker Street Irregular.* London: Methuen, 1965, 278 p.

Tickell, Jerrard. *Odette: The Story of a British Agent.* London: Chapman and Hall, 1949, 334 p.

Walker, David Esdaile. *Lunch with a Stranger.* New York: Norton, 1957, 223 p.

Warren, Charles Esme Thornton and **Benson, James.** *The Broken Column: The Story of James Frederick Wilde's Adventures with the Italian Partisans.* London: Harrap, 1966, 207 p.

Wharton, Bill. *The Real 007.* New York: Pyramid Publications, 1979, 206 p. (Thomas Langridge) (paperback).

Whitwell, John, pseud. *British Agent.* London: Kimber, 1966, 224 p.

Wighton, Charles. *Pin-Stripe Saboteur: The Story of "Robin"—British Agent and French Resistance Leader.* London: Odhams Press, 1959, 256 p.

Winterbotham, Frederick William. *The Nazi Connection.* New York: Harper and Row, 1978, 222 p.

Winterbotham, Frederick William. *Secret and Personal.* London: Kimber, 1969, 192 p.

United States

Caldwell, John Cope and **Gayn, Mark.** *American Agent.* New York: Holt, 1947, 220 p. (John Caldwell in China, 1943-1944).

Coon, Carleton Stevens. *A North Africa Story: The Anthropologist as OSS Agent, 1941-1943.* Ipswich, Mass.: Gambit, 1980, 146 p.

Dreux, William B. *No Bridges Blown.* Notre Dame: University of Notre Dame Press, 1971, 322 p.

Dulles, Allen Welsh. *The Secret Surrender.* New York: Harper and Row, 1966, 268 p.

Dunlop, Richard. *Behind Japanese Lines, with the OSS in Burma.* New York: Rand McNally, 1979, 448 p.

Hefley, James C. and **Hefley, Marti.** *The Secret File on John Birch.* Wheaton, Ill.: Tyndale House, 1980, 231 p.

Higham, Charles. *Errol Flynn: The Untold Story.* Garden City, N.Y.: Doubleday, 1980, 370 p.

Holmes, Wilfred Jay. *Double-edged Secrets: U.S. Naval Intelligence Operations in the Pacific During World War II.* Annapolis, Md.: Naval Institute Press, 1979, 231 p.

Hoover, Calvin Bryce. *Memoirs of Capitalism, Communism, and Nazism.* Durham: Duke University Press, 1965, 302 p.

Hyde, Harford Montgomery. *Cynthia.* New York: Farrar, Straus and Giroux, 1965, 240 p.

Icardi, Aldo. *Aldo Icardi: American Master Spy: A True Story.* Pittsburgh: Stalwart Enterprises, 1954, 275 p.

Ingham, Travis. *Rendezvous by Submarine: The Story of Charles Parsons and the Guerrilla-Soldiers in the Philippines.* Garden City, N.Y.: Doubleday, Doran, 1945, 255 p.

Inks, James M. *Eight Bailed Out.* Edited by Lawrence Klingman. New York: Norton, 1954, 222 p.

Kaufman, Louis; Fitzgerald, Barbara et al. *Moe Berg: Athlete, Scholar, Spy.* Boston: Little, Brown, 1974, 274 p.

Klein, Alexander. *The Counterfeit Traitor.* New York: Holt, 1958, 301 p.

MacDonald, Elizabeth P. *Undercover Girl.* New York: Macmillan, 1947, 305 p.

Moon, Thomas N. and **Eifler, Carl F.** *The Deadliest Colonel.* New York: Vantage Press, 1975, 342 p.

Morgan, William James. *The O.S.S. and I.* New York: Pocket Books, 1958, 196 p. (paperback).

Morgan, William James. *Spies and Saboteurs.* London: Gollancz, 1955, 183 p.

Padover, Saul Kussiel. *Experiment in Germany: The Story of an American Intelligence Officer.* New York: Duell, Sloan and Pearce, 1946, 400 p.

Phillips, Claire and **Goldsmith, Myron B.** *Manila Espionage.* Portland, Oregon: Binfords and Mort, 1947, 226 p ("High-Pockets" is Claire Phillips.).

Tompkins, Peter. *A Spy in Rome.* New York: Simon and Schuster, 1962, 347 p.

Vogeler, Robert Alexander and **White, Leigh.** *I Was Stalin's Prisoner.* New York: Harcourt, Brace, 1952, 314 p.

Warren, William. *The Legendary American: The Remarkable Career and Strange Disappearance of Jim Thompson.* Boston: Houghton Mifflin, 1970, 275 p.

Welch, Robert Henry Winborne. *The Life of John Birch: In the Story of One American Boy, the Ordeal of his Age.* Belmont, Mass.: Western Islands, 1965, 127 p. (paperback).

Wilhelm, Maria. *The Man Who Watched the Rising Sun: The Story of Admiral Ellis M. Zacharias.* New York: F. Watts, 1967, 238 p.

Wynne, Barry. *Count Five and Die.* Told to author by William Eliscu. New York: Ballantine Books, 1958, 152 p. (paperback).

Zacharias, Ellis M. *Secret Missions: The Story of an Intelligence Officer.* New York: Paperback Library, 1961, 351 p. (paperback).

Postwar
General

Aldouby, Zwy and **Ballinger, Jerrold.** *The Shattered Silence: The Eli Cohen Affair.* New York: Lancer Books, 1971, 453 p. (paperback).

Aspin, Leslie and **Aspinall, Trevor.** *I, Kovaks.* London: Everest Books, 1975, 239 p.

Ben-Hanan, Eli. *Our Man in Damascus: Elie Cohn.* New York: Crown, 1969, 192 p.

Benuto, Rita. *Mistress of Cuba: I was a Call Girl and Spy for Castro's Cuba.* Los Angeles: Holloway House, 1967, 318 p. (paperback).

Buitrago Salazar, Evelio. *Zarpazo the Bandit: Memoirs of an Undercover Agent of the Colombian Army.* Translated by M. Murray Lasley. Edited by Russell W. Ramsey. University: University of Alabama Press, 1977, 168 p.

Castro Hidalgo, Orlando. *Spy for Fidel.* Miami: E.A. Seeman, 1971, 110 p.

Clifford, Garry. "Ex-Spy David Phillips Preaches the C.I.A. Story, but Can't Convince his own Daughter," *People,* June 23, 1975, p. 10.

Coffin, William Sloan. *Once to Every Man: A Memoir.* New York: Atheneum, 1977, 344 p.

Dan, Ben. *The Spy from Israel.* London: Vallentine, Mitchell, 1969, 212 p. (Translation of L'Espion qui venait d'Israel: l'affaire Elie Cohen).

De Silva, Peer. *Sub Rosa: The CIA and the Uses of Intelligence.* New York: Quadrangle, 1978, 308 p.

El-Ad, Avri and **Creech, James, III.** *Decline of Honor.* Chicago: Regnery, 1976, 364 p.

Gaucher, Roland. *Le réseau Curiel ou la subversion humanitaire.* Paris: Jean Picollec, 1981, 433 p.

Golan, Aviezer and **Pinkas, Danny.** *Shula, Code Name the Pearl.* New York: Delacorte Press, 1980, 345 p.

Goldberg, Jeff. "Who Killed John Paisley?" *Inquiry, October 15, 1979.*

Henderson, Bruce E. and **Cyr, C.C.** *Double Eagle: The Autobiography of a Polish Spy who Defected to the West.* New York: Bobbs-Merrill, 1979, 227 p. (Mr. "X").

Ignatius, David. "In from the Cold: A Former Master Spy Spins Intriguing Yarns of his Past Intrigues: In CIA's Prime, Rocky Stone Orchestrated Iran Coup, Walked into Syrian Trap." *Wall Street Journal,* October 19, 1979, p. 1+.

Leonhard, Wolfgang. *Child of the Revolution.* Translated by C.M. Woodhouse. Chicago: Regnery, 1958, 447 p.

Lindsey, Robert. *The Falcon and the Snowman: A True Story of Friendship and Espionage.* New York: Simon and Schuster, 1979, 359 p.

Lotz, Wolfgang. *The Champagne Spy: Israel's Master Spy Tells his Story.* New York: St. Martin's Press, 1972, 240 p.

Monat, Pawel and **Dille, John.** *Spy in the U.S.* New York: Harper and Row, 1961, 208 p.

Russell, Richard. "The Spy at the Bottom of the Bay." *Gallery,* May 1981. (John Paisley).

Smith, Colin and **Bhatia, Shyam.** "Stealing the Bomb for Pakistan." *World Press Review,* March 1980, pp. 26–28.

Thyraud de Vosjoli, Monique and **Thyraud de Vosjoli, Philippe.** *Le Comité.* Montréal: Editions de l'Homme, 1975, 315 p.

Fiction

Greene, Graham. *A Sort of Life.* New York: Pocket Books, 1973, 190 p.

Pearson, John. *Alias James Bond: The Life of Ian Fleming.* New York: McGraw-Hill, 1967, 342 p. (paperback edition of *The Life of Ian Fleming*).

Pearson, John. *The Life of Ian Fleming.* New York: McGraw-Hill, 1966, 338 p.

Pelrine, Eleanor and **Pelrine, Dennis.** *Ian Fleming: Man with the Golden Pen.* Wilmington, Delaware: Swan Publishing, 1966, 159 p. (paperback).

Rezette, Ilka and **Pasquiez, Jean Claude.** *Grand-mère agent secret.* Paris: Editions du Dauphin, 1972, 252 p. (paperback).

USSR
General

Bernikow, Louise. *Abel.* New York: Pocket Books, 1971, 319 p. (paperback) (Rudolf Abel).

Dialoguski, Michael. *The Case of Colonel Petrov: How I Weaned a High MVD Official from Communism.* New York: McGraw-Hill, 1955, 238 p. (Vladimir Mikhaelovich Petrov).

Bourke, Seán. *The Springing of George Blake.* New York: Pinnacle Books, 1971, 379 p. (paperback).

Carr, Barbara. *Spy in the Sun.* London: Allan Wingate-Baker, 1970, 255 p. (IUrii Nikolaevich Loginov).

Cookridge, E.H., pseud. (Spiro, Edward). *The Many Sides of George Blake, Esq.: The Complete Dossier.* Princeton, N.J.: Brandon Systems Press, 1970, 254 p.

Donovan, James Britt. *Strangers on a Bridge: The Case of Colonel Abel.* New York: Atheneum, 1964, 432 p. (Rudolf Abel).

Drath, Viola Herms. *Willy Brandt, Prisoner of his Past.* Radnor, Pa.: Chilton Book, 1975, 364 p. (Günter Guillaume).

Germany, Federal Republic of. *Commission Report on Security Questions in Guillaume Case.* Washington: U.S. Joint Publications Research Service, April 16, 1975, 61 p. (Translations on Western Europe, No. 670, JPRS 64559, based on West German Government report dated November 1974) (Günter Guillaume).

Houghton, Harry. *Operation Portland: The Autobiography of a Spy.* London: Hart-Davis, 1972, 164 p.

Huminik, John. *Double Agent.* New York: New American Library, 1967, 181 p.

Hurt, Henry. *Shadrin, the Spy Who Never Came Back.* New York: Reader's Digest Press, 1981, 301 p. (Nicholas Shadrin).

Lonsdale, Gordon Arnold. *Spy: Twenty Years in Soviet Secret Service—The Memoirs of Gordon Lonsdale.* New York: Hawthorn Books, 1965, 220 p.

Massing, Hede. *This Deception.* New York: Duell, Sloan and Pearce, 1951, 335 p. (Autobiography, with commentary also on Alger Hiss).

Moorehead, Alan. *The Traitors: The Double Life of Fuchs, Pontecorvo, and Nunn May.* London: Hamilton, 1952, 222 p. (Klaus Emil Julius Fuchs, Bruno Pontecorvo, and Allan Nunn May) (paperback).

Moorehead, Alan. *The Traitors: The Double Life of Fuchs, Pontecorvo, and Nunn May.* New York: Dell, 1965, 222 p. (paperback).

Murray, John. *A Spy Called Swallow: The True Love Story of Nora, the Russian Agent.* London: W.H. Allen, 1978, 175 p. (Nora Korzhenko Murray).

Petrov, Vladimir Mikhailovich and **Petrov, Evdokia.** *Empire of Fear.* New York: Praeger, 1956, 351 p.

Pilat, Oliver Ramsay. *The Atom Spies.* New York: Putnam, 1952, 312 p. (Harry Gold, Klaus Emil Julius Fuchs, David Greenglass, and Ruth Lee Printz Greenglass).

Pohl-Wannenmacher, Helga. *Red Spy at Night: A True Story of Espionage and Seduction Behind the Iron Curtain.* Translated by Rena Wilson. London: Leo Cooper, 1978, 176 p.

Rönblom, Hans Krister. *The Spy Without a Country.* Translated from the Swedish by Joan Bulman. New York: Coward-McCann, 1965, 222 p. (translation of *Wennerström spionen*) (Stig Wennerström).

Sakharov, Vladimir and **Tosi, Umberto.** *High Treason.* New York: Putnam, 1980, 318 p.

Sigl, Rupert. *In the Claws of the KGB: Memoirs of a Double Agent.* Philadelphia: Dorrance, 1978, 247 p.

Sweden, Justitiedepartementet. *Rapport av Parlamentariska Nämnden i Wennerströmaffären.* Stockholm: Kungl. Boktryckeriet P.A. Norstedt and Söner, 1964, 46 p.

Tesselin, Basile. *Guillaume, l'espion tranquille du chancelier.* Paris: France-empire, 1979, 266 p. (Günther Guillaume).

Tishkov, Arsenii Vasil'evich. *Rudol'f Abel' pered amerikanskim sudom.* Moscow: IUrid. Lit., 1971, 69 p.

U.S. Congress, Senate, Committee on the Judiciary. *The Wennerstroem Spy Case, How it Touched the United States and NATO; Excerpts from the Testimony of Stig Eric Constans Wennerstroem, a Noted Soviet Agent.* A translation prepared for the Subcommittee to Investigate the Administration of the Internal Security Act and Other Internal Security Laws, of the Committee on the Judiciary, United States Senate. 88th Congress, 2d session, Washington: U.S. GPO, 1964, 168 p.

Vassall, William John Christopher. *Vassall: The Autobiography of a Spy.* London: Sidgwick and Jackson, 1975, 200 p.

Vostokov, Vladimir and **Shmelev, Oleg.** *The Resident Agent's Last Mistake.* Washington: U.S. Joint Publications Research Service, no. 55597, March 31, 1972, 218 p. (translation of *Poslednyaya oshibka rezidenta.* Moscow: Ogonek, nos. 38–49, 1965).

West, Rebecca, *pseud. The Vassall Affair.* London: Sunday Telegraph, 1963, 99 p. (William John Christopher Vassall) (paperback).

Whiteside, Thomas. *An Agent in Place: The Wennerström Affair.* New York: Viking Press, 1966, 150 p. (Stig Wennerström).

Alger Hiss—Whittaker Chambers

Andrews, Bert and **Andrews, Peter.** *A Tragedy of History: A Journalist's Confidential Role in the Hiss-Chambers Case.* Washington: R.B., Luce, 1962, 235 p.

Chambers, Whittaker. *Odyssey of a Friend: Letters to William F. Buckley, Jr., 1954–1961.* Edited with notes by William F. Buckley, Jr. n.p.: Privately printed by *National Review*, 1969, 303 p.

Chambers, Whittaker. *Witness.* New York: Random House, 1952, 808 p.

Cook, Fred J. *The Unfinished Story of Alger Hiss.* New York: Morrow, 1958, 184 p.

Cooke, Alistair. *A Generation on Trial: U.S.A. v. Alger Hiss.* New York: Knopf, 1950, 342 p.

De Toledano, Ralph and **Lasky, Victor.** *Seeds of Treason: The True Story of the Hiss-Chambers Tragedy.* New York: Newsweek, 1950, 270 p.

Hiss, Alger. *In re Alger Hiss: Petition for a Writ of Error Coram Nobis.* Edited by E. Tiger. New York: Hill and Wang, 1979, 438 p.

Hiss, Alger. *In the Court of Public Opinion.* New York: Knopf, 1957, 424 p.

Hiss, Anthony. *Laughing Last: Alger Hiss.* Boston: Houghton Mifflin, 1977, 194 p.

Levitt, Morton and **Levitt, Michael.** *A Tissue of Lies: Nixon vs. Hiss.* New York: McGraw-Hill, 1979, 353 p.

Seth, Ronald. *The Sleeping Truth: The Hiss-Chambers Affairs Reappraised.* New York: Hart, 1968, 292 p.

Smith, John Chabot. *Alger Hiss: The True Story.* New York: Holt, Rinehart and Winston, 1976, 485 p.

Weinstein, Allen. *Perjury: The Hiss-Chambers Case.* New York: Knopf, 1978, 674 p.

Zeligs, Meyer A. *Friendship and Fratricide: An Analysis of Whittaker Chambers and Alger Hiss.* New York: Viking Press, 1967, 476 p.

Oleg Penkovsky

Neotvratimoe vozmezdie: po materialam sudebnykh protsessov nad izmennikami Rodiny, Fashistkimi palachami i agentami imperialisticheskikh razvedok. Moscow: Voenizdat, 1974, 352 p.

Penkovskii, Oleg Vladimirovich. *The Penkovsky Papers.* Translated by Peter Deriabin. Garden City, N.Y.: Doubleday, 1965, 411 p.

Penkovskii, Oleg Vladimirovich. *Sudebnyi protsess po ugolovnomu delu agenta angliiskoi i amerikanskoi razvedok grazhdanina SSSR Pen'kovskogo, O.B., i shpiona-sviaznika poddannogo Veliko-britanii Vinna, G.M., 7–11 Maia 1963 goda.* Edited by O. Vadeev and A. Gorshkova. Moscow: Izd-vo Polit. Lit-ry, 1963, 318 p.

Wynne, Greville M. *The Man from Moscow: The Story of Wynne and Penkovsky.* London: Hutchinson, 1967, 222 p.

Kim Philby—Guy Burgess—Donald Maclean

Boyle, Andrew. "Britain's Establishment Spies," *New York Times Magazine,* December 9, 1979.

Boyle, Andrew. *The Fourth Man: The Definitive Account of Kim Philby, Guy Burgess and Donald Maclean and Who Recruited them to Spy for Russia.* New York: Dial Press, 1979, 504 p.

Driberg, Tom. *Guy Burgess: A Portrait with Background.* London: Weidenfeld and Nicolson, 1956, 123 p.

Fisher, John. *Burgess and Maclean: A New Look at the Foreign Office Spies.* London: Hale, 1977, 256 p.

Green, Martin Burgess. *Children of the Sun: A Narrative of "Decadence" in England After 1918.* New York: Basic Books, 1976, 470 p. (literature).

Hoare, Geoffrey. *The Missing Macleans.* London: Cassell, 1955, 182 p.

Mather, John Sidney, ed. *The Great Spy Scandal.* London: Daily Express, 1955, 192 p.

Page, Bruce; Leitch, David et al. *The Philby Conspiracy.* Garden City, N.Y.: Doubleday, 1968, 300 p.

Philby, Eleanor. *Kim Philby: The Spy I Married.* New York: Ballantine Books, 1968, 174 p. (paperback).

Philby, Kim. *My Silent War.* New York: Grove Press, 1968, 262 p.

Purdy, Anthony and **Sutherland, Douglas.** *Burgess and Maclean.* Garden City, N.Y.: Doubleday, 1963, 182 p.

Rees, Goronwy. *A Chapter of Accidents.* New York: Library Press, 1972, 270 p. (autobiographical).

Seale, Patrick and **McConville, Maureen.** *Philby: The Long Road to Moscow.* New York: Simon and Schuster, 1973, 282 p.

Sutherland, Douglas. *The Great Betrayal: The Definitive Story of Blunt, Philby, Burgess, and Maclean.* New York: Time Books, 1980, 174 p.

Thompson, Francis Joseph. *Destination Washington.* London: Hale, 1960, 222 p.

Julius and Ethel Rosenberg

Fineberg, Solomon Andhil. *The Rosenberg Case: Fact and Fiction.* New York: Oceana Publication, 1953, 159 p.

Goldstein, Alvin H. *The Unquiet Death of Julius and Ethel Rosenberg.* New York: Lawrence Hill, 1975, 96 p. (paperback).

Meeropol, Robert and **Meeropol, Michael.** *We are Your Sons: The Legacy of Ethel and Julius Rosenberg* (written by their children). Boston: Houghton Mifflin, 1975, 419 p.

Nizer, Louis. *The Implosion Conspiracy.* Greenwich, Conn.: Fawcett, 1974, 543 p. (paperback).

Root, Jonathan. *The Betrayers: The Life and Death of Julius and Ethel Rosenberg.* New York: Berkley Medallion Books, 304 p. (paperback).

Root, Jonathan. *The Betrayers: The Rosenberg Case—a Reappraisal of an American Crisis.* New York: Coward-McCann, 1963, 305 p.

Rosenberg, Ethel Greenglass. *Death House Letters of Ethel and Julius Rosenberg.* New York: Jero Pub., 1953, 168 p.

Schneir, Walter and **Schneir, Miriam.** *Invitation to an Inquest.* Garden City, N.Y.: Doubleday, 1965, 467 p.

Schneir, Walter and **Schneir, Miriam.** *Invitation to an Inquest.* Baltimore, Md.: Penquin Books, 1973, 487 p. (paperback).

Wexley, John. *The Judgment of Julius and Ethel Rosenberg.* New York: Ballantine Books, 1977, 672 p. (paperback).

Overt Collection

Cole, Wayne S. *Charles A. Lindbergh and the Battle Against American Intervention in World War II.* New York: Harcourt, Brace, Jovanovich, 1974, 298 p.

Davidson-Houston, James Vivian. *Armed Diplomat: A Military Attaché in Russia.* London: Hale, 1959, 191 p.

Gade, John Allyne. *All my Born Days: Experience of a Naval Intelligence Officer in Europe.* New York: Scribner, 1942, 408 p.

Hilton, Richard. *Military Attaché in Moscow.* London: Hollis and Carter, 1949, 231 p.

Lindbergh, Charles Augustus. *Autobiography of Values.* Edited by William Jovanovich and Judith A. Schiff. New York: Harcourt, Brace, Jovanovich, 1977, 423 p.

Lindbergh, Charles Augustus. *The Wartime Journals of Charles A. Lindbergh.* New York: Harcourt, Brace, Jovanovich, 1970, 1038 p.

Mosley, Leonard. *Lindbergh: A Biography.* New York: Dell, 1977, 544 p. (paperback).

Mott, Thomas Bentley. *Twenty Years as Military Attaché.* New York: Oxford University Press, 1937, 342 p.

Parrott, Cecil, Sir. *The Tightrope.* London: Faber and Faber, 1975, 223 p.

Smith, Truman. *Air Intelligence Activities: Office of the Military Attaché, American Embassy, Berlin, Germany, August 1935—April 1939 (with Special Reference to the Services of Colonel Charles A. Lindbergh, Air Corps, Res.).* n.p., 1954-1956, 163 p. (typescript).

Stevens, Leslie Clark. *Russian Assignment.* Boston: Little, Brown, 1953, 568 p.

U.S. War Department, General Staff. *A Guide for Military Attachés.* Washington: Military Intelligence Division, April 21, 1921, 78 p.

Vagts, Alfred. *The Military Attaché.* Princeton, N.J.: Princeton University Press, 1967, 408 p.

Walters, Vernon A. *Silent Missions.* Garden City, N.Y.: Doubleday, 1978, 654 p.

Waters, Wallscourt Hely Hutchinson. *"Secret and Confidential": The Experiences of a Military Attaché.* London: John Murray, 1926, 388 p.

Technical Collection
General

Bartlett, Donald L. and **Steele, James B.** *Empire: The Life, Legend, and Madness of Howard Hughes.* New York: Norton, 1979, 687 p.

Burleson, Clyde W. *The Jennifer Project.* Englewood Cliffs, N.J.: Prentice-Hall, 1977, 179 p.

Burns, Thomas S. *The Secret War for the Ocean Depths: Soviet-American Rivalry for Mastery of the Seas.* New York: Rawson Associates, 1978, 334 p.

Gjessing, Dag T. *Remote Surveillance by Electromagnetic Waves for Air, Water, Land.* Ann Arbor, Mich.: Ann Arbor Science Publishers, 1980, 152 p.

Heaps, Leo. *Operation Morning Light: Terror in the Skies: The True Story of Cosmos 954.* London: Paddington Press, 1978, 208 p.

Jones, Reginald Victor. *Most Secret War.* London: Hamilton, 1978, 556 p.

Kalashnikov, Evgenii Vladimirovich. *Razvedka i tseleukazanie.* Moscow: Voen. Izd-vo, 1967, 69 p.

Paine, Lauran. *The Technology of Espionage.* London: Hale, 1978, 191 p.

Pope, Maurice. *The Story of Archaeological Decipherment: From Egyptian Hieroglyphs to Linear B.* New York: Scribner, 1975, 216 p.

Royal United Services Institute for Defence Studies. *R.U.S.I. and Brassey's Defence Yearbook.* New York: Praeger Publishers, 1974, 338 p.

Tsipis, Kosta. *Tactical and Strategic Antisubmarine Warfare.* Cambridge: MIT Press, 1974, 148 p.

Varner, Roy and **Collier, Wayne.** *A Matter of Risk: The Incredible Inside Story of the CIA's Hughes Glomar Explorer Mission to Raise a Russian Submarine.* New York: Random House, 1978, 258 p.

Whiteside, Thomas. *Computer Capers: Tales of Electronic Thievery, Embezzlement, and Fraud.* New York: Crowell, 1978, 164 p.

Aerial and Photo Reconnaissance

Armengaud. "Modern Air Reconnaissance: The Importance of Unity of Command." *Journal of the Royal United Service Institution,* v. LXXIX (February-November 1934), pp. 700–706. (summary of his article in *Revue Militaire Francaise,* no. 154, April 1934).

Babington-Smith, Constance. *Air Spy: The Story of Photo Intelligence in World War II.* New York: Ballantine Books, 1957, 190 p. (paperback).

Elmhirst, Thomas. "Air Reconnaissance—Its Purpose and Value." *Journal of the Royal United Service Institution,* v. XCVII (February-November 1952), pp. 84–86.

Furniss, Tim. *Man in Space.* London: Batsford Academic and Educational, 1981, 72 p.

Hallam, T.D. *The Spider Web: The Romance of a Flying-Boat Flight in the First World War.* Annapolis, Md.: Nautical and Aviation Publishing, 1979, 278 p.

Heiman, Grover. *Aerial Photography: The Story of Aerial Mapping and Reconnaissance.* New York: Macmillan, 1972, 180 p.

Hochman, Sandra and **Wong, Sybil.** *Satellite Spies: The Frightening Impact of a New Technology: An Investigation.* Indianapolis: Bobbs-Merrill, 1976, 212 p.

Infield, Glenn B. *Unarmed and Unafraid.* New York: Macmillan, 1970, 308 p.

James, Peter N. *Soviet Conquest from Space.* New Rochelle, N.Y.: Arlington House, 1974, 256 p.

Jones, Cecil B. "Photographic Satellite Reconnaissance." *United States Naval Institute Proceedings,* June 1980, pp. 41-51.

Killian, James Rhyne. *Sputnik, Scientists, and Eisenhower: A Memoir of the First Special Assistant to the President for Science and Technology.* Cambridge: M.I.T. Press, 1977, 315 p.

Kistiakowsky, George Bogdan. *A Scientist at the White House: The Private Diary of President Eisenhower's Special Assistant for Science and Technology.* Cambridge: Harvard University Press, 1976, 448 p.

Klass, Philip J. *Secret Sentries in Space.* New York: Random House, 1971, 236 p.

Mackay, C.J. "The Probable Influence of Air Reconnaissance on Strategy and Tactics." *Journal of the Royal United Service Institution,* v. LXVII (February-November 1922), pp. 622–641.

Oberdorfer, Don. "The 'Drigada': An Unwelcome Sighting in Cuba." *Washington Post,* September 9, 1979, pp. 1 and A18.

Oberg, James E. *Red Star in Orbit.* New York: Random House, 1981, 272 p.

Ordway, Frederick Ira and **Sharpe, Mitchell R.** *The Rocket Team.* New York: Crowell, 1979, 462 p.

Powers, Barbara (Moore) with **Diehl, W.W.** *Spy Wife.* New York: Pyramid Books, 1965, 188 p.

Powers, Francis Gary with **Gentry, Curt.** *Operation Overflight: The U-2 Pilot Tells his Story for the First Time.* New York: Holt, Rinehart and Winston, 1970, 375 p.

Powers, Francis Gary, defendant. *The Trial of the U-2: Exclusive Authorized Account of the Court Proceedings of the Case of Francis Gary Powers, Heard Before the Military Division of the Supreme Court of the U.S.S.R., Moscow, August 17, 18, 19, 1960.* Chicago: Translation World Publishers, 1960, 158 p.

Schreyer, W. *Glaz, vvinchennyi v nebo: Khronika vozdushnogo shpionazha.* Translated from the German by V. Cherniask. Moscow: Progress, 1974, 229 p (original: *Augen am Himmel: eine Piraten-Chronik.* Militär-verlag der D.D.R.).

Slessor, J.C. "Air Reconnaissance in Open Warfare: Two Incidents in the Advance to the Aisne in September, 1914." *Journal of the Royal United Service Institution,* v. LXXIX (February-November 1934), pp. 682–699.

Soiuz Zhurnalistov SSSR. *No Return for U-2: Truth About the Provocative Penetration of Soviet Air Space by an American Plane.* Compiled by D. Asanov et al. for the Union of Journalists of the U.S.S.R. Moscow: Foreign Languages Pub. House, 1960, 174 p. (translation of *Agressorov k pozornomu stoibu!*).

Taylor, John William Ransom and **Mondey, David.** *Spies in the Sky.* New York: Scribner, 1972, 128 p.

TerHorst, Jerald F. and **Albertazzie, Ralph.** *The Flying White House: The Story of Air Force One.* New York: Coward, McCann and Geoghegan, 1979, 350 p.

Wise, David and **Ross, Thomas B.** *The U-2 Affair.* New York: Random House, 1962, 269 p.

Signals Intelligence: Ciphers and Codes
General

Allensworth, W.H. and **Spottswood, W.G.** *The Cipher of the War Department.* Washington: U.S. GPO, 1902, 852 p.

Barker, Wayne G. *Cryptanalysis of the Simple Substitution Cipher with Word Divisions Using Non-Pattern Word Lists.* Laguna Hills, Calif.: Aegean Park Press, 1975, 126 p.

Barker, Wayne G., ed. *The History of Codes and Ciphers in the United States Prior to World War I.* Laguna Hills, Calif.: Aegean Park Press, 1978, 159 p.

Bonatz, Heinz. *Die deutsche Marine-Funkaufklärung 1914-1945.* Darmstadt: Wehr und Wissen Verlagsgesellschaft, 1970, 174 p. (Beiträge zur Wehrforschung, v. 20/21).

Candela, Rosario. *The Military Cipher of Commandant Bazeries: An Essay in Decrypting.* New York: Cardanus Press, 1938, 137 p. (Researches in Cryptography and Decrypting, a series edited by Rosario Candela. Issue I).

Carroll, John Millar. *Secrets of Electronic Espionage.* New York: Dutton, 1966, 224 p.

[Childs, James Rives]. *Before the Curtain Falls.* Indianapolis, Bobbs-Merrill, 1932, 333 p. (fiction).

Cryptologia, v. 1, nos. 1, 2, and 3. Laguna Hills, Calif.: Aegean Park Press.

D'Agapeyeff, Alexander. *Codes and Ciphers.* London: Oxford University Press, 1939, 160 p.

Deacon, Richard, *pseud.* (McCormick, Donald). *Love in Code: Or, How to Keep Your Secrets.* London: Eyre Methuen, 1980, 216 p.

D'Imperio, M.E. *The Voynich Manuscript—an Elegant Enigma.* Laguna Hills, Calif.: Aegean Park Press, 1976, 140 p. (paperback).

Ewing, Alfred Washington. *The Man of Room 40: The Life of Sir Alfred Ewing.* London: Hutchinson, 1939, 295 p.

Fitzgerald, Penelope. *The Knox Brothers.* New York: Coward, McCann and Geohegan, 1977, 294 p.

Friedman, William Frederick. *Advanced Military Cryptography.* Laguna Hills, Calif.: Aegean Park Press, 1976, 113 p.

Friedman, William Frederick. *Elementary Military Cryptography.* Laguna Hills, Calif.: Aegean Park Press, 1976, 86 p.

Friedman, William Frederick. *Elements of Cryptanalysis.* Laguna Hills, Calif.: Aegean Park Press, 1976, 172 p.

Friedman, William Frederick. *Military Cryptanalysis, Part I: With New Added Problems for the Student Monoalphabetic Substitution Systems.* Laguna Hills, Calif.: Aegean Park Press, 1980, 149 p.

Friedman, William Frederick. *Solving German Codes in World War I, with an Added Special "Code Problem" for the Student.* Laguna Hills, Calif.: Aegean Park Press, 1977, 142 p.

Friedman, William Frederick, ed. *Cryptography and Cryptanalysis Articles.* Laguna Hills, Calif.: Aegean Park Press, 1976, 2 v.

Friedman, William Frederick and **Mendelsohn, Charles J.** *The Zimmermann Telegram of January 16, 1917, and its Cryptographic Background.* Prepared under the direction of the Chief Signal Officer, War Dept. Laguna Hills, Calif.: Aegean Park Press, 1976, 33 p.

Gaines, Helen Fouché. *Elementary Cryptanalysis: A Study of Ciphers and Their Solution.* Sponsored by American Cryptogram Association. Boston: American Photographic Publishing, 1943, 230 p.

Galland, Joseph Stanislaus. *An Historical and Analytical Bibliography of the Literature of Cryptology.* Evanston, Ill.: Northwestern University, 1945, 209 p. (Northwestern University Studies in the Humanities, no. 10).

Gardner, Martin. *Codes, Ciphers, and Secret Writing.* New York: Simon and Schuster, 1972, 96 p. (Juvenile literature).

Givierge, Marcel. *Course in Cryptography.* Laguna Hills, Calif.: Aegean Park Press, 1978, 164 p. (translation of *Cours de cryptographie*).

Great Britain, War Office, General Staff. *Manual of Cryptography.* Laguna Hills, Calif.: Aegean Park Press, n.d., 96 p. (reproduction of the 1914 edition).

Haldane, Robert A. *The Hidden World.* London: Hale, 1976, 207 p.

Hitt, Parker. *Manual for the Solution of Military Ciphers.* Laguna Hills, Calif.: Aegean Park Press, 1976, 112 p.

James, William Milburne, Sir. *The Code Breakers of Room 40: The Story of Admiral Sir William Hall, Genius of British Counter-intelligence.* New York: St. Martin's Press, 1956, 212 p. (U.S. edition of *The Eyes of the Navy.* London, 1955).

Kahn, David. *The Codebreakers: The Story of Secret Writing.* New York: Macmillan, 1967, 1164 p.

Kahn, David. "Cryptology Goes Public." *Foreign Affairs,* v. 58, no. 1 (Fall 1979), pp. 141-159.

Kerckhoffs, Aug. "La Cryptographie Militaire." Ann Arbor, Mich.: University Microfilms International, 1976, 191 p. (original published in *Journal des Sciences Militaires,* January-February 1883.

Kullback, Solomon. *Statistical Methods in Cryptanalysis.* Laguna Hills, Calif.: Aegean Park Press, 1976, 206 p. (paperback).

Langie, André. *Cryptography.* Translated from the French by J.C.H. Macbeth. London: Constable, 1922, 192 p.

Lerville, Edmond. *Les cahiers secrets de la cryptographie: le chiffre dans l'histoire des histoires du chiffre.* Monaco: Editions du Rocher, 1972, 318 p.

Lysing, Henry, pseud. (Nanovic, John Leonard). *Secret Writing: An Introduction to Cryptograms, Ciphers and Codes.* New York: D. Kemp, 1936, 117 p.

MITRE Corporation, Metrek Division. *Selected Examples of Possible Approaches to Electronic Communication Interception Operations,* by C.W. Sanders, G.F. Sandy et al. Boulder, Colo.: Paladin Press, 1978, 30 p. (typescript).

Moore, Dan Tyler and **Waller, Martha.** *Cloak and Cipher.* Indianapolis: Bobbs-Merrill, 1962, 256 p.

Norman, Bruce. *Secret Warfare: The Battle of Codes and Ciphers.* Washington: Acropolis Books, 1973, 187 p.

Pennycook, Andrew. *Codes and Ciphers.* New York: D. McKay, 1980, 152 p. (juvenile literature).

Pratt, Fletcher. *Secret and Urgent, the Story of Codes and Ciphers.* Garden City, N.Y.: Blue Ribbon Books, 1942, 282 p.

Sacco, Luigi. *Manual of Cryptography.* Laguna Hills, Calif.: Aegean Park Press, 1977, 193 p. (translation of *Manuale di crittografia.* Roma, 1936).

Schooling, J.H. "Secrets in Cipher," *The Pall Mall Magazine,* v. VIII (January-April 1896).

Shulman, David. *An Annotated Bibliography of Cryptography.* New York: Garland, 1976, 388 p.

Smith, Laurence Dwight. *Cryptography, the Science of Secret Writing.* New York: Norton, 1943, 164 p.

Smith, W. Thomas. "Confederate Secret Service Disc." *North South Trader,* v. II, no. 6 (September 1975), pp. 16-19.

Thompson, James Westfall and **Padover, Saul K.** *Secret Diplomacy: Espionage and Cryptography, 1500-1815.* New York: F. Ungar, 1963, 290 p.

Tuchman, Barbara (Wertheim). *The Zimmermann Telegram.* New York: Viking Press, 1958, 244 p.

U.S. Dept. of the Army. *Basic Cryptography.* Washington: U.S. GPO, 1950, 186 p. (TM32-220).

U.S. Naval Education and Training Program Development Center. *Cryptologic Technician M 3 and 2.* Prepared by the Center for the Chief of Naval Education and Training. Pensacola, Fla.: Naval Education and Training Support Command, 1978, 499 p. (NAVEDTRA 10232-B).

Way, Peter. *Codes and Ciphers.* New York: Crown, 1977, 144 p.

Weber, Ralph Edward. *United States Diplomatic Codes and Ciphers, 1775-1938.* Chicago: Precedent, 1979, 633 p.

Wolfe, James Raymond. *Secret Writing: The Craft of the Cryptographer.* New York: McGraw-Hill, 1970, 192 p. (juvenile literature).

Yardley, Herbert O. *The American Black Chamber.* New York: Blue Ribbon Books, [1931], 375 p. (first ed. published by Bobbs-Merrill, 1931).

Yardley, Herbert O. *Yardleygrams.* Indianapolis: Bobbs-Merrill, 1932, 190 p.

Zim, Herbert Spencer. *Codes and Secret Writing.* New York: Morrow, 1964, 154 p.

World War II

Beesly, Patrick. *Very Special Intelligence: The Story of the Admiralty's Operational Intelligence Centre, 1939-1945.* London: Hamilton, 1977, 271 p.

Bell, Ernest L. *An Initial View of Ultra as an American Weapon.* Keene, N.H.: T S U Press, 1977, 110 p.

Bennett, Ralph Francis. "Ultra and Some Command Decisions." *Journal of Contemporary History,* v. 16, no. 1 (January 1981), pp. 131-151.

Bennett, Ralph Francis. *Ultra in the West: The Normandy Campaign of 1944-45.* London: Hutchinson, 1979, 305 p.

Bertrand, Gustave. *Enigma: ou, la plus grande énigme de la guerre 1939-1945.* Paris: Plon, 1973, 295 p.

Calvocoressi, Peter. *Top Secret Ultra.* London: Cassell, 1980, 132 p.

Clark, Ronald William. *The Man Who Broke Purple: The Life of Colonel William F. Friedman, Who Deciphered the Japanese Code in World War II.* London: Weidenfeld and Nicolson, 1977, 271 p.

Farago, Ladislas. *The Broken Seal: The Story of Operation Magic and the Pearl Harbor Disaster.* New York: Random House, 1967, 439 p.

Flicke, Wilhelm F. *War Secrets in the Ether.* Laguna Hills, Calif.: Aegean Park Press, 1977, 2 v.

Flicke, Wilhelm F. *War Secrets in the Ether, Parts I and II.* Translated from the German by Ray W. Pettengill. Washington: National Security Agency, 1953, 271 p. (typescript).

Die Funkaufklärung und ihre Rolle im Zweiten Weltkrieg: e. internat. Tagung in Bonn-Bad Godesberg u. Stuttgart vom 15.–18. November 1978. Hrsg. von Jürgen Rohwer u. Eberhard Jäckel. Stuttgart: Motorbuch-Verlag, 1979, 406 p.

Garlinski, Józef. *The Enigma War.* New York: Scribner, 1979, 219 p. (British edition published under title *Intercept*).

Haldane, Robert A. *The Hidden War.* New York: St. Martin's Press, 1978, 224 p.

Halter, Jon C. *Top Secret Projects of World War II.* New York: Wanderer Books, 1978, 192 p. (juvenile literature).

Hoehling, Adolph A. *The Week before Pearl Harbor.* New York: Norton, 1963, 238 p.

Holmes, Wilfred Jay. *Double-edged Secrets: U.S. Naval Intelligence Operations in the Pacific During World War II.* Annapolis, Md.: Naval Institute Press, 1979, 231 p.

Johnson, Brian. *The Secret War.* New York: Methuen, 1978, 352 p.

Kimmel, Husband Edward. *Admiral Kimmel's Story.* Chicago: Regnery, 1955, 206 p.

Korbonski, Stefan. "The True Story of Enigma—The German Code Machine in World War II." *East European Quarterly,* v. XI, no. 2 (Summer 1977), pp. 227–234.

Lewin, Ronald. *Ultra Goes to War: The Secret Story.* London: Hutchinson, 1978, 397 p.

Montagu, Ewen. *Beyond Top Secret Ultra.* New York: Coward, McCann and Geoghegan, 1978, 192 p.

Morgenstern, George Edward. *Pearl Harbor: The Story of the Secret War.* New York: Devin-Adair, 1947, 425 p.

Streetly, Martin. *Confound and Destroy: 100 Group and the Bomber Support Campaign.* London: Macdonald and Jane's, 1978, 279 p.

Theobald, Robert Alfred. *The Final Secret of Pearl Harbor: The Washington Contribution to the Japanese Attack.* New York: Devin-Adair, 1954, 202 p.

U.S. Dept. of Defense. *The "Magic" Background of Pearl Harbor.* Washington: U.S. GPO, 1977, 5 v.

Van Der Rhoer, Edward. *Deadly Magic: A Personal Account of Communications Intelligence in World War II in the Pacific.* New York: Scribner, 1978, 225 p.

Winterbotham, Frederick William. *The Ultra Secret.* New York: Harper and Row, 1974, 199 p.

Winterbotham, Frederick William. *Operatsiia "Ultra."* Moscow: Voenizdat, 1978, 224 p.

Woytak, Richard A. *On the Border of War and Peace: Polish Intelligence and Diplomacy in 1937–1939 and the Origins of the Ultra Secret.* Boulder, Colo.: East European Quarterly; New York: Columbia University Press, 1979,,141 p. (East European monographs; no. 49).

Post World War II

Barron, John. "A Tale of Two Embassies." *Readers Digest,* December 1979, pp. 116–119.

Brandt, Ed. *The Last Voyage of USS Pueblo.* New York: Norton, 1969, 248 p.

Bucher, Lloyd M. with **Rascovich, Mark.** *Bucher: My Story.* New York: Dell, 1970, 433 p. (paperback).

Crawford, Don. *Pueblo Intrigue: A Journey of Faith.* New York: Pyramid Books, 1969, 113 p. (paperback).

Ennes, James M. *Assault on the Liberty: The True Story of the Israeli Attack on an American Inteligence Ship.* New York: Random House, 1979, 299 p.

Gallery, Daniel V. *The Pueblo Incident.* Garden City, N.Y.: Doubleday, 1970, 174 p.

Harris, Stephen R. with **Hefley, James C.** *My Anchor Held.* Old Tappan, N.J.: F.H. Revell, 1970, 160 p. (Pueblo capture).

Murphy, Edward R. with **Gentry, Curt.** *Second in Command: The Uncensored Account of the Capture of the Spy Ship Pueblo.* New York: Holt, Rinehart and Winston, 1971, 452 p.

"NATO Electronic Spying Devices Listed." Washington: U.S. Joint Publications Research Service, no. 73187, April 9, 1979. (translation from the Bulgarian of article in *Teknichesko Delo,* Sofia, January 27, 1979, p. 10).

O'Ballance, Edgar. *The Electronic War in the Middle East, 1968–70.* Hamden, Conn.: Shoe String Press, 1974, 148 p.

Schumacher, Frederick Carl and **Wilson, George C.** *Bridge of No Return: The Ordeal of the U.S.S. Pueblo.* New York: Harcourt, Brace, Jovanovich, 1971, 242 p.

Simmons, Robert R. *The Pueblo, EC-121, and Mayaguez Incidents: Some Continuities and Changes.* Baltimore: University of Maryland School of Law, 1978, 51 p. (Occasional Papers/Reprints Series in Contemporary Asian Studies, no. 8, 1978).

Windchy, Eugene G. *Tonkin Gulf.* Garden City, N.Y.: Doubleday, 1971, 358 p.

Wiretapping and Eavesdropping

Brown, Robert Michael. *The Electronic Invasion.* New York: J.F. Rider, 1967, 184 p.

Carroll, John Millar. *The Third Listener: Personal Electronic Espionage.* New York: Dutton, 1969, 179 p.

Dash, Samuel; Schwartz, Richard F. *et al. The Eavesdroppers.* New Brunswick, N.J.: Rutgers University Press, 1959, 484 p.

Greulich, Helmut. *Spion in der Streichholzschachtel: Raffinierte Methoden der Abhörtechnik.* Gütersloh: Bertelsmann, 1969, 192 p.

LeMond, Alan and **Fry, Ron.** *No Place to Hide.* New York: St. Martin's Press, 1975, 278 p.

Long, Edward V. *The Intruders: The Invasion of Privacy by Government and Industry.* New York: Praeger, 1967, 230 p.

O'Toole, George. *The Private Sector: Private Spies, Rent-a-Cops, and the Police-Industrial Complex.* New York: Norton, 1978, 250 p.

III. RESEARCH AND ANALYSIS

General

Bovey, Robert. "The Quality of Intelligence Analysis." *American Intelligence Journal,* Winter 1980–1981, pp. 6–11.

Bowen, Russell J.; Halpin, Jeanne A. *et al. Tactical Order of Battle: A State-of-the-Art Survey.* Washington: U.S. Army Research Institute for the Behavioral and Social Sciences, 1975, 120 p.

The Encyclopedia of UFO's edited by Ronald D. Story and J. Richard Greenwell. Garden City, N.Y.: Dolphin Books, 1980, 440 p.

Falls, Cyril. "Studies in Operational Research." *Journal of the Royal United Service Institution,* v. CVIII (February 1963), pp. 62–64.

Gauche, General. *Le Deuxième Bureau au travail (1935–1940).* Paris: Amiot-Dumont, 1953, 239 p. (paperback).

Gazit, Schlomo. "Estimates and Fortune-Telling in Intelligence Work." *International Security,* v. 4, no. 4 (Spring 1980), pp. 36–56.

Godson, Roy, ed. *Analysis and Estimates.* Washington: National Strategy Information Center, 1980, 223 p. (Intelligence Requirements for the 1980s, no. 2) (paperback).

Goldman, Marshall I. *The Enigma of Soviet Petroleum: Half-full or Half-empty.* London: Allen and Unwin, 1980, 214 p.

Holmes, Wilfred Jay. *Double-edged Secrets: U.S. Naval Intelligence Operations in the Pacific During World War II.* Annapolis, Md.: Naval Institute Press, 1979, 231 p.

Hughes, Thomas Lowe. *The Fate of Facts in a World of Men: Foreign Policy and Intelligence-making.* New York: Foreign Policy Association, 1976, 62 p. (Headline series, no. 233).

Irving, David, ed. *Breach of Security: The German Secret Intelligence File on Events Leading to the Second World War.* London: Kimber, 1968, 216 p.

Jackson, Andrew. *Message from the President of the United States Relative to the "Political, Military and Civil Condition of Texas."* U.S. Senate, 24th Congress, 2d Session, December 22, 1836, 36 p.

Jones, Reginald Victor. *Most Secret War.* London: Hamilton, 1978, 556 p.

Jones, Reginald Victor. "Scientific Intelligence." *Journal of the Royal United Service Institution,* v. XCII (February-November 1947), pp. 352–369.

Jones, Reginald Victor. "Scientific Intelligence." *Research 9* (September 1956), pp. 347–352.

Kirkpatrick, Lyman B., Jr. *Captains Without Eyes: Intelligence Failures in World War II.* New York: Macmillan, 1969, 303 p.

Lea, Homer. *The Valor of Ignorance.* New York: Harper and Brothers, 1909, 343 p.

Lee, Asher. "Soviet Intelligence Problems." *Brassey's Annual; the Armed Forces Year-Book,* 1966, pp. 167–174.

McKale, Donald M. *Hitler, the Survival Myth.* New York: Stein and Day, 1981, 270 p.

Medvedev, Zhores Aleksandrovich. *Nuclear Disaster in the Urals.* Translated by George Saunders. New York: Norton, 1979, 214 p.

Morgan, Dan. *Merchants of Grain.* New York: Viking Press, 1979, 387 p.

Platt, Washington. *National Character in Action: Intelligence Factors in Foreign Relations.* New Brunswick, N.J.: Rutgers University Press, 1961, 250 p.

Possony, Stefan T. "U.S. Intelligence at the Crossroads." *Orbis,* v. IX, no. 3 (Fall 1965), pp. 587–612.

Project Blue Book: The Top Secret UFO Findings Revealed. Edited by Brad Steiger. New York: Ballantine Books, 1976, 423 p.

U.S. Defense Intelligence School. *Intelligence Research Methodology: An Introduction to Techniques and Procedures for Conducting Research in Defense Intelligence* by Jerome K. Clauser and Sandra M. Weir. Washington: Defense Intelligence School, May 1976, 382 p.

Wilensky, Harold L. *Organizational Intelligence: Knowledge and Policy in Government and Industry.* New York: Basic Books, 1967, 226 p.

Assessment of Strategic Capability
General

Aspin, Les. "Debate Over U.S. Strategic Forecasts: A Mixed Record." *Strategic Review,* v. VIII, no. 3 (Summer 1980), pp. 29–43.

Barnet, Richard J. *The Giants: Russia and America.* New York: Simon and Schuster, 1977, 190 p.

Betts, Richard K. "Analysis, War, and Decision: Why Intelligence Failures are Inevitable." *World Politics,* v. 31, no. 1 (October 1978). (Brookings General Series Reprint no. 343).

Collins, John M. *Grand Strategy: Principles and Practices.* Annapolis, Md.: Naval Institute Press, 1973, 338 p. (paperback).

Douglass, Joseph D. *Soviet Military Strategy in Europe.* New York: Pergamon Press, 1980, 238 p.

Dupuy, Trevor Nevitt. *Numbers, Prediction, and War: Using History to Evaluate Combat Factors and Predict the Outcome of Battles.* Indianapolis: Bobbs-Merrill, 1979, 244 p.

Englebardt, Stanley L. *Strategic Defenses.* New York: Crowell, 1966, 168 p.

Freedman, Lawrence. *U.S. Intelligence and the Soviet Strategic Threat.* Boulder, Colo.: Westview Press, 1977, 235 p.

Hilsman, Roger. *To Move a Nation: The Politics of Foreign Policy in the Administration of John F. Kennedy.* Garden City, N.Y.: Doubleday, 1967, 602 p.

Holzman, Franklyn D. "Are the Soviets Really Outspending the U.S. on Defense?" *International Security,* v. 4, no. 4 (Spring 1980), pp. 86–104.

Lee, William T. "Debate Over U.S. Strategic Forecasts: A Poor Record." *Strategic Review,* v. VIII, no. 3 (Summer 1980), pp. 44–57.

Lee, William T. "The Soviet Defense Establishment in the '80s." *Air Force,* March 1980, pp. 100–108.

Lee, William Thomas. *Understanding the Soviet Military Threat: How CIA Estimates Went Astray.* New York: National Strategy Information Center, 1977, 73 p.

McGovern, William Montgomery. *Strategic Intelligence and the Shape of Tomorrow.* Chicago: Regnery, 1961, 191 p.

Platt, Washington. *Strategic Intelligence Production: Basic Principles.* New York: Praeger, 1957, 302 p.

Prados, John. *The Soviet Estimate: U.S. Intelligence Analysis and Russian Military Strength.* New York: Dial Press, 1982, 367 p.

Public Broadcasting System Network, WETA TV, Washington, D.C. *World Special: The Red Army. Transcript of World Television Program, May 6, 1981.* Chevy Chase, Md.: Radio TV Reports, May 1981, 23 p. (typescript).

Scoville, Herbert, Jr. *MX: Prescription for Disaster.* Cambridge, Mass.: M.I.T. Press, 1981, 231 p.

Speed, Roger D. *Strategic Deterrence in the 1980s.* Stanford: Hoover Institution Press, 1979, 174 p. (paperback).

Stech, Frank J. "Self-Deception: The Other Side of the Coin." *Washington Quarterly,* Summer 1980, pp. 130–140.

Taylor, Maxwell Davenport. *Precarious Security.* New York: Norton, 1976, 143 p.

U.S. Joint Chiefs of Staff. *Dropshot: The United States Plan for War with the Soviet Union in 1957.* Edited by Anthony Cave Brown. New York: Dial Press, 1978, 330 p.

Arms Control

Bowen, Russell J. "Soviet Research and Development: Some Implications for Arms Control Inspection." *Journal of Conflict Resolution,* v. VII, no. 3 (September 1973), pp. 426–448.

Cox, Arthur M. *The Dynamics of Détente: How to End the Arms Race.* New York: Norton, 1976, 256 p.

Graham, Daniel Orrin. *Shall America be Defended?: SALT II and Beyond.* New Rochelle, N.Y.: Arlington House, 1979, 267 p.

Humphrey, Gordon J. "Analysis and Compliance Enforcement in SALT Verification." *International Security Review,* Spring 1980.

Newhouse, John. *Cold Dawn: The Story of SALT.* New York: Holt, Rinehart and Winston, 1973, 302 p.

Pincus, Walter and **Wilson, George C.** "Dilemma: Saving SALT II." *Washington Post,* September 9, 1979, p. A19.

Smith, Gerard C. *Doubletalk: The Story of the First Strategic Arms Limitations Talks.* Garden City, N.Y. Doubleday, 1980, 556 p.

Talbott, Strobe. *Endgame: The Inside Story of SALT II.* New York: Harper and Row, 1979, 319 p.

Cuba Missile Crisis

Allison, Graham T. *Essence of Decision: Explaining the Cuban Missile Crisis.* Boston: Little, Brown, 1971, 338 p.

Daniel, James and **Hubbell, John G.** *Strike in the West: The Complete Story of the Cuban Crisis.* New York: Holt, Rinehart and Winston, 1963, 180 p.

Detzer, David. *The Brink: Cuban Missile Crisis, 1962.* New York: Crowell, 1979, 299 p.

Dinerstein, Herbert Samuel. *The Making of a Missile Crisis, October 1962.* Baltimore: Johns Hopkins Press, 1976, 302 p. (paperback).

Gleichauf, Justin F. "Red Presence in Cuba: The Genesis of a Crisis." *Army,* November 1979, pp. 34–38.

Manrara, Luis V. *Betrayal Opened the Door to Russian Missiles in Red Cuba.* Miami, Florida: Truth About Cuba Committee 1968, 168 p.

Oberdorfer, Don. "The 'Brigada': An Unwelcome Sighting in Cuba." *Washington Post,* September 9, 1979, pp. 1 and A18.

Schram, Martin. "Response: Avoiding a Crisis Tone." *Washington Post,* September 9, 1979, pp. A18–19.

Pearl Harbor

Air Raid: Pearl Harbor! Recollections of a Day of Infamy. Edited by Paul Stillwell. Annapolis, Md.: Naval Institute Press, 1981, 299 p.

Bartlett, Bruce R. *Cover-up: The Politics of Pearl Harbor, 1941–1946.* New Rochelle, N.Y.: Arlington House, 1978, 189 p.

Farago, Ladislas. *The Broken Seal: The Story of Operation Magic and the Pearl Harbor Disaster.* New York: Random House, 1967, 439 p.

Hoehling, Adolph A. *The Week Before Pearl Harbor.* New York: Norton, 1963, 238 p.

Kimmel, Husband Edward. *Admiral Kimmel's Story.* Chicago: Regnery, 1955, 206 p.

Morgenstern, George Edward. *Pearl Harbor: The Story of the Secret War.* New York: Devin-Adair, 1947, 425 p.

Prange, Gordon William. *At Dawn We Slept: The Untold Story of Pearl Harbor.* New York: McGraw-Hill, 1981, 873 p.

Schuler, Frank and **Moore, Robin.** *The Pearl Harbor Cover-up.* New York: Pinnacle Books, 1976, 277 p. (paperback).

Theobald, Robert Alfred. *The Final Secret of Pearl Harbor: The Washington Contribution to the Japanese Attack.* New York: Devin-Adair, 1954, 202 p.

U.S. Congress, Joint Committee on the Investigation of the Pearl Harbor Attack. *Report of the Joint Committee on the Investigation of the Pearl Harbor Attack, Congress of the United States, Pursuant to S. Con. Res. 27, 79th Congress, a Concurrent Resolution to Investigate the Attack on Pearl Harbor on December 7, 1941, and Events and Circumstances Relating Thereto, and Additional Views of Mr. Keefe, together with Minority Views of Mr. Ferguson and Mr. Brewster* ... Washington: U.S. GPO, 1946, 580 p.

U.S. Department of Defense. *The "Magic" Background of Pearl Harbor.* Washington: Dept. of Defense, U.S.A.: U.S. GPO, 1977, 5 v.

Wohlstetter, Roberta. *Pearl Harbor: Warning and Decision.* Stanford: Stanford University Press, 1963, 426 p.

Studies of Political Stability

Adams, Sam. "Cover-Up: Playing War with Numbers." *Harper's,* May 1975, p. 41.

Brandon, Henry. *Anatomy of Error: The Inside Story of the Asian War on the Potomac, 1954–1969.* Boston: Gambit, 1969, 178 p.

Churba, Joseph. *The Politics of Defeat: America's Decline in the Middle East.* New York: Cyrco Press, 1977, 224 p.

Graham, Robert. *Iran: The Illusion of Power.* New York: St. Martin's Press, 1978, 228 p.

Handel, Michael I. "Surprise and Change in International Politics." *International Security,* v. 4, no. 4 (Spring 1980), pp. 57-85.

Hopkins, Robert. *Warnings of Revolution.* Washington: U.S. Central Intelligence Agency, Center for the Study of Intelligence, March 1980, 11 p. (paperback).

Horowitz, Irving Louis, comp. *The Rise and Fall of Project Camelot: Studies in the Relationship Between Social Science and Practical Politics.* Cambridge, Mass.: M.I.T. Press, 1967, 385 p.

Langer, Walter Charles. *The Mind of Adolf Hitler: The Secret Wartime Report.* New York: Basic Books, 1972, 269 p.

Maclear, Michael. *The Ten Thousand Day War: Vietnam, 1945-1975.* New York: St. Martin's Press, 1981, 368 p.

Rubin, Barry M. *Paved with Good Intentions: The American Experience and Iran.* New York: Oxford University Press, 1980, 426 p.

Selser, Gregorio. *Espionaje en América Latina: el Pentágono y las técnicas sociológicas.* Mexico: n.p., 1967, 414 p. (Colección Documentos, 12) (paperback).

Snepp, Frank. *Decent Interval: An Insider's Account of Saigon's Indecent End.* New York: Random House, 1977, 590 p.

Springer, Michael; Schneier, Edward et al. "Political Intelligence for America's Future." *Annals of the American Academy of Political and Social Science,* v. 388, March 1970, pp. 1-194. (ten articles).

U.S. Congress, House, Permanent Select Committee on Intelligence, Subcommittee on Evaluation. *Iran: Evaluation of U.S. Intelligence Performance Prior to November 1978: Staff Report.* Washington: U.S. GPO, 1979, 8 p.

U.S. Interdepartmental Group for Africa. *The Kissinger Study of Southern Africa: National Security Study Memorandum 39* (secret). Edited and introduced by Mohamed A. El-Khawas and Barry Cohen. Westport, Conn.: L. Hill, 1976, 189 p. (paperback).

IV. COUNTERINTELLIGENCE AND SECURITY

General

Ad Hoc Committee on Forced Labor. *Report for Submission to the Economic and Social Council of the United Nations and the Governing Body of the International Labour Office.* Geneva: United Nations, 1953, 619 p. (United Nations Document E/2431) (paperback).

Adams, Ian. *S: Portrait of a Spy: RCMP Intelligence, the Inside Story.* Agincourt, Ontario: Gage, 1977, 176 p. (novel).

Baraheni, Reza. *The Crowned Cannibals: Writings on Repression in Iran.* New York: Vintage Books, 1977, 279 p. (paperback).

Barker, A.J. *Prisoners of War.* New York: Universe Books, 1975, 249 p.

Benenson, Peter. *Persecution.* Harmondsworth, Middlesex, England: n.p., 1961, 152 p.

Committee for Human Rights in Iran. *Letters from the Great Prison: An Eyewitness Account of Human and Social Conditions in Iran.* Washington: The Committee, 1978, 35 p.

Committee for the Defence of Political Prisoners in Iran. *The Iranian Bulletins: The News Bulletins of the Committee.* London: Index on Censorship, September 1979, 120 p. (paperback).

Dallin, Alexander and **Breslauer, George W.** *Political Terror in Communist Systems.* Stanford, Calif.: Stanford University Press, 1970, 172 p.

Gwyn, David. *Idi Amin: Death-Light of Africa.* Boston: Little, Brown, 1977, 240 p.

Harel, Isser. *The House on Garibaldi Street: The First Full Account of the Capture of Adolf Eichmann, Told by the Former Head of Israel's Secret Service.* New York: Viking Press, 1975, 296 p.

Hauser, Thomas. *The Execution of Charles Horman: An American Sacrifice.* New York: Harcourt, Brace, Jovanovich, 1978, 255 p.

Herrmann, Walter. *Spionen-Schicksal: Inferno.* Berlin: A. Scherl GmbH, 1931, 167 p.

Hill, Cedric Waters. *The Spook and the Commandant.* London: Kimber, 1975, 201 p.

Kremer, J.v. *Le livre noir de l'espionnage: les dessous de la guerre de l'ombre.* Paris: Editions Fleuve Noir, 1955, 222 p.

Kyemba, Henry. *A State of Blood: The Inside Story of Idi Amin.* New York: Grosset and Dunlap, 1977, 288 p.

Latey, Maurice. *Patterns of Tyranny.* New York: Atheneum, 1969, 331 p. (London edition title: *Tyranny: A Study in the Abuse of Power*).

Longstreth, Thomas Morris. *The Silent Force: Scenes from the Life of the Mounted Police of Canada.* New York: Century, 1927, 383 p.

Plate, Thomas and **Darvi, Andrea.** *Secret Police: The Inside Story of a Network of Terror.* Garden City, N.Y.: Doubleday, 1981, 458 p.

Political Prisoners. New York: Facts on File, 1978, 285 p. (Alexander Grant; Lester Sobel).

Rauf, Mohammad Abdur. *Cuban Journal: Castro's Cuba as it Really Is. An Eyewitness Account by an American Reporter.* New York: Crowell, 1964, 231 p.

Timerman, Jacobo. *Prisoner Without a Name, Cell Without a Number.* Translated from the Spanish by Toby Talbot. New York: Knopf, 1981, 164 p. (translation of: *Preso sin Nombre, celda sin número*).

Tinnin, David B. and **Christensen, Dag.** *The Hit Team.* Boston: Little, Brown, 1976, 240 p.

Asia

Amnesty International. *Political Imprisonment in the People's Republic of China: An Amnesty International Report.* London: Amnesty International Publications, 1978, 171 p.

Bao, Ruo-Wang (Jean Pasqualini) and **Chelminski, Rudolph.** *Prisoner of Mao.* New York: Coward, McCann and Geoghegan, 1973, 318 p.

Blakey, Scott. *Prisoner at War: The Survival of Commander Richard A. Stratton.* New York: Penguin Books, 1979, 397 p. (paperback).

Brougher, William Edward. *South to Bataan, North to Mukden: The Prison Diary of Brigadier General W.E. Brougher.* Edited by D. Clayton James. Athens: University of Georgia Press, 1971, 207 p.

Brown, Wallace L. *The Endless Hours: My Two and a Half Years as a Prisoner of the Chinese Communists.* New York: Modern Literary Editions Publishing Co., 1961, 223 p. (paperback).

Deane, Philip. *I should have Died.* New York: Atheneum, 1977, 182 p.

Ford, Robert. *Captured in Tibet.* London: Harrap, 1957, 256 p.

Goodwin, Ralph Burton. *Passport to Eternity.* London: A. Barker, 1956, 192 p.

Hartendorp, A.V.H. *The Santo Tomas Story.* Edited from the Official History of the Santo Tomas Internment Camp by Frank H. Golay. New York: McGraw-Hill, 1964, 446 p.

McDougall, William H. *By Eastern Windows: The Story of a Battle of Souls and Minds in the Prison Camps of Sumatra.* New York: Scribner, 1949, 349 p.

McGee, John Hugh. *Rice and Salt: A History of the Defense and Occupation of Mindanao During World War II.* San Antonio: Naylor, 1962, 242 p.

McGrath, John M. *Prisoner of War: Six Years in Hanoi.* Annapolis, Md.: Naval Institute Press, 1975, 114 p.

Minear, Richard H. *Victors' Justice: The Tokyo War Crimes Trial.* Princeton, N.J.: Princeton University Press, 1971, 229 p.

Pernikoff, Ossip Alexandre Joseph. *"Bushido," the Anatomy of Terror.* New York: Liveright Publishing Corp., 1943, 284 p.

Reel, Adolf Frank. *The Case of General Yamashita.* Chicago: University of Chicago Press, 1949, 323 p. (paperback).

Reynolds, Quentin James. *Quentin Reynolds' Officially Dead: The Story of Commander C.D. Smith.* New York: Random House, 1945, 244 p.

Reynolds, Quentin James. *Officially Dead: The Story of Commander C.D. Smith.* New York: Pyramid Books, 1962, 159 p. (paperback).

Rowe, James N. *Five Years to Freedom.* Boston: Little, Brown, 1971, 467 p.

Statler, Oliver. *Shimoda Story.* New York: Random House, 1969, 627 p.

Tennien, Mark A. *No Secret is Safe Behind the Bamboo Curtain.* New York: Farrar, Straus and Young, 1952, 270 p.

Tokayer, Marvin and **Swarz, Mary.** *The Fugu Plan: The Untold Story of the Japanese and the Jews During World War II.* New York: Paddington Press, 1979, 287 p.

Wignall, Sydney. *Prisoner in Red Tibet.* London: Hutchinson, 1957, 264 p.

East Europe
General

Andrew, Brother; Sherill, John et al. *God's Smuggler.* New York: New American Library, 1967, 240 p.

Bergh, Hendrik van. *Murder to Order.* New York: Devin-Adair, 1967, 127 p.

Dewhurst, Claude Hector. *Close Contact.* Boston: Houghton Mifflin, 1954, 173 p.

Lewis, Flora. *Red Pawn: The Story of Noel Field.* Garden City, N.Y.: Doubleday, 1965, 283 p.

Marku, Michael. *The Red Pioneer.* New York: Comet Press, 1955, 68 p. (fiction).

Mowat, R.C. *Ruin and Resurgence, 1939–1965.* London: Blandford Press, 1966, 406 p.

Shub, Anatole. *An Empire Loses Hope: The Return of Stalin's Ghost.* New York: Norton, 1970, 474 p.

Steven, Stewart. *Operation Splinter Factor.* Philadelphia: Lippincott, 1974, 249 p.

Czechoslovakia

Cecilia, Sister. *The Deliverance of Sister Cecilia, as told to William Brinkley.* New York: Farrar, Straus and Young, 1954, 360 p. (Secular name: Cecilia Agnes Barath).

Kohout, Pavel. *From the Diary of a Counterrevolutionary.* Translated from the Czech by George Theiner. New York: McGraw-Hill, 1972, 307 p.

Komunisticka strana Ceskoslovenska, Ustredni vybor, Komise pro vyrizonvani stranickych rehabilitaci. *The Czechoslovak Political Trials, 1950–1954: The Suppressed Report of the Dubcek Government's Commission of Inquiry.* Edited by Jiri Pelikan. London: Macdonald and Co., 1971, 360 p.

Kovaly, Heda and **Kohak, Erazim.** *The Victors and the Vanquished.* New York: Horizon Press, 1973, 274 p.

Loebl, Eugen. *My Mind on Trial.* New York: Harcourt, Brace, Jovanovich, 1976, 235 p.

Mackenzie, Compton, *Sir. Dr. Benes.* London: Harrap, 1946, 356 p.

Mnacko, Ladislav. *The Seventh Night.* Translated from the Slovak. New York: Dutton, 1969, 220 p.

Saroch, Z. *Na granitse.* Translated from the Czech by A.N. Gus'kov, L.M. Madiakina *et al.* Moscow: Voenizdat, 1974, 150 p. (original: Vystrely Zhranice. Prague: Nase Vojsko, 1972).

Slanska, Josefa. *Report on my Husband.* Translated from the Czech by Edith Pargeter. New York: Atheneum, 1969, 208 p.

Sterling, Claire. *The Masaryk Case.* New York: Harper and Row, 1969, 366 p.

Stransky, Jan. *East Wind over Prague.* New York: Random House, 1951, 245 p.

Valenta, Jiri. *Soviet Intervention in Czechoslovakia, 1968: Anatomy of a Decision.* Baltimore: Johns Hopkins University Press, 1979, 208 p.

German Democratic Republic

Cate, Curtis. *The Ides of August: The Berlin Wall Crisis—1961.* New York: M. Evans, 1978, 534 p.

Knop, Werner Gustav John. *Prowling Russia's Forbidden Zone: A Secret Journey into Soviet Germany.* New York: Knopf, 1949, 200 p.

Löwenthal, Fritz. *News From Soviet Germany.* Translated by Edward Fitzgerald. London: Gollancz, 1950, 343 p.

Riess, Curt. *The Berlin Story.* London: Frederick Muller, 1953, 240 p.

Van Altena, John. *A Guest of the State.* Chicago: Regnery, 1967, 244 p.

Hungary

Bone, Edith. *7 Years' Solitary.* New York: Harcourt, Brace, 1957, 256 p.

Bursten, Martin A. *Escape From Fear.* Syracuse, N.Y.: Syracuse University Press, 1958, 224 p.

Copp, DeWitt S. and **Peck, Marshall.** *Betrayal at the UN: The Story of Paul Bang-Jensen.* New York: Devin-Adair, 1961, 335 p.

Faludy, György. *My Happy Days in Hell.* Translated by Kathleen Szasz. New York: Morrow, 1962, 468 p. (autobiography).

The Hungarian Revolution of 1956 in Retrospect. Edited by Bela K. Kiraly and Paul Jonas. Boulder, Colo.: East European Quarterly, 1978, 158 p.

Ignotus, Paul. *Political Prisoner: With an Epilogue by the Author Bringing his Story up to Date.* New York: Collier Books, 1964, 224 p.

Irving, David. *Uprising! One Nation's Nightmare: Hungary, 1956.* London: Hodder and Stoughton, 1981, 628 p.

Kövágó, József. *You are all Alone.* New York: Praeger, 1959, 259 p.

Lasky, Melvin J. ed. *The Hungarian Revolution: A White Book. The Story of the October Uprising as Recorded in Documents, Dispatches, Eyewitness Accounts, and World-wide Reactions.* New York: Praeger, 1957, 318 p.

Marton, Endre. *The Forbidden Sky.* Boston: Little, Brown, 1971, 306 p.

Mikes, George. *A Study in Infamy: The Operations of the Hungarian Secret Police (AVO).* Based on Secret Documents Issued by the Hungarian Ministry of the Interior. London: Deutsch, 1959, 175 p.

Mikes, George. *The Hungarian Revolution.* London: Deutsch, 1957, 192 p.

Nagy, Ferenc. *The Struggle Behind the Iron Curtain.* Translated from the Hungarian by Stephen K. Swift. New York: Macmillan, 1948, 471 p.

Nyarady, Miklos. *My Ringside Seat in Moscow.* New York: Crowell, 1952, 307 p.

Sovremennyi Vengerskii detektiv. Compiled by O. Gromov; edited by E. Orlov. Translated from the Hungarian. Moscow: Progress, 1974, 543 p. (fiction).

Vali, Rose. *Black Nightshade: The Hungarian Prison Memoirs of Rose Vali.* Narrated in English by Theresa de Kerpely. New York: Morrow, 1965, 288 p.

Poland

Belevich, Anton. *Khatyn': Bol'ignev.* Translated from the Belorussian by V. Zhizhenko. Moscow: Politizdat, 2d ed., 1974, 80 p.

The Dark Side of the Moon. New York: Scribner, 1947, 299 p.

Epstein, Edward Jay. "An Incredible Mole Who Would be Tsar." *Washington Star,* May 17, 1981, p. G-1.

Komorowski, Eugenjusz Andrei and **Gilmore, Joseph L.** *Night Never Ending.* Chicago: Regnery, 1974, 285 p.

Korbonski, Stefan. *Warsaw in Chains.* Translated from the Original Polish by Norbert Guterman. London: Allen and Unwin, 1959, 319 p.

Kot, Stanislaw. *Conversations with the Kremlin, and Dispatches from Russia.* Translated and arranged by H.C. Stevens. London: Oxford University Press, 1963, 285 p.

Mackiewicz, Josef. *The Katyn Wood Murders.* London: Hollis and Carter, 1951, 252 p.

Mikolajczyk, Stanislaw. *The Rape of Poland: Pattern of Soviet Aggression.* New York: Whittlesey House, 1948, 309 p.

Weit, Erwin. *At the Red Summit: Interpreter Behind the Iron Curtain.* Translated by Mary Schofield. New York: Macmillan, 1973, 226 p.

Wittlin, Tadeusz. *Time Stopped at 6:30.* Indianapolis: Bobbs-Merrill, 1965, 317 p.

Zawodny, Janusz Kazimierz. *Death in the Forest: The Story of the Katyn Forest Massacre.* Notre Dame, Ind: University of Notre Dame Press, 1962, 235 p.

Romania

Ciobanu, Vasile et al. (defendants) *Trial of the Group of Spies and Traitors in the Service of Imperialist Espionage.* Bucharest: n.p., 1950, 43 p.

Dunham, Donald Carl. *Zone of Violence: The Brutal, Shocking Story Lived by an American Diplomat Behind the Red Curtain.* New York: Belmont Books, 1962, 188 p.

Samuelli, Annie. *The Wall Between.* Washington: R.B. Luce, 1967, 227 p.

Wurmbrand, Richard. *Christ in the Communist Prisons.* Edited by Charles Foley. New York: Coward-McCann, 1968, 255 p.

Yugoslavia

Doder, Dusko. *The Yugoslavs.* New York: Random House, 1978, 256 p.

Martin, David. *Ally Betrayed: The Uncensored Story of Tito and Mihailovich.* New York: Prentice-Hall, 1946, 372 p.

Prcela, John and **Guldescu, Stanko,** comps. *Operation Slaughterhouse: Eyewitness Accounts of Postwar Massacres in Yugoslavia* Philadelphia: Dorrance, 1970, 557 p.

West Europe
General

Gallonio, Antonio. *Torture of the Christian Martyrs.* Translated and adapted by A.R. Allinson. n.p.: Fredrick Publications, 1959, 243 p.

Messalla, Flavio. *Le mani rosse sulle forze armate.* Rome: Centro Studi e Documentazione Sulla Guerra Psicologica, 1966, 82 p. (paperback).

Pinto, Oreste. *Spy Catcher.* New York: Harper, 1952, 213 p.

Rydenfelt, Sven and **Larsson, Janerik.** *Säkerhetspolisens hemliga register: Om asiktsfrihet och asiktsförföljelse.* Göteborg: Zinderman, 1966, 118 p.

France

Belin, Jean. *Secrets of the Sûreté: The Memoirs of Commissioner Jean Belin.* New York: Putnam, 1950, 277 p.

Bernert, Philippe. *Roger Wybot et la bataille pour la D.S.T.* Paris: Presse de la Cité, 544 p. (paperback).

Carr, John Laurence. *Robespierre: The Force of Circumstance.* New York: St. Martin's Press, 1972, 240 p.

Dark, Sidney. *Twelve Bad Men.* New York: Thomas Y. Crowell, 1929, 351 p.

Dentu, E. ed. *Vingt ans de police: Souvenirs et anecdotes d'un ancien officier de paix.* Paris: Librairie de la Societé des Gens de Lettres, 1881, 311 p.

Du Camp, Maxime. *Paris After the Prussians.* Translated from the French by Philip A. Wilkins. London: Hutchinson, 1940, 288 p.

Dunoyer, Alphonse. *The Public Prosecutor of the Terror, Antoine Quentin Fouquier-Tinville.* Translated from the French by A.W. Evans. New York: Putnam, 1913, 320 p.

Forssell, Nils. *Fouché, the Man Napoleon Feared.* Translated from the Swedish by Ann Barwell. London: Allen and Unwin, 1928, 255 p.

Fouché, Joseph. *The Memoirs of Joseph Fouché, Duke of Otranto, Minister of the General Police of France.* Translated from the French. 2d ed., rev. and cor. London: Gibbings, 1894, 474 p.

Galtier-Boissière, Jean. *Mysteries of the French Secret Police.* Translated by Ronald Leslie-Melville. London: S. Paul, 1938, 292 p.

Guillaume, Gilbert. *Mes missions face à l'Abwehr: Contre-espionnage, 1938–1945.* vol. II. Paris: Plon, 1973, 269 p.

Hentig, Hans von. *Fouché: Ein Beitrag zur Technik der politschen Polizei in nachrevolutionären Perioden.* Tübingen: Mohr, 1919, 46 p.

Kennedy, Michael L. *The Jacobin Club of Marseilles, 1790–1794.* Ithaca, N.Y.: Cornell University Press, 1973, 245 p.

Kerr, Wilfred Brenton. *The Reign of Terror, 1793–4: The Experiment of the Democratic Republic, and the Rise of the Bourgeoisie.* Toronto: University of Toronto Press, 1927, 499 p.

Ladoux, Georges. *Mes souvenirs (contre-espionnage) recueillis et mis au point par Marcel Berger.* Paris: Les Editions de France, 1937, 185 p.

Lenotre, G., *pseud.* (Gosselin, Louis Leon Theodore). *The Tribunal of the Terror: A Study of Paris in 1793–1795.* Translated by Frederic Lees. London: William Heinemann, 1909, 292 p.

Loomis, Stanley. *Paris in the Terror: June 1793–July 1794.* Philadelphia: Lippincott, 1964, 415 p.

Mauriac, Claude. *The Other de Gaulle: Diaries 1944–1954.* Translated from the French by Moura Budberg and Gordon Latta. London: Angus and Robertson, 1973, 378 p.

Memoirs of Monsieur Claude, Chief of Police, Under the Second Empire. Translated by Katherine Prescott Wormeley. Boston: Houghton Mifflin, 1907, 321 p.

Novick, Peter. *The Resistance Versus Vichy: The Purge of Collaborators in Liberated France.* New York: Columbia University Press, 1968, 245 p.

Palmer, Robert Roswell. *Twelve Who Ruled: The Committee of Public Safety, During the Terror.* Princeton: Princeton University Press, 1941, 417 p.

Panzani, Alex. *Une prison clandestine de la police francaise, Arenc.* Paris: F. Maspero, 1975, 102 p.

Scott, Otto J. *Robespierre: The Voice of Virtue.* New York: Mason and Lipscomb, 1974, 266 p. (Maximilien Marie Isidore de Robespierre).

Scott, William. *Terror and Repression in Revolutionary Marseilles.* New York: Harper and Row, 1973, 385 p.

Alfred Dreyfus

Chapman, Guy. *The Dreyfus Case: A Reassessment.* New York: Reynal, 1955, 400 p.

Chapman, Guy. *The Dreyfus Trials.* New York: Stein and Day, 1972, 282 p.

Charpentier, Armand. *The Dreyfus Case.* Translated by J. Lewis May. London: G. Bles, 1935, 278 p.

Dreyfus, Alfred. *Five Years of My Life, 1894–1899.* New York: McClure, Phillips, 1901, 310 p.

Dreyfus, Alfred. *Five Years of My Life, 1894–1899.* New York: Peebles' Press International, 1977, 252 p. (reprint of 1899 original edition with an introduction by Nicholas Halasz).

Dreyfus, Alfred. *Lettres d'un innocent: The Letters of Captain Dreyfus to his Wife.* Translated by L.G. Moreau. New York: Harper, 1899, 234 p.

Halasz, Nicholas. *Captain Dreyfus: The Story of a Mass Hysteria.* New York: Simon and Schuster, 1955, 274 p.

Harding, William. *Dreyfus: The Prisoner of Devil's Island, a Full Story of the Most Remarkable Military Trial and Scandal of the Age.* New York: Associated Publishing Co., 1899, 406 p.

Hoffman, Robert Louis. *More Than a Trial: The Struggle over Captain Dreyfus.* New York: Free Press, 1980, 247 p.

Kayser, Jacques. *L'affaire Dreyfus.* Paris: Gallimard, 1946, 309 p.

Kerkhoff, Johnston D. *Traitor! Traitor! The Tragedy of Alfred Dreyfus.* New York: Greenberg, 1930, 291 p.

Lewis, David L. *Prisoners of Honor: The Dreyfus Affair.* New York: Morrow, 1973, 346 p.

Miquel, Pierre. *Une Enigme? L'affaire Dreyfus.* Paris: Presses Universitaires de France, 1972. 96 p. (paperback).

Miquel, Pierre. *L'affaire Dreyfus.* Paris: Presses Universitaires de France, 1961, 128 p. (paperback).

Mittelstädt, Otto. *Die Affaire Dreyfus: eine kriminalpolitische Studie.* Berlin: J. Guttentag, 1899, 112 p.

Paléologue, Georges Maurice. *An Intimate Journal of the Dreyfus Case.* Translated from the French by Eric Mosbacher. New York: Criterion Books, 1957, 319 p. (translation of *Journal de l'affaire Dreyfus, 1894–1899; l'affaire Dreyfus et le Quai d'Orsay*).

Paléologue, Georges Maurice. *My Secret Diary of the Dreyfus Case, 1894–1899.* Translated from the French by Eric Mosbacher. London: Secker and Warburg, 1957, 230 p.

Snyder, Louis Leo. *The Dreyfus Case: A Documentary History.* New Brunswick, N.J.: Rutgers University Press, 1973, 414 p.

Steinthal, Walter. *Dreyfus.* Translated from the German by Captain Raymond Johnes. London: Allen and Unwin, 1930, 282 p.

Germany, including Nazi Germany
General

Allied Forces, Supreme Headquarters. *Military Government Germany: Supreme Commander's Area of Control. Proclamations, Laws, Ordinances and Notices. Directives and Instructions to German Police.* [Germany]: Reproduced by Ninth U.S. Army, November 7, 1944, 54 p.

Allied Forces, Supreme Headquarters. *Arrest Categories Handbook: Germany.* n.p.: Supreme Headquarters, Allied Expeditionary Force, Office of Assistant Chief of Staff, G-2, Counter-intelligence Sub-division, Evaluation and Dissemination Section, 1945, 31 p.

Borkin, Joseph. *The Crime and Punishment of I.G. Farben.* New York: Free Press, 1978, 250 p.

Cecil, Robert. *The Myth of the Master Race: Alfred Rosenberg and Nazi Ideology.* New York: Dodd, Mead, 1972, 266 p.

Curtin, Daniel Thomas. *The Land of Deepening Shadow: Germany-at-War.* New York: George H. Doran, 1917, 337 p.

Dimitroff, Georgei. *Dimitroff: Briefe und Aufzeichnungen aus der Zeit der Haft und des Leipziger Prozesses.* Paris: Éditions du Carrefour, 1935, 174 p.

Dukes, Paul, Sir. *An Epic of the Gestapo: The Story of a Strange Search.* London: Cassell, 1940, 283 p.

Fitz Gibbon, Constantine. *Denazification.* New York: Norton, 1969, 222 p.

Fredborg, Arvid. *Behind the Steel Wall: A Swedish Journalist in Berlin, 1941–1943.* New York: Viking Press, 1944, 305 p.

Institut für Zeitgeschichte, Munich. *Anatomie des SS-Staates,* von Hans Buchheim [et al.] Olten: Walter-Verlag, 1965, 2 v.

Institut für Zeitgeschichte, Munich. *Anatomy of the SS State* by Helmut Krausnick [et al.] Translated from the German by Richard Barry, Marian Jackson et al. New York: Walker, 1968, 614 p.

Moczarski, Kazimierz. *Conversations with an Executioner.* Edited by Mariana Fitzpatrick. Englewood Cliffs, N.J.: Prentice-Hall, 1981, 282 p.

Nollau, Günther. *Wie sicher ist die Bundesrepublik?* Munich: Bertelsmann, 1976, 206 p.

Petersen, Jan. *Gestapo Trial: A Novel About the German Secret State Police.* Translated from the German by Cyrus Brooks. London: Gollancz, 1939, 286 p.

Reile, Oscar. *L'Abwehr, le contre-espionnage allemand en France.* Translated by René Jouan. Paris: Éditions France-Empire, 1970, 318 p. (paperback).

Russell, Edward Frederick Langley Russell, Baron. *The Scourge of the Swastika: A Short History of Nazi War Crimes.* New York: Ballantine Books, 1956, 244 p. (paperback).

Schoenbaum, David. *The Spiegel Affair.* Garden City, N.Y.: Doubleday, 1968, 239 p.

Tissot, Victor. *La police secrète prussienne.* Paris: Librairie de la Société des Gens de Lettres, 1884, 436 p. (photocopy).

Toliver, Raymond F. and **Scharff, Hanns J.** *The Interrogator: The Story of Hanns Scharff, Luftwaffe's Master Interrogator.* Fallbrook, Calif.: Aero Publishers, 1978, 384 p.

Valtin, Jan. pseud. (Krebs, Richard Julius Herman). *Out of the Night.* New York: Alliance Book Corp., 1941, 749 p.

Veale, Frederick John Partington. *War Crimes Discreetly Veiled.* New York: Devin-Adair, 1959, 240 p.

Vogt, Hannah. *The Burden of Guilt: A Short History of Germany, 1914–1945.* Translated by Herbert Straus. New York: Oxford University Press, 1964, 318 p.

Rudolf Hess

Douglas-Hamilton, James. *Motive for a Mission: The Story Behind Hess's Flight to Britain.* London: Macmillan, 1971, 290 p.

Hess, Rudolf. *Prisoner of Peace.* Translated from the German of Ilse Hess, England-Nurnberg-Spandau by Meyrick Booth. Edited by George Pile. London: Britons Pub., 1954, 151 p.

Hutton, Joseph Bernard. *Hess: The Man and his Mission.* New York: Macmillan, 1970, 262 p.

Manvell, Roger and **Fraenkel, Heinrich.** *Hess: A Biography.* New York: Drake Publishers, 1973, 256 p.

Thomas, Walter Hugh. *The Murder of Rudolf Hess.* New York: Harper and Row, 1979, 224 p.

Adolf Hitler

Kohler, Pauline. *The Woman who Lived in Hitler's House.* New York: Sheridan House, 1940, 216 p. (London edition: *I was Hitler's Maid*).

Ludecke, Kurt Georg Wilhelm. *I Knew Hitler: The Story of a Nazi who Escaped the Blood Purge.* London: Jarrolds Pub., 1938, 715 p.

Minott, Rodney G. *The Fortress that Never was: The Myth of Hitler's Bavarian Stronghold.* New York: Holt, Rinehart and Winston, 1964, 208 p.

Wiedemann, Fritz. *Der Mann, der Feldherr werden wollte: Erlebnisse und Erfahrungen des Vorgesetzten Hitlers im I. Weltkrieg und seines späteren persönlichen Adjutanten.* Velbert: Blick und Bild Verlag für Politische Bildung, 1964, 270 p.

Concentration Camps

Ady-Brille, Benoist. *Les Techniciens de la mort.* Publié par la Fédération nationale des déportés et internés, résistants et patriotes. Paris: Le Livre de Poche, 1979, 414 p. (paperback).

Andrews, Allen. *Exemplary Justice.* London: Harrap, 1976, 238 p. (Stalag Luft 3).

Aziz, Philippe. *Doctors of Death.* Translated from the French by Edouard Bizub and Philip Haentzler. Geneva: Ferni Publishers, 1976, 3 v.

Bernadac, Christian. *Les mannequins nus.* Paris: France-Empire, 1971–73, 3 v. (Auschwitz and Ravensbruck) (paperback).

Best, Sigismund Payne. *The Venlo Incident.* London: Hutchinson, 1950, 260 p.

Bishop, Jack. *In Pursuit of Freedom.* London: Cooper, 1977, 126 p.

Caillou, Alan, *pseud.* (Lyle-Smythe, Alan) *The World is Six Feet Square.* New York: Norton, 1955, 255 p.

Castle, John, *pseud.* (Payne, Ronald Charles and Garrod, John William). *The Password is Courage.* New York: Ballantine Books, 1955, 190 p. (paperback).

Collins, Douglas. *P.O.W.* Richmond Hill, Ont.: Simon and Schuster of Canada, 1969, 292 p. (paperback).

Duke, Florimand with **Swaart, Charles M.** *Name, Rank, and Serial Number.* New York: Meredith Press, 1969, 162 p. (Colditz).

Eggers, Reinhold. *Colditz: The German Side of the Story.* Translated and edited by Howard Gee. New York: Norton, 1961, 190 p.

Fuchs, Gottlieb. *Dolmetscher gesucht. Ein Schweizer als Generaldolmetscher im Sicherheitsdienst in Südfrankreich. Nr. 44 110 in Buchenwald, Harzungen, Dora-Nordhausen, Belsen-Bergen.* Lucerne: n.p., 1947, 76 p.

Gazagnaire, Louis. *Dans la nuit des prisons.* Paris: Editions Sociales, 1973, 247 p.

Guareschi, Giovanni. *My Secret Diary, 1943–1945.* Translated from the Italian by Frances Frenaye. New York: Farrar, Straus and Cudahy, 1958, 234 p.

Hart, Kitty. *I am Alive.* London: Abelard-Schuman, 1962, 159 p. (Oswieçim).

Heimler, Eugene. *Night of the Mist.* New York: Vanguard Press, 1960, 191 p. (autobiographical).

Hoess, Rudolf. *Commandant of Auschwitz: Autobiography.* Translated from the German by Constantine FitzGibbon. Cleveland: World Pub., 1960, 285 p. (Oswieçim).

Joffroy, Pierre. *A Spy for God: The Ordeal of Kurt Gerstein.* Translated by Norman Denny. New York: Harcourt, Brace, Jovanovich, 1971, 319 p. (translation of *L'espion de Dieu*).

Julitte, Pierre. *Block 26: Sabotage at Buchenwald.* Translated from the French by Francis Price. Garden City, N.Y.: Doubleday, 1971, 318 p.

Ka-tzetnik 135633. *Atrocity.* Edited by Lyle Stuart. New York: L. Stuart, 1963, 287 p. (Oswiȩcim) (fiction).

Kielar, Wieslaw. *Anus mundi: wspomnienia oswiecimskie.* New York: Quadrangle, 1980, 312 p.

Kogon, Eugen. *The Theory and Practice of Hell: The German Concentration Camps and the System Behind Them.* Translated by Heinz Norden. New York: Berkley Publishing, 1960, 328 p. (translation of *Der SS-Staat, das System der deutschen Konzentrationslager*) (paperback).

Kurst, Otto. *Auschwitz: The Horrifying Tortures and Deaths in the Most Notorious of the Nazi Extermination Camps.* New York: Hillman Periodicals, 1960, 144 p. (paperback).

Lacaze, André. *The Tunnel.* London: Hamish Hamilton, 1980, 471 p.

Langhoff, Wolfgang. *Rubber Truncheon: Being an Account of Thirteen Months Spent in a Concentration Camp.* Translated from the German of "Die Moorsoldaten" by Lilo Linke. New York: Dutton, 1935, 279 p. (Börgermoor).

Le Brigant. *Les indomptables.* Paris: Berger-Levrault, 1948, 236 p.

Lengyel, Olga. *Hitler's Ovens.* New York: Avon, 1947, 189 p. (Oswiȩcim and Birkenau) (paperback edition of *Five Chimneys: The Story of Auschwitz*).

Levi, Primo. *If This is a Man.* Translated from the Italian by Stuart Woolf. New York: Orion Press, 1959, 205 p. (Oswiȩcim).

Litten, Irmgard Wüst. *Beyond Tears.* New York: Alliance Book, 1940, 325 p.

Massock, Richard Gilbert. *Italy From Within.* New York: Macmillan, 1943, 400 p.

Michel, Jean and **Nucera, Louis.** *Dora.* Translated by Jennifer Kidd. New York: Holt, Rinehart and Winston, 1980, 308 p.

Moen, Petter. *Diary.* Translated from the Norwegian by Kate Austin-Lund. London: Faber and Faber, 1951, 146 p.

Müller, Filip. *Eyewitness Auschwitz: Three Years in the Gas Chambers.* Edited and translated by Susanne Flatauer. New York: Stein and Day, 1979, 180 p.

Nyiszli, Miklos. *Auschwitz: A Doctor's Eyewitness Account.* Translated by Tibère Kremer and Richard Seaver. New York: F. Fell, 1960, 222 p. (translation of *Dr. Mengele boncolóorvosa voltam*).

Pawelozyncka, Anna. *Values and Violence in Auschwitz: A Sociological Analysis.* Translated by Catherine S. Leach. Berkeley: University of California Press, 1979, 170 p.

Piliar, IUrii Evgen'evich. *It All Really Happened.* Translated from the Russian by Percy Ludwick. Moscow: Foreign Languages Pub. House, 1956, 187 p.

Poller, Walter. *Medical Block, Buchenwald: The Personal Testimony of Inmate 996, Block 36.* New York: L. Stuart, 1961, 277 p. (translation of *Arztschreiber in Buchenwald*).

Romilly, Giles and **Alexander, Michael.** *The Privileged Nightmare.* London: Weidenfeld and Nicolson, 1954, 246 p.

Seger, Gerhart Heinrich. *A Nation Terrorized.* Chicago: Reilly and Lee, 1935, 204 p. (Oranienburg).

Sereny, Gitta. *Into That Darkness: From Mercy Killing to Mass Murder.* New York: McGraw Hill, 1974, 380 p.

Soupault, Philippe. *Age of Assassins: The Story of Prisoner No. 1234.* Translated from the French by Hannah Josephson. New York: Knopf, 1946, 315 p.

Steiner, Jean François. *Treblinka.* Translated from the French by Helen Weaver. New York: Simon and Schuster, 1967, 415 p.

Szmaglewska, Seweryna. *Smoke over Birkenau.* Translated from the Polish by Jadwiga Rynas. New York: Holt, 1947, 386 p.

Occupied Areas
General

Adamson, Hans Christian and **Klem, Per.** *Blood on the Midnight Sun.* New York: Norton, 1964, 282 p. (Norway).

Dourlein, Pieter. *Inside North Pole: A Secret Agent's Story.* Translated by F.G. Renier and Anne Cliff. 2d ed. London: Kimber, 1953, 206 p. (Netherlands).

Falla, Francis Walter. *The Silent War.* London: Frewin, 1967, 224 p. (Guernsey).

Gerson, L.D., pseud. (Gern, Peter). *Schreieder und die Spione: der erste deutsche Bericht über das "England-Spiel."* Munich: Münchener Dom-Verlag, 1950, 61 p. (Netherlands).

Giskes, H.J. *London Calling North Pole.* London: Kimber, 1953, 208 p. (Netherlands).

Goris, Jan Albert, ed. and tr. *Belgium Under Occupation.* New York: Moretus Press for the Belgian Government Information Center, 1947, 240 p.

Great Britain, Foreign Office. *Secret German Documents Seized During the Raid on the Lofoten Islands on the 4th of March 1941, Embodying Instructions to the Army on the Control of the Press and on Collaboration with the Gestapo in Dealing with Norwegian Nationals.* London: H.M. Stationery Off., 1941, 28 p.

Knudsen, Harald Franklin. *I was Quisling's Secretary.* London: Britons Publishing, 1967, 192 p. (translation of *Jeg var Quislings sekretaer*).

Lemkin, Raphael. *Axis Rule in Occupied Europe: Laws of Occupation, Analysis of Government, Proposals for Redress.* Washington: Carnegie Endowment for International Peace, Division of International Law, 1944, 674 p.

Myklebost, Tor. *They Came As Friends.* Translated by Trygve M. Ager. Garden City, N.Y.: Doubleday, Doran, 1943, 297 p. (Norway).

Petrow, Richard. *The Bitter Years: The Invasion and Occupation of Denmark and Norway, April 1940–May 1945.* New York: Morrow, 1974, 403 p.

Posthumus, N.W., ed. "The Netherlands During German Occupation." *The Annals of the American Academy of Political and Social Science,* v. 245, May 1946, 231 p.

Psychoundakis, George. *The Cretan Runner: His Story of the German Occupation.* Translated by Patrick Leigh Fermor. London: Murray, 1955, 242 p.

Somerhausen, Anne S. *Written in Darkness: A Belgian Woman's Record of the Occupation, 1940–1945.* New York: Knopf, 1946, 339 p.

Wood, Alan and **Wood, Mary.** *Islands in Danger: The Story of the German Occupation of the Channel Islands, 1940–1945.* New York: Macmillan, 1955, 255 p.

Zeè, Alkè. *Petros' War.* Translated from the Greek by Edward Fenton. New York: Dutton, 1972, 236 p. (fiction).

East Europe

Cooper, Matthew. *The Nazi War Against Soviet Partisans, 1941–1944.* New York: Stein and Day, 1979, 217 p.

Cooper, Matthew. *The Phantom War: The German Struggle Against Soviet Partisans, 1941–1944.* London: Macdonald and Janes, 1979, 219 p.

Documents Accuse. Compiled and commented by B. Baranauskas and K. Ruksenas. Edited by E. Rozauskas. Translated from Lithuanian by L. Valeika and A. Aukstikalniene, from German by Vl. Grodzenskis. English version edited by Vl. Grodzenskis. Vilnius: Gintaras, 1970, 310 p.

Gedye, George Eric Rowe. *Betrayal in Central Europe; Austria and Czechoslovakia: The Fallen Bastions.* New York: Harper, 1939, 499 p. (published in England under the title of *Fallen Bastions*).

Kamenetsky, Ihor. *Secret Nazi Plans for Eastern Europe: A Study of Lebensraum Policies.* New York: Bookman Associates, 1961, 263 p.

Karski, Jan. pseud. *Story of a Secret State.* Boston: Houghton Mifflin, 1944, 391 p.

Mastny, Vojtech. *The Czechs Under Nazi Rule: The Failure of National Resistance, 1939–1942.* New York: Columbia University Press, 1971, 274 p.

Peis, Günter. *The Man Who Started the War.* London: Odhams Press, 1960, 223 p.

Reitlinger, Gerald. *The House Built on Sand: The Conflicts of German Policy in Russia, 1939–1945.* New York: Viking Press, 1960, 459 p.

Russia, Narodnyi komissariat po inostrannym delam. *The Molotov Notes on German Atrocities. Notes sent by V.M. Molotov, People's Commissar for Foreign Affairs, to all Governments with which the U.S.S.R. has Diplomatic Relations.* London: H.M. Stationery Off., 1942, 20 p.

Russia, Narodnyi komissariat po inostrannym delam. *We Shall not Forgive! The Horrors of the German Invasion in Documents and Photographs.* Moscow: Foreign Languages Publishing House, 1942, 144 p.

Szende, Stefan. *The Promise Hitler Kept.* New York: Roy Publishers, 1945, 281 p. (Adolf Folkmann).

Wells, Leon Weliczker. *The Janowska Road.* New York: Macmillan, 1963, 305 p. (autobiograpical).

France

Aron, Robert with **Elgey, Georgette.** *The Vichy Regime, 1940–1944.* Translated by Humphrey Hare. Boston: Beacon Press, 1969, 536 p.

Amouroux, Henri. *Le peuple du désastre, 1939–1940.* vol. 1; *Quarante millions de pétainistes.* vol. 2; *Les beaux jours des collabos.* vol. 3. *La grande histoire des Français sous l'occupation.* Paris: R. Laffont, 1976–1978 (paperback).

Baraduc, Jacques. *Tout ce qu'on vous a caché: les archives secrètes du Reich.* Paris: Editions de l'Elan, 1949, 318 p.

Fuller, Jean Overton. *The German Penetration of SOE: France 1941-1944.* London: Kimber, 1975, 192 p.

Greenwall, Harry James. *When France Fell.* London: Wingate, 1958, 188 p.

Hasquenoph, Marcel. *La Gestapo en France.* Paris: De Vecchi, 1975, 504 p.

Lapierre, Dominique and **Collins, Larry.** *Is Paris Burning?* New York: Pocket Books, 1977, 398 p. (paperback).

Paxton, Robert O. *Vichy France: Old Guard and New Order, 1940-1944.* New York: Norton, 1972, 399 p. (paperback).

Pryce-Jones, David. *Paris in the Third Reich: A History of German Occupation, 1940-1944.* New York: Holt, Rinehart and Winston, 1981, 294 p.

Teissier du Cros, Janet. *Divided Loyalties.* London: Hamilton, 1962, 329 p. (autobiographical).

Toynbee, Arnold Joseph. *The German Terror in France: An Historical Record.* London: Hodder and Stoughton, 1917, 212 p. (paperback).

Walter, Gérard. *Paris Under the Occupation.* Translated from the French by Tony White. New York: Orion Press, 1960, 209 p. (translation of *La vie à Paris sous l'occupation*).

Persecution of the Jews

Baker, Leonard. *Days of Sorrow and Pain: Leo Baeck and the Berlin Jews.* New York: Macmillan, 1978, 396 p.

Bartoszewski, Wladyslaw. *Warsaw Death Ring, 1939-1944.* Translated from the Polish by Edward Rothert. Warsaw: Interpress, 1968, 448 p.

Dawidowicz, Lucy S. *The War Against the Jews, 1933-1945.* New York: Holt, Rinehart and Winston, 1975, 460 p.

Donat, Alexander. *The Holocaust Kingdom: A Memoir.* New York: Holt, Rinehart and Winston, 1965, 361 p.

Dribben, Judith Strick. *A Girl Called Judith Strick.* New York: Pyramid Books, 1972, 413 p. (paperback).

Eisner, Jack. *The Survivor.* Edited by Irving A. Leitnes. New York: Morrow, 1980, 320 p.

Eitinger, Leo. *Concentration Camp Survivors in Norway and Israel.* The Hague: Martinus Nijhoff, 1972, 199 p.

Friedländer, Saul. *Kurt Gerstein, the Ambiguity of Good.* Translated from the French and German by Charles Fullman. New York: Knopf, 1969, 228 p. (translation of *Kurt Gerstein ou l'Ambiguité du bien*).

Gilbert, Martin. *Final Journey: The Fate of the Jews in Nazi Europe.* New York: Mayflower Books, 1979, 224 p.

Hehn, Paul N. *The German Struggle Against Yugoslav Guerrillas in World War II: German Counter-insurgency in Yugoslavia, 1941-1943.* Boulder, Colo.: East European Quarterly, 1979, 153 p.

Hilberg, Raul. *The Destruction of the European Jews.* Chicago: Quadrangle, 1961, 788 p.

Hilberg, Raul, comp. *Documents of Destruction: Germany and Jewry, 1933-1945.* Chicago: Quadrangle Books, 1971, 242 p.

Hillel, Marc and **Henry, Clarissa.** *Of Pure Blood.* Translated from the French by Eric Mosbacher. New York: McGraw-Hill, 1976, 256 p. (translation of *Au nom de la race*).

Jewish Black Book Committee. *The Black Book: The Nazi Crime Against the Jewish People.* New York: Duell, Sloan and Pearce, 1946, 560 p.

Katz, Robert. *Black Sabbath: A Journey Through a Crime Against Humanity.* London: Barker, 1969, 398 p.

Kinnaird, Clark. *This Must not Happen Again! The Black Book of Fascist Horror.* New York: Howell, Soskin, 1945, 157 p.

Knoop, Hans. *The Menten Affair.* Translated from the Dutch by R. and M. Rudnik. New York: Macmillan, 1978, 165 p. (translation of *De zaak Menten*).

Lerner, Lily Gluck and **Stuart, Sandra Lee.** *The Silence.* Secaucus, N.J.: Stuart, 1980, 190 p.

Marrus, Michael Robert and **Paxton, Robert O.** *Vichy France and the Jews.* New York: Basic Books, 1981, 432 p.

Masters, Anthony. *The Summer that Bled: The Biography of Hannah Senesh.* New York: St. Martin's Press, 1972, 349 p.

Morse, Arthur D. *While Six Million Died: A Chronicle of American Apathy.* New York: Random House, 1967, 420 p.

Reitlinger, Gerald. *The Final Solution: The Attempt to Exterminate the Jews of Europe, 1939-1945.* New York: Barnes, 1961, 622 p. (paperback).

Ringelblum, Emmanuel. *Notes from the Warsaw Ghetto: The Journal of Emmanuel Ringelblum.* Edited and translated by Jacob Sloan. New York: McGraw-Hill, 1958, 369 p.

Schleunes, Karl A. *The Twisted Road to Auschwitz: Nazi Policy Toward German Jews, 1933-1939.* Urbana: University of Illinois Press, 1970, 280 p.

Steckel, Charles W. *Destruction and Survival.* Los Angeles: Delmar Pub., 1973, 179 p.

Tushnet, Leonard. *The Pavement of Hell.* New York: St. Martin's Press, 1972, 210 p.

Wasserstein, Bernard. *Britain and the Jews of Europe, 1939-1945.* London: Institute of Jewish Affairs; New York: Oxford University Press, 1979, 389 p.

Weinreich, Max. *Hitler's Professors: The Part of Scholarship in Germany's Crimes Against the Jewish People.* New York: Yiddish Scientific Institute-YIVO, 1946, 291 p. (paperback).

Wiesel, Elie. *Night.* Translated from the French by Stella Rodway. New York: Pyramid Books, 1961, 127 p. (paperback).

Wiesenthal, Simon. *The Murderers Among Us: The Simon Wiesenthal Memoirs.* Edited by Joseph Wechsberg. New York: McGraw-Hill, 1967, 340 p.

Adolf Eichmann

Arendt, Hannah. *Eichmann in Jerusalem: A Report on the Banality of Evil.* Rev. and enl. ed. New York: Viking Press, 1975, 312 p. (paperback).

Clarke, Comer. *Eichmann: The Man and his Crimes.* New York: Ballantine, 1960, 153 p. (paperback).

Donovan, John. *Eichmann, Man of Slaughter.* New York: Avon, 1960, 109 p. (paperback).

Kempner, Robert Max Wasilii, ed. *Eichmann und Komplizen.* Zürich: Europa Verlag, 1961, 451 p.

Linze, Dewey W. *The Trial of Adolf Eichmann.* Los Angeles: Holloway House, 1961, 224 p.

Reynolds, Quentin James; Katz, Ephraim et al. *Minister of Death: The Adolf Eichmann Story.* New York: Viking Press, 1960, 246 p.

Robinson, Jacob. *And the Crooked Shall be Made Straight: The Eichmann Trial, the Jewish Catastrophe, and Hannah Arendt's Narrative.* New York: Macmillan, 1965, 406 p.

Russell, Edward Frederick Langley, *Baron. The Record: The Trial of Adolf Eichmann for his Crimes Against the Jewish People and Against Humanity.* New York: Knopf, 1963, 351 p. (published in London under the title: *The Trial of Adolf Eichmann*).

Zeiger, Henry A., ed. *The Case Against Adolf Eichmann.* New York: New American Library, 1960, 192 p.

Trials at Nuremberg

Bernstein, Victor Heine. *Final Judgment: The Story of Nuremberg.* New York: Boni and Gaer, 1947, 289 p.

Bernstein, Victor Heine. *The Holocaust-Final Judgment.* Indianapolis: Bobbs-Merrill, 1980, 289 p.

Davidson, Eugene. *The Trial of the Germans: An Account of the Twenty-two Defendants Before the International Military Tribunal at Nuremberg.* New York: Macmillan, 1966, 636 p.

Gilbert, G.M. *Nuremberg Diary.* New York: New American Library of World Literature, 1947, 430 p. (paperback).

Goldstein Anatole. *Operation Murder.* Edited by Maximilian Hurwitz. New York: Institute of Jewish Affairs, World Jewish Congress, 1949, 39 p.

Maser, Werner. *A Nation on Trial.* New York: Scribner, 1979, 368 p. (English translation of *Nürnberg: Tribunal d. Sieger.* Dusseldorf: Econ Verlag, 1977, 700 p.).

Miale, Florence R. and **Selzer, Michael.** *The Nuremberg Mind: The Psychology of the Nazi Leaders.* New York: Quadrangle, 1975, 302 p.

Neave, Airey. *On Trial at Nuremberg.* Boston: Little, Brown, 1978, 348 p.

Smith, Bradley F. *Reaching Judgment at Nuremberg.* New York: Basic Books, 1977, 349 p.

Smith, Bradley F. *The Road to Nuremberg.* New York: Basic Books, 1981, 303 p.

Stipp, John L., ed. *The Hitler Conspiracy.* New York: Manor Books, 1977, 271 p. (paperback edition of *Devil's Diary: The Record of Nazi Conspiracy and Aggression.* Yellow Springs, Ohio: Antioch Press, 1955, 236 p.).

War Criminals

Bar-Zohar, Michel. *The Avengers.* Translated from the French by Len Ortzen. New York: Hawthorn Books, 1969, 279 p.

Bezymenskii, Lev Aleksandrovich. *Tracing Martin Bormann.* Translated from the Russian by David Skvirsky and Igor Sokolov. Moscow: Progress Publishers, 1966, 178 p.

Blum, Howard. *Wanted! The Search for Nazis in America.* New York: Quadrangle, 1977, 256 p.

Bower, Tom. *The Pledge Betrayed: America and Britain and the Denazification of Postwar Germany.* Garden City, N.Y.: Doubleday, 1982, 462 p.

Friedmann, Tuvyah. *The Hunter.* Edited and translated by David C. Gross. Garden City, N.Y.: Doubleday, 1961, 286 p. (autobiographical).

Gray, Ronald. *I Killed Martin Bormann!* New York: Lancer Books, 1972, 190 p. (paperback).

Whiting, Charles. *The Hunt for Martin Bormann.* New York: Ballantine Books, 1973, 240 p. (paperback).

Weingartner, James J. *Crossroads of Death: The Story of the Malmédy Massacre and Trial.* Berkeley: University of California Press, 1979, 274 p.

USSR
General

American Jewish Committee. *The Jews in the Eastern War Zone.* New York: American Jewish Committee, 1916, 120 p.

Antonov-Ovseyenko, Anton. *The Time of Stalin: Portrait of a Tyranny.* Translated from the Russian by George Saunders. New York: Harper and Row, 1981, 374 p.

Bilinsky, Yaroslav. *The Second Soviet Republic: The Ukraine After World War II.* New Brunswick, N.J.: Rutgers University Press, 1964, 539 p.

Bortoli, Georges. *The Death of Stalin.* Translated by Raymond Rosenthal. New York: Praeger, 1975, 214 p.

Brzezinski, Zbigniew K. *The Permanent Purge: Politics in Soviet Totalitarianism.* Cambridge: Harvard University Press, 1956, 256 p.

Cholawski, Shalom. *Soldiers from the Ghetto.* San Diego: Barnes, 1980, 182 p.

Dimov, Alexandre. *Les hommes doubles: La vie quotidienne en Union Sovietique.* Translated from Russian by Florence Benoist. Paris: Editions J.-C. Lattés, 1980, 315 p. (paperback).

Granitsa rozhdaet geroev. Compiled by A.V. Davydov, P.A. Ivanchishin *et al.* Moscow: DOSAAF, 1978, 180 p.

Jones, Mervyn. *The Antagonists.* New York: Potter, 1962, 328 p.

Kalme, Albert. *Total Terror: An Exposé of Genocide in the Baltics.* Edited by Walter Arm. New York: Appleton-Century-Crofts, 1951, 310 p.

Koerber, Helene von der Leyen von. *Soviet Russia Fights Crime.* Translated from the German by Mary Fowler. London: Routledge, 1934, 240 p.

Kubatkin, P. *Unichtozhim shpionov i diversantov.* Moscow: n.p., 1941, 16 p. (photocopy).

Lee, Ivy Ledbetter. *USSR (Union of Soviet Socialist Republics): A World Enigma.* New York: Private Printer, 1927, 158 p.

Lewytzkyj, Borys, comp. *The Stalinist Terror in the Thirties: Documentation from the Soviet Press.* Stanford, Calif.: Hoover Institution Press, 1974, 521 p.

Littlepage, John D. and **Bess, Demaree.** *In Search of Soviet Gold.* New York: Harcourt, Brace, 1938, 310 p.

Magidoff, Robert. *In Anger and Pity: A Report on Russia.* Garden City, N.Y.: Doubleday, 1949, 278 p.

Magidoff, Robert. *The Kremlin vs. the People: The Story of the Cold Civil War in Stalin's Russia.* Garden City, N.Y.: Doubleday, 1953, 288 p.

Manning, Clarence Augustus. *Twentieth-Century Ukraine.* New York: Bookman Associates, 1951, 243 p.

Medvedev, Roi Aleksandrovich. *On Stalin and Stalinism.* Translated by Ellen de Kadt. New York: Oxford University Press, 1979, 205 p.

Panos, Chris. *God's Spy.* Plainfield, N.J.: Logos International, 1976, 270 p.

Pogranichnye voiska SSSR: Mai 1945–1950: Sbornik dokumentov i materialov. Compiled by E.D. Solov'ev *et al.* Moscow: Nauka, 1975, 757 p.

Pogranichniki: Sbornik. Compiled by Gennadii A. Anan'ev and Mikhail A. Smirnov. Moscow: Mol. Gvardiia, 1973, 383 p.

Pollock, John Charles. *The Siberian Seven.* Waco, Texas: Word Books, 1979, 267 p.

Scott, John. *Behind the Urals: An American Worker in Russia's City of Steel.* Boston: Houghton Mifflin, 1942, 279 p.

Slovo o pogranichnikakh: Sbornik. Compiled by Nikolai S. Danilov and Vladimir A. Samsonov. Moscow: Sov. Rossiia, 1978, 317 p.

Tolstoy, Nikolai. *Stalin's Secret War.* London: Jonathan Cape, 1981, 463 p.

Trotskii, Lev. *Stalin's Gangsters.* London: New Park Publications, 1978, 84 p.

U.S. Library of Congress, Legislative Reference Service. *The Soviet Empire: Prison House of Nations and Races: A Study in Genocide, Discrimination, and Abuse of Power.* Prepared at the Request of the Subcommittee to Investigate Internal Security Laws of the Committee on the Judiciary, United States Senate, 85th Congress, 2nd session by Joseph G. Whelan, Analyst in Eastern European Affairs. Washington: U.S. GPO, 1958, 72 p.

Utley, Freda. *Lost Illusion.* Chicago: Regnery, 1948, 365 p. (paperback).

The White Sea Canal: Being an Account of the Construction of the New Canal Between the White Sea and the Baltic Sea, written by L. Auerbach, B. Agapov et al. English edition prepared from the Russian version and edited by Amabel Williams-Ellis. London: John Lane, 1935, 356 p.

Concentration Camps, Penal Colonies, and Prisons

Abramowitsch, R. *Die politischen gefangenen in der Sowjet-Union.* Berlin: J.H.W. Dietz Nacht. GmbH, 1930, 52 p.

Artem'ev, Viacheslav Pavlovich. *Rezhim i okhrana ispravitel'no-trudovykh lagerei MVD.* Munich: Institut po Izucheniiu SSSR, 1956, 221 p.

Carmichael, Joel. *Stalin's Masterpiece: The Show Trials and Purges of the Thirties, the Consolidation of the Bolshevik Dictatorship.* New York: St. Martin's Press, 1976, 238 p.

Conquest, Robert. *Kolyma: The Arctic Death Camps.* New York: Viking Press, 1978, 254 p.

Fehling, Helmut M. *One Great Prison: The Story Behind Russia's Unreleased POW's.* Translated by Charles R. Joy. Boston: Beacon Press, 1951, 175 p. (German and Japanese War Prisoners).

International Commission Against Concentration Camp Practices. *Police-state Methods in the Soviet Union,* prepared by the International Commission Against Concentrationist Regimes, under the direction of David Rousset. Translated by Charles R. Joy. Edited by Jerzy G. Gliksman. Boston: Beacon Press, 1953, 64 p.

Kennan, George. *Siberia and the Exile System.* New York: Century, 1891, 2 v.

Khrushchev's Crimes in Ukraine: Mass-Murders of Ukrainian Political Prisoners. London: Ukrainian Publishers, 1962, 93 p. (paperback).

Kosyk, Volodymyr. *Concentration Camps in the USSR.* London: Ukrainian Publishers, 1962, 108 p. (paperback).

Lengyel, Emil. *Siberia.* Garden City, N.Y.: Garden City Publishing, 1943, 416 p.

Neotvratimoe vozmezdie. Po materialam sudebnykh protsessov nad izmennikami Rodiny, Fashistskimi palachami i agentami imperialist. razvedok. Edited by Nikolai F. Chistiakov and Mikhail E. Karyshev. Moscow: Voenizdat, 1973, 352 p.

Os'machka, Teodosii. *Red Assassins: A Factual Story Revealing how the Ukraine lost its Freedom.* Minneapolis: T.S. Denison, 1959, 375 p.

Roeder, Bernhard. *Katorga, an Aspect of Modern Slavery.* Translated by Lionel Kochan. London: Heinemann, 1958, 271 p.

Rupert, Raphael. *A Hidden World.* Edited by Anthony Rhodes. Cleveland: World Pub., 1963, 223 p.

Scholmer, Joseph. *Vorkuta.* Translated from the German by Robert Kee. London: Weidenfeld and Nicolson, 1954, 264 p.

Scholmer, Joseph. *Vorkuta.* Translated from the German by Robert Kee. New York: Holt, 1955, 304 p.

Sedov, Leon, ed. *The Red Book on the Moscow Trial.* London: New Park Publications, 1980, 120 p. (paperback).

Solzhenitsyn, Aleksandr Isaevich. *The Gulag Archipelago, 1918–1956: An Experiment in Literary Investigation.* Translated from the Russian by Thomas P. Whitney. New York: Harper and Row, 1973-78, 3 v.

Taylor, Telford with **Dershowitz, Alan.** *Courts of Terror: Soviet Criminal Justice and Jewish Emigration.* New York: Knopf, 1976, 187 p.

Thomsen, Alexander. *In the Name of Humanity.* Translated and adapted from the Danish by Maurice Michael. New York: Dutton, 1963, 229 p.

Deportation and Repatriation

Bethell, Nicholas William, *Baron. The Last Secret: The Delivery to Stalin of Over Two Million Russians by Britain and the United States.* New York: Basic Books, 1974, 224 p.

Conquest, Robert. *The Nation Killers: The Soviet Deportation of Nationalities.* New York: Macmillan, 1970, 222 p.

Epstein, Julius. *Operation Keelhaul: The Story of Forced Repatriation from 1944 to the Present.* Old Greenwich, Conn.: Devin-Adair, 1973, 255 p.

Nekrich, Aleksandr Moiseevich. *The Punished Peoples: The Deportation and Fate of Soviet Minorities at the End of the Second World War.* Translated from the Russian by George Saunders. New York: Norton, 1978, 238 p.

Tolstoy, Nikolai. *Victims of Yalta.* London: Hodder and Stoughton, 1977, 496 p. (American edition published under the title: *The Secret Betrayal*).

Fiction

Ardamatskii, Vasilii Ivanovich. *Saturn is Almost Invisible.* Translated from the Russian by Fainna Glagoleva. Moscow: Progress Publishers, 1967, 327 p.

Granitsa est' granitsa. Compiled by Gleb Kuzovkin. Lvov: Kameniar, 1975, 301 p.

Karakhanov, Vladimir Evgen'evich. *Prodolzhenie poiska: Sbornik.* Moscow: Mol. Gvardiia, 1977, 239 p.

Korneshov, Lev Konstantinovich. *Skhvatka s nenavist'iu.* Moscow: Molodaia Gvardiia, 1973, 350 p.

Romanov, Nikolai Aleksandrovich. *Granitsa—riadom: Roman.* Moscow: Voenizdat, 1974, 371 p.

Shmel'ov Oleh Mykhailovych and Vostokov, Vladimir Vladimirovich. *Oshibka rezidenta: Roman.* Moscow: Mol. Gvardiia, 2d ed., 1966, 287 p.

Syzonenko, Oleksandr Oleksandrovych. *Zvezdy padaiut v avguste: Povesti.* Translated from the Ukrainian. Moscow: Mol. Gvardiia, 1972, 166 p.

Vasilevskii, Lev Petrovich. *Chekistskie byli: Rasskazy-vospominaniia.* Moscow: Mol. Gvardiia, 1978, 127 p.

Intelligence and Security Services

Chekists about Their Work. Compiled by V. Drozdov and A. Evseev. Washington: U.S. Joint Publications Research Service, no. 55515, March 23, 1972, 85 p. (translation of *Chekisty o svoem trude.* Moscow: Izvestiia, 1965, 126 p.).

Deriabin, Petr Sergeevich. *Watchdogs of Terror: Russian Bodyguards from the Tsars to the Commissars.* New Rochelle, N.Y.: Arlington House, 1972, 448 p.

Dubrovin, Boris Savvovich. *O godakh zabyvaia; Vdali i—riadom. Povesti.* Moscow: Voenizdat, 1973, 336 p.

Egorov, Viktor Georgievich and Parfenov, Lev Ivanovich. *Na Zheleznom vetru.* Moscow: Sov. Rossiia, 1971, 399 p.

Lyons, Eugene. *Our Secret Allies, the Peoples of Russia.* New York: Duell, Sloan and Pearce, 1953, 376 p.

My iz ChK: Sbornik ocherkov. Compiled by N.I. Milovanov. Alma-Ata: Kazakhstan, 1974, 303 p.

Nagornyi, Aleksei Petrovich and Riabov, Gelii Trofimovich. *Povest' ob ugolovnom rozyske.* Moscow: Sov. Rossiia, 1978, 558 p.

Ne zhaleia zhizni: Sbornik. Compiled by N.I. Milovanov. Alma-Ata: Kazakhstan, 1977, 267 p.

Neprimirimye vedut poisk: Ocherki i rasskazy o militsii. Compiled by V. Golovach et al. Minsk: Mastatskaia Literatura, 1978, 207 p.

Nezrimoe srazhenie. Compiled by Gleb Kuzovkin. Lvov: Kamenar, 1976, 211 p.

Pogranichnaia zastava: Sbornik. Compiled by Grigorii Mikhailovich Ignatkovich and V.A. Mel'nichuk. Moscow: Politizdat, 1978, 296 p.

Serge, Victor. *What Everyone Should Know about Repression.* Translated from the French by Judith White. London: New Park Publications; New York: Labor Publications, 1979, 88 p. (original: *Ce que tout révolutionnaire doit savoir sur la répression*).

Solov'ev, Andrei Kuz'mich. *Sebia prodavshie.* Moscow: Molodaia Gvardiia, 1977, 128 p.

Solov'ev, Andrei Kuz'mich. *Volki gibnut v Kapkanakh.* Moscow: Voenizdat, 1976, 253 p.

U.S. Department of the Army. *Rear Area Security in Russia: The Soviet Second Front Behind the German Lines.* Washington: U.S. GPO, 1951, 39 p. (Pamphlet no. 20–240).

Vereeken, Georges. *The GPU in the Trotskyist Movement.* Old Town, Clapham, England: New Park Publications, 1976, 390 p. (original: *La guepeou dans le mouvement trotskyiste.* Paris: La Pensée Universelle, 1975).

Biographies and Case Histories
General

Avinov, Marie. *Marie Avinov: Pilgrimage Through Hell, an Autobiography told by Paul Chavchavadze.* Englewood Cliffs, N.J.: Prentice-Hall, 1968, 275 p.

Barmine, Alexandre. *One Who Survived: The Life Story of a Russian Under the Soviets.* New York: Putnam, 1945, 337 p.

Borodin, Nikolai Mikhailovich. *One Man in his Time.* New York: Macmillan, 1955, 343 p. (autobiography).

Demin, Mikhail. *The Day is Born of Darkness.* Translated from the Russian by Tony Kahn. New York: Knopf, 1976, 368 p.

Dolgun, Alexander and **Watson, Patrick.** *Alexander Dolgun's Story: An American in the Gulag.* New York: Knopf, 1975, 370 p.

Evstifeev, Aleksandr Andrianovich. *Why I Escaped from Soviet Russia by "a Man Without a Country," an Undesirable Alien.* Seattle, Wash.: A. Evstifeef, 1931, 407 p.

Kaledin, Viktor K. *F-l-a-s-h D. 13.* New York: Coward-McCann, 1930, 325 p.

Koudrey, Vladimir. *Once a Commissar.* New Haven: Yale University Press, 1937, 262 p. (autobiography).

Kourdakov, Sergei. *The Persecutor.* Carmel, N.Y.: Guideposts Assoc., 1973, 254 p.

Kravchenko, Viktor Andreevich. *I Chose Freedom: The Personal and Political Life of a Soviet Official.* Garden City, N.Y.: Garden City Publishing Co., 1947, 496 p.

Kravchenko, Viktor Andreevich. *I Chose Justice.* New York: Scribner, 1950, 458 p.

Kravchenko, Viktor Andreevich, *plaintiff. Kravchenko Versus Moscow: The Report of the Famous Paris Case.* London: Wingate, 1950, 253 p. (action for libel by author against Claude Morgan and André Wurmser).

Murray, Nora Korzhenko. *I Spied for Stalin.* London: Pan Books, 1950, 251 p.

Navrozov, Lev. *The Education of Lev Navrozov: A Life in the Closed World Once Called Russia.* New York: Harper's Magazine Press, 1975, 628 p.

Neotvratimoe vozmezdie: po materialam sudebnykh protsessov nad izmennikami Rodiny, Fashistkimi palachami i agentami imperialisticheskikh razvedok. Moscow: Voenizdat, 1974, 352 p.

Piddington, William Ernest Reginald. *Russian Frenzy.* London: Elek Books, 1955, 262 p.

Pirogov, Petr Afanas'evich. *Why I Escaped: The Story of Peter Pirogov.* New York: Duell, Sloan and Pearce, 1950, 336 p.

Porter, Cathy. *Alexandra Kollontai, a Biography: The Lonely Struggle of the Woman Who Defied Lenin.* New York: Dial Press, 1980, 553 p.

Romanov, A.I. *Nights are Longest There: A Memoir of the Soviet Security Services.* Translated by Gerald Brooke. Boston: Little, Brown, 1972, 256 p.

Shalamov, Varlam Tikhonovich. *Kolyma Tales.* Translated from the Russian by John Glad. New York: Norton, 1980, 222 p. (fiction).

Tchernavin, Tatiana. *Escape from the Soviets.* Translated from the Russian by N. Alexander, *pseud.* New York: Dutton, 1934, 320 p.

Tokaev, Grigori Aleksandrovich. *Betrayal of an Ideal.* Translated from the Russian by Alec Brown. Bloomington, Indiana: Indiana University Press, 1955, 298 p. (His Memoirs, pt. 1).

Unishevsky, Vladimir. *Red Pilot: Memoirs of a Soviet Airman.* Translated by Violet M. Macdonald. London: Hurst and Blackett, 1939, 260 p.

Viktorov, Ivan Vasil'evich. *Podpol'shchik, voin, chekist.* Moscow: Izd-vo Polit. Lit-ry, 1963, 79 p. (Mikhail Sergeevich Kedrov).

White, William Lindsay. *The Little Toy Dog: The Story of the Two RB-47 Flyers, Captain John R. McKone and Captain Freeman B. Olmstead.* New York: Dutton, 1962, 304 p.

Zenzinov, Vladimir Mikhailovich. *The Road to Oblivion.* Edited by Isaac Don Levine. New York: R.M. McBride and National Traveller Club, 1931, 250 p.

Forced Labor

Gliksman, Jerzy G. *Tell the West: An Account of his Experiences as a Slave Laborer in the Union of Soviet Socialist Republics.* New York: Gresham Press, 1948, 358 p.

González, Valentin R. and **Gorkin, Julian.** *El Campesino: Life and Death in Soviet Russia.* Translated by Ilsa Barea. New York: International Press Alliance Corp., 1953, 160 p. (paperback).

Herling, Albert Konrad. *The Soviet Slave Empire.* New York: W. Funk, 1951, 230 p.

Herling, Gustaw. *A World Apart.* Translated from the Polish by Joseph Marek. New York: New American Library, 1952, 256 p.

Kitchin, George. *Prisoner of the OGPU.* London: Longmans, Green, 1935, 336 p.

Lied, Jonas. *Prospector in Siberia: The Autobiography of Jones Lied.* New York: Oxford University Press, 1945, 317 p. (London edition title: *Return to Happiness*).

Lipper, Elinor. *Eleven Years in Soviet Prison Camps.* Translated by Richard and Clara Winston. Chicago: Regnery, 1951, 310 p.

Noble, John H. *I was a Slave in Russia: An American Tells his Story.* New York: Devin-Adair, 1958, 182 p. (Vorkuta).

Parvilahti, Unto. *Beria's Gardens: A Slave Laborer's Experiences in the Soviet Utopia.* Translated from the Finnish by Alan Blair. New York: Dutton, 1960, 286 p.

Petrov, Vladimir. *Escape from the Future: The Incredible Adventures of a Young Russian.* Bloomington: Indiana University Press, 1973, 470 p.

Petrov, Vladimir. *Soviet Gold: My Life as a Slave Laborer in the Siberian Mines.* Translated from the Russian by Mirra Ginsburg. New York: Farrar, Straus, 1949, 426 p.

Pidhainy, Semen Aleksandrovich. *Islands of Death.* Toronto: Burns and MacEachern, 1953, 240 p.

Solonevich, Ivan Luk'ianovich. *Russia in Chains: A Record of Unspeakable Suffering.* Translated by Warren Harrow. London: Williams and Norgate, 1938, 2 v.

Solonevich, Ivan Luk'ianovich. *The Soviet Paradise Lost.* Translated by Warren Harrow. New York: Paisley Press, 1938, 314 p. (London edition title: *Russia in Chains*).

Jews

Azbel', Mark IAkovlevich. *Refusenik: Trapped in the Soviet Union.* Edited by Grace Pierce Forbes. Boston: Houghton Mifflin, 1981, 513 p.

Begin, Menachem. *White Nights: The Story of a Prisoner in Russia.* Translated from the Hebrew by Katie Kaplan. New York: Harper and Row, 1979, 240 p.

Samuel, Maurice. *Blood Accusation: The Strange History of the Beiliss Case.* New York: Knopf, 1966, 286 p.

Svirskii, Grigorii. *Hostages: The Personal Testimony of a Soviet Jew.* Translated from the Russian by Gordon Clough. New York: Knopf, 1976, 305 p.

Tager, Aleksandr Semenovich. *The Decay of Czarism: The Beiliss Trial, a Contribution to the History of the Political Reaction During the Last Years of Russian Czarism.* Philadelphia: The Jewish Publication Society of America, 1935, 197 p.

Political Prisoners and Prison Systems

Armonas, Barbara. *Leave Your Tears in Moscow, as told to A.L. Nasvytis.* Philadelphia: Lippincott, 1961, 222 p.

Berger, Joseph. *Nothing but the Truth.* New York: John Day, 1971, 286 p. (London edition has title: *Shipwreck of a Generation*).

Brunovskii, Vladimir Khristianovich. *The Methods of the OGPU.* London: Harper and Brothers, 1931, 255 p.

Chmara, Otaman. *Offenbarungen aus der todeszelle der OGPU, das schicksal des Otaman Chamara.* Goerlitz: Doffmann and Reiber, [post 1920], 67 p.

Ekart, Antoni. *Vanished Without Trace: The Story of Seven Years in Soviet Russia.* London: M. Parrish, 1954, 320 p.

Ettighoffer, Paul Cölestin. *Tovarish.* Translated from the German by M.H. Jerome. London: Hutchinson, 1935, 288 p.

Gabór, Andor. *Spione und Saboteur vor dem Volksgericht in Moskau. Bericht über den Hochverratsprozess gegen Ramsin und Genossen vom 25. November bis 7. Dezember 1930 im Gewerkschafthaus in Moskau. Auf Grund der stenografischen Protokolle zusammengestellt, mit drei Zeichnungen von Deni, Moskau.* Berlin: Neuer Deutscher Verlag, 1931, 128 p. (microfilm).

Ginzburg, Evgeniia Semenovna. *Within the Whirlwind.* Translated by Ian Boland. New York: Harcourt, Brace, Jovanovich, 1981, 423 p.

Gollwitzer, Helmut. *Unwilling Journey: A Diary from Russia.* Translated by E.M. Delacour. Philadelphia: Muhlenberg Press, 1954, 316 p.

Harrison, Marguerite E. Baker. *Unfinished Tales from a Russian Prison.* New York: George H. Doran, 1923, 195 p.

Hunt, Ruth. *East Wind: The Story of Maria Zeitner Linke.* Grand Rapids, Mich.: Zondervan Pub. House, 1976, 240 p.

IAkir, Petr Ionovich. *A Childhood in Prison.* Edited by Robert Conquest. New York: Coward, McCann and Geoghegan, 1973, 155 p.

Ivanov, Razumnik Vasil'evich. *The Memoirs of Ivanov-Razumnik.* Translated and annotated by P.S. Squire. New York: Oxford University Press, 1965, 374 p.

Joffe, Maria. *One Long Night: A Tale of Truth.* Translated by Vera Dixon. Clapham, [Eng.]: New Park Publications, 1978, 248 p.

Khodorovich, Tat'iana Sergeevna. *The Case of Leonid Plyushch.* Translated from the Russian by Marite Sapiets, Peter Reddaway et al. Boulder, Colo.: Westview Press, 1976, 152 p.

Kindermann, Karl Gustav. *In the Toils of the O.G.P.U.* Translated from the German by Gerald Griffin. London: Hurst and Blackett, [1933?], 288 p.

Kopelev, Lev Zalmanovich. *To be Preserved Forever.* Translated and edited by Anthony Austin. Philadelphia: Lippincott, 1977, 268 p.

Krasnov, Nikolai Nikolaevich. *The Hidden Russia: My Ten Years as a Slave Laborer.* New York: Holt, 1960, 341 p.

Kropotkin, Peter Alekseevich, *Kniaz'. In Russian and French Prisons.* New York: Schocken Books, 1971, 387 p.

Kudirka, Simas and **Eichel, Larry.** *For Those Still at Sea.* New York: Dial Press, 1978, 226 p.

Kuznetsov, Eduard. *Prison Diaries.* Translated by Howard Spier. New York: Stein and Day, 1975, 254 p.

Lermolo, Elizabeth. *Face of a Victim.* Translated from the Russian by I.D.W. Talmadge. New York: Harper, 1955, 311 p. (autobiographical).

Lias, Godfrey. *I Survived.* New York: John Day, 1954, 255 p. (Erwin Germanovich).

Muravin, Victor. *The Diary of Vikenty Angarov.* Translated from the Russian by Alan Thomas. New York: Newsweek Books, 1978, 349 p. (fiction).

Panin, Dimitrii Mikhailovich. *The Notebooks of Sologdin.* Translated by John Moore. New York: Harcourt, Brace, Jovanovich, 1976, 320 p.

Pliushch, Leonyd Ivanovych with **Plyushch, Tatyana.** *History's Carnival: A Dissident's Autobiography.* Edited and translated by Marco Carynnyk. New York: Harcourt, Brace, Jovanovich, 1979, 429 p.

Solomon, Michael. *Magadan.* Princeton: Auerbach Publishers, 1971, 243 p.

Tchernavin, Vladimir Vyacheslavovich. *I Speak for the Silent Prisoners of the Soviets.* Translated from the Russian by Nicholas M. Oushakoff. Boston: Hale, Cushman and Flint, 1935, 368 p.

Voinov, Nicholas, *pseud. Outlaw: The Autobiography of a Soviet Waif.* London: Harvill Press, 1955, 243 p.

Wallach, Erica Glaser. *Light at Midnight.* Garden City, N.Y.: Doubleday, 1967, 397 p.

Weissberg, Alexander. *The Accused.* Translated by Edward Fitzgerald. New York: Simon and Schuster, 1951, 518 p.

Wittlin, Tadeusz. *A Reluctant Traveller in Russia.* Translated from the Polish by Noel E.P. Clark. New York: Rinehart, 1952, 280 p.

Trotskyites

Bukharin, Nikolai Ivanovich, *defendant. The Great Purge Trial.* Edited, and with notes, by Robert C. Tucker and Stephen F. Cohen. New York: Grosset and Dunlap, 1965, 725 p.

Bukharin, Nikolai Ivanovich, *defendant. Report of Court Proceedings in the Case of the Anti-Soviet "Bloc of Rights and Trotskyites," Heard Before the Military Collegium of the Supreme Court of the U.S.S.R.,*

Moscow, March 2–13, 1938, in re: N.I. Bukharin, A.I. Rykov, G.G. Yagoda, N.N. Krestinsky, K.G. Rakovsky, A.P. Rosengoltz, V.I. Ivanov, M.A. Chernov, G.F. Grinko, I.A. Zelensky, S.A. Bessonov, A. Ikramov, F. Khodjayev, V.F. Sharangovich, P.T. Zubarev, P.P. Bulanov, L.G. Levin, D.D. Pletnev, I.N. Kazakov, V.A. Maximov-Dikovsky, P.P. Kryuchkov, Charged with Crimes Covered by Articles 58[1]a, 58[2], 58[7], 58[8], and 58[11] of the Criminal Code of the R.S.F.S.R., and Ivanov, Zelensky and Zubarev, in Addition, with Crimes Covered by Article 58[13] of the Criminal Code of the R.S.F.S.R. Verbatim Report. Moscow: People's Commissariat of Justice of the U.S.S.R., 1938, 799 p.

Kalpashnikov, Andrei. *A Prisoner of Trotsky's.* Garden City, N.Y.: Doubleday, Page, 1920, 287 p.

Piatakov, Georgii Leonidovich, defendant. *Report of Court Proceedings in the Case of the Anti-Soviet Trotskyite Centre, Heard Before the Military Collegium of the Supreme Court of the U.S.S.R., Moscow, January 23–30, 1937; in re: Y.L. Pyatakov, K.B. Radek, G.Y. Sokolnikov, L.P. Serebryakov, N.I. Muralov, Y.A. Livshitz, Y.N. Drobnis, M.S. Boguslavsky, I.A. Knyazev, S.A. Rataichak, B.O. Norkin, A.A. Shestov, M.S. Stroilov, Y.D. Turok, I.Y. Hrasche, G.E. Pushin, V.V. Arnold, Accused of Treason Against the Country, Espionage, Acts of Diversion, Wrecking Activities and the Preparation of Terrorist Acts, i.e., of Crimes Covered by Articles 58[1]a, 58[8], 58[9], and 58[11] of the Criminal Code of the R.S.F.S.R. Verbatim Report.* Moscow: People's Commissariat of Justice of the U.S.S.R., 1937, 580 p.

United Kingdom

Bellamy, J.G. *The Tudor Law of Treason: An Introduction.* London: Routledge and Kegan Paul, 1979, 305 p.

Brooke-Hunt, Violet. *Prisoners of the Tower of London: Being an Account of Some who at Divers Times lay Captive Within its Walls.* 2d ed. London: J.M. Dent, 1899, 347 p.

Brust, Harold, pseud. (Cheyney, Peter). *"I Guarded Kings": The Memoirs of a Political Police Officer.* New York: Hillman Curl, 1936, 288 p. (author was a Detective Inspector).

Childs, Wyndham, Sir. *Episodes and Reflections, Being Some Records from the Life of Major-General Sir Wyndham Childs, K.C.M.G., K.B.E., C.B., One Time Second Lieut., 2nd Volunteer Battalion, the Duke of Cornwall's Light Infantry.* London: Cassell, 1930, 287 p.

Cookridge, E.H., pseud. (Spiro, Edward). *Secrets of the British Secret Service: Behind the Scenes of the Work of British Counter-espionage During the War.* London: S. Low, Marston, 1947, 216 p.

Denning, Alfred Thompson Denning, Baron. *The Profumo-Christine Keeler Affair: Lord Denning's Report Presented to Parliament by the Prime Minister.* New York: Marc Publishing, 175 p. (paperback).

Dixon, William Hepworth. *Her Majesty's Tower.* New York: Harper and Brothers, 1869, 263 p.

Du Cann, Charles Garfield Lott. *Famous Treason Trials.* New York: Walker, 1964, 272 p.

Ellis, R.J. *He Walks Alone. The Public and Private Life of Captain Cunningham-Reld, D.F.C., Member of Parliament, 1922–45.* London: W.H. Allen, 1945, 292 p.

Firmin, Stanley. *They Came to Spy.* London: Hutchinson, 1950, 156 p.

Gillman, Peter and **Gillman, Leni.** *"Collar the Lot!": How Britain Interned and Expelled its Wartime Refugees.* London: Quartet Books, 1980, 334 p.

Heym, Stefan. *The Queen Against Defoe, and Other Stories.* New York: L. Hill, 1974, 114 p. (fiction).

Hollis, Christopher. *The Monstrous Regiment.* New York: Minton, Balch, 1930, 250 p.

Irving, Clive; Hall, Ron et al. *Anatomy of a Scandal: A Study of the Profumo Affair.* New York: M.S. Mill, 1963, 227 p.

Keeton, George Williams. *Trial for Treason.* London: Macdonald, 1959, 256 p.

Lampe, David. *The Last Ditch.* New York: Putnam, 1968, 250 p.

Lucas, Norman. *Spycatcher: A Biography of Detective-Superintendent George Gordon Smith.* London: W.H. Allen, 1973, 179 p.

Macready, Nevil, Sir, Bart. *Annals of An Active Life.* London: Hutchinson, 1924, 2 v.

Masterman, John Cecil, Sir. *The Double-Cross System in the War of 1939 to 1945.* New Haven: Yale University Press, 1972, 203 p.

Prebble, John. *Glencoe: The Story of the Massacre.* New York: Holt, Rinehart and Winston, 1966, 336 p.

Rice-Davies, Mandy with **Flack, Shirley.** *Mandy.* London: Joseph, 1980, 223 p.

Robertson, Geoff. *Reluctant Judas: The Life and Death of the Special Branch Informer, Kenneth Lennon.* London: Temple Smith, 1976, 228 p.

Sansom, Alfred William. *I Spied Spies.* London: Harrap, 1965, 271 p.

Sproat, Iain. *Wodehouse at War.* New Haven: Ticknor and Fields, 1981, 167 p.

Thomson, Basil Home, Sir. *La chasse aux espions: mes souvenirs de Scotland Yard, 1914–1919.* Paris: Payot, 1933, 265 p. (paperback).

Thomson, Basil Home, Sir. *Queer People.* London: Hodder and Stoughton, 1922, 320 p.

Waugh, Auberon. *The Last Word: An Eyewitness Account of the Trial of Jeremy Thorpe.* Boston: Little, Brown, 1980, 240 p.

West, Rebecca, pseud. *The New Meaning of Treason.* New York: Viking Press, 1964, 374 p. (trials of William Joyce and John Amery).

Wilkinson, George E. *Special Branch Officer: International Security Assignments of Ex-Superintendent, George Wilkinson.* London: Odhams Press, 1956, 254 p.

United States
General

Beichman, Arnold. "Can Counterintelligence Come in From the Cold?" *Policy Review,* no. 15 (Winter 1981), pp. 93–101.

Coffin, Harold W. *Assignment in Military Intelligence.* Old Town, Maine: Penobscot Press, 1972, 217 p.

Donner, Frank J. *The Un-Americans.* New York: Ballantine Books, 1961, 313 p. (paperback).

Duus, Masayo. *Tokyo Rose: Orphan of the Pacific.* Translated from the Japanese by Peter Duus. New York: Harper and Row, 1979, 248 p.

Forsythe, John William. *Guerrilla Warfare, and Life in Libby Prison.* Edited by Melvin Lee Steadman, Jr. Annandale, Va.: Turnpike Press, 1967, 53 p.

Gansberg, Judith M. *Stalag, U.S.A.: The Remarkable Story of German POWs in America.* New York: Crowell, 1977, 233 p.

Gellermann, William. *Martin Dies.* New York: John Day, 1944, 310 p.

Gentry, Curt. *Frame-up: The Incredible Case of Tom Mooney and Warren Billings.* New York: Norton, 1967, 496 p.

Gill, William J. *The Ordeal of Otto Otepka.* New Rochelle, N.Y.: Arlington House, 1969, 505 p.

Godson, Roy, ed. *Counterintelligence.* Washington: National Strategy Information Center, 1980, 339 p. (Intelligence Requirements for the 1980s; no. 3).

Goodman, Peter. *The Committee: The Extraordinary Career of the House Committee on Un-American Activities.* New York: Farrar, Straus, and Giroux, 1968, 564 p.

Grodzins, Morton. *Americans Betrayed: Politics and the Japanese Evacuation.* Chicago: Univ. of Chicago Press, 1949, 444 p.

Hosokawa, Bill. *Nisei: The Quiet Americans.* New York: Morrow, 1969, 522 p.

Hough, Emerson. *The Web: A Revelation of Patriotism.* Chicago: Reilly and Lee, 1919, 511 p.

Ignatius, David. "Spy Wars: Experts Fear That U.S. Loses Espionage Battle With the Soviet Union." *Wall Street Journal,* October 4, 1979, p. 1+.

Keyes, Harold C. *Tales of the Secret Service.* Cleveland, Ohio: Britton-Gardner Printing Co., 1927, 272 p.

Krammer, Arnold. *Nazi Prisoners of War in America.* New York: Stein and Day, 1979, 338 p.

Marshall, John A. *American Bastille. A History of the Illegal Arrests and Imprisonment of American Citizens During the Late Civil War.* 4th ed. Philadelphia: Evans, Stoddart, 1870, 728 p.

Martin, David C. *Wilderness of Mirrors.* New York: Harper and Row, 1980, 236 p.

O'Toole, George. "America's Secret Police Network." *Penthouse,* December 1976, p. 77+.

Rollins, Richard. *I Find Treason: The Story of an American Anti-Nazi Agent.* New York: Morrow, 1941, 291 p.

Russell, Charles Edmund. *Adventures of the D.C.I., Department of Criminal Investigation.* Garden City, N.Y.: Doubleday, Page, 1927, 280 p.

Schwarzwalder, John. *We Caught Spies.* New York: Duell, Sloan and Pearce, 1946, 296 p.

Strother, French. *Fighting Germany's Spies.* Garden City, N.Y.: Doubleday, Page, 1919, 275 p.

Thorp, Elliott R. *East Wind, Rain: The Intimate Account of an Intelligence Officer in the Pacific, 1939–49.* Boston: Gambit, 1969, 307 p.

U.S. Counter Intelligence Corps School, Baltimore. *History and Mission of the Counter Intelligence Corps in World War II: Special Text.* Baltimore: CIC School, Counter Intelligence Corps Center, 1951, 83 p.

U.S. National Guard, First Service Command, Tactical School, Concord/Sturbridge, Mass. *Manual Available for Security Troops, Including State Guards. Compiled from Material Developed at the First Service*

Command Tactical School and on the Proving Ground of the New England Maneuvers. Prepared by H. Wendell Endicott. Sturbridge, Mass.: The School, November 2, 1942, 92 p.

U.S. Ninth Army. *Counter-Intelligence Handbook.* Headquarters Ninth U.S. Army, APO 339, December 20, 1944, 39 p.

Weglyn, Michi. *Years of Infamy: The Untold Story of America's Concentration Camps.* New York: Morrow, 1976, 351 p. (paperback).

Weyl, Nathaniel. *The Battle Against Disloyalty.* New York: Crowell, 1951, 378 p.

FBI Operations

Archer, Jules. *Superspies: The Secret Side of Government.* New York: Delacorte Press, 1977, 252 p. (juvenile literature).

Ayer, Frederick. *Yankee G-Man.* Chicago: Regnery, 1957, 312 p. (autobiographical).

Brown, Julia Clarice. *I Testify: My Years as an Undercover Agent for the FBI.* Boston: Western Islands, 1966, 293 p.

Calomiris, Angela. *Red Masquerade: Undercover for the F.B.I.* Philadelphia: Lippincott, 1950, 284 p. (autobiographical).

Cochran, Louis. *FBI Man: A Personal History.* New York: Duell, Sloan and Pearce, 1966, 207 p.

Garrow, David J. *The FBI and Martin Luther King, Jr.: From "Solo" to Memphis.* New York: Norton, 1981, 320 p.

Hart, Scott. *Washington at War, 1941–1945.* Englewood Cliffs, N.J.: Prentice-Hall, 1970, 296 p.

Miller, Marion Freed. *I Was a Spy.* Indianapolis: Bobbs-Merrill, 1960, 224 p.

Morros, Boris. *My Ten Years as a Counterspy: As Told to Charles Samuels.* New York: Dell Publishing, 1959, 288 p. (paperback).

Munves, James. *The FBI and the CIA: Secret Agents and American Democracy.* New York: Harcourt, Brace, Jovanovich, 1975, 185 p.

O'Connor, Dick. *G-Men at Work: The Story of America's Fight Against Crime and Corruption.* London: J. Long, 1939, 256 p.

Philbrick, Herbert Arthur. *I Led 3 Lives: Citizen, "Communist," Counterspy.* New York: Grosset and Dunlap, 1952, 323 p.

Purvis, Melvin Horace. *The Violent Years.* New York: Hillman Periodicals, 1960, 159 p. (paperback abridgement of *American Agent.* Garden City, N.Y.: Doubleday, Doran, 1936, 291 p.).

Rashke, Richard L. *The Killing of Karen Silkwood: The Story Behind the Kerr-McGee Plutonium Case.* Boston: Houghton Mifflin, 1981, 407 p.

Schott, Joseph L. *No Left Turns.* New York: Praeger, 1975, 214 p.

Turrou, Leon G. *Where my Shadow Falls: Two Decades of Crime Detection.* Garden City, N.Y.: Doubleday, 1949, 224 p.

V. COVERT ACTION
General

Blackstock, Paul W. *The Strategy of Subversion: Manipulating the Politics of Other Nations.* Chicago: Quadrangle Books, 1964, 351 p.

Ignatius, David. "Should the U.S. Revive Its Covert-Action Capability?" *Wall Street Journal,* November 30, 1979, p. 24.

Julien, Claude. *L'Empire américain.* Paris: B. Grasset, 1968, 419 p.

Langguth, A.J. *Hidden Terrors.* New York: Pantheon Books, 1978, 339 p.

Michie, Allen Andrew. *Voices Through the Iron Curtain: The Radio Free Europe Story.* New York: Dodd, Mead, 1963, 304 p.

Orman, John M. *Presidential Secrecy and Deception: Beyond the Power to Persuade.* Westport, Conn.: Greenwood Press, 1980, 239 p.

Parakal, Pauly V. *The Inside Out of CIA.* New Delhi: Sterling Publishers, 1974, 127 p. (paperback).

Petrusenko, Vitalii Vasil'evich. *A Dangerous Game: CIA and the Mass Media.* Translated from the Russian by Nicolai Kozelsky and Vladimir Leonov. Prague: Interpress, 1979, 190 p.

Phillips, David Atlee. *The Night Watch.* New York: Atheneum, 1977, 309 p. (autobiographical).

Powers, Thomas. "Inside the Department of Dirty Tricks: The CIA at Work." *Atlantic,* v. 244, no. 2 (August 1979), p. 33+.

Rositzke, Harry August. *The CIA's Secret Operations: Espionage, Counterespionage, and Covert Action.* New York: Reader's Digest Press, 1977, 286 p.

Shackley, Theodore. *The Third Option: An American View of Counterinsurgency Operations.* New York: Reader's Digest Press: McGraw-Hill, 1981, 185 p.

Smith, Joseph Burkholder. *Portrait of a Cold Warrior.* New York: Putnam, 1976, 448 p.

Szulc, Tad. *The Illusion of Peace: Foreign Policy in the Nixon Years.* New York: Viking Press, 1978, 822 p.

U.S. Congress, House, Permanent Select Committee on Intelligence, Subcommittee on Oversight. *The CIA and the Media. Hearings, Ninety-fifth Congress, first and second sessions.* Washington: U.S. GPO, 1978, 627 p.

U.S. Congress, Senate, Select Committee to Study Governmental Operations with Respect to Intelligence Activities. *Alleged Assassination Plots Involving Foreign Leaders: An Interim Report of the Select Committee to Study Governmental Operations with Respect to Intelligence Activities, United States Senate: Together with Additional Supplemental and Separate Views.* Washington: U.S. GPO, 1975, 349 p.

U.S. Library of Congress, Congressional Research Service. *Reported Foreign and Domestic Covert Activities of the United States Central Intelligence Agency, 1950-1974.* Compiled by Richard F. Grimmett. Washington: Library of Congress Congressional Research Service, February 18, 1975, 13 p.

Chile

Palacios, Jorge. *Chile: An Attempt at "Historic Compromise": The Real Story of the Allende Years.* Chicago: Banner Press, 1979, 519 p. (paperback).

Petras, James F. and **Morley, Morris.** *The United States and Chile: Imperialism and the Overthrow of the Allende Government.* New York: Monthly Review, 1975, 217 p.

Rojas, Róbinson. *The Murder of Allende and the End of the Chilean Way to Socialism.* Translated from the Spanish by Andrée Conrad. New York: Harper and Row, 1976, 274 p.

U.S. Congress, House, Committee on Foreign Affairs. *United States and Chile During the Allende Years, 1970-1973. Hearings Before the Subcommittee on Inter-American Affairs, U.S. House of Representatives.* Washington: U.S. GPO, 1975, 677 p.

U.S. Congress, Senate, Committee on Foreign Relations. *Multinational Corporations and United States Foreign Policy. Hearings Before the Subcommittee on Multinational Corporations, Committee on Foreign Relations, U.S. Senate, Ninety-third Congress on the International Telephone and Telegraph Co. and Chile, 1970-1971.* Washington: U.S. GPO, 1973, 1091 p.

Uribe Arce, Armando. *The Black Book of American Intervention in Chile.* Translated from the Spanish by Jonathan Casart. Boston: Beacon Press, 1975, 163 p.

Cuba

Ayers, Bradley Earl. *The War That Never Was: An Insider's Account of CIA Covert Operations Against Cuba.* Indianapolis: Bobbs-Merrill, 1976, 235 p.

"An Exclusive Interview with the CIA Superspy Who Engineered Both the Bay of Pigs and Watergate." *Penthouse,* May 1975, p. 50+. (E. Howard Hunt).

Hunt, Howard. *Give us this Day.* New Rochelle, N.Y.: Arlington House, 1973, 235 p.

Johnson, Haynes Bonner with **Artime, Manuel** et al. *The Bay of Pigs: The Leaders' Story of Brigade 2506.* New York: Norton, 1964, 368 p.

Meyer, Karl Ernest and **Szulc, Tad.** *The Cuban Invasion: The Chronicle of a Disaster.* New York: Praeger, 1968, 160 p.

Taylor, Maxwell D. *Operation Zapata: The "Ultrasensitive" Report and Testimony of the Board of Inquiry on The Bay of Pigs.* Frederick, Md.: University Publications of America, Inc., 1981, 367 p.

Thomas, Hugh. *The Cuban Revolution.* New York: Harper and Row, 1977, 755 p. (the final half of the author's encyclopedic work, *Cuba: The Pursuit of Freedom*).

Wyden, Peter. *Bay of Pigs: The Untold Story.* New York: Simon and Schuster, 1979, 352 p.

Mideast and Eastern Mediterranean

Copeland, Miles. *The Game of Nations: The Amorality of Power Politics.* New York: Simon and Schuster, 1969, 318 p.

Eveland, Wilbur. *Ropes of Sand: America's Failure in the Middle East.* New York: Norton, 1980, 382 p.

Katris, John. *Eyewitness in Greece: The Colonels Come to Power.* St. Louis: New Critics Press, 1971, 317 p.

Roosevelt, Kermit. *Countercoup: The Struggle for the Control of Iran.* New York: McGraw-Hill, 1979, 217 p.

Rousseas, Stephen William. *Militärputsch in Griechenland oder im Hintergrund der CIA.* Reinbek b. Hamburg: Rowohlt-Taschenbuch-Verlag, 1968, 154 p.

Stern, Laurence. *The Wrong Horse: The Politics of Intervention and the Failure of American Diplomacy.* New York: Times Books, 1977, 170 p. (Greece, Turkey and Cyprus).

Taub, William L. *Forces of Power.* New York: Grosset and Dunlap, 1979, 255 p. (Greece).

Southeast Asia

Blaufarb, Douglas S. *The Counterinsurgency Era: U.S. Doctrine and Performance, 1950 to the Present.* New York: Free Press, 1977, 356 p.

Critchfield, Richard. *The Long Charade: Political Subversion in the Vietnam War.* New York: Harcourt, Brace and World, 1968, 401 p.

DuBerrier, Hilaire. *Background to Betrayal: The Tragedy of Vietnam.* Boston: Western Islands, 1965, 292 p. (paperback).

Gelb, Leslie H. and **Betts, Richard K.** *The Irony of Vietnam: The System Worked.* Washington: Brookings Institution, 1979, 387 p.

Lansdale, Edward Geary. *In the Midst of Wars: An American's Mission to Southeast Asia.* New York: Harper and Row, 1972, 386 p. (Vietnam and the Philippines).

Scott, Peter Dale. *The War Conspiracy: The Secret Road to the Second Indochina War.* Indianapolis: Bobbs-Merrill, 1972, 238 p.

Winters, Jim. "Tom Dooley: The Forgotten Hero." *Notre Dame Magazine,* May 1979, p. 10+. (Laos and Vietnam).

VI. SUBVERSION
General

Belov, A. and **Shilkin, A.** *Diversiia bez dinamita.* Moscow: Politizdat, 2d ed., 1976, 182 p.

Blackstock, Paul W. *Agents of Deceit: Frauds, Forgeries, and Political Intrigue Among Nations.* Chicago: Quadrangle Books, 1966, 315 p.

Blackstock, Paul W. *The Strategy of Subversion: Manipulating the Politics of Other Nations.* Chicago: Quadrangle Books, 1964, 351 p.

Borkenau, Franz. *The Communist International.* London: Faber and Faber, 1938, 442 p.

Chase, Allan. *Falange: The Axis Secret Arrny in the Americas.* New York: Putnam 1943, 278 p.

The Comintern and the East: The Struggle for the Leninist Strategy and Tactics in National Liberation Movements. Edited by R.A. Ulyanovsky. Translated from the Russian by David Fidlon. Moscow: Progress Publishers, 1979, 516 p.

Conley, Michael Charles. *Mechanics of Subversion.* Boulder, Colo.: Paladin Press, 1966, 130 p. (paperback).

Contacts with the Opposition: A Symposium. Edited by Martin F. Herz. Washington: Institute for the Study of Diplomacy, Edmund A. Walsh School of Foreign Service, Georgetown University, 1979, 72 p.

Dewar, Hugo. *Assassins at Large: Being a Fully Documented and Hitherto Unpublished Account of the Executions Outside Russia Ordered by the GPU.* London: Wingate, 1951, 203 p.

Douglass, Joseph D. "Soviet Disinformation," *Strategic Review,* v. IX, no. 1 (Winter 1981), pp. 16–26.

Drachkovitch, Milorad M. and **Lazitch, Branko,** eds. *The Comintern: Historical Highlights, Essays, Recollections, Documents.* New York: F.A. Praeger, 1966, 430 p. (publication of the Hoover Institution on War, Revolution, and Peace, Stanford University).

Esslin, Martin. "The Art of Black Propaganda: How Not to Write History," *Encounter,* January 1979, pp. 42–49.

Flynn, John Thomas. *The Road Ahead: America's Creeping Revolution.* New York: Committee for Constitutional Government, 1949, 207 p.

Girling, J.L.S. *America and the Third World: Revolution and Intervention.* London: Routledge and K. Paul, 1980, 276 p.

Greig, Ian. *The Assault on the West.* Petersham: Foreign Affairs Publishing, 1968, 357 p.

Hargreaves, Reginald. "Communism and the Resistance Movement." *Journal of the Royal United Service Institution,* v. XCIV (February-November 1949), pp. 393-403.

Hartness, William M. *Communist Cell: Prelude to Takeover.* Laguna Hills, Calif.: Aegean Park Press, 1977, 76 p. (paperback).

Heilbrunn, Otto. *The Soviet Secret Services.* London: Allen and Unwin, 1956, 216 p.

Hutton, Joseph Bernard. *Danger From Moscow.* London: N. Spearman, 1960, 261 p.

Hutton, Joseph Bernard. *The Subverters.* New Rochelle, N.Y.: Arlington House, 1972, 266 p.

The International Communist Movement: Sketch of Strategy and Tactics. Edited by V.V. Zagladin. Washington: U.S. Joint Publications Research Service, nos. 57044-1 and 57044-2, September 18, 1972. 2 v.

King-Hall, Stephen, Sir. *The Communist Conspiracy.* London: Constable, 1953, 239 p.

Kintner, William Roscoe with **Kornfeder, Joseph Z.** *The New Frontier of War:* Political Warfare, Present and Future. Chicago: Regnery, 1962, 362 p.

Kirkpatrick, Lyman B., Jr. and **Sargeant, Howland H.** *Soviet Political Warfare Techniques: Espionage and Propaganda in the 1970s.* New York: National Strategy Information Center, 1972, 82 p.

Kurzman, Dan. *Subversion of the Innocents: Patterns of Communist Penetration in Africa, the Middle East, and Asia.* New York: Random House, 1963, 570 p.

LaCharité, N.A. *Case Studies in Insurgency and Revolutionary Warfare. Volume 1: Cuba, 1953-1959.* Washington: American University, Special Operations Research Office, 1963, 173 p.

Maslowski, Alexander. *Communist World Revolution: The First Ten Years.* n.p.: Center for Study of Communist History, December 1966.

Miksche, Ferdinand Otto. *Secret Forces: The Technique of Underground Movements.* London: Faber and Faber, 1950, 181 p.

Moss, Robert. "Intelligence War: The KGB Lie Machine." *London Daily Telegraph,* August 20, 1979.

New York (State) Legislature, Joint Legislative Committee Investigating Seditious Activities. *Revolutionary Radicalism, its History, Purpose and Tactics with an Exposition and Discussion of the Steps Being Taken to Curb it: Part 1, Revolutionary and Subversive Movements Abroad and at Home.* Report Filed April 24, 1920 in the Senate of the State of New York. Albany: J.B. Lyon, 1920, 1140 p.

Rees, John. *Infiltration of the Media by the KGB and Its Friends.* Washington: Accuracy in Media, April 20, 1978, 37 p.

Skousen, Willard Cleon. *The Naked Communist.* 7th ed. Salt Lake City: Ensign Pub., 1960, 343 p.

Stephan, John J. *The Russian Fascists: Tragedy and Farce in Exile, 1925–1945.* New York: Harper and Row, 1978, 450 p.

Thompson, Robert Grainger Ker, Sir. *Revolutionary War in World Strategy, 1945–1969.* New York: Taplinger Pub., 1970, 171 p.

U.S. Congress, House, Committee on Foreign Affairs. *Report on the Strategy and Tactics of World Communism. Supplement IV: Five Hundred Leading Communists (in the Eastern Hemisphere, excluding the USSR).* Washington: U.S. GPO, 1948, 129 p.

U.S. Congress, House, Committee on Internal Security. *The Theory and Practice of Communism. Hearings. Part I: People's Republic of China; Part II: The Communist Party, USA—Defender of Soviet Anti-Semitism; Part III: EXPOCUBA.* Washington: U.S. GPO, 1973, 2372 p.

U.S. Congress, House, Committee on Un-American Activities. *The Communist Conspiracy: Strategy and Tactics of World Communism. Part 1: Communism Outside the United States.* Washington: U.S. GPO, 1956, 553 p.

U.S. Congress, House, Committee on Un-American Activities. *Manipulation of Public Opinion by Organizations Under Concealed Control of the Communist Party. (National Assembly for Democratic Rights and Citizens Committee for Constitutional Liberties) Report Pursuant to H. Res. 8, 87th Congress, and Public Law 601, 79th Congress.* Washington: U.S. GPO, 1961, 218 p., v. 1.

U.S. Congress, House, Permanent Select Committee on Intelligence, Subcommittee on Oversight. *Soviet Covert Action (the Forgery Offensive).* 96th Congress, 2d session. Washington: U.S. GPO, 1980, 245 p.

U.S. Marine Corps Schools, Quantico, Virginia. *Guerrilla Warfare.* Quantico: Extensive School, Marine Corps Educational Center, Marine Corps Schools, 1954, 29 p. (Supp. material NAVMC-4764; SM-17).

Vidor, John. *Spying in Russia.* London: J. Long, 1929, 284 p

Wachsman, Z.H. *Trail Blazers for Invasion.* New York: Frederick Ungar, 1943, 284 p.

Wang, Chüeh-yüan. *The Russian Communists' Strategies and Tactics for World Revolution.* Taipei, Taiwan: World Anti-Communist League, China Chapter, 1976, 128 p.

Wolfe, Lawrence. *Sabotage.* London: Nicholson and Watson, 1942, 190 p.

World Committee for the Victims of German Fascism. *The Brown Network: The Activities of the Nazis in Foreign Countries.* New York: Knight Publications, 1936, 309 p.

Zacharias, Ellis M. with **Farago, Ladislas.** *Behind Closed Doors: The Secret History of the Cold War.* New York: Putnam, 1950, 367 p.

Africa

The Attempted Communist Subversion of Africa Through Nkrumah's Ghana. Washington: Subcommittee to Investigate the Administration of the Internal Security Act and Other Internal Security Laws of the Committee on the Judiciary, U.S. Senate, 1972, 215 p.

Barker, Peter. *Operation Cold Chop: The Coup that Toppled Nkrumah.* Accra: Accra Ghana Pub., 1969, 210 p.

Batson, Alfred. *African Intrigue.* Garden City, N.Y.: Garden City Publishing Co., 1935, 307 p.

Greig, Ian. *The Communist Challenge to Africa: An Analysis of Contemporary Soviet, Chinese and Cuban Policies.* Richmond, Surrey: Foreign Affairs Publishing, 1977, 306 p.

Hughes, John. *The New Face of Africa South of the Sahara.* New York: Longmans, Green, 1961, 296 p.

Ignat'ev, Oleg Konstantinovich. *Secret Weapon in Africa.* Translated from the Russian by David Fidlon. Moscow: Progress Publishers, 1977, 188 p.

Nkrumah's Subversion in Africa: Documentary Evidence of Nkrumah's Interference in the Affairs of Other African States. Accra, Ghana: Ministry of Information, 1966, 91 p.

O'Ballance, Edgar. *The Secret War in the Sudan, 1955–1972.* London: Faber, 1977, 174 p.

Weyl, Nathaniel. *Traitors' End: The Rise and Fall of the Communist Movement in Southern Africa.* New Rochelle, N.Y.: Arlington House, 1970, 261 p.

Asia
General

Flynn, John Thomas. *While You Slept: Our Tragedy in Asia and Who Made it.* New York: Devin-Adair, 1951, 192 p.

Jacobs, Daniel Norman. *Borodin, Stalin's Man in China.* Cambridge: Harvard University Press, 1981, 369 p.

Kaznacheev, Aleksandr IUr'evich. *Inside a Soviet Embassy: Experiences of a Russian Diplomat in Burma.* Edited by Simon Wolin. Philadelphia: Lippincott, 1962, 250 p.

Lamour, Catherine. *Enquête sur une armée secrète.* Paris: Editions du Seuil, 1975, 285 p.

Netherlands East Indies. *Ten Years of Japanese Burrowing in the Netherlands East Indies.* New York: Netherlands Information Bureau, 1942, 132 p.

Norodom Sihanouk Varman. *King of Cambodia. My War with the CIA: The Memoirs of Prince Norodom Sihanouk as related to Wilfred Burchett.* New York: Pantheon Books, 1972, 271 p.

Prudnikov, Mikhail Sidorovich. *Operatsiia "Feniks": Povest'.* Moscow: Voenizdat, 1975, 255 p.

Randolph, R. Sean and **Thompson, W. Scott.** *Thai Insurgency: Contemporary Developments.* Beverly Hills, Calif.: Sage Publications, 1981, 88 p. (Washington Papers, 81).

Malaya

British Association of Malaya. *The Civil Defence of Malaya: A Narrative of the Part Taken in it by the Civilian Population of the Country in the Japanese Invasion.* Compiled by a Committee under the Chairmanship of Sir George Maxwell . . . from information received from persons who were in Malaya at the time. London: Hutchinson, 1944, 128 p.

Campbell, Arthur. *Jungle Green.* London: Allen and Unwin, 1953, 214 p.

Campbell, Arthur. *Jungle Green.* Boston: Little, Brown, 1954, 298 p.

Clutterbuck, Richard L. *The Long, Long War: Counterinsurgency in Malaya and Vietnam.* New York: Praeger, 1966, 206 p.

Henniker, M.C.A. *Red Shadow Over Malaya.* Edinburgh: Blackwood, 1955, 302 p.

Thompson, Robert Grainger Ker, Sir. *Defeating Communist Insurgency: The Lessons of Malaya and Vietnam.* New York: Praeger, 1966, 171 p.

Philippines

Kerkvliet, Benedict J. *The Huk Rebellion: A Study of Peasant Revolt in the Philippines.* Berkeley: University of California Press, 1977, 305 p.

Pomeroy, William J. *The Forest: A Personal Record of the Huk Guerrilla Struggle in the Philippines.* New York: International Publishers, 1963, 224 p.

Romulo, Carlos Peña. *Crusade in Asia: Philippine Victory.* New York: J. Day, 1955, 309 p.

Scaff, Alvin H. *The Philippine Answer to Communism.* Stanford: Stanford University Press, 1955, 165 p.

Valeriano, Napoleon D. and **Bohannan, Charles T.R.** *Counter-Guerrilla Operations: The Philippine Experience.* New York: Praeger, 1962, 275 p.

Vietnam

Asprey, Robert B. *War in the Shadows: The Guerrilla in History.* Garden City, N.Y.: Doubleday, 1975, 2 v.

Clutterbuck, Richard L. *The Long, Long War: Counterinsurgency in Malaya and Vietnam.* New York: Praeger, 1966, 206 p.

Radványi, János. *Delusion and Reality: Gambits, Hoaxes, and Diplomatic One-Upmanship in Vietnam.* South Bend, Ind.: Gateway Editions, 1978, 295 p.

Thompson, Robert Grainger Ker, Sir. *Defeating Communist Insurgency: The Lessons of Malaya and Vietnam.* New York: Praeger, 1966, 171 p.

Tru' ó'ng-Chinh. *Primer for Revolt: The Communist Take-Over in Viet-Nam.* New York: Praeger, 1963, 213 p. (facsimile edition of *The August Revolution* and *The Resistance Will Win*).

Võ Nguyên Giàp. *Guerre du peuple, armée du peuple.* Paris: F. Maspero, 1966, 231 p. (paperback).

Võ Nguyên Giàp. *People's War, People's Army: The Viet Cong Insurrection Manual for Underdeveloped Countries.* New York: Praeger, 1962, 217 p.

Europe
General

Frölich, Paul. *Rosa Luxemburg: Her Life and Work.* Translated by Edward Fitzgerald. London: Gollancz, 1940, 336 p.

Lajolo, Davide. "Secret History of Italian Communist Party Revealed." Washington: U.S. Joint Publications Research Service, no. 64633, April 28, 1975, 80 p. (translation from the Italian of articles appearing in *Il Mundo,* Milan on March 6, 13, 20, and 27, 1975).

Os'machka, Teodosii. *Red Assassins: A Factual Story Revealing how the Ukraine Lost its Freedom.* Minneapolis: T.S. Denison, 1959, 375 p.

Rothschild, Joseph. *The Communist Party of Bulgaria: Origins and Development, 1883–1936.* New York: Columbia University Press, 1959, 354 p.

Zarubica, Mladin. *The Year of the Rat: A Chronicle.* New York: Harcourt, Brace and World, 1964, 213 p. (fiction)..

Czechoslovakia

Bittman, Ladislav. *The Deception Game: Czechoslovak Intelligence in Soviet Political Warfare.* Syracuse, N.Y.: Syracuse University Research Corp., 1972, 246 p.

Kozak, Jan. *And Not a Shot is Fired.* Translated from the original Czech. New Canaan, Conn.: Long House, 1962, 48 p. (American edition of author's guidebook: "How Parliament Can Play a Revolutionary Part in the Transition to Socialism, and the Role of the Popular Masses.").

Kozak, Jan. *The New Role of National Legislative Bodies in the Communist Conspiracy.* [Print of the] Committee on Un-American Activities, House of Representatives, 87th Congress, 1st session. Washington: U.S. GPO, 1961, 47 p. (reprint of "How Parliament Can Play a Revolutionary Part in the Transition to Socialism" and "The Role of the Popular Masses.").

France

DeMontmorency, Alec. *The Enigma of Admiral Darlan.* New York: Dutton, 1943, 194 p.

Gaucher, Roland. *Histoire secrète du Parti communiste francais: 1920–1974.* Paris: A. Michel, 1974, 704 p. (paperback).

Johnson, Severance. *The Enemy Within: Hitherto Unpublished Details of the Great Conspiracy to Corrupt and Destroy France.* Translations by Edgard Léon. New York: James A. McCann, 1919, 297 p.

Rossi, A., pseud. (Tasca, Angelo). *A Communist Party in Action: An Account of the Organization and Operations in France.* Translated and edited by Willmoore Kendall. New Haven: Yale University Press, 1949, 301 p.

Tiersky, Ronald. *French Communism, 1920–1972.* New York: Columbia University Press, 1974, 425 p.

Torrès, Henry. *Campaign of Treachery: A Dramatic Review and a Brilliant Analysis of Fifth Column Warfare in Europe.* New York: Dodd, Mead, 1942, 256 p.

Germany

Ehrt, Adolf. *Communism in Germany: The Truth About the Communist Conspiracy on the Eve of the National Revolution.* Berlin: Eckhart-Verlag, 1933, 179 p. (paperback).

Erdstein, Erich and **Bean, Barbara.** *Inside the Fourth Reich.* New York: St. Martin's Press, 1977, 220 p.

Grunberger, Richard. *Red Rising in Bavaria.* London: Barker, 1973, 164 p.

Hoettl, Wilhelm. *The Secret Front: The Story of Nazi Political Espionage.* Translated from the German by R.H. Stevens. New York: Praeger, 1954, 327 p.

Horchem, Hans Josef. *Die roten Maulwürfe: Tatsachenbericht aus der Arbeit des Verfassungsschutzes gegen die kommunistische Untergrundtätigkeit.* Donauwörth: L. Auer, 1964, 127 p. (paperback).

Jong, Louis de. *The German Fifth Column in the Second World War.* Chicago: University of Chicago Press, 1956, 308 p.

Julitte, Pierre. *Block 26: Sabotage at Buchenwald.* Translated from the French by Francis Price. Garden City, N.Y.: Doubleday, 1971, 318 p.

Littlejohn, David. *The Patriotic Traitors: The History of Collaboration in German-Occupied Europe, 1940–1945.* Garden City, N.Y.: Doubleday, 1972, 391 p.

Meyer-Leviné, Rosa. *Leviné: The Life of a Revolutionary.* Farnborough: Saxon House, 1973, 225 p.

Nationale Front des Demokratischen Deutschland. *Braunbuch. Kriegs-und Naziverbrecher in der Bundesrepublik und in Westberlin. Staat, Wirtschaft, Verwaltung, Armee, Justiz, Wissenschaft.* Herausgeber: Nationalrat der Nationalen Front des demokratischen Deutschland, Dokumentationszentrum der Staatlichen Archivverwaltung der DDR. Berlin: Staatsverlag der Deutschen Demokratischen Republic, 1965, 387 p.

Oechsner, Frederick Cable; Grigg, Joseph W. *et al. This is the Enemy.* Boston: Little, Brown, 1942, 364 p.

Riess, Curt. *The Nazis go Underground.* Garden City, N.Y.: Doubleday, Doran, 1944, 210 p.

Sayers, Michael and **Kahn, Albert E.** *The Plot Against the Peace: A Warning to the Nation!* New York: Dial Press, 1945, 258 p.

Spivak, John Louis. *Secret Armies: The New Technique of Nazi Warfare.* New York: Modern Age Books, 1939, 160 p.

Tatsachen über Westberlin: Subversion, Wirtschaftskrieg, Revanchismus Gegen die Sozialistischen Staaten 2. Aufl. Herausgeber: Allgemeiner Deutscher Nachrichtendienst, *et al.* Berlin: Deutscher Militärverlag, 1962, 176 p. (paperback).

U.S. Department of State. *Confuse and Control: Soviet Techniques in Germany.* Washington: U.S. GPO, 1951, 108 p. (paperback).

Greece

Brown, Demetra Vaka. *In the Heart of German Intrigue.* Boston: Houghton Mifflin, 1918, 377 p. (U.S. edition of *Constantine, King and Traitor.* London: J. Lane).

Kousoulas, Dimitrios George. *Revolution and Defeat: The Story of the Greek Communist Party.* New York: Oxford University Press, 1965, 306 p.

Myers, Edmund Charles Wolf. *Greek Entanglement.* London: R. Hart-Davis, 1955, 289 p.

O'Ballance, Edgar. *The Greek Civil War, 1944–1949.* New York: Praeger, 1966, 237 p.

United Kingdom

Baillie-Stewart, Norman. *The Officer in the Tower, as told to John Murdoch.* London: Frewin, 1967, 304 p.

Chester, Lewis and **Young, Hugo.** *The Zinoviev Letter.* Philadelphia: Lippincott, 1968, 218 p.

Courtney, Anthony. *Sailor in a Russian Frame.* London: Johnson, 1968, 256 p.

Deacon, Richard, *pseud.* (McCormick, Donald.) *The British Connection: Russia's Manipulation of British Individuals and Institutions.* London: Hamilton, 1979, 291 p.

Mure, David, *Master of Deception: Tangled Webs in London and the Middle East.* London: Kimber, 1980, 284 p.

Mure, David. *Practise to Deceive.* London: Kimber, 1977, 270 p.

Pincher, Chapman, *Inside Story: A Documentary of the Pursuit of Power.* New York: Stein and Day, 1979, 400 p.

Wheatley, Dennis. *Stranger than Fiction.* London: Hutchinson, 1959, 364 p.

White, John Baker. *The Red Network.* London: St. Clements Press, 1953, 38 p.

Williams, Francis. *War by Revolution.* New York: Viking Press, 1941, 158 p.

Latin America
General

Debray, Régis, *Strategy for Revolution.* Essays translated from the French. Edited by Robin Blackburn. London: Monthly Review Press, 1975, 254 p.

Diederich, Bernard. *Somoza, and the Legacy of U.S. Involvement in Central America.* New York: Dutton, 1981, 352 p.

Diederich, Bernard. *Trujillo: The Death of the Goat.* Boston: Little, Brown, 1978, 264 p.

Farago, Ladislas. *Aftermath: Martin Bormann and the Fourth Reich.* New York: Simon and Schuster, 1974, 479 p. (paperback).

Fernàndez Artucio, Hugo. *The Nazi Underground in South America.* New York: Farrar and Rinehart, 1942, 311 p.

Hilton, Stanley E. *Hitler's Secret War in South America, 1939-1945.* Baton Rouge, Louisiana: Louisiana State University Press, 1981, 353 p.

Immerman, Richard H. "Guatemala as Cold War History." *Political Science Quarterly.* v. 95, no. 4 (Winter 1980-81), pp. 629-653.

Katz, Friedrich. *The Secret War in Mexico: Europe, the United States and the Mexican Revolution.* Portions translated by Loren Goldner. Chicago: University of Chicago Press, 1981, 659 p.

Lartéguy, Jean with **Sapin, Louis.** *Les Guérilleros.* Paris: Presses Pocket, 1967, 376 p. (paperback).

Macdonald, Norman Pemberton. *Hitler over Latin America.* London: Jarrolds, 1940, 259 p.

Sharp, Roland Hall. *South America Uncensored: Jungles of Fascism, Genuine Good-Neighborliness, Portrait of a Continent, In Search of Frontiers.* New York: Longmans, Green, 1945, 363 p.

Cuba

Bartos, Robert E. *The Soviet Penetration of Cuba.* [Oberammergau?], Germany: n.p., 1962, 59 p.

Bellani Nazeri, Rodolfo. *La tumba del "Che."* Buenos Aires: Impr. López, 1968, 204 p. (fiction) (paperback).

Crouch, Thomas W. *A Yankee Guerrillero: Frederick Funston and the Cuban Insurrection, 1896-1897.* Memphis: Memphis State University Press, 1975, 165 p.

Dorschner, John and **Fabricio, Roberto.** *The Winds of December.* New York: Coward, McCann and Geoghegan, 1980, 552 p.

Franqui, Carlos. *Diary of the Cuban Revolution.* Translated by Georgette Felix et al. New York: Viking Press, 1980, 546 p.

Guevara, Ernesto. *Che Guevara on Guerrilla Warfare.* New York: Praeger, 1962, 85 p.

Guevara, Ernesto. *La Guerra de guerrillas.* Bogota, Colombia: Ediciones, Juventud Combatiente, 1960, 157 p.

Guevara, Ernesto. *Guerrilla Warfare.* New York: Monthly Review Press, 1961, 127 p.

Guevara, Ernesto. *Pasajes de la guerra revolucionaria.* Havana: Unión de Escritores y Artistas de Cuba, 1963, 126 p.

Guevara, Ernesto. *Reminiscences of the Cuban Revolutionary War.* Translated by Victoria Ortiz. New York: M.R. Press, 1968, 287 p. (paperback).

Harris, Richard. *Death of a Revolutionary: Che Guevara's Last Mission.* New York: Norton, 1970, 219 p.

Hodges, Donald C., ed. *The Legacy of Che Guevara: A Documentary Study.* Documents translated by Ernest C. Rehder and Donald C. Hodges. London: Thames and Hudson, 1977, 216 p.

Lavretsky, I., pseud. (Grigulevich, Iosif Romual'dovich). *Ernesto Che Guevara.* Translated from the Russian by A.B. Eklof. Moscow: Progress Publishers, 1976, 310 p.

Matthews, Herbert Lionel. *Revolution in Cuba: An Essay in Understanding.* New York: Scribner, 1975, 468 p.

Navarro, Anthony. *Tocayo.* Westport, Conn.: Sandown Books, 1981, 270 p.

Pflaum, Irving Peter. *Tragic Island: How Communism Came to Cuba.* Englewood Cliffs, N.J.: Prentice-Hall, 1961, 196 p.

Taber, Robert. *M-26: Biography of a Revolution.* New York: L. Stuart, 1961, 348 p.

Youngblood, Jack and **Moore, Robin.** *The Devil to Pay.* New York: Coward McCann, 1961, 320 p.

Mideast

"Activist Groups of Eastern Turkey." Washington: U.S. Joint Publications Research Service, no. 74441, West Europe Report no. 1489, October 1979, 109 p. (translation from the Turkish of Articles in *Aydinlik,* Istanbul, January 18-July 1979).

"Mojahedin Publish Soviet Espionage Papers." Washington: U.S. Joint Publications Research Service, June 1979 (translation of article in *Keyhan,* Tehran, June 16, 1979, pp. 1, 5.).

United States

Bealle, Morris Allison. *Red Rat Race: The Unexpurgated, Bare-knuckled, No-Punches-Pulled, Story of World Communism's Infiltration into American Public Life, our Schools, our Press, our Books, our Movies, and Other Mediums of Public Information.* Washington: Columbia Pub., 1953, 287 p.

Bentley, Elizabeth. *Out of Bondage: The Story of Elizabeth Bentley.* New York: Devin-Adair, 1951, 311 p.

Budenz, Louis Francis. *The Bolshevik Invasion of the West: Account of the Great Political War for a Soviet America.* Linden, N.J.: Bookmailer, 1966, 270 p.

Budenz, Louis Francis. *This is My Story.* New York: McGraw-Hill, 1947, 379 p.

Burnham, James. *The Web of Subversion: Underground Networks in the U.S. Government.* New York: John Day, 1954, 248 p.

California, Legislature, Senate, Fact-Finding Committee on Un-American Activities in California. *Fifth Report Accompanied by Supplement with Title: Final Report.* Sacramento: 1949, 709 p.

Charney, George. *A Long Journey.* Chicago: Quadrangle Books, 1968, 340 p.

Coán, Blair *The Red Web: An Underground Political History of the United States from 1918 to the Present Time, Showing how Close the Government is to Collapse, and Told in an Understandable Way.* Chicago: Northwest Pub., 1925, 301 p.

Davis, David Brion, comp. and ed. *The Fear of Conspiracy: Images of Un-American Subversion from the Revolution to the Present.* Ithaca, N.Y.: Cornell University Press, 1971, 369 p.

Decter, Moshe. "The Great Deception." *American Heritage,* v. XIII, no. 1 (December 1961), pp. 73–84.

Diamond, Sander A. *The Nazi Movement in the United States, 1924–1941.* Ithaca, N.Y.: Cornell University Press, 1974, 380 p.

Dies, Martin. *The Trojan Horse in America.* New York: Dodd, Mead, 1940, 366 p.

Dilling, Elizabeth Kirkpatrick. *The Red Network: A "Who's Who" and Handbook of Radicalism for Patriots.* Kenilworth, Ill.: The Author, 1934, 352 p.

Dilling, Elizabeth Kirkpatrick. *The Roosevelt Red Record and its Background.* Kenilworth, Ill.: The Author, 1936, 439 p.

Dodd, Bella Visono. *School of Darkness.* New York: Devin-Adair, 1963, 264 p. (autobiography) (paperback).

Draper, Theodore. *The Roots of American Communism.* New York: Viking Press, 1957, 298 p.

Gates, John, pseud. (Regenstreif, Sol). *The Story of an American Communist.* New York: Nelson, 1958, 221 p.

Gitlow, Benjamin. *I Confess: The Truth About American Communism.* New York: Dutton, 1940, 611 p.

Gitlow, Benjamin. *The Whole of Their Lives: Communism in America, a Personal History and Intimate Portrayal of its Leaders.* New York: Scribner, 1948, 387 p.

Gornick, Vivian. *The Romance of American Communism.* New York: Basic Books, 1977, 265 p.

Great Britain, Foreign Office. *Sworn Statement by Horst von der Goltz, Alias Bridgeman Taylor.* London: H.M. Stationery Office, 1916, 7 p. (Great Britain Foreign Office, Miscellaneous no. 13, 1916. Parliament. Papers by Command, no. 8232).

Hoke, Henry Reed. *It's a Secret.* New York: Reynal and Hitchcock, 1946, 312 p.

Hoover, John Edgar. *The Communist Party Line.* Prepared for the Subcommittee to Investigate the Administration of the Internal Security Act and Other Internal Security Laws of the Committee on the Judiciary, United States Senate, 87th Congress, 1st session. Washington: U.S. GPO, 1961, 6 p.

Hoover, John Edgar. *J. Edgar Hoover Speaks Concerning Communism.* Compiled by James D. Bales. Nutley, N.J.: Craig Press, 1970, 324 p.

Hoover, John Edgar. *Masters of Deceit: The Story of Communism in America and How to Fight it.* New York: Holt, 1958, 374 p.

Hoover, John Edgar. *A Study of Communism.* New York: Holt, Rinehart and Winston, 1962, 212 p.

Johnson, Neil M. *George Sylvester Viereck, German-American Propagandist.* Urbana: University of Illinois Press, 1972, 282 p.

Landon, Maxwell. *Masters of Stupidity.* New York: Vantage Press, 1964, 280 p.

Lavine, Harold. *Fifth Column in America.* New York: Doubleday, Doran, 1940, 240 p.

Luce, Phillip Abbott. *Road to Revolution: Communist Guerrilla Warfare in the U.S.A.* San Diego, Calif.: Viewpoint Books, 1967, 174 p.

Lyons, Eugene. *The Red Decade: The Stalinist Penetration of America.* Indianapolis: Bobbs-Merrill, 1941, 423 p.

Massachusetts, Special Commission on Communism, Subversive Activities and Related Matters Within the Commonwealth. *Interim Report, Fourth Interim Report* and *Fifth Interim Report.* Boston: Wright and Potter, 1955, 3 v.

Morris, Robert. *Self Destruct: Dismantling America's Internal Security.* New Rochelle, N.Y.: Arlington House, 1979, 348 p.

Mowery, Edward J. *Efforts by Communist Conspiracy to Discredit the Federal Bureau of Investigation and its Director. A Series of Articles Documented from the Newark, N.J., Star-Ledger, February 1-9, 1959.* Washington: U.S. GPO, 1959, 27 p.

Musmanno, Michael Angelo. *Across the Street from the Courthouse.* Philadelphia: Dorrance, 1954, 411 p.

Schofield, William Greenough. *Treason Trail.* Chicago: Rand McNally, 1961, 266 p.

Spivak, John L. *Honorable Spy.* New York: Modern Age Books, 1939, 149 p. (paperback).

Spolansky, Jacob. *The Communist Trail in America.* New York: Macmillan, 1951, 227 p.

Stowe, Leland. *Target: You.* New York: Knopf, 1949, 288 p.

Stripling, Robert E. *The Red Plot Against America.* Edited by Bob Considine. Drexel Hill, Pa.: Bell, 1949, 282 p.

Tully, Andrew. *White Tie and Dagger.* New York: Morrow, 1967, 257 p.

Turrou, Leon G. *Nazi Spies in America,* as told to David G. Wittels. New York: Random House, 1939, 299 p.

Turrou, Leon G. *The Nazi Spy Conspiracy in America.* London: Harrap, 1939, 276 p.

Tyson, James L. *Target America: The Influence of Communist Propaganda on U.S. Media.* Chicago: Regnery Gateway, 1981, 284 p.

U.S. Congress, House, Committee on Un-American Activities. *Communist Activities in the Peace Movement (Women Strike for Peace and Certain Other Groups). Hearings ... December 11-13, 1962, including index,* 87th Congress, 2d session. Washington: U.S. GPO, 1963, 2 v.

U.S. Congress, House, Committee on Un-American Activities. *The Communist-led Riots Against the House Committee on Un-American Activities in San Francisco, Calif., May 12-14, 1960; Report no. 2228,* 86th Congress, 2d session. Washington: U.S. GPO, 1960, 22 p.

U.S. Congress, House, Committee on Un-American Activities. *Communist Political Subversion: The Campaign to Destroy the Security Programs of the United States Government. Report no. 1182,* 85th Congress, 1st session. Washington: U.S. GPO, 1957, 97 p.

U.S. Congress, House, Committee on Un-American Activities. *Guide to Subversive Organizations and Publications.* Washington: U.S. GPO, 2 v. (revised editions: 1957 and 1961).

U.S. Congress, House, Committee on Un-American Activities. *The Northern California District of the Communist Party: Structure, Objectives, Leadership. Part 2. Hearings ...* 86th Congress, 2d session. Washington: U.S. GPO, 1960, pp. 1999-2081.

U.S. Congress, House, Committee on Un-American Activities. *Organized Communism in the United States. House Report no. 1724.* 85th Congress, 2d session. Washington: U.S. GPO, 1958, 153 p.

U.S. Congress, House, Committee on Un-American Activities. *Report on the Communist Party of the United States as an Advocate of Overthrow of Government by Force and Violence. Investigation of Un-American Activities in the United States. House Report no. 1920 on Public Law 601 (section 121, subsection Q (2))* 80th Congress, 2d session. Washington: U.S. GPO, 1948, 160 p.

U.S. Congress, House, Committee on Un-American Activities. *Thirty Years of Treason: Excerpts from Hearings. ... 1938-1968.* Edited by Eric Bentley. New York: Viking Press, 1971, 991 p.

U.S. Congress, House, Committee on Un-American Activities. *Violations of State Department Regulations and Pro-Castro Propaganda Activities in the United States. Hearings.* 88th Congress, 1st session. Washington: U.S. GPO, 1963. pt. 3 only.

U.S. Congress, House, Special Committee on Un-American Activities. *Investigation of Un-American Propaganda Activities in the United States. Hearings. ... on H. Res. 282, to Investigate (1) the Extent, Character, and Objects of Un-American Propaganda Activities in the United States, (2) the Diffusion Within the United States of Subversive and Un-American Propaganda that is Instigated from Foreign Countries or of a Domestic Origin and Attacks the Principle of the Form of Government as Guaranteed by our Constitution, and (3) all Other Questions in Relation Thereto that Would aid Congress in any Necessary Remedial Legislation.* 78th Congress, 1st session. Washington: U.S. GPO, v. 15 (June–July 1943).

U.S. Congress, House, Special Committee on Un-American Activities. *Investigation of Un-American Propaganda Activities in the United States: Appendix, part II, a Preliminary Digest and Report on the*

Un-American Activities of Various Nazi Organizations and Individuals in the United States, Including Diplomatic and Consular Agents of the German Government. H. Res. 282. 76th Congress, 3d session. Washington: U.S. GPO, 1940, pp. 969-1382.

U.S. Congress, Senate, Committee on the Judiciary, Subcommittee to Investigate the Administration of the Internal Security Act and Other Internal Security Laws. *Scope of Soviet Activity in the United States. Hearing* ... 84th Congress, 2d session. Washington: U.S. GPO, 1956, Pts. 1-42. (hearings held February 8, 1956-November 29, 1957).

U.S. Federal Bureau of Investigation. *Communist Target: Youth. Communist Infiltration and Agitation Tactics. A Report by J. Edgar Hoover, Director, Illustrating Communist Strategy and Tactics in the Rioting which Occurred During House Committee on Un-American Activities Hearings, San Francisco, May 12-14, 1960.* Washington: U.S. GPO, 1960, 18 p.

U.S. War Department, General Staff. *Propaganda in its Military and Legal Aspects.* Washington: Military Intelligence Branch, Executive Division, General Staff, [1918?], 187 p.

Voros, Sandor. *American Commissar.* Philadelphia: Chilton Co., Book Division, 1961, 477 p.

Whitney, Richard Merrill. *Reds in America: The Present Status of the Revolutionary Movement in the United States Based on Documents Seized by the Authorities in the Raid Upon the Convention of the Communist Party at Bridgman, Michigan, August 22, 1922, Together with Descriptions of Numerous Connections and Associations of the Communists Among the Radicals, Progressives and Pinks.* New York: Beckwith Press, 1924, 287 p.

VII. INTELLIGENCE SUPPORT
General

Bennett, Edward M.; Degan, James et al., eds. *Military Information Systems: The Design of Computer-aided Systems for Command.* New York: Praeger, 1964, 180 p.

Berger, David L. *Industrial Security.* Los Angeles: Security World Pub., 1979, 361 p.

Cothren, Marion Benedict. *Pigeon Heroes: Birds of War and Messengers of Peace.* New York: Coward-McCann, 1944, 47 p.

Felix, Christopher, pseud. *A Short Course in the Secret War.* New York: Dutton, 1963, 314 p.

Koplowitz, Wilfred D. *Teaching Intelligence: A Survey of College and University Courses on the Subject of Intelligence.* Washington: National Intelligence Study Center, 1980, 90 p.

McCormick, Donald. *The Master Book of Spies: The World of Espionage, Master Spies, Tortures, Interrogations, Spy Equipment, Escapes, Codes and How You Can Become a Spy.* New York: F. Watts, 1974, 190 p.

O'Brien-Twohig, Michael. *Diplomatic Courier.* London: Elek Books, 1960, 220 p.

Robbins, Christopher. *Air America.* New York: Putnam, 1979, 323 p.

Shif, Ze'ev. "Finding of Secret Documents in the Trash is Only One Manifestation of Lax Security." English translation by U.S. Joint Publications Research Service. *Ha'aretz,* Tel Aviv, June 25, 1979, p. 11.

Shurtleff, Bertrand Leslie. *AWOL: K-9 Commando.* Indianapolis: Bobbs-Merrill, 1944, 284 p.

U.S. Air Combat Intelligence School, Quonset Point, R.I. *The Life and Times of the Air Combat Intelligence School.* New Haven: Private Printer, 1946, 121 p.

Wheeler-Holohan, V. *The History of the King's Messengers.* New York: Dutton, 1934, 291 p.

Bibliographies

Bibliography of Open-Source Intelligence Literature. Washington: Defense Intelligence School, 1973, 48 p.

Blackstock, Paul W. and **Schaf, Frank L., Jr.** *Intelligence, Espionage, Counterespionage, and Covert Operations: A Guide to Information Sources.* Detroit: Gale Research, 1978, 255 p.

Galland, Joseph Stanislaus. *An Historical and Analytical Bibliography of the Literature of Cryptology.* Evanston, Ill.: Northwestern University, 1945, 209 p. (Northwestern University Studies in the Humanities, no. 10).

Grierson, Philip. *Books on Soviet Russia, 1917–1942: A Bibliography and a Guide to Reading.* London: Methuen, 1943, 354 p.

Gunzenhäuser, Max. *Geschichte des geheimen Nachrichtendienstes (Spionage, Sabotage und Abwehr): Literaturbericht und Bibliographie.* Frankfurt am Main: Bernard and Graefe, 1968, 434 p.

Harris, William Robert. *Intelligence and National Security: A Bibliography with Selected Annotations.* Cambridge, Mass.: n.p., 1968, 3 v.

Mickolus, Edward F. *The Literature of Terrorism (A Selectively Annotated Bibliography).* Westport, Conn.: Greenwood Press, 1980, 553 p.

Murphy, Harry J. *Where's What: Sources of Information for Federal Investigators.* New York: Warner Books, 1976, 452 p. (paperback).

Seth, Ronald. *Encyclopedia of Espionage.* Garden City, N.Y.: Doubleday, 1974, 718 p.

Shaffer, Harry G. *English Language Periodic Publications on Communism: An Annotated Index.* New York: Columbia University Press, 1971, 23 p.

Shulman, David. *An Annotated Bibliography of Cryptography.* New York: Garland Pub., 1976, 388 p.

Smith, Edward Ellis with **Lednicky, Rudolf.** *The Okrana—the Russian Department of Police: A Bibliography.* Stanford, Calif: Hoover Institution on War, Revolution, and Peace, 1967, 280 p.

U.S. Central Intelligence Agency. *CIA Subject Headings and Classed Schedules for Law, Communism and the Communist Parties, Intelligence and Security.* Issued by the Office of Central Reference. 1st rev. ed. Washington: Central Intelligence Agency, November 1960, 39 p.

U.S. Library of Congress, Congressional Research Service. *Soviet Intelligence and Security Services. 1964-1970: A Selected Bibliography of Soviet Publications, with Some Additional Titles from Other Sources.* Washington: U.S. GPO, 1972, 289 p.

U.S. Office of Strategic Services. *Espionage and Counter-espionage: A Bibliography.* Washington: n.p. 1943, 49 p. (typescript).

Interrogation Techniques and Behavior Modification

Bain, Donald. *The Control of Candy Jones.* Chicago: Playboy Press, 1976, 267 p.

Beck, F., *pseud.* and **Godin, W.,** *pseud. Russian Purge and the Extraction of Confession.* Translated from the Original German by Eric Mosbacher and David Porter. New York: Viking Press, 1951, 277 p.

Becket, James. *Barbarism in Greece: A Young American Lawyer's Inquiry into the Use of Torture in Contemporary Greece, with Case Histories and Documents.* New York: Walker, 1970, 147 p.

Bloch, Sidney and **Reddaway, Peter.** *Psychiatric Terror: How Soviet Psychiatry is Used to Suppress Dissent.* New York: Basic Books, 1977, 510 p.

Brown, J.A.C. *Techniques of Persuasion, From Propaganda to Brainwashing.* Baltimore: Penguin Books, 1968, 325 p. (paperback).

Camellion, Richard. *Behavior Modification: The Art of Mind Murdering.* Boulder, Colo.: Paladin Press, 1978, 129 p. (paperback).

Deely, Peter. *Beyond Breaking Point.* London: Barker, 1971, 239 p.

Dulov, Ateist Vasil'evich. *Fundamentals of Psychological Analysis in Preliminary Investigation.* Washington: U.S. Joint Publications Research Service, no. 61685, April 8, 1974, 136 p. (English translation of *Osnovy psikhologicheskogo analiza na predvaritel'nom sledstvii*).

Fireside, Harvey. *Soviet Psychoprisons.* New York: Norton, 1979, 201 p.

Fisher, Seymour. *The Use of Hypnosis in Intelligence and Related Military Situations.* Washington: Bureau of Social Science Research, December 1958, 25 p. (typescript).

The Gangrene. Translated from the French by Robert Silvers. New York: L. Stuart, 1960, 96 p.

Goff, Kenneth. *Brain-washing: A Synthesis of the Russian Textbook on Psychopolitics.* Boulder, Colo.: Paladin Press, [197-], 64 p. (paperback).

Gris, Henry and **Dick, William.** *The New Soviet Psychic Discoveries.* New York: Warner Books, 1979, 448 p. (paperback).

Marks, John D. *The Search for the "Manchurian Candidate."* New York: Times Books, 1979, 242 p.

Medvedev, Zhores Aleksandrovich and **Medvedev, Roy A.** *A Question of Madness.* Translated from the Russian by Ellen de Kadt. New York: Norton, 1979, 223 p. (paperback).

Meerloo, Joost. *The Rape of the Mind: The Psychology of Thought Control, Menticide and Brainwashing.* Cleveland: World Publishing, 1956, 320 p.

Nekipelov, Viktor. *Institute of Fools: Notes from Serbsky.* Edited and translated from the Russian by Marco Carynnyk and Marta Horban. New York: Farrar, Straus, Giroux, 1980, 292 p.

Os'machka, Teodosii. *Red Assassins: A Factual Story Revealing How the Ukraine Lost its Freedom.* Minneapolis: T.S. Denison, 1959, 375 p.

Rogge, Oetje John. *Why Men Confess.* New York: Nelson, 1959, 298 p.

Scheflin, Alan W. and **Opton, Edward M., Jr.** *The Mind Manipulators: A Non-fiction Account.* New York: Paddington Press, 1978, 359 p.

Schrag, Peter. *Mind Control.* New York: Pantheon Books, 1978, 327 p.

U.S. Congress, Senate, Select Committee on Intelligence. *Project MKULTRA, the CIA's Program of Research in Behavioral Modification. Joint Hearing of the Select Committee on Intelligence and the Subcommittee on Health and Scientific Research, Committee on Human Resources.* 95th Congress, 1st session. Washington: U.S. GPO, 1977, 169 p.

Medical

Gibson, Frank. *Cloak and Doctor.* Jericho, N.Y.: Exposition Press, 1974, 208 p. (fiction).

Sava, George, *pseud.* (Bankoff, George Alexis). *Secret Surgeon.* London: Kimber, 1979, 189 p.

Personnel Investigation and Recruitment

Bridges, Burtis C. *Practical Fingerprinting.* New York: Funk and Wagnalls, 1942, 374 p.

Cavanagh, John; Frank, Sally et al. "Princeton in the CIA's Service," The Daily Princetonian, November 12, 1979, pp. 6-7.

Fuqua, Paul Q. and **Wilson, Jerry V.** Security Investigator's Handbook. Houston: Gulf Pub., 1979, 222 p.

Gugas, Chris. The Silent Witness: A Polygraphist's Casebook. Englewood Cliffs, N.J.: Prentice-Hall, 1979, 254 p.

Lykken, David Thoreson. A Tremor in the Blood: Uses and Abuses of the Lie Detector. New York: McGraw-Hill, 1981, 317 p.

Miller, Arthur Raphael. The Assault on Privacy: Computers, Data Banks, and Dossiers. Ann Arbor: University of Michigan Press, 1971, 333 p.

Press, Sylvia. The Care of Devils. New York: Bantam Books, 1966, 218 p. (paperback).

Rowan, Ford. Technospies: The Secret Network that Spies on You, and You. New York: Putnam, 1978, 262 p.

Rudd, Hughes. My Escape from the CIA, and Other Improbable Events. New York: Dutton, 1976, 253 p. (paperback).

"The Spy That Came out of the Computer." German International, no. 8, 1979.

Volkman, Ernest. "Spies on Campus." Penthouse, October 1979, p. 64+.

U.S. Congress, House, Permanent Select Committee on Intelligence. Subcommittee on Oversight. Pre-employment Security Procedures of the Intelligence Agencies. Hearings of the 96th Congress, 1st session. Washington: U.S. GPO, 1980, 213 p.

U.S. Congress, House, Permanent Select Committee on Intelligence, Subcommittee on Oversight. Security Clearance Procedures in the Intelligence Agencies. Staff Report. Washington: U.S. GPO, September 1979, 34 p.

U.S. Office of Strategic Services. Assessment of Men: Selection of Personnel for the Office of Strategic Services. New York: Rinehart, 1948, 541 p.

Training

The Black Bag Owner's Manual. Boulder, Colo.: Paladin Press, 1978, 3 pts. (Pt. 1: "Spookcentre"; Pt. 2: "The Hit Parade"; Pt. 3: "False Face").

Chandler, Stedman and **Robb, Robert W.** Front-line Intelligence. Washington: Infantry Journal Press, 1946, 183 p.

George, Willis De Vere. Surreptitious Entry. New York: D. Appleton-Century, 1946, 214 p.

Graham, Fred P. The Alias Program. Boston: Little, Brown, 1977, 239 p.

Gubbins, Colin McVean, Sir. The Art of Guerrilla Warfare. San Francisco: Interservice, 1981, 18 p.

Gubbins, Colin McVean, Sir. Partisan Leader's Handbook. San Francisco: Interservice, 1981, 34 p.

Harris, Don R. with **Maxfield, Mike** and **Hollady, Glennie.** Basic Elements of Intelligence. Prepared for the Organized Crime Desk, Enforcement Program Division, Office of Regional Operations. Law Enforcement Assistance Administration, U.S. Dept. of Justice. Rev. ed. Washington: U.S. GPO, 1976, 165 p.

Kremer, J.v. with **B. 9834.** Le livre noir de l'espionnage: les dessous de la guerre de l'ombre. Paris: Editions Fleuve Noir, 1955, 222 p.

Krotz, David. How to Hide Almost Anything. New York: Morrow, 1975, 157 p.

Lewis, David. Sexpionage: The Exploitation of Sex by Soviet Intelligence. New York: Harcourt, Brace, Jovanovich, 1976, 174 p.

Locks, Picks, and Clicks. Boulder, Colo.: Paladin Press, 1974, 69 p. (typescript).

Mashiro, N. Black Medicine: The Dark Art of Death, the Vital Points of the Human Body in Close Combat. Boulder, Colo.: Paladin Press, 1978, 92 p.

Minnery, John. How to Kill. Edited by Robert K. Brown and Peder C. Lund. Boulder, Colo.: Paladin Press, 1973-1979, 4 v.

Observation and Description: Counter Intelligence Corps. San Francisco: Interservice, 1981, 54 p.

OSS Sabotage and Demolition Manual. Boulder, Colo.: Paladin Press, 1974, 319 p.

The Paper Trip I: For a New You Through New ID. Edited by Cathy Clark. Fountain Valley, Calif.: Eden Press, 1971, 82 p.

The Paper Trip II: For a New You Through New ID. Fountain Valley, Calif.: Eden Press, 1980, 160 p.

Police Guide to Lock Picking and Improvised Lock Picks. Cornville, Ariz.: Desert Publications, 1976, 60 p.

Prikhodko, I.E. Characteristics of Agent Communications and of Agent Handling in the United States of America. San Francisco: Interservice, 1981, 40 p.

Roper, Carl. *Agent's Handbook of Black Bag Operations.* Cornville, Ariz.: Desert Publications, 1978, 64 p.

Russell, Charles Edmund. *Espionage and Counter-espionage, M.1.-4: A Series of Lectures Prepared for the Regular Army, National Guard, and Reserve Officers of the U.S.A., and Delivered Before these Officers of the New York Corps Area; with an Appendix Containing Chapters on Spies, Propaganda, Codes and Ciphers, and Espionage and Counter-espionage in Government Departments.* Garden City, N.Y.: Country Life Press, 1926, 263 p.

Special Air Service Regiment Patrol Techniques. San Francisco: Interservice, 1981, 73 p.

Thomas, Shipley. *S-2 in Action.* Harrisburg, Pa.: The Military Service Publishing, 1940, 128 p.

Townsend, Elias Carter. *Risks: The Key to Combat Intelligence.* Harrisburg, Pa.: Military Service Pub., 1955, 82 p.

Undercover Operations. San Francisco: Interservice, 1981, 29 p. (paperback).

U.S. Air Force, Air Training Command. *Intelligence Fundamentals. Volume 2: Processing Intelligence.* Montgomery, Alabama: U.S.A.F. Extension Course Institute, June 1953, 81 p.

U.S. Air Force, Air Training Command. *Intelligence Operations Specialist. Volume 1: Background Intelligence.* Montgomery, Alabama: U.S.A.F. Extension Course Institute, September 1953, 99 p.

U.S. Air Force, Continental Air Command. *Con AC Manual, no. 20450. Intelligence Operations Specialist.* Mitchell AFB, N.Y.: March 15, 1954, [210] p.

U.S. Department of the Army. *Combat Intelligence.* Washington: U.S. GPO, February 1951, 314 p. (FM30-5).

U.S. Department of the Army. *Intelligence Interrogation.* Boulder, Colo.: Paladin Press, 1967, 97 p. (FM30-15).

U.S. Marine Corps Schools, Quantico, Virginia. *Basic Combat Intelligence.* Quantico: Extension School, Marine Corps Educational Center, 1955, 88 p.

U.S. Office of Strategic Services. *Operational Group Field Manual,* April 25, 1944. San Francisco: Interservice, 1981, 25 p.

U.S. War Department. *Examination of Enemy Personnel, Repatriates, Civilians, Documents, and Materiel.* Washington: U.S. GPO, 1945, 52 p. (FM30-15).

U.S. War Department. *Infantry Field Manual: Headquarters Company, Intelligence and Signal Communication, Rifle Regiment.* Washington: U.S. GPO, 1942, 78 p. (FM7-25).

U.S. War Department. *Military Intelligence: Combat Intelligence.* Washington: U.S. GPO, 1946, 98 p. (FM30-5).

U.S. War Department. *Military Intelligence: Examination of Enemy Personnel, Repatriates, Documents, and Materiel.* Washington: U.S. GPO, 1943, 28 p. (FM30-15).

U.S. War Department, Chief of Staff. *Basic Field Manual: Military Intelligence, Combat Intelligence.* With Change no. 1, January 2, 1941. Washington: U.S. GPO, 1940, 36 p. (FM30-5).

U.S. War Department, Chief of Staff. *Technical Manual: Post, Camp, and Station Intelligence, Zone of the Interior.* Washington: U.S. GPO, March 3, 1941, 15 p. (TM30-230).

Wade, G.A. *Intelligence and Liaison.* n.p.: Aldershot, Gale and Polden, [1942?], 35 p.

Wagner, Arthur Lockwood. *The Service of Security and Information.* 3d ed. Kansas City, Mo.: Hudson-Kimberly, 1893, 244 p.

Whipp, Derek. *Street and Guerrilla Fighting.* San Francisco: Interservice, 1981, 47 p.

Weapons and Equipment

Bell, Leslie. *Sabotage! The Story of Lt.-Col. J. Elder Wills.* London: T.W. Laurie, 1957, 189 p.

CIA Ammunition and Explosives Supply Catalog, July 1, 1966. Boulder, Colo.: Paladin Press, [post 1966], 81 p.

CIA Explosives for Sabotage Manual. Boulder, Colo.: Paladin Press, 1976, 66 p.

CIA Special Weapon Supply Catalog. Boulder, Colo.: Paladin Press, 60 p.

Dewar, Michael. *Internal Security Weapons and Equipment of the World.* New York: Scribner, 1979, 128 p.

Errand, Jeremy. *Secret Passages and Hiding-places.* Newton Abbot, England: David and Charles, 1974, 200 p.

Great Britain, The War Office. *Enemy Sabotage Equipment (Identification).* London: The War Office, December 1943, 104 p.

Hoy, Michael. *Exotic Weapons: An Access Book.* Mason, Mich.: Loompanics, 1977, 37 p.

Kates, James. "The Spy Radio That Became CB." *C B Magazine,* June 1979, pp. 24-42.

McLean, Donald B. *The Plumber's Kitchen: The Secret Story of American Spy Weapons.* Wickenburg, Ariz.: Normount Technical Publications, 1975, 282 p.

Puy-Montbrun, Déodat. *Les Armes des espions.* Paris: Ballard, 1974, 298 p.

Saxon, Kurt. *The Poor Man's James Bond: The Complete "Militant's Formulary" and Much More.* Harrison, Arkansas: Atlan Formularies, 1972, 146 p.

Scriven, George Percival. *The Transmission of Military Information. An Outline of the Service of a Corps of Intelligence, or of a Signal Corps, Under Modern Conditions Affecting the Transmission of Military Information to Troops in the Field, and to the Coast Defense.* Governor's Island, N.Y.: Wynkoop Hallenbeck Crawford, 1908, 153 p.

Seagrave, Sterling. *Yellow Rain: A Journey Through the Terror of Chemical Warfare.* New York: M. Evans, 1981, 316 p.

Truby, J. David. *How Terrorists Kill: The Complete Terrorist Arsenal.* Edited by Devon Christensen. Boulder, Colo.: Paladin Press, 1978, 87 p. (paperback).

Truby, J. David. *The Quiet Killers.* Boulder, Colo.: Paladin Press, 1972, 79 p.

Truby, J. David. *Silencers, Snipers, and Assassins: An Overview of Whispering Death.* Edited by Robert K. Brown and Peder Lund. Boulder, Colo.: Paladin Press, 1972, 209 p.

VIII. LEGAL AND MORAL CONSIDERATIONS
General

Baxter, Richard, "So-Called 'Underprivileged Belligerency'": Spies, Guerrillas and Saboteurs." *British Year Book of International Law,* 1951, pp. 323-345.

Berman, Jerry J. and **Halperin, Morton H.,** eds. *The Abuses of Intelligence Agencies.* Washington: Center for National Security Studies, 1975, 185 p. (paperback).

Bok, Sissela. *Lying: Moral Choice in Public and Private Life.* New York: Vintage Books, 1979, 354 p.

Burn, Michael. *The Debatable Land: A Study of the Motives of Spies in Two Ages.* London: Hamilton, 1970, 285 p.

Godfrey, E. Drexel, Jr. "Ethics and Intelligence." *Foreign Affairs,* v. 56, no. 3 (April 1978), pp. 624-642.

Godson, Roy. "Intelligence Reform in the United States: The Proposed Charter." *World Affairs,* Summer 1980, p. 3.

Grodzins, Morton. *The Loyal and the Disloyal: Social Boundaries of Patriotism and Treason.* Chicago: University of Chicago Press, 1956, 319 p.

Killen, Frederick S. *The Question of America's Intelligence Gathering Capabilities: An Examination of the Intelligence Community's Ability to Provide Information Concerning Impending Terrorist Actions.* Santa Ana, Calif.: The Author, 1979, 338 p.

Lane, Mark. *The Strongest Poison.* New York: Hawthorn Books, 1980, 494 p.

Lefever, Ernest W. and **Godson, Roy.** *The CIA and the American Ethic: An Unfinished Debate.* Washington: Ethics and Public Policy Center, Georgetown University, 1979, 161 p.

McCarthy, Eugene J. *America Revisited: 150 Years After Tocqueville.,* Garden City: N.Y.: Doubleday, 1978, 256 p.

Morris, George. *CIA and American Labor: The Subversion of the AFL-CIO's Foreign Policy.* New York: International Publishers, 1967, 159 p.

Pritt, Denis Nowell. *Spies and Informers in the Witness Box.* London: B. Hanison, 1958, 96 p.

Stanger, Roland J., ed. *Essays on Espionage and International Law* by Quincy Wright and Others. Columbus: Ohio State University Press, 1962, 101 p.

Congressional Oversight

Franck, Thomas M. and **Weisband, Edward.** *Foreign Policy by Congress.* New York: Oxford University Press, 1979, 357 p.

Joyce, Martin H., III. *Executive Intelligence Oversight: A History and Assessment.* August 27, 1979, 17 p. (typescript).

Latimer, Thomas K. "U.S. Intelligence and the Congress." *Strategic Review,* v. VII, no. 3 (Summer 1979), pp. 47-55.

McNamee, Michael D.; Sandler, Norman D. et al. *Congressional Oversight of the Central Intelligence Agency: Observations and Analysis.* Cambridge, Mass.: Center for International Studies, Mass. May 1974, 55 p. (typescript).

Sandler, Norman Davis. *28 Years of Looking the Other Way: Congressional Oversight of the Central Intelligence Agency, 1947-1975.* Cambridge, Mass.: Center for International Studies, May 1975, 309 p. (typescript).

Silberman, Laurence H. *Testimony on Electronic Surveillance for National Security Purposes.* Washington: American Enterprise Institute, 1978, 11 p. (statement of Laurence H. Silberman before the House Permanent Select Committee on Intelligence, February 8, 1978).

U.S. Congress, House, Committee on Armed Services, Special Subcommittee on Intelligence. *Inquiry into the Alleged Involvement of the Central Intelligence Agency in the Watergate and Ellsberg Matters. Report, 93d Congress, 1st session. October 23, 1973.* Washington: U.S. GPO, 1973, 23 p.

U.S. Congress, Senate, Select Committee on Intelligence. *National Intelligence Reorganization and Reform Act of 1978: Hearing . . . on S. 2525. . . . held April 4–August 3, 1978.* 95th Congress, 2d session. Washington: U.S. GPO, 1978, 1101 p.

U.S. Congress, Senate, Select Committee on Intelligence. *Report . . .* no. 96–141, Covering the Period May 16, 1977–December 31, 1978, 95th Congress. 96th Congress, 1st session. Washington: U.S. GPO, 1979, 75 p.

U.S. Congress, Senate, Select Committee to Study Government Operations with Respect to Intelligence Activities. *Final Report . . . Book V. The Investigation of the Assassination of President John F. Kennedy: Performance of the Intelligence Agencies, April 23, 1976.* 94th Congress, 2d session. Washington: U.S. GPO, 1976, 106 p.

U.S. Congress, Senate, Select Committee to Study Government Operations with Respect to Intelligence Activities. *Final Report . . . Book VI. Supplementary Reports on Intelligence Activities, April 23, 1976,* 94th Congress, 2d session. Washington: U.S. GPO, 1976, 378 p.

Uses and Abuses of Intelligence

Aitken, Jonathan. *Officially Secret.* London: Weidenfeld and Nicolson, 1971, 236 p.

Administrative Secrecy in Developed Countries. Edited by Donald C. Rowat. London: Macmillan, 1979, 364 p.

Barth, Alan. *Government by Investigation.* New York: Viking Press, 1955, 231 p.

Barth, Alan. *The Loyalty of Free Men.* New York: Viking Press, 1951, 253 p.

Blackstock, Nelson. *Cointelpro: The FBI's Secret War on Political Freedom.* Edited by Cathy Perkus. New York: Monad Press, 1975, 190 p. (paperback).

Brenton, Myron. *The Privacy Invaders.* New York: Coward-McCann, 1964, 240 p.

Buitrago, Ann Mari and **Immerman, Leon Andrew.** *Are You Now or Have You Ever Been in the FBI Files? How to Secure and Interpret Your FBI Files.* New York: Grove Press, 1981, 227 p. (paperback).

Colby, William E. "When TV Probes, Can the Government Keep a Secret?" *TV Guide,* February 12, 1977, pp. 2–6.

Cowan, Paul; Egleson, Nick et al. *State Secrets: Police Surveillance in America.* New York: Holt, Rinehart and Winston, 1974, 333 p.

Cox, Arthur M. *The Myths of National Security: The Peril of Secret Government.* Boston: Beacon Press, 1975, 231 p.

Elliff, John T. *The Reform of FBI Intelligence Operations, Written Under the Auspices of the Police Foundation.* Princeton, N.J.: Princeton University Press, 1979, 248 p.

Foreign Intelligence, Legal and Democratic Controls. Public Policy Forum no. 37, December 11, 1979. Peter Hackes, moderator; Les Aspin et al. participating. Washington: American Enterprise Institute, 1980, 37 p.

Franck, Thomas M. and **Weisband, Edward,** eds. *Secrecy and Foreign Policy.* New York: Oxford University Press, 1974, 453 p.

French, Scott R. *The Big Brother Game.* Secaucus, N.J.: L. Stuart, 1975, 237 p. (paperback).

Friedrich, Carl Joachim. *The Pathology of Politics: Violence, Betrayal, Corruption, Secrecy, and Propaganda.* New York: Harper and Row, 1972, 287 p.

Galnoor, Itzhak, ed. *Government Secrecy in Democracies.* New York: New York University Press, 1977, 317 p.

Garrison, Omar V. *Spy Government: The Emerging Police State in America.* New York: L. Stuart, 1967, 277 p.

Gross, Bertram Myron. *Friendly Fascism: The New Face of Power in America.* New York: M. Evans, 1980, 410 p.

Hain, Peter. *Policing the Police.* London: John Calder Publishers, 1979, 198 p.

Halperin, Morton H. "National Security and Civil Liberties." *Foreign Policy,* no. 21 (Winter 1975–1976), pp. 125–160.

Halperin, Morton H. and **Hoffman, Daniel.** *Freedom vs. National Security: Secrecy and Surveillance.* New York: Chelsea House, 1977, 594 p.

Halperin, Morton H. et al. *The Lawless State: The Crimes of the U.S. Intelligence Agencies.* New York: Penguin Books, 1976, 328 p.

Halperin, Morton H. and **Hoffman, Daniel N.** *Top Secret: National Security and the Right to Know.* Washington: New Republic Books, 1977, 158 p.

Investigating the FBI. Edited by Pat Watters and Stephen Gillers. New York: Ballantine Books, 1974, 472 p. (paperback).

Kim, Young Hum, comp. *The Central Intelligence Agency: Problems of Secrecy in a Democracy.* Lexington, Mass.: Heath, 1968, 113 p.

LeMond, Alan and **Fry, Ron.** *No Place to Hide.* New York: St. Martin's Press, 1975, 278 p.

Morgan, Richard E. *Domestic Intelligence: Monitoring Dissent in America.* Austin: University of Texas Press, 1980, 194 p.

Neier, Aryeh. *Dossier: The Secret Files They Keep on You.* New York: Stein and Day, 1975, 216 p.

Orman, John M. *Presidential Secrecy and Deception: Beyond the Power to Persuade.* Westport, Conn.: Greenwood Press, 1980, 239 p.

Packard, Vance Oakley. *The Naked Society.* New York: D. McKay, 1964, 369 p.

Reed, Fred. "The Other Side of Secrecy." *Washington Post,* October 10, 1979, p. A21.

The Right to Privacy. Edited by Grant S. McClellan. New York: H.W. Wilson, 1976, 240 p.

Schorr, Daniel. *Clearing the Air.* Boston: Houghton Mifflin, 1977, 333 p.

Schrag, Peter. *Test of Loyalty: Daniel Ellsberg and the Rituals of Secret Government.* New York: Simon and Schuster, 1974, 414 p.

Sherick, L.G. *How to Use the Freedom of Information Act (FOIA).* New York: Arco, 1978, 138 p. (paperback).

Shils, Edward Albert. *The Torment of Secrecy: The Background and Consequences of American Security Policies.* New York: Free Press, 1956, 238 p.

Smith, Robert Ellis. *Privacy: How to Protect What's Left of It.* Garden City, N.Y.: Anchor Press/Doubleday, 1979, 346 p.

State Research. *Review of Security and the State 1978, Articles by Its Working Group,* Tony Bunyan, Ian Blunt et al. London: Julian Friedmann Books, 1978, 156 p.

Supperstone, Michael. *Brownlie's Law of Public Order and National Security.* 2d ed. London: Butterworths, 1981, 415 p.

Surveillance and Espionage in a Free Society: A Report by the Planning Group on Intelligence and Security to the Policy Council of the Democratic National Committee. Edited by Richard H. Blum. New York: Praeger, 1972, 319 p.

Szulc, Tad. "How Nixon Used the C.I.A." *New York Magazine,* January 20, 1975, pp. 28-33.

Theoharis, Athan G. *Spying on Americans: Political Surveillance from Hoover to the Huston Plan.* Philadelphia: Temple University Press, 1978, 331 p.

U.S. Central Intelligence Agency. *Director's Report of December 24, 1974 to the President of the United States Covering Matters Related to the New York Times Article of December 22 Alleging CIA Involvement in Massive Illegal Domestic Intelligence Effort.* Washington: July 8, 1975. (press release).

U.S. Commission on CIA Activities Within the United States. *Report to the President.* Washington: U.S. GPO, 1975, 299 p.

U.S. Commission on Government Security. *Report* [Pursuant to Public Law 304, 84th Congress]. New York: Da Capo Press, 1971, 807 p. (commonly known as the Wright report).

U.S. Congress, Senate, Committee on the Judiciary. *Freedom of Information Act. Source Book: Legislative Materials, Cases, Articles.* 93rd Congress, 2d session. Washington: U.S. GPO, 1974, 432 p.

U.S. Congress, Senate, Committee on the Judiciary, Subcommittee on Constitutional Rights. *Military Surveillance of Civilian Politics: A Report.* Washington: U.S. GPO, 1973, 150 p.

Weinberg, Steve. *Trade Secrets of Washington Journalists: How to Get the Facts About What's Going on in Washington.* Washington: Acropolis Books, 1981, 253 p.

Weinstein, Allen. "Open Season on 'Open Government.' " *New York Times Magazine,* June 10, 1979, p. 32+.

Westin, Alan F. *Privacy and Freedom.* New York: Atheneum, 1967, 487 p.

Wise, David. *The American Police State: The Government Against the People.* New York: Random House, 1976, 437 p.

Wise, David. *The Politics of Lying: Government Deception, Secrecy, and Power.* New York: Random House, 1973, 415 p.

Wolfe, Alan. *The Seamy Side of Democracy: Repression in America.* New York: D. McKay, 1973, 306 p.

Woodward, Bob and **Armstrong, Scott.** *The Brethren: Inside the Supreme Court.* New York: Simon and Schuster, 1979, 467 p.

Zemach, Yaacov A. *Political Questions in the Courts: A Judicial Function in Democracies—Israel and the United States.* Detroit: Wayne State University Press, 1976, 296 p.

Zuckerman, Solly, *Sir. Scientists and War: The Impact of Science on Military and Civil Affairs.* New York: Harper and Row, 1967, 177 p.

IX. CRITICISMS AND EXPOSÉS

Agee, Philip. *Inside the Company: CIA Diary.* Harmondsworth, Middlesex, England: Penguin Books, 1975, 639 p. (paperback).

Agee, Philip. *Za kulisami TsRU.* Translated from the English by L. Kashina. Moscow: Voenizdat, 1979, 464 p. (abridged Russian language edition of *Inside the Company: CIA Diary*).

Ashman, Charles. *The CIA-Mafia Link.* New York: Manor Books, 1975, 234 p. (paperback).

Bowart, Walter H. *Operation Mind Control: Our Secret Government's War Against its own People.* New York: Dell, 1978, 317 p. (paperback).

The CIA File. Edited by Robert L. Borosage and John Marks. New York: Grossman Publishers, 1975, 236 p.

Chomsky, Noam and **Herman, Edward S.** *The Washington Connection and Third World Fascism.* Boston: South End Press, 1979, 441 p.

Conference on the CIA and World Peace, Yale University, 1975. *Uncloaking the CIA.* Edited by Howard Frazier. New York: Free Press, 1978, 288 p.

Corson, William. *The Armies of Ignorance: The Rise of the American Intelligence Empire.* New York: Dial Press/J. Wade, 1977, 640 p.

Counter-Spy, v. 2, no. 3 (Spring/Summer 1975). Washington: Fifth Estate Security Education, 64 p.

Dirty Work: The CIA in Western Europe. Edited by Philip Agee and Louis Wolf. Secaucus, N.J.: L. Stuart, 1978, 734 p.

Dirty Work 2: The CIA in Africa. Edited by Ellen Ray et al. Secaucus, N.J.: L. Stuart, 1979, 523 p.

Ellsworth, Robert F. and **Adelman, Kenneth L.** "Foolish Intelligence." *Foreign Policy*, no. 36 (Fall 1979), pp. 147–159.

Fidler, Richard. *RCMP: The Real Subversives.* Toronto, Ontario: Vanguard, 1978, 91 p. (paperback).

Garwood, Darrell. *American Shadow: The Real Case Against the CIA.* Stafford, Va.: Dan River Press, 1980, 247 p.

Gulley, Bill and **Reese, Mary Ellen.** *Breaking Cover.* New York: Simon and Schuster, 1980, 288 p.

Hinckle, Warren and **Turner, William W.** *The Fish is Red: The Story of the Secret War Against Castro.* New York: Harper and Row, 1981, 373 p.

James, Peter N. *The Air Force Mafia.* New Rochelle, N.Y.: Arlington House, 1975, 347 p.

Kelly, John. *CIA Penetration: U.S. Police Departments.* Paper delivered at the annual Political Science Association Convention, August 30, 1980, 18 p. (typescript).

McGarvey, Patrick J. *CIA: The Myth and the Madness.* New York: Saturday Review Press, 1972, 240 p.

Marchetti, Victor and **Marks, John D.** *The CIA and the Cult of Intelligence.* New York: Knopf, 1974, 398 p.

Phillips, David Atlee. "Old Boys Never Talk—Until Now." *Washingtonian*, October 1979, pp. 65–70.

Poelchau, Warner, ed. *White Paper White Wash: Interviews with Philip Agee on the CIA and El Salvador.* New York: Deep Cover Books, 1981, 101 p.

Prouty, Leroy Fletcher. *The Secret Team: The CIA and Its Allies in Control of the United States and the World.* Englewood Cliffs, N.J.: Prentice-Hall, 1973, 496 p.

Safire, William L. *Before the Fall: An Inside View of the Pre-Watergate White House.* New York: Ballantine Books, 1977, 910 p. (paperback).

Snepp, Frank. *Decent Interval: An Insider's Account of Saigon's Indecent End.* New York: Random House, 1977, 590 p.

Stockwell, John. *In Search of Enemies: A CIA Story.* New York: Norton, 1978, 285 p.

Tully, Andrew. *CIA, the Inside Story.* New York: Morrow, 1962, 276 p.

Western Goals Foundation. *Broken Seals. A Western Goals Foundation Report of the Attempts to Destroy the Foreign and Domestic Intelligence Capabilities of the United States.* Alexandria, Va.: Western Goals, 1980, 110 p. (paperback).

Wise, David and **Ross, Thomas B.** *The Invisible Government.* New York: Random House, 1964, 375 p.

SECOND PART

INTELLIGENCE RELATED TOPICS

I. ANTI-COMMUNIST AND OTHER EXTREMIST MOVEMENTS
General

Archer, Jules. *Treason in America: Disloyalty Versus Dissent.* New York: Hawthorn Books, 1971, 198 p.

Beals, Carleton, *Brass-Knuckle Crusade: The Great Know-Nothing Conspiracy, 1820–1860.* New York: Hastings House, 1960, 312 p.

Carlson, John Roy, *pseud.* (Derounian, Arthur). *The Plotters.* New York: Dutton, 1946, 408 p.

Caute, David. *The Great Fear: The Anti-Communist Purge Under Truman and Eisenhower.* New York: Simon and Schuster, 1978, 697 p.

Colwell, Wayne A. "Committee of Vigilance, San Francisco, 1856." *Military Collector and Historian,* v. XXV, no. 1 (Spring 1973), pp. 28–29.

Jensen, Joan M. *The Price of Vigilance.* New York: Rand McNally, 1968, 367 p.

Johnson, Paul. *Enemies of Society.* New York: Atheneum, 1977, 278 p.

Jones, J. Harry, Jr. *The Minutemen.* Garden City, N.Y.: Doubleday, 1968, 426 p. (revised edition published in 1969 under title: *A Private Army*).

Knauff, Ellen Raphael. *The Ellen Knauff Story.* New York: Norton, 1952, 242 p.

Latham, Earl. *The Communist Controversy in Washington: From the New Deal to McCarthy.* Cambridge: Harvard University Press, 1966, 446 p.

Lens, Sidney. *The Futile Crusade: Anti-Communism as American Credo.* Chicago: Quadrangle Books, 1964, 256 p.

McWilliams, Carey. *A Mask for Privilege: Anti-Semitism in America.* Boston: Little, Brown, 1948, 299 p.

Murray, Robert K. *Red Scare: A Study of National Hysteria, 1919 1920.* Minneapolis: University of Minnesota Press, 1955, 337 p.

O'Sullivan, Frank Dalton. *The Poison Pen of Jersey.* Chicago: The O'Sullivan Publishing House, 1936, 301 p.

Rader, Melvin Miller. *False Witness.* Seattle: University of Washington Press, 1979, 209 p. (paperback).

Schappes, Morris Urman, ed. *A Documentary History of the Jews in the United States, 1654–1875.* New York: Schocken Books, 1971, 766 p. (paperback).

Strong, Donald Stuart. *Organized Anti-Semitism in America: The Rise of Group Prejudice During the Decade 1930–40.* Washington: American Council on Public Affairs, 1941, 191 p.

Wechsler, James Arthur. *The Age of Suspicion.* New York: Random House, 1953, 333 p. (autobiographical).

John Birch Society

Broyles, J. Allen. *The John Birch Society: Anatomy of a Protest.* Boston: Beacon Press, 1964, 169 p.

Epstein, Benjamin R. and **Forster, Arnold.** *The Radical Right: Report on the John Birch Society and its Allies.* New York: Random House, 1967, 239 p.

Grove, Gene. *Inside the John Birch Society.* Greenwich, Conn.: Fawcett Publications, 1961, 160 p.

John Birch Society. *Blue Book.* Belmont, Mass.: Western Islands Publishers, 176 p.

Schomp, Gerald. *Birchism Was My Business.* New York: Macmillan, 1970, 189 p.

Welch, Robert Henry Winborne. *The Politician.* Belmont, Mass.: n.p., 1963, 140 p.

Ku Klux Klan

Haas, Ben. *KKK.* Evanston, Ill.: Regency Books, 1963, 158 p.

Jackson, Kenneth T. *The Ku Klux Klan in the City, 1915–1930.* New York: Oxford University Press, 1967, 326 p.

Schappes, Morris Urman, ed. *A Documentary History of the Jews in the United States, 1654–1875.* New York: Schocken Books, 1971, 766 p. (paperback).

Sims, Patsy. *The Klan.* New York: Stein and Day, 1978, 355 p.

McCarthy and McCarthyism
General

Anderson, Jack and **Boyd, James.** *Confessions of a Muckraker: The Inside Story of Life in Washington During the Truman, Eisenhower, Kennedy and Johnson Years.* New York: Random House, 1979, 354 p.

Anderson, Jack and **May, Ronald W.** *McCarthy: The Man, the Senator, the "ism."* Boston: Beacon Press, 1952, 431 p.

Buckley, William Frank and **Bozell, L. Brent.** *McCarthy and his Enemies: The Record and its Meaning.* Chicago: Regnery, 1954, 413 p.

Cogley, John. *Report on Blacklisting.* New York: Fund for the Republic, 1956, 2 v. (paperback).

Feuerlicht, Roberta Strauss. *Joe McCarthy and McCarthyism: The Hate That Haunts America.* New York: McGraw-Hill, 1972, 160 p.

Foster, Jane. *An Unamerican Lady.* London: Sidgwick and Jackson, 1980, 253 p.

Fried, Richard M. *Men Against McCarthy.* New York: Columbia University Press, 1976, 428 p.

Matusow, Harvey Marshall. *False Witness.* New York: Cameron and Kahn, 1955, 255 p.

Pearson, Drew. *Diaries, 1949–1969.* Edited by Tyler Abell. New York: Holt, Rinehart and Winston, 1974, 592 p.

Rees, David. *Harry Dexter White: A Study in Paradox.* New York: Coward, McCann and Geoghegan, 1973, 506 p.

Rovere, Richard Halworth. *Senator Joe McCarthy.* New York: Harcourt, Brace, 1959, 280 p.

Rovere, Richard Halworth. *Senator Joe McCarthy.* New York: Harper and Row, 1973, 280 p.

Case Studies: Owen Lattimore and J. Robert Oppenheimer

Chevalier, Haakon Maurice. *Oppenheimer: The Story of a Friendship.* New York: G. Braziller, 1965, 219 p.

Curtis, Charles Pelham. *The Oppenheimer Case: The Trial of a Security System.* New York: Simon and Schuster, 1955, 281 p.

Flynn, John Thomas. *The Lattimore Story.* New York: Devin-Adair, 1953, 118 p. (paperback).

Goodchild, Peter. *J. Robert Oppenheimer: Shatterer of Worlds.* London: British Broadcasting Corp., 1980, 301 p.

Kipphardt, Heinar. *In the Matter of J. Robert Oppenheimer: A Play Freely Adapted on the Basis of the Documents.* Translated by Ruth Spiers. New York: Hill and Wang, 1968, 127 p. (paperback).

Lattimore, Owen. *Ordeal by Slander.* Boston: Little, Brown, 1950, 236 p.

Major, John. *The Oppenheimer Hearing.* New York: Stein and Day, 1971, 336 p.

Stern, Philip M. with **Green, Harold P.** *The Oppenheimer Case: Security on Trial.* New York: Harper and Row, 1969, 591 p.

Stern, Philip M. with **Green, Harold P.** *The Oppenheimer Case: Security on Trial.* London: Hart-Davis, 1971, 591 p.

U.S. Atomic Energy Commission. *In the Matter of J. Robert Oppenheimer: Transcript of Hearing Before Personnel Security Board, Washington, D.C., April 12, 1954, through May 6, 1954.* Washington: U.S. GPO, 1954, 992 p.

Wilson, Thomas Williams, Jr. *The Great Weapons Heresy.* Boston: Houghton Mifflin, 1970, 275 p. (J. Robert Oppenheimer).

Hearings

U.S. Congress, Senate, Committee on Government Operations. *Army Personnel Actions Relating to Irving Peress. Hearings Before the Permanent Subcommittee on Investigations of the Committee on Government Operations.* 84th Congress, 1st session. Washington: U.S. GPO, 1955, 7 pts. (Hearings held March 15-31, 1955).

U.S. Congress, Senate, Committee on Government Operations. *Army Signal Corps—Subversion and Espionage. Hearings Before the Permanent Subcommittee on Investigations of the Committee on Government Operations . . . Pursuant to S. Res. 40.* 83d Congress, 1st session; 84th Congress, 1st session. Washington: U.S. GPO, 1954, pts. 1-7. (Hearings held October 22, 1953-March 11, 1954).

U.S. Congress, Senate, Committee on Government Operations. *Army Signal Corps—Subversion and Espionage. Report of the Committee on Government Operations made by its Permanent Subcommittee on Investigations.* 84th Congress, 1st session. Washington: U.S. GPO, 1955, 33 p. (Report no. 230).

U.S. Congress, Senate, Committee on Government Operations. *Austrian Incident. Hearings Before the Permanent Subcommittee on Investigations of the Committee on Government Operations . . . Pursuant to S. Res. 40, a Resolution Authorizing the Committee on Government Operations to Employ Additional Personnel and Increasing the Limit of Expenditures.* May 29, June 5 and 8, 1953. 83d Congress, 1st session. Washington: U.S. GPO, 1953, 75 p.

U.S. Congress, Senate, Committee on Government Operations. *Communist Infiltration in the Army. Hearing Before the Permanent Subcommittee on Investigations of the Committee on Government Operations . . . Pursuant to S. Res. 40.* 83d Congress, 1st-2d session. Washington: U.S. GPO, 1953–1954, 4 pts. (Hearings held September 28, 1953—November 15, 1954).

U.S. Congress, Senate, Committee on Government Operations. *Special Senate Investigation on Charges and Countercharges Involving: Secretary of the Army Robert T. Stevens, John G. Adams, H. Struve Hensel and Senator Joe McCarthy, Roy M. Cohn, and Francis P. Carr. Hearings Before the Special Subcommittee on Investigations of the Committee on Government Operations . . . Pursuant to S. Res. 189.* 83d Congress, 2d session. Washington: U.S. GPO, 1954, pts. 27–61, 63–71. (Hearings held March 16-June 17, 1954).

U.S. Congress, Senate, Committee on Government Operations. *State Department—File Survey. Hearings Before the Subcommittee on Investigations of the Committee on Government Operations . . . Pursuant to S. Res. 40, A Resolution Authorizing the Committee on Government Operations to Employ Temporary Additional Personnel and Increasing the Limit of Expenditures.* 83d Congress, 1st session. Washington: U.S. GPO, 1953, 2 pts.

U.S. Congress, Senate, Committee on Government Operations. *State Department, File Survey: Interim Report of the Committee on Government Operations made by its Senate Permanent Subcommittee on Investigations Pursuant to S. Res. 40.* 83d Congress, 1st session. Washington: U.S. GPO, 1953, 19 p.

U.S. Congress, Senate, Committee on Government Operations. *State Department Information Program; Information Centers. Hearings of the Committee on Government Operations made by its Senate Permanent Subcommittee on Investigations pursuant to S. Res. 40.* 83d Congress, 2d session. Washington: U.S. GPO, 1953, pts. 1-4, 7-8.

U.S. Congress, Senate, Committee on Government Operations. *State Department Information Program— Voice of America. Hearings Before the Permanent Subcommittee on Investigations of the Committee on Government Operations . . . Pursuant to S. Res. 40, a Resolution Authorizing the Committee on Government Operations to Employ Temporary Additional Personnel and Increasing the Limit of Expenditures.* 83d Congress, 1st session. Washington: U.S. GPO, 1953, pts. 1-8.

U.S. Congress, Senate, Committee on Government Operations. *Subversion and Espionage in Defense Establishments and Industry. Hearings Before the Permanent Subcommittee on Investigations of the Committee on Government Operations . . . Pursuant to S. Res. 40.* 83d Congress, 1st session; 84th Congress, 1st session. Washington. U.S. GPO, 1954-1955, 8 pts.

U.S. Congress, Senate, Committee on Government Operations. *Subversion and Espionage in Defense Establishments and Industry. Report of the Committee on Government Operations, Made by its Senate Permanent Subcommittee on Investigations pursuant to S. Res. 189.* 84th Congress, 1st session. Washington: U.S. GPO, 1955, 15 p.

U.S. Congress, Senate, Committee on Government Operations. *Voice of America. Report of the Committee on Government Operations Made by its Senate Permanent Subcommittee on Investigations, Pursuant to S. Res. 40.* 83d Congress, 2d session. Washington: U.S. GPO, 1954, 14 p.

U.S. Congress, Senate, Committee on Government Operations. *Waste and Mismanagement in Voice of America Engineering Projects: Report of the Committee on Government Operations Made by its Senate Permanent Subcommittee on Investigations Pursuant to S. Res. 40.* 83d Congress, 2d session. Washington: U.S. GPO, 1954, 11 p..

U.S. Congress, Senate, Committee on the Judiciary. *Institute of Pacific Relations. Hearings Before the Subcommittee to Investigate the Administration of the Internal Security Act and Other Internal Security*

Laws of the Committee on the Judiciary. 82d Congress, 1st–2d sessions. Washington: U.S. GPO, 1952, pt. 14, May 2 and June 20, 1952.

U.S. Congress, Senate, Committee on the Judiciary. *Interlocking Subversion in Government Departments: The Harry Dexter White Papers. Hearing Before the Subcommittee to Investigate the Administration of the Internal Security Act and Other Internal Security Laws of the Committee on the Judiciary.* 84th Congress, 1st session. Washington: U.S. GPO, August 30, 1955, pt. 30, p. 2415–2860.

U.S. Congress, Senate, Committee on Rules and Administration. *Investigation of Senator Joseph R. McCarthy. Hearings Before the Subcommittee on Privileges and Elections of the Committee on Rules and Administration on S. Res. 187, a Resolution to Investigate Senator Joseph R. McCarthy to Determine Whether Expulsion Proceedings Should be Instituted Against Him.* 82d Congress, 1st and 2d sessions. Washington: U.S. GPO, 1952, pt. 1, 320 p.

U.S. Congress, Senate, Committee on Rules and Administration. *Maryland Senatorial Election of 1950; Report of the Subcommittee on Privileges and Elections to the Committee on Rules and Administration ... Pursuant to S. Res. 250, 81st Congress, 2d session, Relative to the Duties Imposed Upon the Committee by Subsection (0) (1) (D) of Rule XXV of the Standing Rules of the Senate on Senatorial Campaign Expenditures.* 82d Congress, 1st session. Washington: U.S. GPO, 1951, 39 p.

U.S. Congress, Senate, Select Committee to Study Censure Charges. *Report of the Select Committee to Study Censure Charges ... Pursuant to the Order on S. Res. 301 and Amendments, a Resolution to Censure the Senator from Wisconsin, Mr. McCarthy.* 83d Congress, 2d session. Washington: U.S. GPO, 1954, 68 p.

II. ASSASSINATIONS
General

Agirre, Julen. *Operation Ogro: The Execution of Admiral Luis Carrero Blanco.* Translated from the Spanish by Barbara Probst Solomon. New York: Quadrangle, 1975, 196 p.

Avner, *pseud.* (Gruszow, Avner). *Memoirs of An Assassin.* Translated from the French by Burgo Partridge. New York: Pyramid Books, 1960, 160 p. (paperback).

Bell, J. Bowyer. *Assassin!* New York: St. Martin's Press, 1979, 310 p.

Bornstein, Joseph. *The Politics of Murder.* New York: Sloane, 1950, 295 p.

Camellion, Richard. *Assassination: Theory and Practice.* Boulder, Colo.: Paladin Press, 1977, 161 p.

Démaret, Pierre and **Plume, Christian.** *Target de Gaulle: The True Story of the 31 Attempts on the Life of the French President.* Translated from the French by Richard Barry. New York: Dial Press, 1975, 293 p.

Dinges, John and **Landau, Saul.** *Assassination on Embassy Row.* New York: Pantheon Books, 1980, 411 p. (Orlando Letelier).

Donoghue, Mary Agnes. *Assassination: Murder in Politics.* Canoga Park, Calif.: Major Books, 1975, 192 p.

Donovan, Robert J. *The Assassins.* New York: Harper, 1955, 300 p.

Franzius, Enno. *History of the Order of Assassins.* New York: Funk and Wagnalls, 1969, 261 p.

Freed, Donald and **Landis, Fred Simon.** *Death in Washington: The Murder of Orlando Letelier.* Westport, Conn.: Lawrence Hill, 1980, 254 p.

Garrett, Jane. *The Triumphs of Providence: The Assassination Plot, 1696.* Cambridge, Eng.: Cambridge University Press, 1980, 289 p.

Gribble, Leonard Reginald. *Hands of Terror: Notable Assassinations of the Twentieth Century.* London: F. Muller, 1960, 228 p.

Hirsch, Phil, ed. *The Death Dealers: Stories.* New York: Pyramid Books, 1960, 192 p.

Johnson, Francis. *Famous Assassinations of History from Philip of Macedon, 336 B.C. to Alexander of Serbia, A.D. 1903.* Chicago: A.C. McClurg, 1903, 434 p.

Leek, Sybil and **Sugar, Bert R.** *The Assassination Chain.* New York: Corwin Books, 1976, 342 p.

Levine, Isaac Don. *The Mind of an Assassin.* New York: New American Library of World Literature, 1960, 190 p. (paperback).

McConnell, Brian. *The History of Assassination.* Nashville: Aurora Publishers, 1970, 359 p.

Paine, Lauran. *The Assassins' World.* New York: Taplinger, 1975, 208 p.

Slattery, T.P. *The Assassination of D'Arcy McGee.* Garden City, N.Y.: Doubleday, 1968, 527 p.

Solar, Edmundo del. *Orlando Letelier: Biographical Notes and Comments.* Translated into English from Spanish by Caridad Inda and Maria del Solar. New York: Vantage Press, 1978, 90 p.

Turner, William W. and **Christian, John G.** *The Assassination of Robert F. Kennedy: A Searching Look at the Conspiracy and the Cover-Up, 1968-1978.* New York: Random House, 1978, 397 p.

Wood, Clement. *The Man Who Killed Kitchener: The Life of Fritz Joubert Duquesne, 1879-.* New York: W. Faro, 1932, 429 p.

John F. Kennedy

Anson, Robert Sam. *"They've Killed the President!" The Search for the Murderers of John F. Kennedy.* New York: Bantam Books, 1975, 408 p. (paperback).

The Assassinations: Dallas and Beyond. A Guide to the Cover-Ups and Investigations. Edited by Peter Dale Scott, Paul L. Hoch *et al.* New York: Vintage Books, 1976, 552 p. (paperback).

Blakey, George Robert and **Billings, Richard N.** *The Plot to Kill the President.* New York: Times Books, 1981, 428 p.

Buchanan, Thomas G. *Who Killed Kennedy?* London: Secker and Warburg, 1964, 192 p.

Buggé, Brian K. *The Mystique of Conspiracy: Oswald, Castro, and the CIA.* Staten Island, N.Y.: Buggé, 1978, 135 p.

Canfield, Michael and **Weberman, Alan J.** *Coup d'état in America: The CIA and the Assassination of John F. Kennedy.* New York: Third Press, 1975, 314 p.

Committee to Investigate Assassinations. *Coincidence or Conspiracy by Bernard Fensterwald, Jr.* New York: Kensington Publishing Corp., 1977, 592 p. (paperback).

Crawford, Curtis; Kempton, Murray et al. *Critical Reactions to the Warren Report.* New York: Marzani and Munsell, 1964, 65 p.

Eddowes, Michael. *The Oswald File.* New York: C.N. Potter, 1977, 240 p.

Epstein, Edward Jay. *Counterplot.* New York: Viking Press, 1969, 182 p.

Epstein, Edward Jay. *Legend: The Secret World of Lee Harvey Oswald.* New York: McGraw-Hill, 1978, 382 p.

Ford, Gerald R. and **Stiles, John R.** *Portrait of the Assassin.* New York: Ballantine Books, 1966, 560 p. (paperback).

Fox, Sylvan. *The Unanswered Questions About President Kennedy's Assassination.* New York: Award Books, 1975, 237 p. (paperback).

Garrison, Jim. *A Heritage of Stone.* New York: Berkley Pub., 1975, 224 p. (paperback).

Hepburn, James. *Verschwörung: Die Hintergründe des politischen Mords in den USA.* Düsseldorf—Vienna: Econ Verlag, 1968, 383 p.

Joesten, Joachim. *Oswald: Assassin or Fall Guy?* New York: Marzani and Munsell, 1964, 158 p.

Kantor, Seth. *The Ruby Cover-Up.* New York: Kensington Pub., 1978, 450 p. (paperback edition of *Who Was Jack Ruby?*).

Kantor, Seth. *Who Was Jack Ruby?* New York: Everest House, 1978, 242 p.

Lane, Mark. *Rush to Judgment: A Critique of the Warren Commission's Inquiry into the Murders of President John F. Kennedy, Officer J.D. Tippit, and Lee Harvey Oswald.* Greenwich, Conn.: Fawcett Publications, 1967, 396 p.

Lewis, Richard Warren. *The Scavengers and Critics of the Warren Report: The Endless Paradox. Based on an Investigation by Lawrence Schiller.* New York: Dell, 1967, 219 p. (paperback).

Lifton, David S. *Best Evidence: Disguise and Deception in the Assassination of John F. Kennedy.* New York: Macmillan, 1980, 747 p.

McDonald, Hugh C. *Appointment in Dallas: The Final Solution to the Assassination of JFK, as told to Geoffrey Bocca.* New York: H. McDonald, 1975, 211 p.

McDonald, Hugh C. and **Moore, Robin.** *L.B.J. and the J.F.K. Conspiracy.* Westport, Conn.: CONDOR, 1979, 242 p. (paperback).

McMillan, Priscilla Johnson. *Marina and Lee.* New York: Harper and Row, 1977, 527 p.

Meagher, Sylvia. *Accessories After the Fact: The Warren Commission, the Authorities, and the Report.* New York: Random House, 1976, 477 p. (paperback).

Miller, Tom. *The Assassination Please Almanac.* Chicago: Regnery, 1977, 284 p. (paperback).

Morrow, Robert D. *Betrayal.* Chicago: Regnery, 1976, 229 p.

Oglesby, Carl. *The Yankee and Cowboy War: Conspiracies from Dallas to Watergate.* Mission, Kan.: Sheed Andrews and McMeel, 1977, 372 p.

O'Toole, George. *The Assassination Tapes. An Electronic Probe into the Murder of John F. Kennedy and the Dallas Coverup.* New York: Penthouse Press, 1975, 265 p.

Roberts, Charles. *The Truth About the Assassination.* New York: Grosset and Dunlap, 1967, 128 p.

Roffman, Howard. *Presumed Guilty.* South Brunswick, N.J.: Barnes, 1976, 299 p.

Summers, Anthony. *Conspiracy.* New York: McGraw-Hill, 1980, 640 p.

U.S. Congress, House, Select Committee on Assassinations. *Final Assassination Report.* New York: Bantam Books, 1979, 792 p. (paperback).

U.S. Congress, Senate, Select Committee to Study Governmental Operations with Respect to Intelligence Activities. *Final Report ... Book V. The Investigation of the Assassination of President John F, Kennedy: Performance of the Intelligence Agencies,* April 23, 1976. 94th Congress, 2d session. Washington: U.S. GPO, 1976, 106 p.

U.S. Warren Commission. *Report on the Warren Commission on the Assassination of President Kennedy.* New York: Bantam Books, 1964, 726 p. (paperback).

Warren, Earl. *The Memoirs of Earl Warren.* Garden City, N.Y.: Doubleday, 1977, 394 p.

Weisberg, Harold. *Oswald in New Orleans: Case of Conspiracy with the C.I.A.* New York: Canyon Books, 1967, 404 p. (paperback).

Weisberg, Harold. *Whitewash: The Report on the Warren Report.* New York: Dell Publishing, 1966, 368 p. (paperback).

Weisberg, Harold. *Whitewash II: The FBI Secret Service Cover-up.* Hyattstown, Md.: n.p. 1966, 250 p.

Weisberg, Harold. *Whitewash IV: Top Secret JFK Assassination Transcript with a Legal Analysis by Jim Lesar.* Frederick, Md.: Weisberg, 1974, 224 p.

Martin Luther King, Jr.

Lane, Mark and **Gregory, Dick.** *Code Name "Zorro": The Murder of Martin Luther King, Jr.* Englewood Cliffs, N.J.: Prentice-Hall, 1977, 314 p.

Lane, Mark and **Gregory, Dick.** *Code Name "Zorro": The Murder of Martin Luther King, Jr.* New York: Pocketbooks, 1978, 408 p. (paperback).

U.S., Congress, House, Select Committee on Assassinations. *The Final Assassination Report.* New York: Bantam Books, 1979, 792 p. (paperback).

Abraham Lincoln

Balsiger, Dave and **Sellier, Charles E., Jr.** *The Lincoln Conspiracy.* Los Angeles, Calif.: Schick Sunn Classic Books, 1977, 320 p. (paperback).

Carter, Samuel. *The Riddle of Dr. Mudd.* New York: Putnam, 1974, 380 p.

Garrett, Richard B. "End of a Manhunt." *American Heritage,* v. XVII, no. 4 (June 1966), p. 40.

Roscoe, Theodore. *The Web of Conspiracy: The Complete Story of the Men Who Murdered Abraham Lincoln.* Englewood Cliffs, N.J.: Prentice-Hall, 1959, 562 p.

Stern, Philip Van Doren. *The Man Who Killed Lincoln: The Story of John Wilkes Booth and His Part in the Assassination.* New York: Random House, 1939, 376 p.

Weichmann, Louis J. *A True History of the Assassination of Abraham Lincoln and of the Conspiracy of 1865.* New York: Knopf, 1975, 492 p.

Leon Trotsky

Fourth International. *How the GPU Murdered Trotsky.* London: The Committee, 1976, 104 p.

Fourth International. *Trotsky's Assassin at Large.* London: New Park Publications, 1977, 40 p.

Payne, Pierre Stephen Robert. *The Life and Death of Trotsky.* New York: McGraw-Hill, 1977, 498 p.

Serge, Victor and **Trotsky, Natalia Sedova.** *The Life and Death of Leon Trotsky.* Translated by Arnold J. Pomerans. New York: Basic Books, 1975, 296 p.

III. CENSORSHIP

Allard, Paul. *Les dessous de la guerre révélés par les comités secrets.* Paris: Les Editions de France, 1932, 238 p. (paperback).

Brownrigg, Douglas Egremont Robert, Sir. *Indiscretions of the Naval Censor.* London: Cassell, 1920, 279 p.

Calvocoressi, Peter with **Bristow, Ann.** *Freedom to Publish: A Report on Obstacles to Freedom in Publishing, Prepared for the Congress of the International Publishers Association,* Stockholm, May 1980. Stockholm: Almqvist and Wiksell International, 1980, 106 p. (paperback).

Graham-Yooll, Andrew. *The Press in Argentina, 1973–1978.* London: Writers and Scholars Educational Trust, May 1979, 171 p. (typescript).

Heise, Juergen Arthur. *Minimum Disclosure: How the Pentagon Manipulates the News.* New York: Norton, 1979, 221 p.

Herrmann, Elisabeth M. *Zur Theorie und Praxis der Presse in der Sowjetischen Besatzungszone Deutschlands. Berichte und Dokumente.* Berlin: Colloquium Verlag, 1963, 158 p.

Koop, Theodore Frederic. *Weapon of Silence.* Chicago: University of Chicago Press, 1946, 304 p.

Laqueur, Walter Ze'ev. *The Terrible Secret: An Investigation into the Suppression of Information About Hitler's 'Final Solution.'* London: Weidenfeld and Nicolson, 1980, 262 p.

Lendvai, Paul. *The Bureaucracy of Truth: How Communist Governments Manage the News.* London: Burnett Books, 1981, 285 p.

Mayr, Josef Karl. *Metternichs geheimer Briefdienst: Postlogen und Postkurse.* Vienna: Verlag Adolf Hulzhausens, 1935. 131 p.

Medvedev. Zhores Aleksandrovich. *The Medvedev Papers: Fruitful Meetings Between Scientists of the World; and, Secrecy of Correspondence Is Guaranteed by Law.* Translated from the Russian by Vera Rich. London: Macmillan, 1971, 471 p.

Mitchell, Richard H. *Thought Control in Prewar Japan.* Ithaca, N.Y.: Cornell University Press, 1976, 226 p.

Mock, James Robert. *Censorship, 1917.* Princeton, N.J.: Princeton University Press, 1941, 250 p.

Newton, V.M., Jr. "The Iron Curtain in America." *Look,* February 18, 1958, pp. 113-116.

Seldes, George. *You Can't Print That! The Truth Behind the News, 1918-1928.* New York: Payson and Clarke, 1929, 465 p.

U.S. War Department. *Military Intelligence: Military Censorship.* Washington: U.S. GPO, September 15, 1944, 73 p. (FM30-28).

Vladimirov, Leonid. *The Russian Space Bluff.* Translated from Russian by David Floyd. London: Tom Stacey, 1971, 192 p.

Young, Eugene Jared. *Looking Behind the Censorships.* Philadelphia: Lippincott, 1938, 368 p.

IV. CRIME AND CORRUPTION
General

Berdin, Richard. *Code Name Richard.* Translated and edited by Jeannette and Richard Seaver. New York: Dutton, 1974, 309 p.

Chapman, Edward Arnold. *Free Agent: Being the Further Adventures of Eddie Chapman.* London: Wingate, 1955, 223 p.

Du Plessis, J.H. *Diamonds are Dangerous: The Adventures of an Agent of the International Diamond Security Organization.* New York: John Day, 1961, 250 p.

Fleming, Ian. *The Diamond Smugglers.* New York: Collier Books, 1957, 124 p. (paperback).

Hirsch, Richard. *Crimes that Shook the World.* New York: Duell, Sloan and Pearce, 1949, 224 p.

Kalimtgis, Konstandinos; Goldman, David et al. *Dope, Inc.: Britain's Opium War Againt the U.S.* New York: New Benjamin Franklin House, 1978, 406 p. (paperback).

Lamour, Catherine and **Lamberti, Michel R.** *The Second Opium War.* Translated by Peter and Betty Ross. London: Penguin Books, 1974, 278 p.

Proal, Louis Joseph Cyrille. *Political Crime.* New York: D. Appleton, 1898, 355 p.

Sillitoe, Percy, Sir. *Cloak Without Dagger.* 2d ed. London: Cassell, 1955, 206 p. (autobiography).

Whittemore, L.H. *Peroff: The Man Who Knew Too Much.* New York: Morrow, 1975, 315 p.

Asia

Bresler, Fenton S. *The Chinese Mafia.* New York: Stein and Day, 1980, 227 p.

Candlin, A.H. Stanton. *Psycho-chemical Warfare: The Chinese Communist Drug Offensive Against the West.* New Rochelle, N.Y.: Arlington House, 1974, 540 p.

Hamburger, Gerd, pseud. (Schermann, Rudolf). *The Peking Bomb: The Psychochemical War Against America.* Translated by Sarah Banks Forman. Washington: R.B. Luce, 1975, 256 p.

McCoy, Alfred W. with **Read, Cathleen B.** et al. *The Politics of Heroin in Southeast Asia.* New York: Harper and Row, 1972, 464 p.

Europe

Brokhin, Yuri. *Hustling on Gorky Street: Sex and Crime in Russia Today.* Translated from the Russian by E.B. Kane and Yuri Brokhin. New York: Dial Press, 1975, 203 p.

Ducloux, Louis. *From Blackmail to Treason: Political Crime and Corruption in France, 1920-1940.* Translated by Ronald Matthews. London: A. Deutsch, 1958, 240 p.

Grombach, John V. *The Great Liquidator.* Garden City, N.Y.: Doubleday, 1980, 408 p.

The Man Who Plays Alone. Translated from the Italian by Antonia Cowan. New York: Pantheon Books, 1969, 367 p.

Pinnock, Geoffrey. *Dark Paths: The Story of Modern Contraband Running in Europe.* London: Nicholson and Watson, 1938, 263 p.

Sturt-Penrose, Barrie and **Courtiour, Roger.** *The Pencourt File.* New York: Harper and Row, 1978, 423 p.

Trevor-Roper, Hugh Redwald. *Hermit of Peking: The Hidden Life of Sir Edmund Backhouse.* New York: Knopf, 1977, 316 p.

United States
General

Baker, Robert Gene with **King, Larry L.** *Wheeling and Dealing: Confessions of a Capitol Hill Operator.* New York: Norton, 1978, 296 p.

Boettcher, Robert B. and **Freedman, Gordon L.** *Gifts of Deceit: Sun Myung Moon, Tongsun Park, and the Korean Scandal.* New York: Holt, Rinehart and Winston, 1980, 402 p.

Daley, Robert. *Prince of the City: The True Story of a Cop who Knew too Much.* Boston: Houghton Mifflin, 1978, 311 p. (Robert Leuci).

Davidson, William. *Collura: Actor with a Gun.* New York: Simon and Schuster, 1977, 221 p.

Dewey, Thomas Edmund. *Twenty Against the Underworld.* Edited by Rodney Campbell. Garden City, N.Y.: Doubleday, 1974, 504 p.

Eisenberg, Dennis; Dan, Uri et al. *Meyer Lansky: Mogul of the Mob.* New York: Paddington Press, 1979, 346 p.

Epstein, Edward Jay. *Agency of Fear: Opiates and Political Power in America.* New York: Putnam, 1977, 352 p.

Jacobs, Donald Harry. *A Scientist and his Experiences with Corruption and Treason in the U.S. Military-Industrial Establishment.* Victoria, British Columbia: Jacobs Instrument Co., 1969, 649 p.

Rosenberg, Philip and **Grosso, Sonny.** *Point Blank.* New York: Grosset and Dunlap, 1978, 315 p. (fiction).

Rosenberg, Philip. *The Spivey Assignment: A Double Agent's Infiltration of the Drug Smuggling Conspiracy.* New York: Holt, Rinehart and Winston, 1979, 313 p.

Selmier, Dean and **Kram, Mark.** *Blow Away.* New York: Viking Press, 1979, 273 p.

Vizzini, Sal with **Fraley, Oscar** et al. *Vizzini: The Secret Lives of America's Most Successful Undercover Agent.* New York: Arbor House, 1972, 330 p.

Waller, Leslie. *Hide in Plain Sight: The True Story of How the United States Government and Organized Crime Kept a Man from his own Children.* New York: Delacorte Press, 1976, 275 p.

Watergate Affair

"American Character: Trial and Triumph." *Harper's,* October 1974, pp. 39–76.

Bergier, Jacques. *L'espionnage politique.* Paris: A. Michel, 1973, 231 p.

Dash, Samuel. *Chief Counsel: Inside the Ervin Committee—the Untold Story of Watergate.* New York: Random House, 1976, 275 p.

Dean, John Wesley. *Blind Ambition: The White House Years.* New York: Simon and Schuster, 1976, 415 p.

Fields, Howard. *High Crimes and Misdemeanors: "Wherefore Richard M. Nixon ... Warrants Impeachment." The Dramatic Story of the Rodino Committee.* New York: Norton, 1978, 330 p.

Frost, David. *"I Gave Them a Sword". Behind the Scenes of the Nixon Interviews.* New York: Morrow, 1978, 320 p.

Haldeman, Harry R. and **DiMona, Joseph.** *The Ends of Power.* New York: Quadrangle, 1978, 326 p.

Higgins, George V. *The Friends of Richard Nixon.* Boston: Little, Brown, 1975, 295 p.

Hunt, Howard. *Undercover: Memoirs of an American Secret Agent.* New York: Berkley Pub., 1974, 338 p.

Klein, Herbert G. *Making it Perfectly Clear.* Garden City, N.Y.: Doubleday, 1980, 464 p.

Kurland, Philip B. *Watergate and the Constitution.* Chicago: University of Chicago Press, 1978, 261 p.

Lasky, Victor. *It Didn't Start with Watergate.* New York: Dial Press, 1977, 438 p.

Liddy, G. Gordon. *Will: The Autobiography of G. Gordon Liddy.* New York: St. Martin's Press, 1980, 374 p.

McCord, James W. *A Piece of Tape: The Watergate Story, Fact and Fiction.* Rockville, Md.: Washington Media Services, 1974, 329 p.

Mankiewicz, Frank. *Perfectly Clear: Nixon From Whittier to Watergate.* New York: Quadrangle, 1973, 239 p.

Mollenhoff, Clark R. *Game Plan for Disaster: An Ombudsman's Report on The Nixon Years.* New York: Norton, 1976, 384 p.

Oglesby, Carl. *The Yankee and Cowboy War: Conspiracies from Dallas to Watergate.* Mission, Kan.: Sheed Andrews and McMeel, 1977, 372 p.

Schell, Jonathan. *The Time of Illusion.* New York: Knopf, 1976, 392 p.

Sirica, John J. *To Set the Record Straight: The Break-in, the Tapes, the Conspirators, the Pardon.* New York: Norton, 1979, 394 p.

Stans, Maurice H. *The Terrors of Justice: The Untold Side of Watergate.* New York: Everest House, 1978, 478 p.

Szulc, Tad. *Compulsive Spy: The Strange Career of E. Howard Hunt.* New York: Viking Press, 1974, 180 p.

Tretick, Stanley and **Shannon, William V.** *They Could not Trust the King: Nixon, Watergate, and the American People.* New York: Macmillan, 1974, 197 p.

U.S. Congress, House, Committee on Armed Services, Special Subcommittee on Intelligence. *Inquiry into the Alleged Involvement of the Central Intelligence Agency in the Watergate and Ellsberg Matters.* Report, 93d Congress, 1st session. October 23, 1973. Washington, U.S. GPO, 1973, 23 p.

White, Theodore Harold. *Breach of Faith: The Fall of Richard Nixon.* New York: Atheneum Publishers, 1975, 373 p.

110

V. ESCAPE AND EVASION
General

Barron, John. *MiG Pilot: The Final Escape of Lieutenant Belenko.* New York: Reader's Digest Press, 1980, 224 p. (Viktor Belenko).

Boleslavski, Richard and **Woodward, Helen.** *Way of the Lancer.* Indianapolis: Bobbs-Merrill, 1932, 316 p.

Brook-Shepherd, Gordon. *The Storm Petrels: The Flight of the First Soviet Defectors.* New York: Harcourt, Brace, Jovanovich, 1978, 241 p.

Campbell-Shaw, Donald. *Pimpernel in Prague.* London: Odhams Press, 1959, 192 p.

Cecilia, *Sister. The Deliverance of Sister Cecilia, as told to William Brinkley.* New York: Farrar, Strauss and Young, 1954, 360 p.

Churchill, Randolph Spencer. *The Young Churchill.* New York: Lancer Books, 335 p. (a shortened version of *Winston S. Churchill. Volume 1: Youth, 1874-1900) (paperback).*

Davenport, Basil, *ed. Great Escapes.* New York: Sloane, 1952, 409 p.

Deacon, Richard, *pseud.* (McCormick, Donald). *Escape!* London: British Broadcasting Corp., 1980, 192 p. (including Kim Philby, Alfred Hinds, Donald Woods).

Dengler, Dieter. *Escape from Laos:* San Rafael, Calif.: Presidio Press, 1979, 211 p.

Durnford, Hugh George Edmund. *The Tunnellers of Holzminden.* Cambridge: The University Press, 1930, 199 p.

Foote, Morris C. "Narrative of an Escape from a Rebel Prison Camp." *American Heritage,* v. XI, no. 4 (June 1960), pp. 65-75.

Gazit, Shlomo. "Risk, Glory, and the Rescue Operation." *International Security,* v. 6, no. 1 (Summer 1981), pp. 111-135.

Hewson, Maurice. *Escape from the French: Captain Hewson's Narrative, 1803-1809.* Edited by Antony Brett-James. Exeter, Devon, England: Webb and Bower, 1981, 192 p.

Hirsch, Phil, *ed. Through Enemy Lines.* New York: Pyramid Books, 1967, 173 p. (paperback).

Kasenkina, Oksana Stepanovna. *Leap to Freedom.* Philadelphia: Lippincott, 1949, 295 p.

Kennedy, John de Navarre. *In the Shadow of the Cheka.* New York: Macaulay, 1935, 320 p.

Kilbourne, Jimmy W. *Escape and Evasion: 17 Stories of Downed Pilots Who Made it Back.* New York: Macmillan, 1973, 165 p.

Larsen, Egon. *A Flame in Barbed Wire: The Story of Amnesty International.* New York: Norton, 1979, 152 p.

McSwigan, Marie. *All Aboard for Freedom!* New York: Dutton, 1954, 249 p.

O'Brien, Pat. *Outwitting the Hun: My Escape from a German Prison Camp.* New York: Harper and Brothers, 1918, 283 p.

Palen, Lewis Stanton. *The White Devil of the Black Sea.* New York: Minton, Balch and Co., 1924, 298 p. (fiction).

Pelletier, Jean and **Adams, Claude.** *The Canadian Caper.* New York: Morrow, 1981, 239 p.

Philipson, Lorrin and **Llerena, Rafael.** *Freedom Flights: Cuban Refugees Talk About Life Under Castro and how They Fled his Regime.* New York: Random House, 1980, 201 p.

Pyke, Geoffrey. *To Ruhleben—and Back: A Great Adventure in Three Phases.* London: Constable, 1916, 246 p.

Reader's Digest True Stories of Great Escapes. Pleasantville, N.Y.: Reader's Digest Association 1977, 608 p.

Reid, Patrick R., *ed. My Favourite Escape Stories.* Guildford, England: Lutterworth Press, 1975, 176 p.

Richards, Guy. *The Rescue of the Romanovs: Newly Discovered Documents Reveal How Czar Nicholas II and the Russian Imperial Family Escaped.* Old Greenwich, Conn.: Devin-Adair, 1975, 215 p.

Sareen, C.L. *Bid for Freedom: U.S.S.R. vs. Tarasov.* Englewood Cliffs, N.J.: Prentice-Hall, 1966, 199 p.

Smith, C.A., ed. *Escape from Paradise, by Seven who Escaped and One who did not.* London: Hollis and Carter, 1954, 243 p.

Sunderman, James F., ed. *Air Escape and Evasion.* New York: F. Watts, 1963, 289 p.

Winchester, Barry. *Beyond the Tumult.* New York: Scribner, 1971, 207 p.

World War II
General

Bird, William Richard. *The Two Jacks: The Amazing Adventures of Major Jack M. Veness and Major Jack L. Fairweather.* Toronto: Ryerson Press, 1954, 209 p.

Doward, Jan S. *The Seventh Escape.* Mountain View, Calif.: Pacific Press Pub. Association, 1968, 119 p.

Ford, Herbert. *Flee the Captor.* Nashville: Southern Pub. Association, 1966, 373 p.

Gazel, Stefan F. *To Live and Kill.* London: Jarrolds, 1958, 215 p.

Gordon, Harry. *Die like the Carp! The Story of the Greatest Prison Escape Ever.* Stanmore, Australia: Cassell Australia, 1978, 240 p.

Jones, Francis S. *The Double Dutchman: A Story of Wartime Escape and Intrigue.* New Zealand: Dunmore Press, 1977, 191 p.

Lowrie, Donald Alexander. *The Hunted Children.* New York: Norton, 1963, 256 p.

McDougall, William H. *Six Bells off Java: A Narrative of one Man's Private Miracle.* New York: Scribner, 1948, 222 p.

Padev, Michael. *Escape from the Balkans.* Indianapolis: Bobbs-Merrill, 1943, 311 p.

Petrov, Vladimir. *My Retreat from Russia.* New Haven: Yale University Press, 1950, 357 p.

Scriabine, Helene. *After Leningrad: From the Caucasus to the Rhine, August 9, 1942-March 25, 1945. A Diary of Survival During World War II.* Translated and edited by Norman Luxenburg. Carbondale: Southern Illinois University Press, 1978, 190 p.

Tsuji, Masanobu. *Underground Escape.* A translation from the Japanese. Tokyo: R. Booth and T. Fukuda, 1952, 298 p.

Williams, Eric Ernest, ed. *Great Escape Stories.* New York: R.M. McBride, 1959, 256 p.

German

Bauer, Josef Martin. *As far as my Feet will Carry me.* Translated by Lawrence P.R. Wilson. New York: Random House, 1957, 347 p.

Magener, Rolf. *Prisoners' Bluff.* Translated from the German by Basil Creighton. New York: Dutton, 1955, 250 p.

Moore, John Hammond. *The Faustball Tunnel: German POWs in America and their Great Escape.* New York: Random House, 1978, 268 p.

Pabel, Reinhold. *Enemies are Human.* Philadelphia: Winston, 1955, 248 p. (autobiographical).

Strasser, Otto and Stern, Michael. *Flight from Terror.* New York: R.M. McBride, 1943, 361 p.

Jewish Rescue and Escape Efforts

Aliav, Ruth and Mann, Peggy. *The Last Escape: The Launching of the Largest Secret Rescue Movement of all Time.* Garden City, N.Y.: Doubleday, 1973, 518 p.

Bertelsen, Aage. *October '43.* Translated by Milly Lindholm and Willy Agtby. New York: Putnam, 1954, 246 p.

Bierman, John. *Righteous Gentile: The Story of Raoul Wallenberg, Missing Hero of the Holocaust.* New York: Viking Press, 1981, 218 p.

Brand, Joel. *Desperate Mission: Joel Brand's Story as told by Alex Weissberg.* Translated from the German by Constantine FitzGibbon and Andrew Foster-Melliar. New York: Criterion Books, 1958, 310 p.

Derogy, Jacques. *Le cas Wallenberg.* Enquéte de Fred Kupferman et Ariane Misrachi. Paris: Ramsay, 1980, 246 p.

Eliav, Arie L. *The Voyage of the Ulua.* Translated from the Hebrew by Israel I. Taslitt. New York: Pyramid Books, 1970, 240 p. (paperback).

Flender, Harold. *Rescue in Denmark.* New York: Manor Books, 1964, 223 p. (paperback).

Friedman, Philip. *Their Brothers' Keepers.* New York: Holocaust Library, 1978, 232 p.

Gruber, Ruth. *Destination Palestine: The Story of the Haganah Ship, Exodus, 1947.* New York: Current Books, 1948, 128 p.

Hallie, Philip Paul. *Lest Innocent Blood be Shed: The Story of the Village of Le Chambon, and How Goodness Happened There.* New York: Harper and Row, 1979, 304 p.

Kimche, Jon and **Kimche, David.** *The Secret Roads: The "Illegal" Migration of a People, 1938-1948.* London: Secker and Warburg, 1954, 223 p.

Kulkielko, Renya. *Escape from the Pit.* New York: Sharon Books, 1947, 189 p.

Lambert, Gilles. *Operation Hazalah.* Translated by Robert Bullen and Rosette Letellier. Indianapolis: Bobbs-Merrill, 1974, 235 p.

Leboucher Fernande. *Incredible Mission.* Translated by J.F. Bernard. Garden City, N.Y.: Doubleday, 1969, 165 p.

Perl, William R. *The Four-Front War: From the Holocaust to the Promised Land.* New York: Crown, 1979, 376 p.

Ramati, Alexander. *The Assissi Underground: The Priests who Rescued Jews, as told by Rufino Niccacci.* New York: Stein and Day, 1978, 181 p.

Stone, Isidor F. *Underground to Palestine.* New York: Pantheon Books, 1978, 260 p.

Thomas, Gordon and **Morgan, Max.** *Voyage of the Damned.* New York: Stein and Day, 1974, 317 p.

Werbell, Frederick E. and **Clarke, Thurston.** *Lost Hero: The Mystery of Raoul Wallenberg.* New York: McGraw-Hill, 1982, 284 p.

Support Lines

Brason, John. *Secret Army.* London: British Broadcasting Corporation, 1977, 256 p. (paperback).

Caskie, Donald C. *The Tartan Pimpernel.* London: Oldbourne, 1957, 270 p.

Connell, Charles. *The Hidden Catch.* London: Elek Books, 1955, 176 p.

Derry, Sam. *The Rome Escape Line: The Story of the British Organization in Rome for Assisting Escaped Prisoners-of-War, 1943-1944.* London: Harrap, 1960, 239 p.

Les Evasions, le prix de la liberté. Témoignages, Paris: Denoël, 1965, 185 p.

Foot, Michael Richard Daniel and **Langley, J.M.** *MI 9: Escape and Evasion, 1939-1945.* London: Bodley Head, 1979, 365 p.

Foot, Michael Richard Daniel and **Langley, J.M.** *MI 9: Escape and Evasion, 1939-1945.* Boston: Little, Brown, 1980, 351 p.

Gold, Mary Jane. *Crossroads Marseilles, 1940.* Garden City, N.Y.: Doubleday, 1980, 412 p.

Hanson, Stan E. *Underground out of Holland.* London: Ian Allan, 1977, 191 p.

Hutton, Clayton. *Official Secret: The Remarkable Story of Escape Aids, Their Invention, Production, and the Sequel.* New York: Crown, 1961, 212 p.

Neave, Airey. *The Escape Room.* New York: Tower Publications, 1969, 286 p. (paperback).

Neave, Airey. *Saturday at M.I.9: A History of Underground Escape Lines in North-West Europe in 1940-5 by a Leading Organiser at M.I.9.* London: Hodder and Stoughton, 1969, 327 p.

Neave, Airey. *They Have Their Exits.* New York: Beagle Books, 1971, 189 p. (paperback).

Shiber, Etta Kahn. *Paris-Underground.* New York: Scribner, 1943, 392 p.

Tartière, Dorothy Blackman with **Werner, M.R.** *The House Near Paris: An American Woman's Story of Traffic in Patriots.* New York: Simon and Schuster, 1946, 318 p.

United Kingdom/United States

Beeson, George. *Five Roads to Freedom.* London: L. Cooper, 1977, 123 p.

Brickhill, Paul and **Norton, Conrad.** *Escape to Danger.* London: Faber and Faber, 1946, 341 p.

Calnan, T.D. *Free as a Running Fox.* New York: Dial Press, 1970, 323 p. (autobiographical).

Chrisp, John. *The Tunnellers of Sandborstal.* London: Hale, 1959, 172 p.

Crawley, Aidan. *Escape from Germany: A History of R.A.F. Escapes During the War.* London: Collins, 1956, 318 p.

Dominy, John. *The Sergeant Escapers.* London: Allan, 1974, 136 p.

Dunbar, John. *Escape Through the Pyrenees.* New York: Norton, 1955, 176 p. (autobiographical).

Embry, Basil Edward, *Sir. Wingless Victory: The Story of Sir Basil Embry's Escape from Occupied France in the Summer of 1940, related by Anthony Richardson.* London: Odhams Press, 1950, 256 p.

Fry, Varian. *Surrender on Demand.* New York: Random House, 1945, 243 p.

Graham, Burton. *Escape from the Nazis.* Secaucus, N.J.: Castle Books, 1975, 120 p.

Instone, Gordon. *Freedom the Spur.* London: Burke, 1953, 256 p.

Lang, Derek. *Return to St. Valéry: The Story of an Escape Through Wartime France and Syria.* London: Cooper, 1974, 192 p.

Millar, George Reid. *Horned Pigeon.* London: W. Heinemann, 1946, 443 p.

Newby, Eric. *When the Snow Comes, They will Take you Away.* New York: Scribner, 1971, 221 p. (fiction).

Orna, Joseph with **Popham, Hugh.** *The Escaping Habit.* London: Futura Publications, 1976, 143 p.

Pape, Richard. *Boldness be my Friend.* London: Elek, 1953, 309 p.

Purvis, James. *Escape: The Dramatic True Story of the Man No Concentration Camp Could Hold, from the Diary of Bernard Lipman.* New York: Manor Books, 1979, 221 p. (paperback).

Reid, Patrick R. *Escape from Colditz: The Two Classic Escape Stories—The Colditz Story and Men of Colditz.* Philadelphia: Lippincott, 1953, 622 p.

Smith, Sydney. *Mission Escape.* New York: Popular Library, 1968, 240 p. (paperback).

Teare, T.D.G. *Evader.* London: Hodder and Stoughton, 1954, 256 p.

Thrower, Derek. *The Lonely Path to Freedom.* London: Hale, 1980, 159 p.

Whitcomb, Edgar D. *Escape from Corregidor.* Chicago: Regnery, 1958, 274 p.

Williams, Elvet. *Arbeitskommando.* London: Gollancz, 1975, 256 p.

Williams, Eric Ernest. *The Wooden Horse.* New York: Bantam Books, 1951, 246 p. (paperback).

VI. FOREIGN RELATIONS
General

Archer, Jules. *The Russians and the Americans.* New York: Hawthorn Books, 1975, 220 p.

Bloodworth, Dennis and **Bloodworth, Ching Ping.** *The Chinese Machiavelli: 3,000 Years of Chinese Statecraft.* New York: Dell Publishing, 1977, 346 p.

Cabot, John Moors. *First Line of Defense: Forty Years' Experience of a Career Diplomat.* Washington: School of Foreign Service, Georgetown University, 1979, 167 p.

Copeland, Miles. *The Game of Nations: The Amorality of Power Politics.* New York: Simon and Schuster, 1969, 318 p.

Davies, John Paton. *Dragon by the Tail: American, British, Japanese, and Russian Encounters with China and one Another.* New York: Norton, 1972, 448 p.

Drachkovitch, Milorad M. and **Lazitch, Branko,** eds. *The Comintern: Historical Highlights, Essays, Recollections, Documents.* New York; Stanford, Calif.: Praeger, 1966, 430 p. (Hoover Institution publication).

Drucker, Peter Ferdinand. *Adventures of a Bystander.* New York: Harper and Row, 1979, 344 p.

Dukes, Paul, Sir. *Come Hammer, Come Sickle!* London: Cassell, 1947, 187 p.

Dzélépy, Eleuthère Nicolas. *Sekret Cherchillia.* Moscow: Progress, 1975, 308 p. (Russian edition of *Le secret de Churchill: vers la troisième guerre mondiale, 1945*).

Girling, J.L.S. *America and the Third World: Revolution and Intervention.* London: Routledge and K. Paul, 1980, 276 p.

Haykal, Muhammad Hasanayn. *The Cairo Documents: The Inside Story of Nasser and his Relationship with World Leaders, Rebels, and Statesmen.* Garden City, N.Y.: Doubleday, 1973, 360 p.

Laffin, John. *The Dagger of Islam.* New York: Bantam Books, 1981, 213 p. (paperback).

Little, Richard. *Intervention: External Involvement in Civil Wars.* London: M. Robertson, 1975, 236 p.

Lockhart, Robert Hamilton Bruce. *The Diaries of Sir Robert Bruce Lockhart.* Edited by Kenneth Young. London: Macmillan, 1973, 2 v.

Louis, Victor E. *The Coming Decline of the Chinese Empire.* New York: Quadrangle, 1979, 198 p.

McGeoch, I.L.M. "National Security and Grand Strategy." *Journal of the Royal United Service Institution,* v. CX (February-November 1965), pp. 64–67.

Markel, Lester *et al. Public Opinion and Foreign Policy.* New York: Harper, 1949, 227 p. (publication of the Council on Foreign Relations).

Monnet, Jean. *Mémoires.* Paris: Fayard, 1976, 830 p. (paperback).

Murphy, Robert Daniel. *Diplomat Among Warriors.* Garden City, N.Y.: Doubleday, 1964, 470 p.

Rubin, Barry M. *The Great Powers in the Middle East, 1941-1947: The Road to the Cold War.* London: Cass, 1980, 254 p.

Schlesinger, Arthur Meier, Jr. *The Imperial Presidency.* Boston: Houghton Mifflin, 1973, 505 p.

Siu, Ralph Gun Hoy. *The Craft of Power.* New York: Wiley, 1979, 255 p.

Thompson, Kenneth W. *Morality and Foreign Policy.* Baton Rouge: Louisiana State University Press, 1980, 197 p.

The United States and Iran: A Documentary History. Edited by Yonah Alexander and Allan Nanes, Frederick, Md.: Aletheia Books, 1980, 524 p.

Vorontsov, Vladilen Borisovich. *Delo "Amereisha": Polit. Stolknoveniia v SShA po problemam Kitaia.* Moscow: Mezhdunar. Otnosheniia, 1974, 205 p.

Pre-20th Century

Barker, Nancy Nichols. *The French Experience in Mexico, 1821-1861: A History of Constant Misunderstanding.* Chapel Hill: University of North Carolina Press, 1979, 264 p.

Baschet, Armand. *Les archives de Venise. Histoire de la chancellerie secrète. Le Sénat, le cabinet des ministres, le Conseil des dix et les inquisiteurs d'état dans leurs rapports avec la France, d'après des recherches faites aux sources originales, pour servir à l'étude de l'histoire de la politique et de la diplomatie.* Paris: H. Plon, 1870, 2 pts.

Carter, Charles Howard. *The Secret Diplomacy of the Hapsburgs, 1598–1625.* New York: Columbia University Press, 1964, 321 p.

Cowles, Virginia Spencer. *The Russian Dagger: Cold War in the Days of the Czars.* New York: Harper and Row, 1969, 351 p.

De Conde, Alexander. *The Quasi-War: The Politics and Diplomacy of the Undeclared War with France, 1797–1801.* New York: Scribner, 1966, 498 p.

Frischauer, Paul. *Beaumarchais, Adventurer in the Century of Women.* Translated by Margaret Goldsmith. New York: Viking Press, 1935, 312 p.

Fülöp-Miller, René. *The Power and Secret of the Jesuits.* Translated by F.S. Flint and D.F. Tait. New York: Viking Press, 1930, 523 p.

Lewis, Lesley. *Connoisseurs and Secret Agents in Eighteenth Century Rome.* London: Chatto and Windus, 1961, 282 p.

Nelson, Anna Louise Kaster. *The Secret Diplomacy of James K. Polk During the Mexican War, 1846–1947.* Ann Arbor, Mich.: University Microfilms, 1976, 308 p.

Les petits papiers secrèts des Tuileries et de Saint-Cloud étiquetés par un collectionneur. Edited by E. Dentu. Paris: E. Dentu, 1871, 324 p.

Read, Conyers. *Mr. Secretary Walsingham and the Policy of Queen Elizabeth.* Oxford: The Clarendon Press, 1925, 3 v.

Zweig, Stefan. *Joseph Fouché. Bildnis eines politischen Menschen.* Frankfurt, Germany: S. Fischer, 1952, 228 p. (paperback).

20th Century Through World War II

Antrobus, George Pollock. *King's Messenger, 1918–1940, Memoirs of a Silver Greyhound.* London: H. Jenkins, 1941, 250 p.

Carsten, Francis Ludwig. *The Reichswehr and Politics, 1918 to 1933.* Berkeley: University of California Press, 1973, 427 p. (paperback).

Carsten, Francis Ludwig. "The Reichswehr and the Red Army, 1920–1933." *Journal of the Royal United Service Institution,* v. CVIII (February 1963), pp. 248–255.

Chandos, Oliver Lyttelton, 1st Viscount. *Memoirs.* London: Bodley Head, 1962, 446 p.

Colville, John Rupert. *Winston Churchill and his Inner Circle.* New York: Wyndham Books, 1981, 287 p.

Dallek, Robert. *Franklin D. Roosevelt and American Foreign Policy, 1932–1945.* New York: Oxford University Press, 1979, 657 p.

De Santis, Hugh. *The Diplomacy of Silence: The American Foreign Service, the Soviet Union, and the Cold War, 1933–1947.* Chicago: University of Chicago Press, 1980, 270 p.

Divine, Robert A. *Eisenhower and the Cold War.* New York: Oxford University Press, 1981, 181 p. (paperback).

Donovan, Robert J. *Conflict and Crisis: The Presidency of Harry S. Truman, 1945–1948.* New York: Norton, 1977, 473 p.

Dulles, Eleanor Lansing. *Eleanor Lansing Dulles: Chances of a Lifetime, a Memoir.* Englewood Cliffs, N.J.: Prentice-Hall, 1980, 390 p.

Filchner, Wilhelm. *Sturm über Asien, erlebnisse eines diplomatischen geheimagenten.* Berlin: Neufeld and Henius, 1924, 310 p.

Forrestal, James. *The Forrestal Diaries.* Edited by Walter Millis with E.S. Duffield. New York: Viking Press, 1951, 581 p.

Gordon, Harold J. *The Reichswehr and the German Republic, 1919–1926.* Princeton: Princeton University Press, 1957, 478 p.

Hilger, Gustav and **Meyer, Alfred G.** *The Incompatible Allies: A Memoir-History of German-Soviet Relations, 1918–1941.* New York: Macmillan, 1953, 350 p.

Klay, Andor. *Daring Diplomacy: The Case of the First American Ultimatum.* Minneapolis: University of Minnesota Press, 1957, 246 p.

Lockhart, Robert Hamilton Bruce. *Guns or Butter.* Boston: Little, Brown, 1938, 439 p.

Lockhart, Robert Hamilton Bruce. *Retreat from Glory.* New York: Garden City Publishing Co., 1938, 348 p.

Mackenzie, Compton, *Sir. Dr. Benes.* London: Harrap, 1946, 356 p.

Mastny, Vojtech. *Russia's Road to the Cold War: Diplomacy, Warfare, and the Politics of Communism, 1941-1945.* New York: Columbia University Press, 1979, 409 p.

Mowat, R.C. *Ruin and Resurgence, 1939-1965.* London: Blandford Press, 1966, 406 p.

Nagy, Ferenc. *The Struggle Behind the Iron Curtain.* Translated from the Hungarian by Stephen K. Swift. New York: Macmillan, 1948, 471 p.

Paris, Henri Robert Ferdinand Marie Louis Philippe de Bourbon-Orléans, *Comte de. Mémoires d'exil et de combats.* Paris: M. Jullian, 1979, 367 p.

Piggott, Francis Stewart Gilderoy. *Broken Thread: An Autobiography.* Aldershot, Eng.: Gale and Polden, 1950, 424 p.

Roskill, Stephen Wentworth. *Hankey: Man of Secrets.* New York: St. Martin's Press, 1971, 672 p.

Witte, Emil. *Revelations of a German Attaché: Ten Years of German American Diplomacy.* Translated from the German by Florence C. Taylor. New York: George H. Doran, 1916, 264 p.

Post World War II
General

Brandt, Willy. *People and Politics: The Years 1960-1975.* Translated from the German by J. Maxwell Brownjohn. Boston: Little, Brown, 1978, 524 p.

Cervenka, Zdenek and **Rogers, Barbara.** *The Nuclear Axis: Secret Collaboration between West Germany and South Africa.* New York: Times Books, 1978, 464 p.

Cooley, John K. "The Libyan Menace." *Foreign Policy,* no. 42 (Spring 1981), pp. 74-93.

Cooper, Chester L. *The Lion's Last Roar: Suez, 1956.* New York: Harper and Row, 1978, 310 p.

Flamini, Roland. *Pope, Premier, President: The Cold War Summit that Never Was.* New York: Macmillan, 1980, 227 p.

Helms, Cynthia. *An Ambassador's Wife in Iran.* New York: Dodd, Mead, 1981, 212 p.

Lazo, Mario. *Dagger in the Heart: American Policy Failures in Cuba.* New York: Twin Circle Publishing, 1970, 447 p.

Neff, Donald. *Warriors at Suez.* New York: Linden Press, 1981, 279 p.

Seton-Watson, Hugh. *Neither War nor Peace: The Struggle for Power in the Postwar World.* New York: Praeger, 1960, 504 p.

Smith, Arthur Lee. *Churchill's German Army: Wartime Strategy and Cold War Politics, 1943-1947.* Beverly Hills: Sage Publications, 1977, 159 p.

Szulc, Tad. "Lisbon and Washington: Behind Portugal's Revolution." *Foreign Policy,* no. 21 (Winter 1975-76), pp. 3-62.

Trautman, Kathleen. *Spies Behind the Pillars, Bandits at the Pass.* New York: D. McKay, 1972, 244 p.

USSR

Dedijer, Vladimir. *The Battle Stalin Lost: Memoirs of Yugoslavia, 1948-1953.* New York: Grosset and Dunlap, 1972, 341 p. (paperback).

Falemi, Faramarz S. *The U.S.S.R. in Iran: The Background History of Russian and Anglo-American Conflict in Iran, its Effect on Iranian Nationalism and the Fall of the Shah.* Cranbury, N.J.: Barnes, 1980, 219 p.

Haykal, Muhammad Hasanayn. *The Sphinx and the Commissar: The Rise and Fall of Soviet Influence in the Middle East.* New York: Harper and Row, 1978, 304 p.

Khrushchev, Nikita Sergeevich. *Khrushchev Remembers: The Last Testament.* Translated and edited by Strobe Talbott. Boston: Little, Brown, 1974, 602 p. (the second and concluding volume of the author's oral memoirs, begun in *Khrushchev Remembers,* 1970).

Krammer, Arnold. *The Forgotten Friendship: Israel and the Soviet Bloc, 1947-1953.* Urbana: University of Illinois Press, 1974, 224 p.

Menon, Kumara Padmanabha Sivasankara. *The Flying Troika: Extracts from a Diary by K.P.S. Menon, India's Ambassador to Russia, 1952-1961.* London: Oxford University Press, 1963, 330 p.

Mnacko, Ladislav. *The Seventh Night.* New York: Dutton, 1969, 220 p.

Schwartz, Harry. *The Red Phoenix: Russia Since World War II.* New York: Praeger, 1961, 427 p. (paperback).

Zacharias, Ellis M. with **Farago, Ladislas.** *Behind Closed Doors: The Secret History of the Cold War.* New York: Putnam, 1950, 367 p.

USSR/United States

Containment: Documents on American Policy and Strategy, 1945-1950. Edited by Thomas H. Etzold and John Lewis Gaddis. New York: Columbia University Press, 1978, 449 p.

Larson, Thomas B. *Soviet-American Rivalry.* New York: Norton, 1978, 308 p.

Smith, Walter Bedell. *My Three Years in Moscow.* Philadelphia: Lippincott, 1949, 346 p.

Yergin, Daniel. *Shattered Peace: The Origins of the Cold War and the National Security State.* Boston: Houghton Mifflin, 1977, 526 p.

United States

Agafonova, Galina Aleksandrovna. *Sovet natsional'noi bezopasnosti SShA: Istoriia sozdaniia i nach. period deiatel'nosti, 1947-1960 gg.* Moscow: Nauka, 1977, 136 p.

Bachrack, Stanley D. *The Committee of One Million: "China Lobby" Politics, 1953-1971.* New York: Columbia University Press, 1976, 371 p.

Ball, George W. *Diplomacy for a Crowded World: An American Foreign Policy.* Boston: Little, Brown, 1976, 356 p.

Betts, Richard K. *Soldiers, Statesmen, and Cold War Crises.* Cambridge: Harvard University Press, 1977, 292 p.

Blechman, Barry M.; Kaplan, Stephen S. et al. *Force Without War: U.S. Armed Forces as a Political Instrument.* Washington: Brookings Institution, 1978, 584 p.

Brown, Seyom. *The Crises of Power: An Interpretation of United States Foreign Policy During the Kissinger Years.* New York: Columbia University Press, 1979, 170 p.

Cline, Ray S. "Policy Without Intelligence." Foreign Policy, no. 17 (Winter 1974-75), pp. 121-135.

Golan, Matti. *The Secret Conversations of Henry Kissinger: Step-by-Step Diplomacy in the Middle-East.* Translated by Ruth Geyra Stern and Sol Stern. New York: Quadrangle, 1976, 280 p.

Goldwater, Barry Morris. *With no Apologies: The Personal and Political Memoirs of United States Senator Barry M. Goldwater.* New York: Morrow, 1979, 320 p.

Hedley, John Hollister. *Harry S. Truman, the 'Little' Man from Missouri.* Woodbury, N.Y.: Barron's, 1979, 353 p.

Kennan, George Frost. *The Cloud of Danger: Current Realities of American Foreign Policy.* Boston: Little, Brown, 1977, 234 p.

Kissinger, Henry Alfred. *White House Years.* Boston: Little, Brown, 1979, 1521 p.

Lundestad, Geir. *America, Scandinavia, and the Cold War, 1945-1959.* New York: Columbia University Press, 1980, 434 p.

McLellan, David S. *Dean Acheson: The State Department Years.* New York: Dodd, Mead, 1976, 466 p.

Morris, Roger. *Uncertain Greatness: Henry Kissinger and American Foreign Policy.* New York: Harper and Row, 1977, 312 p.

Mosley, Leonard. *Dulles: A Biography of Eleanor, Allen and John Foster Dulles and their Family Network.* New York: Dial Press, 1978, 530 p.

Nixon, Richard Milhous. *The Real War.* New York: Warner Books, 1980, 341 p.

Paterson, Thomas G. *On Every Front: The Making of the Cold War.* New York: Norton, 1979, 210 p.

Schlesinger, Arthur Meier, Jr. *Robert Kennedy and his Times.* Boston: Houghton Mifflin, 1978, 1066 p.

Sheehan, Edward R.F. *The Arabs, Israelis, and Kissinger: A Secret History of American Diplomacy in the Middle East.* New York: Readers Digest Press, 1976, 287 p.

Slomich, Sidney J. *The American Nightmare.* New York: Macmillan, 1971, 285 p.

Trewhitt, Henry L. *McNamara.* New York: Harper and Row, 1971, 307 p.

Truman, Margaret. *Harry S. Truman.* New York: Pocket Books, 1974, 660 p. (paperback).

Walton, Richard J. *Cold War and Counterrevolution: The Foreign Policy of John F. Kennedy.* Baltimore, Md.: Penguin Books, 1973, 250 p. (paperback).

VII. LAW ENFORCEMENT

Police: International and Municipal

Fooner, Michael. *Inside Interpol: Combatting World Crime Through Science and International Police Cooperation.* New York: Coward, McCann and Geoghegan, 1975, 48 p.

Garrison, Omar V. *The Secret World of Interpol.* New York: Ralston-Pilot, 1976, 237 p.

Gollomb, Joseph. *Master Man Hunters.* New York: Macaulay, 1926, 315 p.

Gough, William Charles. *From Kew Observatory to Scotland Yard: Being Experiences and Travels in 28 Years of Crime Investigating.* London: Hurst and Blackett, 1927, 284 p.

Harbottle, Michael. *The Blue Berets.* Harrisburg, Pa.: Stockpole Books, 1972, 157 p.

Lambert, Derek. *Blackstone.* New York: Bantam Books, 1974, 198 p.

Lee, Peter G. *Interpol.* New York: Stein and Day, 1976, 204 p.

Meldal-Johnsen, Trevor and **Young, Vaughn.** *The Interpol Connection: An Inquiry into the International Criminal Police Organization.* New York: Dial Press, 1979, 303 p.

Scott, Harold Richard, *Sir. Scotland Yard.* New York: Random House, 1955, 256 p.

Seth, Ronald. *The Special: The Story of the Special Constabulary in England, Wales and Scotland.* London: Gollancz, 1961, 239 p.

Stead, Philip John. *The Police of Paris:* London: Staples Press, 1957, 224 p.

Tullett, Tom. *Inside Interpol.* London: F. Muller, 1963, 223 p.

Vidocq, Eugène François. *Vidocq: The Personal Memoirs of the First Great Detective.* Edited and translated by Edwin Gile Rich. Boston: Houghton Mifflin, 1935, 433 p. (1859 edition under title: *Memoirs of Vidocq: The Principal Agent of the French Police).*

Private Detectives

Dodge, Fred. *Under Cover for Wells Fargo: The Unvarnished Recollections of Fred Dodge.* Edited by Carolyn Lake. Boston: Houghton Mifflin, 1969, 280 p.

Horan, James David. *The Pinkertons: The Detective Dynasty that Made History.* New York: Bonanza Books, 1967, 564 p.

Kahn, Joan, *comp. Trial and Terror.* London: Hamish Hamilton, 1975, 569 p.

Orrmont, Arthur. *Master Detective: Allan Pinkerton.* New York: J. Messner, 1965, 191 p.

Pringle, Patrick. *The Thief-Takers.* London: Museum Press, 1958, 224 p.

Rowan, Richard Wilmer. *The Pinkertons: A Detective Dynasty.* Boston: Little, Brown, 1931, 350 p.

U.S. Federal Agencies

Baughman, Urbanus Edmund with **Robinson, Leonard Wallace.** *Secret Service Chief.* New York: Harper, 1961, 266 p.

Burnham, George Pickering. *Memoirs of the United States Secret Service.* New York: Shepard and Dillingham, 1872, 436 p. (Col. H.C. Whitley).

Colby, Carroll B. *Secret Service: History, Duties, and Equipment.* New York: Coward-McCann, 1966, 48 p. (juvenile literature).

Hynd, Alan. *The Giant Killers.* New York: R.M. McBride, 1945, 317 p.

McIlhany, William H. *Klandestine: The Untold Story of Delmar Dennis and his Role in the FBI's War Against the Ku Klux Klan.* New Rochelle, N.Y.: Arlington House, 1975, 255 p.

Makris, John N. *The Silent Investigators: The Great Untold Story of the United States Postal Inspection Service.* New York: Dutton, 1959, 319 p.

Messick, Hank. *Secret File.* New York: Putnam, 1969, 378 p.

Ottenberg, Miriam. *The Federal Investigators.* New York: Pocket Books, 1963, 423 p. (paperback).

Purvis, Melvin Horace. *American Agent.* Garden City, N.Y.: Doubleday, Doran, 1936, 291 p.

Roark, Garland. *The Coin of Contraband: The True Story of United States Customs Investigator Al Scharff.* New York: Modern Literary Editions, 1964, 382 p. (paperback).

Rowe, Gary Thomas. *My Undercover Years with the Ku Klux Klan.* New York: Bantam Books, 1976, 216 p.

Smith, Graham. *Something to Declare: 1000 Years of Customs and Excise.* London: Harrap, 1980, 230 p.

Starling, Edmund William. *Starling of the White House: The Story of the Man Whose Secret Service Detail Guarded Five Presidents from Woodrow Wilson to Franklin D. Roosevelt, as told to Thomas Sugrue.* New York: Simon and Schuster, 1946, 334 p.

Tully, Andrew. *Treasury Agent: The Inside Story.* New York: Pyramid Books, 1960, 288 p. (paperback).

Villano, Anthony with **Astor, Gerald.** *Brick Agent: Inside the Mafia for the FBI.* New York: Ballantine Books, 1978, 248 p. (paperback).

Whitley, Hiram C. *In It, by H.C. Whitley, Late Chief of the Secret Service Division of the United States Treasury.* Cambridge: Riverside Press, 1894, 322 p.

Wilson, Frank John and **Day, Beth.** *Special Agent: A Quarter Century with the Treasury Department and the Secret Service.* New York: Holt, Rinehart and Winston, 1965, 250 p.

Wilson, James Q. *The Investigators: Managing FBI and Narcotics Agents.* New York: Basic Books, 1978, 228 p.

Woodward, Patrick Henry. *Guarding the Mails; or, The Secret Service of the Post-Office Department. Being a Record of Mail Robberies and Their Detection. Embracing Sketches of Wonderful Exploits of Special Agents in the Detection, Pursuit and Capture of Depredators upon the Mails, with a Complete Description of the Many Means and Complicated Contrivances of the Wily and Unscrupulous to Defraud the Public.* Hartford, Conn.: J.P. Fitch, 1882, 568 p.

VIII. POLITICAL DISSENT, INCLUDING SECRET SOCIETIES
General

Acton, Harold Mario Mitchell. *The Pazzi Conspiracy: The Plot Against the Medici.* London: Thames and Hudson, 1979, 128 p.

Feuer, Lewis Samuel. *The Conflict of Generations: The Character and Significance of Student Movements.* New York: Basic Books, 1969, 543 p.

Kolosov, L. and **Petrov, N.** *Immortality of Those who Have Fallen.* Washington: U.S. Joint Publications Research Service, no. 55490, March 21, 1972, 34 p. (serial article from *Izvestiya*, Moscow, October 8–10, 1969).

Kuper, Leo. *Passive Resistance in South Africa.* New Haven: Yale University Press, 1957, 256 p. (paperback).

Lamb, Harold. *The Crusades: The Flame of Islam.* Garden City, N.Y.: International Collectors Library, 1931, 473 p.

Mackenzie, Norman Ian, *ed. Secret Societies.* London: Aldus, 1967, 350 p.

Packe, Michael St. John. *Orsini: The Story of a Conspirator.* Boston: Little, Brown, 1957, 213 p. (U.S. edition of *The Bombs of Orsini.* London).

Pike, D.W. *Secret Societies: Their Origin, History and Ultimate Fate.* New York: Oxford University Press, 1939, 152 p.

Procopius. *History of the War: Secret History and Buildings.* Edited by Averil Cameron. New York: Twayne Publishers, [post 1967], 351 p.

Salmon, John Hearsey McMillan. *Cardinal de Retz: The Anatomy of a Conspirator.* New York: Macmillan, 1970, 447 p.

Webster, Nesta Helen. *Secret Societies and Subversive Movements.* 7th ed. London: Britons Pub. Society, 1955, 419 p.

Wilkins, Ivor and **Strydom, Hans.** *The Broederbond.* New York: Grosset and Dunlap, 1979, 458 p.

Williams, Hugh Noel. *A Fair Conspirator, Marie de Rohan, Duchesse de Chevreuse.* New York: Scribner, 1813, 351 p.

Young, George Frederick. *The Medici.* New York: The Modern Library, 1933, 824 p.

France

Aron, Raymond, *The Elusive Revolution: Anatomy of a Student Revolt.* Translated by Gordon Clough. New York: Praeger, 1969, 20 p.

Bourdé, Guy. *La Défaite du Front populaire.* Paris: F. Maspéro, 1977, 359 p.

Duclos, Charles Pinot. *Secret Memoirs of the Regency: The Minority of Louis XV.* Translated from the French by E. Jules Méras. New York: Sturgis and Walton, 1910, 343 p.

Erlanger, Philippe. *The King's Minion: Richelieu, Louis XIII, and the Affair of Cinq-Mars.* Translated from the French by Gilles and Heather Cremonesi. Englewood Cliffs, N.J.: Prentice-Hall, 1972, 247 p.

Kravetz, Marc, *comp.* with **Bellour, Raymond** *et al. L'insurrection étudiante 2–13 mai 1968, ensemble critique et documentaire.* Paris: Union Générale d'Editions, 1968, 511 p. (paperback).

Philpin de Piépape, Léonce Marie Gabriel. *The Princess of Strategy: The Life of Anne Louise Bénédicte de Bourbon-Condé, Duchesse du Maine.* Translated from the French by J. Lewis May. London: J. Lane, 1911, 415 p.

Rioux, Jean Pierre. *Révolutionnaires du Front populaire: Choix de documents, 1935–1938.* Paris: Union Général d'Editions, 1973, 444 p.

Schnapp, Alain, *comp.* and **Vidal-Naquet, Pierre.** *The French Student Uprising, November 1967-June 1968: An Analytical Record.* Translated by Maria Jolas. Boston: Beacon Press, 1971, 654 p.

USSR

Bonavia, David. *Fat Sasha and the Urban Guerilla: Protest and Conformism in the Soviet Union.* New York: Atheneum, 1973, 193 p.

Brumberg, Abraham, comp. *In Quest of Justice: Protest and Dissent in the Soviet Union Today.* New York: Praeger, 1970, 477 p.

Bukovskii, Vladimir Konstantinovich. *To Build a Castle: My Life as a Dissenter.* Translated by Michael Scammell. New York: Viking Press, 1979, 438 p.

De Mauny, Erik. *Russian Prospect: Notes of a Moscow Correspondent.* New York: Atheneum, 1970, 320 p.

Dilas, Milovan. *Tito: The Story from Inside.* Translated by Vasilije Kojić and Richard Hayes. New York: Harcourt, Brace, Jovanovich, 1980, 185 p.

Gaucher, Roland. *Opposition in the U.S.S.R., 1917-1967.* Translated by Charles Lam Markmann. New York: Funk and Wagnalls, 1969, 547 p.

Germany, Federal Republic of, Bundesministerium für Gesamtdeutsche Fragen. *2 × 2 = 8: The Story of a Group of Young Men in the Soviet Zone of Germany.* Compiled and revised by Rainer Hildebrandt. Bonn: Federal Ministry for All-German Affairs, 1961, 64 p.

Gerstenmaier, Cornelia I. *The Voices of the Silent.* Translated from the German by Susan Hecker. New York: Hart Pub., 1972, 587 p.

Medvedev, Roi Aleksandrovich. *On Soviet Dissent: Interviews with Piero Ostellino.* Translated from the Italian by William A. Packer. Edited by George Saunders. New York: Columbia University Press, 1980, 158 p.

Reddaway, Peter, comp. and ed. *Uncensored Russia: The Human Rights Movement in the Soviet Union.* London: Cape, 1972, 499 p.

Rothberg, Abraham. *The Heirs of Stalin: Dissidence and the Soviet Regime, 1953-1970.* Ithaca, N.Y.: Cornell University Press, 1972, 450 p.

Rubenstein, Joshua. *Soviet Dissidents: Their Struggle for Human Rights.* Boston: Beacon Press, 1980, 304 p.

Solzhenitsyn, Aleksandr Isaevich. *The Oak and the Calf: Sketches of Literary Life in the Soviet Union.* Translated from the Russian by Harry Willetts. New York: Harper and Row, 1980, 568 p.

Steinberg, Julien, ed. *Verdict of Three Decades: From the Literature of Individual Revolt Against Soviet Communism, 1917-1950.* New York: Duell, Sloan and Pearce, 1950, 634 p.

Ulam, Adam Bruno. *Russia's Failed Revolutions: From the Decembrists to the Dissidents.* New York: Basic Books, 1981, 453 p.

Young, Gordon. *The House of Secrets: Russian Resistance to the Soviet Regime Today.* New York: Duell, Sloan and Pearce, 1959, 179 p.

United Kingdom

Cowan, Samuel. *The Gowrie Conspiracy and its Official Narrative.* London: S. Low, Marston and Co., 1902, 264 p.

Davison, Meredith Henry Armstrong. *The Casket Letters: A Solution to the Mystery of Mary, Queen of Scots, and the Murder of Lord Darnley.* Washington: University Press, 1965, 352 p.

Defoe, Daniel. *An Account of the Riots, Tumults, and Other Treasonable Practices: With Some Remarks Shewing the Necessity of Strengthening the Laws Against Riots, Humbly Offered to the Consideration of the Parliament.* Ann Arbor, Mich.: Xerox University Microfilms, 1975, 26 p. (original published by J. Baker, London: 1715).

Derry, John Wesley. *Charles James Fox.* New York: St. Martin's Press, 1972, 454 p.

Earle, Peter. *The World of Defoe.* New York: Atheneum, 1977, 353 p.

Goodman, Anthony. *The Loyal Conspiracy: The Lords Appellant Under Richard II.* London: Routledge and K. Paul, 1971, 212 p.

Minto, William. *Daniel Defoe.* London: Macmillan, 1902, 179 p.

Mosley, Oswald, Sir. *My Life.* New Rochelle, N.Y.: Arlington House, 1968, 521 p.

Pollock, John. *The Popish Plot. A Study in the History of the Reign of Charles II.* London: Duckworth and Co., 1903, 419 p.

Trevelyan, George Otto, Sir. *The Early History of Charles James Fox.* New York: Harper and Brothers, 1902, 470 p.

Trevelyan, George Otto, *Sir. George the Third and Charles Fox: The Concluding Part of The American Revolution.* New York: Longmans, Green, 1912-14, 2 v.

United States

Boyd, Julian Parks. *Number 7: Alexander Hamilton's Secret Attempts to Control American Foreign Policy, with Supporting Documents.* Princeton: Princeton University Press, 1964, 166 p.

Green, Thomas Marshall. *The Spanish Conspiracy: A Review of Early Spanish Movements in the Southwest, Containing Proofs of the Intrigues of James Wilkinson and John Brown; of the Complicity Therewith of Judges Sebastian, Wallace, and Innes; the Early Struggles of Kentucky for Autonomy; the Intrigues of Sebastian in 1795-7, and the Legislative Investigation of his Corruption.* Gloucester, Mass.: P. Smith, 1967, 406 p.

Kelner, Joseph and **Munves, James.** *The Kent State Coverup.* New York: Harper and Row, 1980, 305 p.

Methvin, Eugene H. *The Riot Makers: The Technology of Social Demolition.* New Rochelle, N.Y.: Arlington House, 1970, 586 p.

Milton, George Fort. *The Age of Hate: Andrew Johnson and the Radicals.* New York: Coward-McCann, 1930, 787 p.

Sale, Kirkpatrick. *SDS.* New York: Random House, 1973, 752 p.

Smith, Le Roy Foster and **Johns, E.B.** *Pastors, Politicians, Pacifists.* Chicago: The Constructive Educational Publishing Co., 1927, 222 p.

Taylor, John. *Disunion Sentiment in Congress in 1794: A Confidential Memorandum Hitherto Unpublished, Written ... for James Madison.* Edited by Gaillard Hunt. Washington: W.H. Lowdermilk, 1905, 23 p.

Williams, Thomas Harry. *Lincoln and the Radicals.* Madison: The University of Wisconsin Press, 1941, 413 p.

IX. PSYCHOLOGICAL WARFARE
General

Arbatov, Georgi. *The War of Ideas in Contemporary International Relations: The Imperialist Doctrine, Methods and Organization of Foreign Political Propaganda.* Translated from the Russian by David Skvirsky. Moscow: Progress Publishers, 1973, 313 p.

Atkinson, James David. *The Edge of War.* Chicago: Regnery, 1960, 318 p.

Barclay, Cyril Nelson. *The New Warfare.* London: W. Clowes, 1953, 65 p.

Bogardus, Emory Stephen. *The Making of Public Opinion.* New York: Association Press, 1951, 265 p.

Bruge, André. *Le Poison rouge, guerre sans frontières.* Nice: The Author, 1969, 227 p. (paperback).

Chakhotin, Sergei. *The Rape of the Masses: The Psychology of Totalitarian Political Propaganda.* Translated by E.W. Dickes. New York: Alliance Book Corp., 1940, 310 p.

Childs, Harwood Lawrence and **Whitton, John B.,** eds. *Propaganda by Short Wave.* Princeton: Princeton University Press, 1942, 355 p.

Clews, John C. *Communist Propaganda Techniques.* New York: Praeger, 1965, 326 p.

Crossman, Richard Howard Stafford. "Psychological Warfare." *Journal of the Royal United Service Institution,* v. XCVII (February–November 1952), pp. 319–332.

Doob, Leonard William. *Propaganda: Its Psychology and Technique.* New York: Holt, 1943, 424 p.

Dovring, Karin. *Road to Propaganda: The Semantics of Biased Communication.* New York: Philosophical Library, 1959, 158 p.

Dyer, Murray. *The Weapon on the Wall: Rethinking Psychological Warfare.* Baltimore: Johns Hopkins Press, 1959, 269 p.

Ellul, Jacques. *Propaganda: The Formation of Men's Attitudes.* Translated from the French by Konrad Kellen and Jean Lerner. New York: Knopf, 1965, 328 p.

Fourth International. *Accomplices of the GPU by the International Committee of the Fourth International.* London: New Park Publications, 1976, 24 p

Fourth International. *Dossier of a Double Agent: The Lies of Joseph Hansen by the International Committee of the Fourth International.* London: New Park Publications, 1978, 36 p.

Hale, Julian Anthony Stuart. *Radio Power: Propaganda and International Broadcasting.* Philadelphia: Temple University Press, 1975, 196 p.

Huang Chih-hsing and **Chen Ying-leu.** *Psychological Warfare: Theories and Application.* Translated by Lee Wah-chung. Hong Kong: Chi Hsing Press Branch, 1955, 257 p.

Hummel, William Castle and **Huntress, Keith.** *The Analysis of Propaganda.* New York: Sloane, 1949, 222 p.

Institute for Propaganda Analysis, Inc., New York. *The Fine Art of Propaganda.* Prepared by Alfred McClung Lee and Elizabeth Briant Lee. New York: Harcourt, Brace, 1939, 141 p. (paperback).

Knightley, Phillip. *The First Casualty: From the Crimea to Vietnam—The War Correspondent as Hero, Propagandist and Myth Maker.* New York: Harcourt, Brace, Jovanovich, 1975, 465 p.

Langdon-Davies, John. *Fifth Column.* London: J. Murray, 1940, 60 p.

Lean, Edward Tangye. *Voices in the Darkness: The Story of the European Radio War.* London: Secker and Warburg, 1943, 243 p.

Lerner, Daniel, ed. *Propaganda in War and Crisis: Materials for American Policy.* New York: G.W. Stewart, 1951, 500 p.

Linebarger, Paul Myron Anthony. *Psychological Warfare.* Washington: Infantry Journal Press, 1948, 259 p.

Martin, Leslie John. *International Propaganda: Its Legal and Diplomatic Control.* Gloucester, Mass.: n.p., 1969, 284 p. (reprint of the 1958 edition published by the University of Minnesota Press).

Movimiento Argentino Antiimperialista de Solidaridad Latinoamericana: *La CIA, qué es? qué hace en América Latina?* Buenos Aires: Ediciones Voz Latinoamericana. 1974, 44 p.

Murty, B.A. *Propaganda and World Public Order: The Legal Regulation of the Ideological Instrument of Coercion.* New Haven: Yale University Press, 1968, 310 p.

Narodno-trudovoi soiuz, Sektor inostrannykh del. *NTS (Bund Russicher Solidaristen): Die revolutionäre Organisation der russischen Widerstandsbewegung.* Herausgeber: NTS, Sektion für Auswärtige Angelegenheiten. 4 Aufl. Frankfurt: Possev-Verlag, 1965, 62 p.

Owen, David. *Battle of Wits: A History of Psychology and Deception in Modern Warfare.* London: Cooper, 1978, 207 p.

Reed, John. *The Sisson Documents.* New York: Liberator Pub., 1918, 17 p.

Riegel, Oscar Wetherhold. *Mobilizing for Chaos: The Story of the New Propaganda.* New Haven: Yale University Press, 1934, 231 p.

Saenz, Gabriel. *19 años de agresiones de la CIA contra América Latina.* Mexico, D.F.: n.p. 1967, 91 p.

Scheurig, Bodo. *Free Germany: The National Committee and the League of German Officers.* Translated from the German by Herbert Arnold. Middletown, Conn.: Wesleyan University Press, 1969, 311 p.

Schneider, Hannes. *Secret Service, die Bedrohung der Welt, Beiträge zur Geschichte und Praxis des englischen Geheimdienstes, von Feldmarschal-Leutnant A. v. Urbanski, dr. R. Kutsch, Kontreadmiral a.d. Arno Spindler, Hans L. Walther.* Nuremburg: J.L. Schrag, 1940, 160 p. (paperback).

Seth, Ronald. *The Truth-Benders: Psychological Warfare in the Second World War.* London: Frewin, 1969, 204 p.

Strausz-Hupé, Robert. *Axis America: Hitler Plans our Future.* New York: Putnam, 1941, 274 p.

Sturminger, Alfred. *3000 Jahre politische Propaganda.* Vienna: Herold, 1960, 468 p.

Vidal, Pierre. *La C.I.A. américaine, bande de criminels internationaux.* [n.p.: n.p., 197?], 51 p.

Wagner, Ernst Karl and **Cortigiano, Franco,** eds. *Im Schatten der Vergangenheit. Deutschen Soldaten in der Propaganda der italienischen Kommunisten.* Cologne: Markus-Verlag, 1969, 158 p. (paperback).

Watson, Peter. *War on the Mind: The Military Uses and Abuses of Psychology.* New York: Basic Books, 1978, 534 p.

Germany including Nazi Germany

Barth von Wehrenalp, Erwin. *Auf den Spuren des secret Service.* Berlin-Leipzig. Nibelungenverlag, 1940, 93 p. (propaganda about British intelligence).

Farago, Ladislas and **Gittler, Lewis Frederick,** eds. *German Psychological Warfare: Survey and Bibliography,* with the cooperation of Prof. Gordon W. Allport, Dr. John G. Beebe-Center *et al.* New York: Committee for National Morale, 1941, 133 p.

Zeman, Zbynek A.B. *Nazi Propaganda.* New York: Oxford University Press, 1964, 226 p.

Soviet and East European
General

American Business Consultants, Inc. *Red Channels: The Report of Communist Influence in Radio and Television.* New York: Counterattack, 1950, 213 p.

Araldsen, O.P. "Norway and Soviet Psychological Warfare." *Journal of the Royal United Service Institution,* v. CVI (February–November 1961), pp. 585–588.

Arbatov, Georgi. *The War of Ideas in Contemporary International Relations: The Imperialist Doctrine, Methods and Organization of Foreign Political Propaganda.* Translated from the Russian by David Skvirsky. Moscow: Progress Publishers, 1973, 313 p.

Barghoorn, Frederick Charles. *Soviet Foreign Propaganda.* Princeton, N.J.: Princeton University Press, 1964, 329 p.

Buzek, Antony. *How the Communist Press Works.* New York: Praeger, 1964, 287 p.

Dunham, Donald Carl. *Kremlin Target: U.S.A.: Conquest by Propaganda.* New York: Washburn, 1961, 274 p.

Hartel, Gunther E. *The Red Herring.* New York: I. Obolensky, 1962, 177 p.

Kirkpatrick, Evron Maurice, ed. *Year of Crisis: Communist Propaganda Activities in 1956.* New York: Macmillan, 1957, 414 p.

Kruglak, Theodore Eduard. *The Two Faces of TASS.* Minneapolis: University of Minnesota Press, 1962, 263 p.

Lasswell, Harold Dwight and **Blumenstock, Dorothy.** *World Revolutionary Propaganda: A Chicago Study.* New York: Knopf, 1939, 393 p.

Maxwell, Lucia Ramsey. *The Red Juggernaut.* Washington: Library Press, 1932, 218 p.

Reisky-Dubnic, Vladimir. *Communist Propaganda Methods: A Case Study on Czechoslovakia.* New York: Praeger, 1960, 287 p.

Die Rote Armee: ein Sammelbuch. Aufsäze von Trotzki [*et al.*]. Hamburg: Verlag C. Hoym, 1923, 134 p.

Shackford, R.H. The Truth about Soviet Lies. Washington: Public Affairs Press, 1962, 224 p.

Trotskii, Lev. *The Stalin School of Falsification.* Translated by John G. Wright. London: New Park Publications, 1974, 263 p. (paperback).

U.S. Congress, House, Committee on Un-American Activities. *Communist Propaganda, and the Truth about Conditions in Soviet Russia (Testimony of David P. Johnson). Hearing . . . May 22, 1962.* 87th Congress, 2d session. Washington: U.S. GPO, 1962, pp. 939–987.

Works of Propaganda

Artemov, Vladimir L'vovich and **Semenov, V.** *Bi-Bi-Si-istoriia, apparat, metody radio propagandy.* Moscow: Iskusstvo, 1978, 256 p.

Biahun, Vladzimir Iakaulevich. *Vtorzhenie bez oruzhiia.* Moscow: Mol. Gvardiia, 1977, 176 p.

Cherniavskii, Vitalii Gennadievich. *Shpion no. 1: pamflet o shefe razvedki SShA Dzhone Alekse Makkoune.* Ann Arbor, Mich.: University Microfilms International, 1976, 46 p. (original published by Polit. Lit-ry, Moscow, 1963). (John A. McCone).

Goliakov, Sergei. *Spy College at Chateau Pourtalet.* Moscow: Novosti, [post 1966], 46 p. (translation of *Diversiya v shato purtale*).

John, Otto. *Ich wählte Deutschland.* [Berlin?]: Ausschuss für Deutsche Einheit, 1954, 47 p.

Laloy, Emile, ed. *Les documents secrets des archives du Ministère des affaires étrangères de Russie, publiés par les bolcheviks.* Paris: Editions Bossard, 1919, 197 p.

Mader, Julius. *Who's Who in CIA: Ein biographisches Nachschlagewerk über 3000 Mitarbeiter der zivilen und militärischen Geheimedienstzweige der USA in 20 Staaten.* Berlin: n.p., 1968, 591 p.

Nikolaev, Ivan Petrovich. *Pod Zheleznoi piatoi.* Moscow: Mol. Gvardiia, 1978, 175 p.

Panfilov, Artem Flegontovich and **Karchevskii, IUrii.** *Subversion by Radio: Radio Free Europe and Radio Liberty.* Moscow: Novosti, 1974, 188 p.

Panfilov, Artem Flegontovich. *Za kulisami "Radio Svoboda."* Moscow: Mezhdunarodnye Otnosheniia, 1974, 192 p.

Petrusenko, Vitalii Vasil'evich. *Tainoe stanovitsia iavnym: TSRU i sredstva massovoi inform.* Moscow: Mysl', 1978, 223 p.

Prague, Ustav pro Mezinarodni Politku a Ekonomii. *Beware! German Revenge-seekers Threaten Peace.* Prague: Orbis, 1959, 78 p.

Provocateurs falsificateurs fabricants d'opinion: le trust de la press Axel Springer au service des ultras. Berlin: L'Union des Journalistes Allemands (VDJ), 1963, 84 p.

Razvedchiki razoblachaiut . . . Compiled by V. Zarechnyi. Moscow: Molodaia Gvardiia, 1977, 176 p.

Reuben, Wliam A. *The Atom Spy Hoax.* New York: Action Books, 1955, 504 p.

Russia, Sovetskoe Informatsionnoe Biuro. *Caught in the Act: Facts about U.S. Espionage and Subversion against the U.S.S.R.* Moscow: n.p., 1960, [159] p. (translation of *Poimany s polichnym*).

Russia, Sovetskoe Informatsionnoe Biuro. *Con las manos en la masa: datos sobre el espionaje y labor de zapa de los Estados Unidos Contra la U.R.S.S.* Montevideo: Ediciones Pueblos Unidos, 1961, 160 p.

Strzhizhovskii, Lev Fedorovich. *Streliaet pressa Shpringera.* Moscow: Politizdat, 1978, 78 p.

Tarasov, Konstantin Sergeevich. *Tainaia voina imperializma SShA v Latinskoi Amerike.* Moscow: Politizdat, 1978, 214 p.

Vachnadze, Georgii Nikolaevich. *Antenny napravleny na Vostok.* Moscow: Politizdat, 1977, 239 p.

Vasil'ev, V.N. et al. *Sekrety sekretnykh sluzhb SShA: Sbornik.* Moscow: Politizdat, 1973, 303 p.

United Kingdom

Jacob, Ian. "The British Broadcasting Corporation in Peace and War." *Journal of the Royal United Service Institution.* v. XCIV (February–November 1949), pp. 379–389.

Jacob, Ian. "The Coduct of External Broadcasting." *Journal of the Royal United Service Institution,* v. CIII (February 1958), pp. 172–183.

Stewart-Smith, D.G. *No Vision Here: Non-Military Warfare in Britain.* Petersham, Sydney, Australia: Foreign Affairs Publishing, 1965, 142 p.

Stuart, Campbell, *Sir. Secrets of Crewe House: The Story of a Famous Campaign.* London: Hodder and Stoughton, 1920, 240 p.

United States

Barrett, Edward W. *Truth is our Weapon.* New York: Funk and Wagnalls, 1953, 355 p.

Butterfield, Lyman H. "Psychological Warfare in 1776: the Jefferson-Franklin Plan to Cause Hessian Desertions." *Proceedings of the American Philosophical Society,* v. 94, no. 3 (June 1950), pp. 233-241.

Dizard, Wilson P. *The Strategy of Truth: The Story of the U.S. Information Service.* Washington: Public Affairs Press, 1961, 213 p.

Hapgood, Norman, ed. *Professional Patriots: Material Assembled by Sidney Howard and John Hearley, an Exposure of the Personalities, Methods and Objectives Involved in the Organized Effort to Exploit Patriotic Impulses in These United States and After the Late War.* New York: A. and C. Boni, 1927, 210 p.

Holt, Robert T. and **Van de Velde, Robert W.** *Strategic Psychological Operations and American Foreign Policy.* Chicago: University of Chicago Press, 1960, 243 p.

Meyerhoff, Arthur E. *The Strategy of Persuasion: The Use of Advertising Skills in Fighting the Cold War.* New York: Coward-McCann, 1965, 191 p.

Sorensen, Thomas C. *The Word War: The Story of American Propaganda.* New York: Harper and Row, 1968, 337 p.

Thomson, Charles Alexander Holmes. *Overseas Information Service of the United States Government.* Washington: Brookings Institution, 1948, 397 p.

World War I

Blankenhorn, Heber. *Adventures in Propaganda: Letters from an Intelligence Officer in France.* Boston: Houghton Mifflin, 1919, 166 p.

Bruntz, George G. *Allied Propaganda and the Collapse of the German Empire in 1918.* New York: Arno Press, 1972, 246 p. (reprint of 1938 Hoover War Library publication).

Hanak, Harry. *Great Britain and Austria-Hungary During the First World War: A Study in the Formation of Public Opinion.* New York: Oxford University Press, 1962, 312 p.

Hillis, Newell Dwight. *The Blot on the Kaiser's Scutcheon.* New York: Fleming H. Revell Co., 1918, 193 p.

Lasswell, Harold Dwight. *Propaganda Technique in World War I.* Cambridge, Mass.: M.I.T. Press, 1971, 233 p.

Mock, James Robert and **Larson, Cedric.** *Words that won the War: The Story of the Committee on Public Information, 1917-1919.* Princeton: Princeton University Press, 1939, 372 p.

Ogg, David. "German Naval Propaganda." *Journal of the Royal United Service Institution,* v. LXV (February 1920), pp. 1-22.

Peterson, Horace Cornelius. *Propaganda for War: The Campaign Against American Neutrality, 1914-1917.* Norman: University of Oklahoma Press, 1939, 357 p.

Ponsonby, Arthur Ponsonby, *Baron. Falsehood in War-time, Containing an Assortment of Lies Circulated Throughout the Nations During the Great War.* London: Allen and Unwin, 1928, 192 p. (paperback).

Roetter, Charles. *The Art of Psychological Warfare, 1914-1945.* New York: Stein and Day, 1974, 199 p.

Rogerson, Sidney. *Propaganda in the Next War.* London: G. Bles, 1938, 187 p.

Viereck, George Sylvester. *Spreading Germs of Hate.* New York: H. Liveright, 1930, 327 p.

Wanderscheck, Hermann. *Die englische Lügenpropaganda im Weltkrieg und Heute.* Berlin: Junker and Dünnhaupt, 1940, 70 p.

Whitehouse, Vira Boarman. *A Year as a Government Agent.* New York: Harper and Brothers, 1920, 316 p.

World War II

Baird, Jay W. *The Mythical World of Nazi War Propaganda, 1939-1945.* Minneapolis: University of Minnesota Press, 1974, 329 p.

Balfour, Michael Leonard Graham. *Propaganda in War, 1939-1945: Organisations, Policies, and Publics, in Britain and Germany.* London: Routledge and Kegan Paul, 1979, 520 p.

Bennett, Jeremy. *British Broadcasting and the Danish Resistance Movement, 1940-1945: A Study of the Wartime Broadcasts of the B.B.C. Danish Service.* Cambridge: Cambridge University Press, 1966, 266 p.

Buchbender, Ortwin and **Schuh, Horst,** comps. *Heil Beil!: Flugbattpropaganda im Zweiten Weltkrieg: Dokumentation und Analyse.* Stuttgart: Seewald Verlag, 1974, 214 p. (paperback).

Burlingame, Roger. *Don't Let Them Scare You: The Life and Times of Elmer Davis.* Westport, Conn.: Greenwood Press, 1961, 352 p.

Carroll, Wallace. *Persuade or Perish.* Boston: Houghton Mifflin, 1948, 392 p.

Colby, Benjamin. *'Twas a Famous Victory.* New Rochelle, N.Y.: Arlington House, 1974, 221 p.

Cole, John Alfred. *Lord Haw-Haw and William Joyce: The Full Story.* New York: Farrar, Strauss and Giroux, 1965, 316 p.

Cruikshank, Charles Greig. *The Fourth Arm: Psychological Warfare, 1938-1945.* London: Davis-Poynter, 1977, 200 p.

Delmer, Sefton. *Black Boomerang.* New York: Viking Press, 1962, 303 p.

Ettlinger, Harold. *The Axis on the Air.* Indianapolis: Bobbs-Merrill, 1943, 318 p.

Germany, Auswärtiges Amt. *Allied Intrigue in the Low Countries: Further Documents Concerning the Anglo-French Policy of Extending the War.* Full text of White Book, no. 5, published by the German Foreign Office. New York: German Library of Information, 1940, 46 p.

Goebbels, Joseph. *Final Entries, 1945: The Diaries of Joseph Goebbels.* Edited by Hugh Trevor-Roper. Translated from the German by Richard Barry. New York: Avon Books, 1979, 453 p. (paperback).

Haffner, Sebastian. *Offensive Against Germany.* London: Seeker and Warburg, 1941, 126 p.

Hardy, Alexander G. *Hitler's Secret Weapon: The "Managed" Press and Propaganda Machine of Nazi Germany.* New York: Vantage Press, 1967, 350 p.

Herzstein, Robert Edwin. *The War that Hitler Won: The Most Infamous Propaganda Campaign in History.* New York: Putnam, 1978, 491 p.

Kato, Masuo. *The Lost War: A Japanese Reporter's Inside Story.* New York: Knopf, 1946, 264 p.

Kris, Ernst and **Speier, Hans.** *German Radio Propaganda: Report on Home Broadcasts During the War.* New York: Oxford University Press, 1944, 529 p.

Lavine, Harold and **Wachsler, James.** *War Propaganda and the United States.* New Haven: Yale University Press, 1940, 363 p.

Lerner, Daniel. *Psychological Warfare Against Nazi Germany: The Sykewar Campaign, D Day to VE Day.* Cambridge, Mass.: M.I.T. Press, 1971, 377 p.

McLaine, Ian. *Ministry of Morale: Home Front Morale and the Ministry of Information in World War II.* London: Allen and Unwin, 1979, 325 p.

Margolin, Leo Jay. *Paper Bullets, a Brief Story of Psychological Warfare in World War II.* New York: Froben Press, 1946, 149 p.

Reimann, Viktor. *Goebbels.* Translated from the German by Stephen Wendt. Garden City, N.Y.: Double-day, 1976, 352 p.

Rhodes, Anthony Richard Ewart. *Propaganda: The Art of Persuasion in World War II.* Edited by Victor Margolin. New York: Chelsea House Publishers, 1976, 319 p.

Roetter, Charles. *The Art of Psychological Warfare, 1914-1945.* New York: Stein and Day, 1974, 199 p.

Rolo, Charles James. *Radio Goes to War: The "Fourth Front."* London: Faber and Faber, 1943, 245 p.

Rutherford, Ward. *Hitler's Propaganda Machine.* London: Bison Books, 1978, 192 p.

Rutledge, Brett, pseud. (Paul, Elliot Harold). *The Death of Lord Haw Haw, no. 1 Personality of World War no. 2: Being an Account of the Last Days of the Foremost Nazi Spy and news Commentator, the Mysterious English Traitor.* New York: Random House, 1940, 306 p. (fiction).

Scheel, Klaus. *Krieg über Atherwellen: NS-Rundfunk und Monopole, 1933-1945.* Berlin: Deutscher Verlag der Wissenschaften, 1970, 316 p.

Sington, Derrick and **Weidenfeld, Arthur.** *The Goebbels Experiment: A Study of the Nazi Propaganda Machine.* New Haven: Yale University Press, 1943, 274 p.

Sywottek, Jutta. *Mobilmachung für den totalen Krieg: Die Propagandistische Vorbereitung der deutschen Bevölkerung auf den Zweiten Weltkrieg.* Opladen: Westdeutscher Verlag, 1976, 398 p. (paperback).

Taylor, Edmund. *The Strategy of Terror: Europe's Inner Front.* Boston: Houghton Mifflin, 1940, 277 p.

Taylor, Richard. *Film Propaganda: Soviet Russia and Nazi Germany.* New York: Barnes and Noble, 1979, 265 p.

Willis, Jeffrey Robert. *The Wehrmacht Propaganda Branch: German Military Propaganda and Censorship During World War II.* Ann Arbor, Mich.: University Microfilms, 1976, 305 p.

Winkler, Allan M. *The Politics of Propaganda: The Office of War Information, 1942-1945.* New Haven: Yale University Press, 1978, 230 p.

Zeman, Abynek A.B. *Selling the War: Art and Propaganda in World War II.* London: Orbis Books, 1978, 120 p.

X. UNCONVENTIONAL WARFARE
General

Bergeron, Louis and **Kosseleck, Reinhart.** *L'âge des révolutions européennes (1870-1948).* Paris: Bordas, 1973, 282 p.

Casey, Douglas, R. *The International Man: The Complete Guidebook to the World's Last Frontiers: For Freedom Seekers, Investors, Adventurers, Speculators, and Expatriates.* Alexandria, Virginia: Alexandria House Books, 1979, 133 p.

Chaliand, Gérard. *Revolution in the Third World: Myths and Prospects.* New York: Viking Press, 1977, 195 p.

Crozier, Brian. *The Rebels: A Study of Post-War Insurrections.* Boston: Beacon Press, 1962, 256 p.

Ellis, John. *Armies in Revolution.* London: Croom Helm, 1973, 278 p.

Goodspeed, Donald J. *The Conspirators: A Study of the Coup d'Etat.* New York: Viking Press, 1961, 252 p.

Hobsbawn, Eric. J. *Primitive Rebels: Studies in Archaic Forms of Social Movement in the 19th and 20th Centuries.* New York: W.W. Norton, 1965, 202 p. (paperback).

Hoehling, Adolph A. *Who Destroyed the Hindenburg?* New York: Popular Library, 1962, 241 p.

Luttwak, Edward. *Coup d'Etat: A Practical Handbook.* New York: Knopf, 1969, 209 p.

MacCloskey, Monro. *Alert the Fifth Force: Counterinsurgency, Unconventional Warfare, and Psychological Operations of the United States Air Force in Special Air Warfare.* New York: R. Rosen Press, 1969, 190 p.

Malaparte, Curzio. *Coup d'Etat: The Technique of Revolution.* Translated by Sylvia Saunders. New York: Dutton, 1932, 251 p.

Matthews, Blayney F. *The Specter of Sabotage.* Los Angeles: Lymanhouse, 1941, 256 p.

"Partisan Warfare." *Journal of the Royal United Service Institution,* v. XXVI (1883), pp. 135-164.

Ramsay, Archibald H. Maule. *The Nameless War.* London: Britons Pub. Society, 1962, 120 p.

Sanger, Richard Harlakenden. *Insurgent Era: New Patterns of Political, Economic, and Social Revolution* Washington: Potomac Books, 1970, 235 p.

Suskind, Richard. *By Bullet, Bomb, and Dagger: The Story of Anarchism.* New York: Macmillan, 1971, 182 p.

White, John Baker. *Sabotage is Suspected.* London: Evans Bros., 1957, 224 p.

Wilkinson, Burke, comp. *Cry Sabotage! True Stories of 20th Century Saboteurs.* Scarsdale, N.Y.: Bradbury Press, 1972, 265 p.

Guerrillas

Al-Rayyis, Riyad Najib and **Nahas, Dunia.** *Guerrillas for Palestine.* London: Croom Helm, 1976, 155 p.

American Academy of Political and Social Science, Philadelphia. *Unconventional Warfare.* Edited by J.K. Zawodny. Philadelphia, 1962, 180 p.

Bell, J. Bowyer. *The Myth of the Guerrilla: Revolutionary Theory and Malpractice.* New York: Knopf, 1971, 285 p.

Bell, J. Bowyer. *On Revolt: Strategies of National Liberation.* Cambridge: Harvard University Press, 1976, 272 p.

Blacker, Irwin R. ed. *Irregulars, Partisans, Guerrillas: Great Stories from Rogers' Rangers to the Haganah.* New York: Simon and Schuster, 1954, 487 p.

Campbell, Arthur. *Guerrillas: A History and Analysis.* New York: John Day, 1968, 345 p.

Chateau-Jobert, Pierre. *Doctrine d'action contrerévolutionaire.* Vouillé: Diffusion de la pensée française, 1972, 348 p. (paperback).

Clutterbuck, Richard L. *Guerrillas and Terrorists.* London: Faber and Faber, 1977, 125 p.

Cross, James Eliot. *Conflict in the Shadows: The Nature and Politics of Guerrilla War.* London: Constable, 1964, 180 p.

Dach Bern, H. von. *Total Resistance.* Translated by Hans Lienhard. Edited by Robert K. Brown. Boulder, Colo.: Panther Publications, 1965, 173 p.

Dobson, Christopher. *Black September: Its Short, Violent History.* New York: Macmillan, 1974, 179 p. (Fedayeen).

Ellis, John. *A Short History of Guerrilla Warfare.* New York: St. Martin's Press, 1976, 220 p.

Fleming, Peter. "Unorthodox Warriors." *Journal of the Royal United Service Institution,* v. CIV (February--November 1959), pp. 378–389.

Galula, David. *Counterinsurgency Warfare: Theory and Practice.* New York: Praeger, 1964, 143 p.

Gann, Lewis H. *Guerrillas in History.* Stanford: Hoover Institution Press, 1971, 99 p.

The Guerrilla Reader: A Historical Anthology. Edited by Walter Laqueur. New York: New American Library, 1977, 246 p.

Heilbrunn, Otto. "Guerrillas in Pitched Battle." *Journal of the Royal United Service Institution,* v. CX (February–November 1965), pp. 166–169.

Heilbrunn, Otto. "Guerrillas in the 19th Century." *Journal of the Royal United Service Institution,* v. CVIII (February 1963), pp. 145–148.

Heilbrunn, Otto. *Partisan Warfare.* New York: Praeger, 1962, 199 p.

Heilbrunn, Otto. *Warfare in the Enemy's Rear.* New York: Praeger, 1964, 231 p.

Hodges, Donald Clark and **Shanab, Robert Elias Abu,** eds. *NLF. National Liberation Fronts, 1960-1970.* New York: Morrow, 1972, 350 p.

Kitson, Frank. *Bunch of Five.* London: Faber, 1977, 306 p.

Laqueur, Walter Ze'ev. *Guerrilla: A Historical and Critical Study.* Boston: Little, Brown, 1976, 462 p.

Lockwood, Rupert. *Guerrilla Paths to Freedom.* London: Angus and Robertson, 1942, 83 p.

Maclean, Fitzroy. "The Setting for Guerrilla Warfare." *Journal of the Royal United Service Institution,* v. CVIII (February 1963), pp. 206–212.

Marighella, Carlos. *Minimanual of the Urban Guerrilla.* Boulder, Colo.: Paladin Press, 1978, 42 p.

The Marine Corps Gazette. *The Guerrilla, and How to Fight Him: Selections.* Edited by T.N. Greene. New York: Praeger, 1962 and 1964, 310 p.

Moss, Robert. *Urban Guerrillas: The New Face of Political Violence.* London: Maurice Temple Smith, 1972, 288 p.

Ney, Virgil. *Notes on Guerrilla War: Principles and Practices.* Washington: Command Publications, 1961, 185 p.

Oatts, L.B. "Guerrilla Warfare." *Journal of the Royal United Service Institution,* v. XCIV (February–November 1949), pp. 192–196.

O'Ballance, Edgar. *Language of Violence: The Blood Politics of Terrorism.* San Rafael, Calif.: Presidio Press, 1979, 365 p. (Fedayeen).

O'Neill, Bard E. *Revolutionary Warfare in the Middle East: The Israelis vs. the Fedayeen.* Boulder Colo.: Paladin Press, 1974, 140 p.

Osanka, Franklin Mark. ed. *Modern Guerrilla Warfare: Fighting Communist Guerrilla Movements, 1941-1961.* New York: Free Press of Glencoe, 1962, 519 p.

Paget, Julian. *Counter-Insurgency Operations (Techniques of Guerrilla Warfare).* New York: Walker, 1967, 189 p. (London edition title: *Counter-Insurgency Campaigning*).

Paret, Peter and **Shy, John W.** *Guerrilla y contraguerrilla.* Edited by Jorge Alvarez. Translated by Carlos Peralta. Buenos Aires: Carlos Peralta, 1964, 176 p. (paperback).

Paret, Peter and **Shy, John W.** *Guerrillas in the 1960's.* New York: Praeger, 1962, 82 p.

Paret, Peter and **Shy, John W.** *Guerrillas in the 1960's.* 2d ed. New York: Praeger, 1962, 98 p.

Pomeroy, William J., comp. *Guerrilla Warfare and Marxism: A Collection of Writings from Karl Marx to the Present on Armed Struggles for Liberation and for Socialism.* New York: International Publishers, 1968, 336 p.

Pryce-Jones, David. *The Face of Defeat: Palestinian Refugees and Guerrillas.* New York: Holt, Rinehart and Winston, 1972, 179 p.

Pustay, John S. *Counterinsurgency Warfare.* New York: Free Press, 1965, 236 p.

Revolutionary Guerrilla Warfare. Edited by Sam C. Sarkesian. Chicago: Precedent Pub., 1975, 623 p.

Robinson, Donald B., *comp. The Dirty Wars: Guerrilla Actions and Other Forms of Unconventional Warfare.* New York: Delacorte Press, 1968, 356 p.

Schiff, Zeev and **Rothstein, Raphael.** *Fedayeen: Guerrillas Against Israel.* New York: McKay, 1972, 246 p.

Standing, Percy Cross. *Guerrilla Leaders of the World, from Charette to De Wet.* London: S. Paul, 1913, 294 p.

Sully, François. *Age of the Guerrilla: The New Warfare.* New York: Avon Books, 222 p. (paperback).

Taber, Robert. *The War of the Flea: A Study of Guerrilla Warfare Theory and Practice.* New York: L. Stuart, 1965, 192 p.

Thayer, Charles Wheeler. *Guerrilla.* London: M. Joseph, 1964, 221 p.

Towards a Citizens' Militia: Anarchist Alternatives to NATO and the Warsaw Pact. Sanday, England: Cienfuegos Press, 1980, 28 p.

Trinquier, Roger. *La guerra moderna y la lucha contra las guerrillas.* Barcelona: Editorial Herder, 1965, 187 p. (Spanish edition of: *La guerre moderne.* Paris: La Table ronde, 1961, 196 p.).

Trinquier, Roger. *Modern Warfare: A French View of Counterinsurgency.* Translated from the French by Daniel Lee. New York: Praeger, 1964, 115 p.

United States Naval Institute. *Studies in Guerrilla Warfare.* Annapolis: n.p., 1963, 89 p.

Mercenaries

Banks, John. *The Wages of War: The Life of a Modern Mercenary.* London: Cooper, 1978, 112 p.

Burchett, Wilfred G. and **Roebuck, Derek.** *The Whores of War: Mercenaries Today.* Harmondsworth: Penguin, 1977, 240 p.

Mallin, Jay and **Brown, Robert K.** *Merc: American Soldiers of Fortune.* New York: New American Library, 1980, 184 p. (paperback).

Smith, Colin. *Carlos: Portrait of a Terrorist.* New York: Holt, Rinehart and Winston, 1976, 312 p.

Sultan, Ali. *And They Died.* London: Sampson Low, Marston and Co., 1930, 244 p.

Terrorists

Alexander, Joseph H. "Countering Tomorrow's Terrorism." *United States Naval Institute Proceedings,* July 1981, pp. 45-50.

Alexander, Yonah; Browne, Marjorie Ann et al., eds. *Control of Terrorism: International Documents.* New York: Crane, Russak, 1979, 215 p.

Alexander, Yonah; Carlson, David et al., eds. *Terrorism: Theory and Practice.* Boulder, Colo.: Westview Press, 1979, 280 p.

Bell, J. Bowyer. *A Time of Terror: How Democratic Societies Respond to Revolutionary Violence.* New York: Basic Books, 1978, 292 p.

Bell, J. Bowyer. *Transnational Terror.* Washington: American Enterprise Institute for Public Policy, 1979, 91 p.

Burton, Anthony. *Urban Terrorism: Theory, Practice and Response.* New York: Free Press, 1975, 259 p.

Chapman, Robert D. and **Chapman, M. Lester.** *The Crimson Web of Terror.* Boulder, Colo.: Paladin Press, 1980, 155 p.

Clarke, Thurston. *By Blood and Fire: The Attack on the King David Hotel.* London: Hutchinson, 1981, 347 p.

Clutterbuck, Richard L. *Guerrillas and Terrorists.* London: Faber and Faber, 1977, 125 p.

Clutterbuck, Richard L. *Living with Terrorism.* London: Faber and Faber, 1975, 160 p.

Cohen, Geulah. *Woman of Violence: Memoirs of a Young Terrorist, 1943-1948.* Translated from the Hebrew by Hillel Halkin. New York: Holt, Rinehart and Winston, 1966, 275 p. (Lohame Herut Yisrael).

Cooley, John K. "The Libyan Menace." *Foreign Policy,* no. 42 (Spring 1981), pp. 74-93.

Demaris, Ovid. *Brothers in Blood: The International Terrorist Network.* New York: Scribner, 1977, 441 p.

Dobson, Christopher and **Payne, Ronald.** *The Carlos Complex: A Study in Terror.* New York: Putnam, 1977, 254 p.

Dobson, Christopher and **Payne, Ronald.** *The Terrorists: Their Weapons, Leaders and Tactics.* New York: Facts on File, 1979, 238 p.

Ebersole, John F. "International Terrorism and the Defense of Offshore Facilities." *Drilling-DCW,* no. 514 (November 1979), pp. 30+.

Fromkin, David. "The Strategy of Terrorism." *Foreign Affairs,* v. 53, no. 4 (July 1975), pp. 683–698.

Gaucher, Roland. *Les terroristes.* Paris: A. Michel, 1965, 372 p.

Hacker, Frederick J. *Crusaders, Criminals, Crazies: Terror and Terrorism in our Time.* New York: Bantam Books, 1978, 395 p. (paperback).

International School on Disarmament and Research on Conflicts, 5th, Urbino, Italy, 1974. *International Terrorism and World Security: [Proceedings].* Edited by David Carlton and Carlo Schaerf. New York: Wiley, 1975, 332 p.

International Terrorism in the Contemporary World. Edited by Marius H. Livingston with Lee Bruce Kress et al. Westport, Conn.: Greenwood Press, 1978, 522 p.

Joesten, Joachim. *The Red Hand: The Sinister Account of the Terrorist Arm of the French Right-Wing "Ultras"—in Algeria and on the Continent.* London: Abelard-Schuman, 1962, 200 p.

Katz, Doris Kaplan. *The Lady was a Terrorist, During Israel's War of Liberation.* New York: Shiloni Pub., 1953, 192 p. (Irgun Zvai Leumi).

Killen, Frederick S. *The Question of America's Intelligence Gathering Capabilities: An Examination of the Intelligence Community's Ability to Provide Information Concerning Impending Terrorist Actions.* Santa Ana, Calif.: The Author, 1979, 338 p.

Kupperman, Robert H. and **Trent, Darrell M.** *Terrorism: Threat, Reality, Response.* Stanford: Hoover Institution Press, Stanford University, 1979, 450 p.

Laqueur, Walter, ed. *The Terrorism Reader: A Historical Anthology.* New York: New American Library, 1978, 291 p. (paperback).

McKnight, Gerald. *The Mind of the Terrorist.* London: Joseph, 1974, 182 p.

Mardor, Meir. *Strictly Illegal.* Translated by H.A.G. Shmucklev. London: Hale, 1957, 239 p. (Haganah).

Parry, Albert. *Terrorism: From Robespierre to Arafat.* New York: Vanguard Press, 1976, 624 p.

Payne, Pierre Stephen Robert. *Zero: The Story of Terrorism.* New York: John Day, 1950, 270 p.

The Politics of Terrorism. Edited by Michael Stohl. New York: M. Dekker, 1979, 419 p.

Schamis, Gerardo Jorge. *War and Terrorism in International Affairs.* Translated by Danielle Salti. New Brunswick, N.J.: Transaction Books, 1980, 89 p.

Schreiber, Jan Edward. *The Ultimate Weapon: Terrorists and World Order.* New York: Morrow, 1978, 218 p.

Schultz, Richard H., Jr. and **Sloan, Stephen,** eds. *Responding to the Terrorist Threat: Security and Crisis Management.* Elmsford, N.Y.: Pergamon Press, 1980, 261 p.

Slater, Leonard. *The Pledge.* New York: Simon and Schuster, 1970, 350 p. (Haganah).

Sloan, Stephen. *Simulating Terrorism.* Norman: University of Oklahoma Press, 1981, 158 p.

Sterling, Claire. *The Terror Network: The Secret War of International Terrorism.* New York: Holt, Rinehart, and Winston, 1981, 357 p.

Ten Years of Terrorism: Collected Views. Edited by Jennifer Shaw et al. New York: Crane, Russak, 1979, 192 p.

Terrorism. Edited by Michael Wallace and Gene Brown. New York: Arno Press, 1979, 378 p.

U.S. Congress, Senate, Committee on the Judiciary. *Soviet Terrorism in Free Germany. Hearing Before the Subcommittee to Investigate the Administration of the Internal Security Act and Other Internal Security Laws . . . Testimony of Theodor Hans, September 21, 1960.* 86th Congress, 2d session. Washington: U.S. GPO, 1960, 39 p.

Wilkinson, Paul. *Terrorism and the Liberal State.* New York: Wiley, 1977, 257 p.

Zionist Organization of America. *Hagana: A History of Jewish Resistance.* New York: Zionist Organization of America, Education Department, 1946, 16 p.

Africa

Attwood, William. *The Reds and the Blacks: A Personal Adventure.* New York: Harper and Row, 1967, 341 p.

Baldwin, William W. *Mau Mau Man-Hunt: The Adventures of the only American who has Fought the Terrorists in Kenya.* New York: Dutton, 1957, 252 p. (autobiographical).

Croker, G.W. "Mau Mau." *Journal of the Royal United Service Institution,* v. C (February–November 1955), pp. 47–53.

Dempster, Chris and **Tomkins, Dave.** *Fire Power.* New York: St. Martin's Press, 1980, 491 p.

Driver, C.J. *Elegy for a Revolutionary.* London: Faber, 1969, 214 p.

Erskine, George. "Kenya-Mau Mau." *Journal of the Royal United Service Institution,* v. CI, (February–November 1956), pp. 11–22.

Grundy, Kenneth W. *Guerrilla Struggle in Africa: An Analysis and Preview.* New York: Grossman, 1971, 204 p.

Henderson, Ian with **Goodhart, Philip.** *Man Hunt in Kenya.* Garden City, N.Y.: Doubleday, 1958, 240 p.

Hoare, Michael, *Congo Mercenary.* London: Hale, 1978, 318 p.

Holman, Dennis. *Bwana Drum.* London: W.H. Allen, 1964, 198 p.

Leakey, Louis Seymour Bazett. *Defeating Mau Mau.* London: Methuen, 1954, 151 p.

Martin, David and **Johnson, Phyllis.** *The Struggle for Zimbabwe: The Chimurenga War.* London: Faber and Faber, 1981, 378 p.

Nkrumah, Kwame, *Pres. Ghana. Handbook of Revolutionary Warfare: A Guide to the Armed Phase of the African Revolution.* New York: International Publishers, 1969, 128 p. (paperback).

Nugent, John Peer. *Call Africa 999.* New York: Coward-McCann, 1965, 255 p.

Raeburn, Michael. *We are Everywhere: Narrative from Rhodesian Guerillas.* New York: Random House, 1978, 209 p.

Seale, Patrick and **McConville, Maureen.** *The Hilton Assignment.* New York: Praeger, 1973, 236 p.

Smiley, David with **Kemp, Peter.** *Arabian Assignment.* London: Cooper, 1975, 248 p.

Steiner, Rolf with **Cox, Steve.** *The Last Adventurer.* Boston: Little, Brown, 1978, 275 p.

Asia and the Pacific

Chou Wen-ching. *How to put an end to Communist Armed Struggle in Rural Area.* Taipei, Taiwan: World Anti-Communist League, China Chapter, August 1979, 62 p.

Follett, Helen Thomas. *Men of the Sulu Sea.* New York: Scribner, 1945, 250 p.

Ghassemlou, A.R.; Roosevelt, A. et al. *People Without a Country: The Kurds and Kurdistan.* Translated from the French by Michael Pallis. London: Zed Press, 1980, 246 p. (paperback).

Hauner, Milan. "One Man Against the Empire. The Faqir of Ipi and the British in Central Asia on the Eve of and During the Second World War." *Journal of Contemporary History,* v. 16, no. 1 (January 1981), pp. 183–212.

Lambrick, H.T., ed. *The Terrorist.* Translated by the editor. London: Benn, 1972, 246 p.

Lattimore, Owen. *Nomads and Commissars: Mongolia Revisited.* New York: Oxford University Press, 1962, 238 p.

Mangeot, Sylvain. *Manchurian Adventure: The Story of Lobsang Thondup.* New York: Morrow, 1975, 279 p.

Peissel, Michel. *The Secret War in Tibet.* Boston: Little, Brown, 1972, 258 p.

Sinha, Satyanarayan. *Operation Himalayas: To Defend Indian Sovereignty.* New Delhi: S. Chand, 1975, 200 p.

Sivaram, M. *The Road to Delhi.* Rutland, Vt.: C.E. Tuttle, 1967, 264 p.

Wildman, Edwin. *Aguinaldo: A Narrative of Filipino Ambitions.* Boston: Lothrop, 1901, 374 p.

Zornow, William F. "Funston Captures Aguinaldo." *American Heritage,* v. IX, no. 2 (February 1958), p. 24.

Europe

Becker, Jillian. *Hitler's Children: The Story of the Baader-Meinhof Terrorist Gang.* Philadelphia: Lippincott, 1977, 322 p.

Benes, Edvard, *Pres., Czechoslovak Republic. My War Memoirs.* Translated from the Czech by Paul Selver. Boston: Houghton Mifflin, 1928, 512 p.

Bookchin, Murray. *The Spanish Anarchists: The Heroic Years, 1868-1936.* New York: Harper and Row, 1978, 344 p. (paperback).

Calmes, Albert. *Histoire contemporaine du Grand-Duché de Luxembourg. Volume 2: Le Grand-Duché de Luxembourg dans la révolution belge, 1830–1939.* Brussels: L'Edition Universelle, 1939, 423 p.

Caserta, John. *The Red Brigades: Italy's Agony.* New York: Manor Books, 1978, 240 p. (paperback).

Faÿ, Bernard. *Revolution and Freemasonry, 1680–1800.* Boston: Little, Brown, 1935, 349 p.

Fleming, Marie. *The Anarchist Way to Socialism: Elysée Reclus and Nineteenth-Century European Anarchism.* Totowa, N.J.: Rowman and Littlefield, 1979, 299 p.

Irving, David. *Uprising! One Nation's Nightmare: Hungary, 1956.* London: Hodder and Stoughton, 1981, 628 p.

Lansdowne, Henry William Edmund Petty FitzMaurice, 6th Marquis of, ed. *The Secret of the Coup d'Etat: Unpublished Correspondence of Prince Louis Napoleon, MM. de Morny, de Flahault, and others, 1848 to 1852* ... a study by Philip Guedalla. New York: Putnam, 1924, 362 p.

Lasky, Melvin J., ed. *The Hungarian Revolution: A White Book. The Story of the October Uprising as Recorded in Documents, Dispatches, Eye-witness Accounts, and World-wide Reactions.* New York: Praeger, 1957, 318 p.

MacDermott, Mercia. *Apostle of Freedom: A Portait of Vasil Levsky Against a Background of Nineteenth Century Bulgaria.* New York: Barnes, 1968, 407 p.

Maliniak, Thierry. "Instability in Spain." Washington: U.S. Joint Publications Research Service, 1981, 26 p. (translated from *Le Monde* (Paris), March 19, 1981, pp. 1, 6).

Paret, Peter. *Internal War and Pacification: The Vendée, 1789–1796.* Princeton, N.J.: Center of International Studies, Woodrow Wilson School of Public and International Affairs, Princeton University, 1961, 73 p.

Smith, Arthur Douglas Howden. *Fighting the Turk in the Balkans: An American's Adventures with the Macedonian Revolutionists.* New York: Putnam, 1908, 369 p.

Taylor, Alan John Percivale. *Revolutions and Revolutionaries.* London: Hamilton, 1980, 165 p.

Tellez, Antonio. *Sabate: Guerrilla Extraordinary.* Translated from the Spanish by Stuart Christie. London: Davis-Paynter, 1974, 183 p.

Todorov, Kosta. *Balkan Firebrand: The Autobiography of a Rebel, Soldier and Statesman.* New York: Ziff-Davis, 1943, 340 p.

Ireland: North and South

Barry, Tom B. *Guerrilla Days in Ireland.* Dublin: Irish Press, 1949, 228 p.

Bell, J. Bowyer. *The Secret Army: The IRA, 1916–1979.* Cambridge, Mass.: M.I.T. Press, 1974, 434 p.

Bennett, Richard. *The Black and Tans.* Boston: Houghton Mifflin, 1960, 228 p.

Boyle, Andrew. *The Riddle of Erskine Childers.* London: Hutchinson, 1977, 351 p.

Butler, Ewan. *Barry's Flying Column.* London: Leo Cooper, 1971, 165 p.

Coogan, Timothy Patrick. *The I.R.A.* New York: Praeger, 1970, 373 p.

Dangerfield, George. *The Damnable Question: A Study in Anglo-Irish Relations.* Boston: Little, Brown, 1976, 400 p.

Escouflaire, Rodolphe C. *Ireland an Enemy of the Allies?* New York: Dutton, 1920, 268 p. (translation of *L'Irlande—ennemie?*).

Figgis, Darrell. *Recollections of the Irish War.* Garden City, N.Y.: Doubleday, Doran, 1925, 308 p.

FitzGibbon, Constantine. *Red Hand: The Ulster Colony.* New York: Warner Paperback Library, 1973, 400 p.

Fitzpatrick, William John. *Secret Service Under Pitt.* New York: Longmans, Green, 1892, 390 p.

Gwynn, Denis Rolleston. *Traitor or Patriot: The Life and Death of Roger Casement.* New York: J. Cape and H. Smith, 1931, 444 p.

Henry, Robert Mitchell. *The Evolution of Sinn Fein.* Freeport, N.Y.: Books for Libraries Press, 1971, 284 p.

Inglis, Brian. *Roger Casement.* New York: Harcourt, Jovanovich, 1973, 448 p.

Irish Republican Army. *Notes on Guerrilla Warfare.* Boulder, Colo.: Paladin Press, 1979, 38 p.

Lennhoff, Eugen. *De Valera.* Lubeck: C. Coleman, 1933, 69 p.

Lyons, Francis Stewart Leland. *Culture and Anarchy in Ireland. 1890–1939.* New York: Oxford University Press, 1979, 184 p.

MacColl, René. *Roger Casement: A New Judgment.* New York: Norton, 1957, 328 p.

McHugh, Roger Joseph, ed. *Dublin, 1916.* New York: Hawthorn Books, 1966, 399 p.

MacStiofáin, Seán. *Revolutionary in Ireland.* London: G. Cremonesi, 1975, 372 p.

Monteith, Robert. *Casement's Last Adventure.* Revised ed. Dublin: M.F. Moynihan, 1953, 266 p.

Murdoch, Iris. *Aloe i Zelenoe.* Translated from English by M. Lorie. Moscow: Progress, 1968, 287 p. (original: *The Red and the Green.* London, 1965) (fiction).

O Broin, Léon. *The Prime Informer: A Suppressed Scandal.* London: Sidgwick and Jackson, 1971, 174 p.

O Broin, Léon. *Revolutionary Underground: The Story of the Irish Republican Brotherhood, 1858-1924.* Totowa, N.J.: Rowan and Littlefield, 245 p.

Pakenham, Thomas. *The Year of Liberty: The Story of the Great Irish Rebellion of 1798.* Englewood Cliffs, N.J.: Prentice-Hall, 1969, 416 p.

Reid, Benjamin Lawrence. *The Lives of Roger Casement.* New Haven: Yale University Press, 1976, 532 p.

Ryan, Desmond. *The Rising: The Complete Story of Easter Week.* Dublin: Golden Eagle Books, 1957, 276 p.

Sheehy-Skeffington, Francis. *Michael Davitt: Revolutionary, Agitator and Labour Leader.* Boston: Dana Estes, 1909, 291 p.

Styles, George. *Bombs Have no Pity: My War Against Terrorism, as told to Bob Perrin.* London: Luscombe, 1975, 187 p.

Thompson, William Irwin. *The Imagination of an Insurrection. Dublin, Easter, 1916: A Study of an Ideological Movement.* New York: Oxford University Press, 1967, 262 p.

Wilkinson, Burke. *The Zeal of the Convert.* Washington: R.B. Luce, 1976, 256 p.

Mediterranean and Mideast

Byford-Jones, W. *Grivas and the Story of EOKA.* London: Hale, 1959, 192 p.

Eudes, Dominique. *The Kapetanios: Partisans and Civil War in Greece, 1943-1949.* Translated from the French by John Howe. New York: Monthly Review Press, 1972, 381 p.

Fatemi, Faramarz S. *The U.S.S.R. in Iran: The Background History of Russian and Anglo-American Conflict in Iran, its Effect on Iranian Nationalism and the Fall of the Shah.* Cranbury, N.J.: Barnes, 1980, 219 p.

Forbis, William H. *Fall of the Peacock Throne: The Story of Iran.* New York: Harper and Row, 1980, 305 p.

Grivas, George. *General Grivas on Guerrilla Warfare.* Translated by A. Pallis. New York: Praeger, 1962, 109 p. (original: *Agon EOKA kai antartopolemos*).

Grivas, George. *Guerrilla Warfare and EOKA's Struggle: A Politico-Military Study.* London: Longmans, Green, 1964, 109 p. (translation of *Agon E.O.K.A. kai antartopolemos*).

Grivas, George. *The Memoirs of General Grivas.* Edited by Charles Foley. New York: Praeger, 1965, 226 p.

Hoveyda, Fereydoun. *The Fall of the Shah.* Translated by Roger Liddell. New York: Wyndham Books, 1980, 221 p.

Ignatius, David. "The Coup Against 'Countercoup': How a Book Disappeared." *Wall Street Journal,* November 6, 1979, p 1.

Maccoby, Hyam. *Revolution in Judaea: Jesus and the Jewish Resistance.* New York: Taplinger Pub., 1980, 256 p.

Saikal, Amin. *The Rise and Fall of the Shah.* Princeton, N.J.: Princeton University Press, 1980, 279 p.

Shiragian, Arshavir. *The Legacy: Memoirs of an Armenian Patriot.* Translated by Sonia Shiragian. Boston: Hairenik Press, 1976, 217 p.

Stockton, Bayard. *Phoenix with a Bayonet: A Journalist's Interim Report on the Greek Revolution.* Ann Arbor, Mich.: Georgetown Publications, 1971, 306 p.

Theodorakis, Mikis. *Journals of Resistance.* Translated from the French by Graham Webb. London: Hart-Davis McGibbon, 1973, 334 p.

Woodhouse, Christopher Montague. *The Struggle for Greece, 1941-1949.* London: Hart-Davis, MacGibbon, 1976, 324 p.

United Kingdom

Caraman, Philip. *Henry Garnet, 1555-1606, and the Gunpowder Plot.* New York: Farrar, Straus, 1964, 466 p.

Durst, Paul. *Intended Treason: What Really Happened in the Gunpowder Plot.* Cranbury, N.J.: Barnes, 1970, 352 p.

Herring, Francis. *Mischeefes Mysterie: or, Treasons Master-Peece, the Powder-Plot.* New York: Da Capo Press, 1971, 121 p.

Jardine, David. *A Narrative of the Gunpowder Plot.* London: J. Murray, 1857, 344 p.

Kemp, Hilary. *The Jacobite Rebellion.* London: Almark, 1975, 160 p.

Parkinson, Cyril Northcote. *Gunpowder: Treason and Plot.* New York: St. Martin's Press, 1976, 139 p.

Sidney, Philip. *A History of the Gunpowder Plot: The Conspiracy and its Agents.* London: The Religious Tract Society, 1905, 313 p.

Latin America

Béjar Rivera, Héctor. *Peru 1965: Notes on a Guerrilla Experience.* Translated by William Rose. New York: Monthly Review Press, 1970, 142 p.

Broderick, Walter J. *Camilo Torres: A Biography of the Priest-Guerrillero.* New York: Doubleday, 1975, 370 p.

Gilio, Maria Esther. *The Tupamaros.* Translated from the Spanish by Anne Edmondson. London: Secker and Warburg, 1972, 198 p.

Gott, Richard. *Guerrilla Movements in Latin America.* Garden City, N.Y.: Doubleday, 1971, 626 p.

Guevara, Ernesto. *La guerra per bande: Ernesto "Che" Guevara.* Translated by Adele Faccio. Milan: Edizioni Avanti!, 1961, 164 p. (paperback).

Jackson, Geoffrey. *Surviving the Long Night: An Autobiographical Account of a Political Kidnapping.* New York: Vanguard Press, 1974, 225 p.

MacEóin, Gary. *Revolution Next Door: Latin America in the 1970's.* New York: Holt, Rinehart and Winston, 1971, 243 p.

Rojas Rodríguez, Marta and **Calderón, Mirta Rodríguez,** eds. *Tania: The Unforgettable Guerrilla.* New York: Random House, 1971, 212 p.

The Tupamaros: Urban Guerrillas of Uruguay. New York: Times Change Press, 1970, 48 p. (English language edition of: ¿Quienes son los tupamaros? Bogota: Ediciones Zureca, 1971).

Traven, B. *General from the Jungle.* Translated by Desmond Vesey. New York: Hill and Wang, 1972, 280 p. (fiction).

USSR

Martovych, Oleh R., *pseud. Ukrainian Liberation Movement in Modern Times.* Edinburgh: Scottish League for European Freedom, [1972?], 176 p. (paperback).

Percec, Gustav. *Durch Lug and Trug: Durch Gewalt: Durch Morde—zur Unterjochung Kroatiens und zum neuerlichen Weltkrieg.* Vienna: Kroatischer Korrespondenz "Gric," 1931, 71 p.

Perventsev, Arkadii Alekseevich. *Sekretnyi front: Roman.* Moscow: Voenizdat, 1972, 399 p.

Polianych, B. *Stril unochi: sensatsiina povist'.* Philadelphia: Konotop, 1974, 107 p.

United States/Canada

Brackenridge, Henry Marie. *History of the Western Insurrection, 1794.* New York: Arno Press, 1969, 336 p.

Broehl, Wayne G. *The Molly Maguires.* Cambridge: Harvard University Press, 1964, 409 p.

Davis, William Watts Hart. *The Fries Rebellion, 1798-99.* New York: Arno Press, 1969, 143 p.

Evans, William McKee. *To Die Game: The Story of the Lowry Band, Indian Guerrillas of Reconstruction.* Baton Rouge: Louisiana State University Press, 1971, 282 p.

Grathwohl, Larry and **Reagan, Frank.** *Bringing Down America: An FBI Informer with the Weathermen.* New Rochelle, N.Y.: Arlington House, 1976, 191 p.

"Guerrilla War in the U.S.A.; 1965-1970." *Scanlan's,* v. I, no. 8 (January 1971), pp. 1-96.

Halliday, E.M. "Geronimo!" *American Heritage,* v. XVII, no. 4, (June 1966), p. 56.

Hoffman, Anita and **Hoffman, Abbie.** *To America with Love: Letters from the Underground.* New York: Stonehill Pub., 1976, 206 p.

Horsmanden, Daniel. *The New York Conspiracy.* Boston: Beacon Press, 1971, 491 p. (reprint of *The New-York Conspiracy, or A History of the Negro Plot, with the Journal of the Proceedings Against the Conspirators at New-York in the Years 1741–2.* New York: Southwick and Pelsue, 1810, 385 p.).

Howe, George Locke. "The Tragedy of King Philip and the Destruction of the New England Indians." *American Heritage,* v. X, no. 1 (December 1958), pp. 65–80.

Lewis, Arthur H. *Lament for the Molly Maguires.* New York: Harcourt, Brace and World, 1964, 308 p.

Miller, Linus Wilson. *Notes of an Exile to Van Dieman's Land: Comprising Incidents of the Canadian Rebellion in 1838, Trial of the Author in Canada ... and Transportation to Van Dieman's Land.* New York: Johnson Reprint Corp., 1968, 378 p. (reprint of 1846 edition).

Myers, John Myers. *San Francisco's Reign of Terror.* Garden City, N.Y.: Doubleday, 1966, 301 p.

Oppenheimer, Martin. *The Urban Guerrilla.* Chicago: Quadrangle Books, 1969, 188 p.

Payne, Cril. *Deep Cover: An FBI Agent Infiltrates the Radical Underground.* New York: Newsweek Books, 1979, 348 p.

Pinkerton, Allan. *The Mollie Maguires and the Detectives.* Gloucester, Mass.: Peter Smith, n.d., 552 p.

Thompson, Daniel Pierce. *The Green Mountain Boys: A Historical Tale of the Early Settlement of Vermont.* Revised ed. Boston: Lee and Shepard, 1890, 2 v.

Vaughan, Alden T. "The 'Horrid and Unnatural Rebellion' of Daniel Shays." *American Heritage,* v. XVII, no. 4 (June 1966), pp. 50–53.

Weems; John Edward. *Men Without Countries: Three Adventurers of the Early Southwest.* Boston: Houghton Mifflin, 1969, 272 p.

XI. WARFARE

Military Strategy
General

Army Times, eds. *The Tangled Web: True Stories of Deception in Modern Warfare.* Washington: R.B. Luce, 1963, 199 p.

Beaumont, Roger A. *Military Elites.* Indianapolis: Bobbs-Merrill, 1974, 251 p.

Davies, Edward. *The Art of War and England Traynings.* New York: Da Capo Press, 1968, 121 p.

Duncan, K., Jr. "The Service of Security: Suggested Changes in the Nomenclature of Covering Detachments." *Journal of the United States Infantry Association,* v. III′, no. 3 (January 1907), pp. 89–94.

Friedrich II, *King of Prussia. Frederick the Great: Instructions for his Generals.* Translated by Brigadier General Thomas R. Phillips. Harrisburg, Pa.: Stackpole, 1960, 104 p.

Fuller, John Frederick Charles. *The Conduct of War, 1789–1961: A Study of the Impact of the French, Industrial, and Russian Revolutions on War and its Conduct.* New Brunswick, N.J.: Rutgers University Press, 1961, 352 p.

Guyénot, Jules Grégoire. *Guerre moderne. Service d'état-major.* Paris: L. Baudoin, 1886, 272 p.

Jervey, Henry. *Warfare of the Future.* New York: Collier, 1917, 384 p.

Luvaas, Jay. *The Education of an Army: British Military Thought, 1815–1940.* London: Cassell, 1965, 454 p.

Maurice, Frederick Barton, *Sir. British Strategy: A Study of the Application of the Principles of War.* London: Constable, 1929, 243 p.

Military History Symposium (U.S.), 2d, U.S. Air Force Academy, 1968. *Command and Commanders in Modern Warfare: Proceedings.* Edited by William Geffen. 2d. ed. enl. Washington: U.S. GPO, 1971, 340 p.

Napoléon I. *Napoleon and Modern War: His Military Maxims.* rev. ed. Harrisburg, Pa.: Military Service Publishing Co., 1943, 158 p.

Nelson, Otto Lauren. *National Security and the General Staff.* Washington: Infantry Journal Press, 1946, 608 p.

Rothenburg, Gunther Erich. *The Art of Warfare in the Age of Napoleon.* Bloomington: Indiana University Press, 1978, 272 p.

St. Privat. *German Sources.* Translated by Harry Bell. Fort Leavenworth, Kan.: Staff College Press, 1914, 498 p.

Schurman, Donald M. *The Education of a Navy: The Development of British Naval Strategic Thought, 1867–1914.* London: Cassell, 1965, 213 p.

Skizze eines Vortrages über Generalstabswissenschaft, von J. v. H. Stuttgart: Verlag von Franz Köhler, 1854, 340 p.

Spaulding, Oliver Lyman; Nickerson, Hoffman et al. *Warfare: A Study of Military Methods From the Earliest Times.* New York: Harcourt, Brace, 1925, 601 p.

Turney-High, Harry Holbert. *Primitive War: Its Practice and Concepts.* Columbia: University of South Carolina Press, 1949, 277 p.

U.S. President's Advisory Commission on Universal Training. *A Program for National Security, May 29, 1947. Report.* Washington: U.S. GPO, 1947, 453 p.

Vegetius Renatus, Flavius. *The Foure Bookes of Martiall Policye.* New York: Da Capo Press, 1968, 66 p.

Camouflage

Barkas, Geoffrey with **Barkas, Natalie.** *The Camouflage Story, from Aintree to Alamein.* London: Cassell, 1952, 216 p.

Bell, Leslie. *Sabotage! The Story of Lt.-Col. J. Elder Wills.* London: T.W. Laurie, 1957, 189 p.

Bird, W.D. "Things are not Always What They Seem." *Journal of the Royal United Service Institution,* v. LXVII (February–November 1922), pp. 682-687.

Chesney, Clement Hope Rawdon and **Huddlestone, J.** *The Art of Camouflage.* London: Hale, 1941, 252 p.

Hampshire, A. Cecil. *The Phantom Fleet.* London: Kimber, 1962, 157 p.

Hartcup, Guy. *Camouflage: A History of Concealment and Deception in War.* Newton Abbot, Devon, England: David and Charles, 1979, 160 p.

Maskelyne, Jasper. *Magic—Top Secret.* New York: S. Paul, 1949, 191 p.

Moore, William L. with **Berlitz, Charles.** *The Philadelphia Experiment: Project Invisibility. An Account of a Search for a Secret Navy Wartime Project that May Have Succeeded—too Well.* New York: Grosset and Dunlap, 1979, 177 p. (The Eldridge).

Reit, Seymour. *Masquerade: The Amazing Camouflage Deceptions of World War II.* New York: Hawthorn Books, 1978, 255 p.

White, O.W. "Camouflage and Cover From View." *Journal of the Royal United Service Institution,* v. LXVI (February–November 1921), pp. 419-429.

Employment of Forces
General

Andrews, Lincoln Clarke. *Fundamentals of Military Service.* Philadelphia: Lippincott, 1916, 428 p.

Gordon, John William, Jr. *Special Forces for Desert Warfare: British Improvisation, 1915-1943.* Ann Arbor, Mich.: Xerox University Microfilms, 1976, 301 p.

Hackett, John Winthrop, *Sir.* "The Employment of Special Forces." *Journal of the Royal United Service Institution,* v. XCVII (February–November 1952), pp. 26-41.

Heilbrunn, Otto. *Warfare in the Enemy's Rear.* New York: Praeger, 1964, 231 p.

U.S. Army, Chief of Field Artillery. *Command and Staff Functions.* Fort Sill, Okla.: The Field Artillery School, 1931, 126 p.

U.S. Army Infantry School, Fort Benning, Georgia. *Ranger Handbook.* Boulder, Colo.: Paladin Press, November 1969, 206 p.

U.S. War Department. *Field Service Regulations, United States Army, 1923.* Washington: U.S. GPO, 1924, 195 p.

Wieczorek, George A. "Technical Training for Line Officers in the Use and Construction of Military Lines of Information." *Journal of the United States Infantry Association,* v. IV, no. 5 (March 1908), pp. 739-743.

Wilbraham, R. with **Cust, Edward,** *Sir.* "Outpost Duties." A Lecture Before the Royal United Service Institution on Friday, January 24, 1862. *Journal of the Royal United Service Institution,* v. VI (1863), pp. 60-83.

Air Forces and Airborne Troops

Foxley-Morris, C.N. "The Use of Air Power in Security Operations." *Journal of the Royal United Service Institution,* v. XCIX (February–November 1954), pp. 554-558.

Hickey, Michael. *Out of the Sky: A History of Airborne Warfare.* New York: Scribner, 1979, 286 p.

MacCloskey, Monro. *Alert the Fifth Force: Counterinsurgency, Unconventional Warfare, and Psychological Operations of the United States Air Force in Special Air Warfare.* New York: R. Rosen Press, 1969, 190 p.

Merglen, Albert. *La Guerre de l'inattendu, opérations subversives, aéroportées et amphibies.* Grenoble: Arthaud, 1966, 242 p.

U.S. Department of the Army. *Armored Cavalry Platoon and Troop, Air Cavalry Troop, and Divisional Armored Cavalry Squadron.* Washington: n.p., 1961, 354 p.

Weeks, John S. *Assault from the Sky: A History of Airborne Warfare.* Newton Abbot, Devon, England: Westbridge Books, 1978, 192 p.

Amphibious and Naval Forces

Hampshire, A. Cecil. *The Phantom Fleet.* London: Kimber, 1962, 157 p. (paperback).

Keyes, Roger John Brownlow Keyes, *Baron. Amphibious Warfare and Combined Operations.* Cambridge, England: The University Press, 1943, 110 p.

Merglen, Albert. *La Guerre de l'inattendu, opérations subversives, aéroportées et amphibies.* Grenoble: Arthaud, 1966, 242 p.

Moore, William L. with **Berlitz, Charles.** *The Philadelphia Experiment: Project Invisibility. An Account of a Search for a Secret Navy Wartime Project that May Have Succeeded—too Well.* New York: Grosset and Dunlap, 1979, 177 p. *(The Eldridge).*

Schurman, Donald M. *The Education of a Navy: The Development of British Naval Strategic Thought, 1867-1914.* London: Cassell, 1965, 213 p.

Vagts, Alfred. *Landing Operations: Strategy, Psychology, Tactics, Politics, from Antiquity to 1945.* Harrisburg, Pa.: Military Service Publishing Co., 1946, 831 p.

Cavalry

Baker, Valentine. "Organization and Employment of Cavalry." *Journal of the Royal United Service Institution,* v. XVII, 1874, pp. 375-410.

Fraser, Keith. "European Cavalry." *Army and Navy Quarterly,* v. I, no. 1 (January 1885), pp. 1-16.

Graves, [Major]. "The Functions of Cavalry in Modern War." *Army and Navy Quarterly,* v. I, no. 3 (July 1885), pp. 328-344 and v. I, no. 4 (October 1885), pp. 405-421.

Pelet-Narbonne, von. *Cavalry on Service, Illustrated by the Advance of the German Cavalry Across the Mosel in 1870.* Translated by Major D'A. Legard. London: Hugh Rees, 1906, 350 p.

Piekalkiewicz, Janusz. *The Cavalry of World War II.* New York: Stein and Day, 1980, 256 p. (translation of *Pferd und Reiter im II Weltkrieg*).

"Synopsis of the History of Cavalry." *Journal of the Royal United Service Institution,* v. XVIII (1875), pp. 3-15.

Wrangle, Gustav, *Graf. The Cavalry in the Russo-Japanese War: Lessons and Critical Considerations.* Translated from the German by J. Montgomery. London: H. Rees, 1907, 90 p. (Austrian cavalry).

Commandos

Churchill, T.B.L. "The Value of Commandos." *Journal of the Royal United Service Institution,* v. XCV (February-November 1950), pp. 85-90.

Cohen, Eliot A. *Commandos and Politicians: Elite Military Units in Modern Democracies.* Cambridge: Center for International Affairs, Harvard University, 1978, 136 p.

Garrett, Richard. *The Raiders: The Elite Strike Forces that Altered the Course of War and History.* London: David and Charles, 1980, 224 p.

Vagts, Alfred. *Landing Operations: Strategy, Psychology, Tactics, Politics, from Antiquity to 1945.* Harrisburg, Pa.: Military Service Publishing Co., 1946, 831 p.

Privateers

Andrews, Kenneth R. *Elizabethan Privateering: English Privateering during the Spanish War, 1585-1603.* Cambridge: University Press, 1964, 297 p.

Eastman, Ralph Mason. *Some Famous Privateers of New England.* Boston: State Street Trust Co., 1928, 87 p.

Jackson, Melvin H. *Privateers in Charleston, 1793-1796: An Account of a French Palatinate in South Carolina.* Washington: U.S. GPO, 1969, 160 p.

Marryat, Frederick. *The Privateersman. Adventures, by Sea and Land, in Civil and Savage Life, One Hundred Years ago.* London: J.M. Dent, 1896, 327 p.

National Commands and Commanders
China

U.S. Defense Intelligence Agency. *The Chinese Armed Forces Today: The U.S. Defense Intelligence Agency Handbook of China's Army, Navy and Air Force.* Englewood Cliffs, N.J.: Prentice-Hall, 1979, 240 p. (published in 1976 under title: *Handbook on the Chinese Armed Forces*).

France

Belloc, Hilaire. *Richelieu: A Study.* Philadelphia: Lippincott, 1929, 392 p.

La Gorce, Paul Marie de. *The French Army: A Military-Political History.* Translated by Kenneth Douglas. New York: G. Braziller, 1963, 568 p.

Germany

Addington, Larry. *The Blitzkreig Era and the German General Staff, 1865-1941.* New Brunswick, N.J.: Rutgers University Press, 1971, 285 p.

Allen, Charles Russell. *Heusinger of the Fourth Reich.* New York: Marzani and Munsell, 1963, 320 p. (paperback).

Demeter, Karl. *The German Officer-Corps in Society and State, 1650-1945.* Translated from the German by Angus Malcolm. New York: Praeger, 1965, 414 p.

Forster, Thomas Manfred. *NVA: Die Armee der Sowjetzone.* Cologne: Markus-Verlag, 1964, 287 p.

Görlitz, Walter. *History of the German General Staff, 1657-1945.* Translated by Brian Battershaw. New York: Praeger, 1959, 508 p. (paperback).

Riess, Curt. *The Self-Betrayed: Glory and Doom of the German Generals.* New York: Putnam, 1942, 402 p.

Whitton, Frederick Ernest. *Moltke.* London: Constable, 1921, 326 p.

USSR/Russia

Beskrovnyi, Liubomir Grigor'evich. *Russkaia armiia i flot v deviatnadtsatom veke: Voen.-Ekon. potentsial Rossii.* Moscow: Nauka, 1973, 616 p.

Gorbatov, Aleksandr Vasil'evich. *Years off my Life: The Memoirs of General of the Soviet Army.* Translated by Gordon Clough and Anthony Cash. New York: Norton, 1965, 222 p.

Liddell Hart, Basil Henry, ed. *The Red Army: The Red Army, 1918 to 1945, the Soviet Army, 1946 to the Present.* New York: Harcourt, Brace, 1956, 480 p. (London ed. title: *The Soviet Army*).

Mackintosh, John Malcolm. *Juggernaut: A History of the Soviet Armed Forces.* New York: Macmillan, 1967, 320 p.

Scott, Harriet Fast and **Scott, William F.** *The Armed Forces of the USSR.* Boulder, Colo.: Westview Press, 1979, 439 p.

Shatsillo, Kornelii Fedorovich. *Rossiia pered pervoi mirovoi voinoi: vooruzh. sily tsarisma v 1905-1914 gg.* Moscow: Nauka, 1974, 110 p.

United Kingdom

Gerahty, Tony. *Who Dares Win: The Story of the Special Air Service, 1950-1980.* London: Arms and Armour Press, 1980, 249 p.

Norton, G.G. *The Red Devils: The Story of the British Airborne Forces.* Harrisburg, Pa.: Stackpole Books, 1971, 260 p.

Warner, Philip. *The Special Air Service.* London: Kimber, 1978, 285 p.

Wood, Derek. *Attack Warning Red: The Royal Observer Corps and the Defence of Britain, 1925 to 1975.* London: Macdonald and Jane's, 1976, 357 p.

United States

DuPre, Flint O. *Hap Arnold: Architect of American Air Power.* New York: Macmillan, 1972, 144 p.

Hewes, James E. *From Root to McNamara: Army Organization and Administration, 1900-1963.* Washington: U.S. GPO, 1975, 452 p.

Hittle, James Donald. *The Military Staff, Its History and Development.* Harrisburg, Pa.: Military Service Pub. Co., 1949, 286 p.

Ingersoll, Lurton Dunham. *A History of the War Department of the United States.* Washington: F.B. Mohun, 1880, 613 p.

Mollenhoff, Clark R. *The Pentagon: Politics, Profits and Plunder.* New York: Putnam, 1967, 450 p.

Roosevelt, Theodore. *The Rough Riders.* New York: Putnam, 1900, 300 p.

Scriven, George Percival. *The Service of Information, United States Army. A Review of the Nature, Use, Field of Service, and Organization of the Signal Corps of the Army, with an Outline of its Methods and Technical Apparatus, and Notes on the Service of Information and the Organization of the Aviation Service of the Leading Foreign Armies.* Washington: U.S. GPO, 1915, 179 p.

Ward, Harry M. *The Department of War, 1781-1795.* Pittsburgh: University of Pittsburgh Press, 1962, 287 p.

Weigley, Russell Frank. *History of the United States Army.* New York: Macmillan, 1967, 688 p.

Yarmolinsky, Adam. *The Military Establishment: Its Impacts on American Society.* New York: Harper and Row, 1971, 434 p.

XII. WARS
General

Andrews, Kenneth R. *Elizabethan Privateering: English Privateering During the Spanish War, 1585-1603.* Cambridge: University Press, 1964, 297 p.

Barker, A.J. *The Civilizing Mission: A History of the Italo-Ethiopian War of 1935-1936.* New York: Dial Press, 1968, 383 p.

Bradford, Ernle Dusgate Selby. *The Great Siege.* London: Hodder and Stoughton, 1916, 256 p.

Clendenen, Clarence Clemens. *Blood on the Border: The United States Army and the Mexican Irregulars.* New York: Macmillan, 1969, 390 p.

Dodge, Theodore Ayrault. *Hannibal: A History of the Art of War Among the Carthaginians and Romans Down to the Battle of Pydna, 168 B.C., With a Detailed Account of the Second Punic War.* Boston: Houghton Mifflin, 1891, 682 p.

Hanighen, Frank Cleary, ed. *Nothing but Danger.* New York: National Travel Club, 1939, 285 p.

Heathcote, T.A. *The Afghan Wars, 1839-1919.* London: Osprey, 1980, 224 p.

Nash, Howard Pervear. *The Forgotten Wars: The Role of the U.S. Navy in the Quasi War with France and the Barbary Wars, 1798-1805.* South Brunswick, N.J.: Barnes, 1968, 308 p.

Parkman, Francis. *History of the Conspiracy of Pontiac, and the War of the North American Tribes Against the English Colonies After the Conquest of Canada.* Boston: Little, Brown, 1855, 630 p.

Read, Jan. *The New Conquistadors.* London: Evans Brothers, 1980, 175 p.

Schnepf, Edwin A. and **Price, Alden.** *Hunter/Killer.* North Hollywood, Calif: All Star Books, 1965, 192 p. (paperback).

Stirling, Walter Francis. *Safety Last.* London: Hollis and Carter, 1954, 251 p. (autobiographical).

Wrench, Evelyn, *Sir. Francis Yeats-Brown, 1886-1944.* London: Eyre and Spottiswoode, 1948, 256 p. (fiction).

American Revolution
General

Augur, Helen. *The Secret War of Independence.* New York: Duell, Sloan and Pearce, 1955, 381 p.

Bendiner, Elmer. *The Virgin Diplomats.* New York: Knopf, 1976, 257 p.

Boudinot, Elias. *Journal of Events in the Revolution.* New York: Arno Press, 1968, 97 p. (Reprint of the 1894 edition).

Bridenbaugh, Carl. *The Spirit of '76: The Growth of American Patriotism Before Independence.* New York: Oxford University Press, 1975, 162 p.

Brown, Wallace. *The Good Americans: The Loyalists in the American Revolution.* New York: Morrow, 1969, 302 p.

Crary, Catherine S., comp. *The Price of Loyalty: Tory Writings From the Revolutionary Era.* New York: McGraw-Hill, 1973, 481 p.

Einstein, Lewis. *Divided Loyalties: Americans in England During the War of Independence.* London: Gobden-Sanderson, 1933, 469 p.

France. *The Treaties of 1778, and Allied Documents.* Edited by Gilbert Chinard. Baltimore: Johns Hopkins Press, 1928, 70 p. (Historical Documents. Institut Français de Washington, v. 1).

Garrison, Webb B. *Sidelights on the American Revolution.* Nashville: Abingdon Press, 1974, 176 p.

Griffith, Samuel B. *In Defense of the Public Liberty: Britain, America, and the Struggle for Independence, From 1760 to the Surrender at Yorktown in 1781.* Garden City, N.Y.: Doubleday, 1976, 725 p.

Kammen, Michael G. *A Rope of Sand: The Colonial Agents, British Politics, and the American Revolution.* Ithaca, N.Y.: Cornell University Press, 1968, 349 p.

Kemble, Stephen. *The Kemble Papers ... 1773-1789.* New York: New-York Historical Society, 1884-1885, 2 v.

Maier, Pauline. *The Old Revolutionaries: Political Lives in the Age of Samuel Adams.* New York: Knopf, 1980, 309 p.

Meng, John J. "A Footnote to Secret Aid in the American Revolution." *American Historical Review,* v. XLIII (July 1938), pp. 791-795.

Minutes of a Conspiracy Against the Liberties of America. New York: Arno Press, 1969, 111 p. (reprint of the 1776, London edition; see below).

Minutes of the Trial and Examination of Certain Persons, in the Province of New York, Charged With Being Engaged in a Conspiracy Against the Authority of the Congress, and the Liberties of America. London: J. Bew, 1776, 45 p. (an account of the Hickey plot, later cited as a "clumsy Tory forgery").

Montross, Lynn. *The Reluctant Rebels: the Story of the Continental Congress, 1774-1789.* New York: Harper, 1950, 467 p.

New York (State), Commission for Detecting and Defeating Conspiracies, 1777-1778. *Minutes ... Albany County Sessions, 1778-1781.* Edited by Victor H. Paltsits. New York: Da Capo Press, 1972, 3 v.

New York (State), Commission for Detecting and Defeating Conspiracies, 1777-1778. *Minutes of the Committee and of the First Commission ... December 11, 1776—September 23, 1778 ... To Which is Added Minutes of the Council of Appointment, State of New York, April 2, 1778—May 3, 1779 ... New York: New-York Historical Society, 1924-1925, 2 v.* (Collections of the Society for the year 1924-25, v. LVII-LVIII).

New York (State), Division of Archives and History. *The American Revolution in New York: Its Political, Social and Economic Significance.* Edited by Alexander C. Flick. Albany, N.Y.: University of the State of New York, 1926, 371 p.

Sanders, Jennings Bryan. *Evolution of Executive Departments of the Continental Congress, 1774-1789.* Gloucester, Mass.: Peter Smith, 1971, 213 p.

Scott, Kenneth, comp. *Rivington's New York Newspaper: Excerpts From a Loyalist Press, 1773-1783.* New York: New-York Historical Society, 1973, 470 p.

[Sears, Robert]. *The Pictorial History of the American Revolution With a Sketch of the Early History of the Country, the Constitution of the United States, and a Chronological Index.* Boston: Lee and Shepard, [187-], 433 p.

Sisson, Daniel. *The American Revolution of 1800.* New York: Knopf, 1974, 468 p.

Stevens, Benjamin Franklin, comp. *B.F. Stevens' Facsimiles of Manuscripts in European Archives Relating to America, 1773-1783. With Descriptions, Editorial Notes, Collations, References and Translations.* Wilmington, Del.: Mellifont Press, 1970, 25 v. (reprint from the 1898, London edition).

Thomson, Buchanan Parker. *Spain, Forgotten Ally of the American Revolution.* North Quincy, Mass.: Christopher Pub. House, 1976, 260 p.

Tryon County, New York, Committee of Safety. *The Minute Book of the Committee ...* Edited by Samuel Ludlow Frey. New York: Dodd, Mead, 1895, 151 p.

U.S. Continental Congress. *Secret Journals of the Acts and Proceedings of Congress, From the First Meeting Thereof to the Dissolution of the Confederation, by the Adoption of the Constitution of the United States.* New York: Johnson Reprint Corporation, 1967, 4 v.

U.S. Department of State. *The Diplomatic Correspondence of the American Revolution ...* Edited by Jared Sparks. Boston: N. Hale, Gray and Bowen; New York: Carvill et al., 1829-30, 12 v.

U.S. Department of State. *The Revolutionary Diplomatic Correspondence of the United States.* Edited by Francis Wharton. Washington: U.S. GPO, 1889, 6 v. (designed to correct, complete and enlarge the 1829-1830 edition).

Van Tyne, Claude Halstead. "French Aid Before the Alliance of 1778." *American Historical Review,* October 1925, pp. 20-40.

Warren, Charles. *Odd Byways in American History.* Cambridge, Mass.: Harvard University Press, 1942, 269 p.

Webb, Samuel Blachley. *Correspondence and Journals ...* Collected and edited by Worthington Chauncey Ford. Lancaster, Pa.: Wickersham Press, 1893-94, 3 v.

Conduct of Military Operations
General

American Heritage, eds. *The American Heritage Book of the Revolution.* Editor in charge: Richard M. Ketchum. Narrative by Bruce Lancaster with a chapter by J.H. Plumb. New York: American Heritage, 1958, 384 p.

Bass, Robert Duncan. *Gamecock: The Life and Campaigns of General Thomas Sumter.* New York: Holt, Rinehart and Winston, 1961, 289 p.

Casey, William J. *Where and How the War Was Fought: An Armchair Tour of the American Revolution.* New York: Morrow, 1976, 352 p.

Clinton, Henry, *Sir. The American Rebellion: Sir Henry Clinton's Narrative of His Campaigns, 1775-1782, With an Appendix of Original Documents.* Edited by William B. Willcox. New Haven: Yale University Press, 1954, 658 p.

Clinton, Henry, *Sir.* "Original Documents: Sir Henry Clinton's Original Secret Record of Private Daily Intelligence." Contributed by Dr. Thomas Addis Emmett. *The Magazine of American History,* v. X (1883), p. 327+; v. XI (1884), p. 53+.

Coakley, Robert W. and **Conn, Stetson.** *The War of the American Revolution: Narrative, Chronology, and Bibliography.* Washington: U.S. GPO, 1975, 257 p.

Commager, Henry Steele and **Morris, Richard B.,** eds. *The Spirit of 'Seventy-six: The Story of the American Revolution as Told by Participants.* Indianapolis: Bobbs-Merrill, 1958, 2 v.

De Peyster, John Watts. *Major General Philip Schuyler, and the Burgoyne Campaign in the Summer of 1777.* Address before the New-York Historical Society. New York: Holt Brothers, printers, 1877, 26 p.

Fleming, Thomas J. *1776, Year of Illusions.* New York: Norton, 1975, 525 p.

Ford, Worthington Chauncey, ed. *Defences of Philadelphia in 1777.* New York: Da Capo Press, 1971, 300 p. (reprint of 1897 edition).

Fowler, William M. *Rebels Under Sail: The American Navy During the Revolution.* New York: Scribner, 1976, 356 p.

Jameson, J.F. "St. Eustatius in the American Revolution." *American Historical Review,* July 1903, pp. 683-708.

Johnston, Henry Phelps. *The Yorktown Campaign and the Surrender of Cornwallis, 1781.* New York: Da Capo Press, 1971, 206 p.

Lancaster, Bruce. *From Lexington to Liberty: The Story of the American Revolution.* Garden City, N.Y.: Doubleday, 1955, 470 p.

Lee, Henry. *Memoirs of the War in the Southern Department of the United States.* Edited by Robert E. Lee. New York: Arno Press, 1969, 620 p. (reprint of the 1869 edition).

Lossing, Benson John. *The Pictorial Field-Book of the Revolution: Or, Illustrations, by Pen and Pencil, of the History, Biography, Scenery, Relics, and Traditions of the War for Independence.* New York: Harper, 1850, 2 v.

Rathbun, Jonathan. *Narrative of Jonathan Rathbun.* [With the Narratives of Rufus Avery and Stephen Hempstead, Including the Narrative of Thomas Herttell.] New York: New York Times, 1971, 59 p. (reprint of the 1911 edition published as Extra no. 15 of the *Magazine of History;* account of battle of Groton Heights).

The Revolution Remembered: Eyewitness Accounts of the War for Independence. Edited by John C. Dann. Chicago: University of Chicago Press, 1980, 446 p.

Stephenson, O.W. "The Supply of Gunpowder in 1776." *American Historical Review,* v. XXX, no. 18 (January 1925), pp. 271-281.

Thacher, James. *Military Journal of the American Revolution.* New York: New York Times, 1969, 538 p. (reprint of 1862 edition).

Trevelyan, George Otto, *Sir. George the Third and Charles Fox, the Concluding Part of the American Revolution.* New York: Longmans, Green, 1912-1914. 2 v.

United States, Naval History Division. *Naval Documents of the American Revolution.* Edited by William Bell Clark and William James Morgan (v. 5). Washington: U.S. GPO, 1964-1972, 6 v.

Ward, Christopher. *The War of the Revolution.* Edited by John Richard Alden. New York: Macmillan, 1952, 989 p. (Based on the author's *The Delaware Continentals, 1776-1783*).

Winsor, Justin, ed. *The American Revolution: A Narrative, Critical and Bibliographical History.* New York: Sons of Liberty Publication, 1972, 1138 p. (compiled from his *Narrative and Critical History of America*).

Canadian Invasion

Carroll, Charles. *Journal of Charles Carroll, 1776.* New York: New York Times, 1969, 110 p. (reprint of 1876 edition).

Hatch, Robert McConnell. *Thrust for Canada: The American Attempt on Quebec in 1775-1776.* Boston: Houghton Mifflin, 1979, 295 p.

Henry, John Joseph. *Account of Arnold's Campaign Against Quebec.* New York: New York Times, 1968, 198 p. (reprint of 1877 edition).

Henry, John Joseph. *An Accurate and Interesting Account of the Hardships and Sufferings of that Band of Heroes, who Traversed the Wilderness in the Campaign Against Quebec in 1775.* Lancaster, Pa.: Printed by William Greer, 1812, 225 p.

Jones, Charles Henry. *History of the Campaign for the Conquest of Canada in 1776, from the Death of Montgomery to the Retreat of the British Army under Sir Guy Carleton.* New York: Research Reprints, 1970, 234 p. (reprint of 1882 edition published by Porter and Coates, Philadelphia).

Verreau, Hospice Anthelme Jean Baptiste, *comp.* and *ed. Invasion du Canada: Collection de memoires.* ... Montreal: E. Senecal, 1873, 2 v.

Massachusetts

De Bernière, Henry. *Gage's Instructions: Thomas Gage.* New York: Arno Press, 1971, 20 p. (reprint of the 1779 edition).

Fleming, Thomas J. *Now We are Enemies.* New York: St. Martin's Press, 1960, 383 p.

Ketchum, Richard M. *The Battle for Bunker Hill.* Garden City, N.Y.: Doubleday, 1962, 232 p.

Massachusetts (Colony), Provincial Congress, February–May 1775. *A Narrative of the Excursion and Ravages of the King's Troops under the Command of General Gage.* New York: New York Times, 1968, 23 p. (reprint of 1775 edition).

Revere, Paul. Letter from Joseph Warren commissioning Paul Revere as messenger to Lexington, dáted April 29, 1775, Cambridge (photocopy).

New Jersey

Fleming, Thomas J. *The Forgotten Victory: The Battle for New Jersey—1780.* New York: Reader's Digest Press and Dutton, 1973, 350 p.

Lundin, Charles Leonard. *Cockpit of the Revolution: The War for Independence in New Jersey.* Princeton: Princeton University Press, 1940, 463 p. (The Princeton History of New Jersey, v. 2).

New York

Bliven, Bruce. *Under the Guns: New York: 1775–1776.* New York: Harper and Row, 1972, 397 p.

Dawson, Henry Barton. *The Sons of Liberty in New York.* A paper read before the New-York Historical Society, May 3, 1859. Poughkeepsie: Platt and Schram, Printers, 1859, 118 p. (manuscript).

Johnston, Henry Phelps. *The Campaign of 1776 around New York and Brooklyn.* New York: Da Capo Press, 1971, 209 p.

Pryer, Charles. *The "Neutral Ground."* New York: Putnam, 1898, 443 p.

Shepherd, William Robert. *The Battle of Harlem Heights.* New York: Putnam, 1898, 383 p.

South Carolina

Corkran, David H. *The Carolina Indian Frontier.* Columbia: University of South Carolina Press, 1970, 71 p.

Weigley, Russell Frank. *The Partisan War: The South Carolina Campaign of 1770–1782.* Columbia: University of South Carolina Press, 1970, 77 p.

Biographies and Case Histories
General

Aitken, James, *defendant. The Whole of the Proceedings Upon the Trial of James Hill, Otherwise James Hind, Otherwise John Hind, Otherwise James Acksan, Commonly Called, John the Painter, on Thursday, March the 6th, 1777. At the Assizes, Held at the Castle at Winchester, for the County of Hants ... Taken in Short Hand by William Blanchard.* London: Printed for J. Wenman, [1777?], 1 p.

Callahan, North. *Daniel Morgan, Ranger of the Revolution.* New York: Holt, Rinehart and Winston, 1961, 342 p.

Caughey, John Walton. *Bernardo de Gálvez in Louisiana, 1776–1783.* Berkeley, Calif.: University of California Press, 1934, 290 p.

Cutter, William. *The Life of Israel Putnam, Major-General in the Army of the American Revolution.* 5th ed. Boston: J. Philbrick, 1854, 383 p.

Dabney, Virginia. "Jack Jouett's Ride." *American Heritage,* v. XIII, no. 1 (December 1961), pp. 56-59.

Deane, Silas. *The Deane Papers . . . 1774-1790.* New York: New-York Historical Society, 1887-90, 5 v. (Society Collections, v. XIX-XXIII).

James, Coy Hilton. *Silas Deane, Patriot or Traitor?* East Lansing: Michigan State University Press, 1975, 152 p.

Jay, John. *John Jay. Volume 1: The Making of a Revolutionary: Unpublished Papers, 1745-1780.* Edited by Richard B. Morris, Floyd M. Shumway *et al.* New York: Harper and Row, 1975, 866 p. (from the collections of Columbia University Libraries).

Lafayette, Marie Joseph Paul Yves Roch Gilbert du Motier, *Marquis de. Lafayette in the Age of the American Revolution: Selected Letters and Papers, 1776-1790. Volume 1: December 7, 1776—March 30, 1778.* Edited by Stanley J. Idzerda, Roger E. Smith *et al.* Ithaca, N.Y.: Cornell University Press, 1977, 487 p.

Lee, Richard Henry. *The Letters of Richard Henry Lee.* Collected and edited by James Curtis Ballagh. New York: Da Capo Press, 1970, 2 v.

Lee, William. *Letters of William Lee, 1776-1783.* Edited by Worthington Chauncey Ford. New York: Arno Press, 1971, 3 v.

McKone, Frank E. *General Sullivan: New Hampshire Patriot.* New York: Vantage Press, 1977, 434 p.

Martyn, Charles. *The Life of Artemas Ward, the First Commander-in-Chief of the American Revolution.* New York: A. Ward, 1921, 334 p.

Roche, John Francis. *Joseph Reed: A Moderate in the American Revolution.* New York: AMS Press, 1968, 298 p. (xerox copy).

Walworth, Mansfield Tracy. "Colonel John Hardin." *Historical Magazine,* v. V, 2d series, no. 4 (April 1869), pp. 233-237.

Ethan Allen

Allen, Ethan. *The Narrative of Colonel Ethan Allen.* New York: Corinth, [1961], 131 p. (reprint of *A Narrative of Colonel Ethan Allen's Captivity, 1779*).

Holbrook, Stewart Hall. *Ethan Allen.* Portland, Oregon: Binfords and Mort, 1958, 283 p.

Pell, John. *Ethan Allen.* Boston: Houghton Mifflin, 1929, 331 p.

Pierre Augustin Caron de Beaumarchais

Grendel, Frederic. *Beaumarchais: The Man Who Was Figaro.* Translated from the French by Roger Greaves. New York: Crowell, 1977, 305 p. (original: *Beaumarchais; ou, La calomnie,* Paris: Flammarion).

Kite, Elizabeth Sarah. *Beaumarchais and the War of American Independence.* Boston: R.G. Badger, 1918, 2 v.

Lemaître, Georges Edouard. *Beaumarchais.* New York: Knopf, 1949, 362 p.

Loménie, Louis Léonard de. *Beaumarchais and his Times. Sketches of French Society in the Eighteenth Century from Unpublished Documents.* Translated by Henry S. Edwards. New York: Harper and Brothers, 1857, 460 p.

Ruskin, Ariane. *Spy for Liberty: The Adventurous Life of Beaumarchais, Playwright and Secret Agent for the American Revolution.* New York: Pantheon Books, 1965, 178 p.

Benjamin Franklin

Augur, Helen. *The Secret War of Independence.* New York: Duell, Sloan and Pearce, 1955, 381 p.

Clark, William Bell. *Ben Franklin's Privateers: A Naval Epic of the American Revolution.* Baton Rouge: Louisiana State University Press, 1956, 198 p.

Currey, Cecil B. *Code Number 72/Ben Franklin: Patriot or Spy?* Englewood Cliffs, N.J.: Prentice-Hall, 1972, 331 p.

Morse, John Torrey. *Benjamin Franklin.* Boston: Houghton Mifflin, 1898, 444 p. (v. I of *American Statesmen . . .*).

Schoenbrun, David. *Triumph in Paris: The Exploits of Benjamin Franklin.* New York: Harper and Row, 1976, 420 p.

George III, King of Britain

George III, *King of Great Britain, 1738-1820. The Correspondence of King George the Third with Lord North from 1768 to 1783.* Edited by W. Bodham Donne. New York: Da Capo Press, 1971, 2 v. (reprint of 1867, London edition).

George III, *King of Great Britain, 1738-1820. The Letters.* Edited by Bonamy Dobrée. New York: Funk & Wagnalls, 1968, 293 p.

Trevelyan, George Otto, Sir. *George the Third and Charles Fox, the Concluding Part of the American Revolution.* New York: Longmans, Green, 1912-1914, 2 v.

Alexander Hamilton

Atherton, Gertrude Franklin Horn. *The Conqueror: Being the True and Romantic Story of Alexander Hamilton.* New York: Macmillan, 1902, 546 p. (fiction).

Hendrickson, Robert A. *Hamilton.* New York: Mason/Charter, 1976, 2 v.

Mitchell, Broadus. *Alexander Hamilton: The Revolutionary Years.* New York: Crowell, 1970, 386 p. (paperback).

Francis Marion

Dean, Sidney Walter. *Knight of the Revolution.* Philadelphia: Macrae-Smith, 1941, 312 p. (Francis Marion).

Rankin, Hugh F. *Francis Marion: The Swamp Fox.* New York: Crowell, [1973], 346 p.

Scheer, George F. "The Elusive Swamp Fox." *American Heritage,* v. IX, no. 3 (April 1958), pp. 40-47.

Weems, Mason Locke. *The Life of General Francis Marion, a Celebrated Partisan Officer, in the Revolutionary War, Against the British and Tories in South Carolina and Georgia.* New York: P.M. Davis, 1835, 252 p.

George Washington

Davis, Burke. *George Washington and the American Revolution.* New York: Random House, 1975, 497 p.

Freeman, Douglas Southall. *George Washington, a Biography.* New York: Scribner, 1948-57, 7 v.

Heusser, Albert Henry. *George Washington's Map Maker: A Biography of Robert Erskine.* Edited by Hubert G. Schmidt. New Brunswick, N.J.: Rutgers University Press, [1966], 268 p. (reprint of *The Forgotten General,* 1928).

Kitman, Marvin. *George Washington's Expense Account.* New York: Ballantine Books, 1970, 336 p. (paperback).

Knollenberg, Bernard. *Washington and the Revolution, a Reappraisal; Gates, Conway, and the Continental Congress.* New York: Macmillan, 1941, 269 p.

Knox, Dudley Wright. *The Naval Genius of George Washington.* Boston: Houghton Mifflin, 1932, 137 p.

Richter, Victor W. *General Washington's Body Guards.* Detroit: Concord Society, 1924, 24 p. (Society Historical Bulletin, no. 3).

U.S. Library of Congress, Manuscript Division. *Calendar of the Correspondence of George Washington, Commander in Chief of the Continental Army, with the Officers* ... Prepared from the original manuscripts by John C. Fitzpatrick. Washington: U.S. GPO, 1915, 3 v. (of a 4 v. set).

Washington, George. *Journal of Colonel George Washington, Commanding a Detachment of Virginia Troops, Sent by Robert Dinwiddie, Lieutenant Governor of Virginia, Across the Alleghany Mountains, in 1754, to Build Forts at the Head of the Ohio.* ... Edited by J.M. Toner. Albany, N.Y.: J. Munsell's, 1893, 273 p.

Washington, George. *The Journal of Major George Washington: An Account of His First Official Mission, Made as Emissary From the Governor of Virginia to the Commandant of the French Forces on the Ohio, October 1753-January 1754.* New York: Holt, for Colonial Williamsburg, Va., 1972, 41 p. (facsimile edition).

War of 1812

Barnes, James. *A Loyal Traitor: A Story of the War of 1812.* New York: Harper, 1899, 306 p. (fiction).

Beirne, Francis F. *The War of 1812.* New York: Dutton, 1949, 410 p.

Berton, Pierre. *The Invasion of Canada. Volume 1: 1812-1813.* Boston: Little, Brown, 1980, 363 p.

Coggeshall, George. "Journal of the Letter-of-Marque Schooners David Porter and Leo." *American Heritage,* v. VIII, no. 6 (October 1957), pp. 65–85.

Snider, Charles Henry Jeremiah. *Under the Red Jack: Privateers of the Maritime Provinces of Canada in the War of 1812.* London: M. Hopkinson, 1928, 268 p.

Mexican War

Bauer, Karl Jack. *The Mexican War, 1846–1848.* New York: Macmillan, 1974, 454 p.

Bill, Alfred Hoyt. *Rehearsal for Conflict: The War with Mexico, 1846–1848.* New York: History Book Club, 1947, 342 p.

Jenkins, John Stilwell. *History of the War Between the United States and Mexico, from the Commencement of Hostilities, to the Ratification of the Treaty of Peace.* Auburn, N.Y.: Derby, Miller; Buffalo: Derby and Hewson, 1848, 506 p.

Smith, George Winston and **Judah, Charles,** comps. *Chronicles of the Gringos: The U.S. Army in the Mexican War, 1846–1848; Accounts of Eyewitnesses and Combatants.* Albuquerque: University of New Mexico Press, 1968, 523 p.

American Civil War
General

Adams, Ephraim Douglass, *Great Britain and the American Civil War.* New York: Russell and Russell, [1958?], 2 v.

Bill, Alfred Hoyt. *The Beleaguered City, Richmond, 1861-1865.* New York: Knopf, 1946, 313 p.

Buckmaster, Henrietta, pseud. *Flight to Freedom: The Story of the Underground Railroad.* New York: Crowell, 1958, 217 p.

Cheek, William F. *Black Reistance Before the Civil War.* Beverly Hills, Calif.: Glencoe Press, 1970, 161 p.

Hynd, Alan. *Arrival: 12:30, the Baltimore Plot Against Lincoln.* Camden, N.J.: Nelson, 1967, 127 p. (fiction).

Leech, Margaret. *Reveille in Washington, 1860-1865.* New York: Harper, 1941, 483 p.

Logan, John Alexander. *The Great Conspiracy: Its Origin and History.* New York: A.R. Hart, 1886, 810 p.

Marshall, John A. *American Bastille: A History of the Illegal Arrests and Imprisonment of American Citizens during the Late Civil War.* 4th ed. Philadelphia: Evans, Stoddart, 1870, 728 p.

Milton, George Fort. *Abraham Lincoln and the Fifth Column.* New York: Vanguard Press, 1942, 364 p.

Salisbury, Allen. *The Civil War and the American System: America's Battle with Britain, 1860-1876.* New York: Campaigner, 1978, 440 p. (paperback).

Thompson, Samuel Bernard. *Confederate Purchasing Operations Abroad.* Gloucester, Mass.: Peter Smith, 1973, 137 p.

Conduct of Military Operations
General

Benson, Blackwood Ketcham. *A Friend with the Countersign.* New York: Macmillan, 1901, 455 p. (fiction).

Brownlee, Richard S. *Gray Ghosts of the Confederacy: Guerrilla Warfare in the West, 1861–1865.* Baton Rouge: Louisiana State University Press, 1958, 274 p.

Catton, Bruce. *Glory Road.* Garden City, N.Y.: Doubleday, 1952, 389 p.

Catton, Bruce. *Mr. Lincoln's Army.* Garden City, N.Y.: Doubleday, 1962, 363 p.

Catton, Bruce. *A Stillness at Appomattox.* Garden City, N.Y.: Doubleday, 1953, 438 p.

Eisenschiml, Otto. *The Hidden Face of the Civil War.* Indianapolis: Bobbs-Merrill, 1961, 319 p.

Jones, Virgil Carrington. *Gray Ghosts and Rebel Raiders.* New York: Holt, 1956, 431 p.

Kelsey, D.M. *Deeds of Daring by Both Blue and Gray: Thrilling Narratives of Personal Adventure ... on Each Side the Line during the Great Civil War.* Cincinnati: Forshee and McMakin, 1883, 608 p.

Lord, Francis Alfred. *They Fought for the Union.* New York: Bonanza Books, 1960, 375 p.

McBarron, H. Charles; Elting, John R. et al. "Balloon Corps; United States Army, 1861-1863." *Military Collector and Historian,* v. XXVIII, no. 1 (Spring 1976), pp. 16-18.

Scheips, Paul J. "Union Signal Communications: Innovation and Conflict." *Civil War History,* v. 9, no. 4 (December 1963), pp. 300-421.

Wilson, Charles Morrow. "The Hit-and-Run Raid." *American Heritage,* v. XII, no. 5 (August 1961), pp. 28-31. (St. Albans, Vermont).

Naval

Bigelow, John. *France and the Confederate Navy, 1862-1868: An International Episode.* New York: Harper, 1888, 247 p.

Cochran, Hamilton. *Blockade Runners of the Confederacy.* Indianapolis: Bobbs-Merrill, 1958, 350 p.

Delaney, Norman C. *John McIntosh Kell of the Raider Alabama.* University: University of Alabama Press, 1973, 270 p.

Groh, George W. "Last of the Rebel Raiders." *American Heritage,* v. X, no. 1 (December 1958), p. 48+.

Hay, David and **Hay, Joan.** *The Last of the Confederate Privateers.* New York: Crescent Books, 1977, 178 p.

Horner, Dave. *The Blockade-Runners: True Tales of Running the Yankee Blockade of the Confederate Coast.* New York: Dodd, Mead, 1968, 241 p.

Roberts, Walter Adolphe. *Semmes of the Alabama.* Indianapolis: Bobbs-Merrill, 1938, 320 p. (Raphael Semmes).

Robinson, William Morrison. *The Confederate Privateers.* New Haven: Yale University Press, 1928, 372 p.

Semmes, Raphael. *The Confederate Raider Alabama.* Gloucester, Mass.: Peter Smith, 1969, 464 p.

Semmes, Raphael. *Rebel Raider, Being an Account of Raphael Semmes's Cruise in the C.S.S. Sumter; Composed in large part of extracts from Semmes's Memoirs of Service Afloat, Written in the Year 1869.* Edited by Harpur Allen Gosnell. Chapel Hill: University of North Carolina Press, 1948, 218 p.

United States, Naval History Division. *Civil War Naval Chronology, 1861-1865.* Washington: U.S. GPO, 1971, 477 p.

Biographies and Case Histories
General

Campbell, Holen Jones. *Confederate Courier.* New York: St. Martin's Press, 1965, 301 p. (John Harrison Surratt).

Edwards, John Newman. *Noted Guerrillas: Or, the Warfare of the Border, Being a History of the Lives and Adventures of Quantrell, Bill Anderson, George Todd, Dave Poole, Fletcher Taylor, Peyton Long, Oll Shepherd, Arch Clements, John Maupin, Tuck and Woot Hill, Wm. Gregg, Thomas Maupin, the James Brothers, the Younger Brothers, Arthur McCoy, and Numerous other well Known Guerrillas of the West.* Dayton, Ohio: Morningside Bookshop, 1976, 488 p. (facsimile of 1877 edition).

Jeffries, C.C. *Terry's Rangers.* New York: Vantage Press, 1962, 139 p. (Benjamin Franklin Terry).

Johnson, Adam Rankin. *The Partisan Rangers of the Confederate States Army.* Edited by William J. Davis. Louisville, Ky.: G.G. Fetter, 1904, 476 p. (memoirs).

Kean, Robert Garlinck Hill. *Inside the Confederate Government: The Diary of Robert Garlick Hill Kean, Head of the Bureau of War.* Edited by Edward Younger. New York: Oxford University Press, 1957, 241 p.

Meade, Robert Douthat. *Judah P. Benjamin, Confederate Statesman.* New York: Oxford University Press, 1943, 432 p.

Meredith, Roy. *The World of Mathew Brady: Portraits of the Civil War Period.* Los Angeles: Brooke House, 1976, 240 p.

Peavey, James Dudley, ed. *Confederate Scout, Virginia's Frank Stringfellow.* Onancock, Va.: Eastern Shore, 1956, 62 p.

Roske, Ralph Joseph and **Van Doren, Charles.** *Lincoln's Commando: The Biography of Commander W.B. Cushing, U.S.N.* New York: Harper, 1957, 310 p.

Sensing, Thurman. *Champ Ferguson, Confederate Guerilla.* Nashville, Tenn.: Vanderbilt University Press, 1942, 256 p.

Swanberg, W.A. "Was the Secretary of War a Traitor?" *American Heritage,* v. XIV, no. 2 (February 1963), pp. 34-37. (John B. Floyd).

Walker, Jeanie Mort. *Life of Capt. Joseph Fry, the Cuban Martyr. Being a Faithful Record of his Remarkable Career from Childhood to the Time of his Heroic Death at the Hands of Spanish Executioners; Recounting his Experience as an Officer in the U.S. and Confederate Navies, and Revealing much of the Inner History and Secret Marine Service of the Late Civil War in America.* Hartford: J.B. Burr, 1875, 589 p.

Wise, Winifred Esther. *Lincoln's Secret Weapon.* New York: Chilton, 1961, 195 p. (Anna Ella Carroll).

John Brown

Furnas, Joseph Chamberlain. *The Road to Harpers Ferry.* New York: W. Sloane, 1959, 477 p.

Greene, Laurence. *The Raid, a Biography of Harpers Ferry.* New York: Holt, 1953, 246 p.

Redpath, James. *The Public Life of Capt. John Brown . . . with an Auto-biography of his Childhood and Youth.* Boston: Thayer and Eldridge, 1860, 407 p.

John Morgan

Brown, Dee Alexander. *The Bold Cavaliers: Morgan's 2nd Kentucky Cavalry Raiders.* Philadelphia: Lippincott, 1959, 353 p.

Duke, Basil Wilson. *A History of Morgan's Cavalry.* Edited by Cecil Fletcher Holland. Bloomington: Indiana University Press, 1960, 595 p.

Dunn, Byron Archibald. *Raiding with Morgan.* Chicago: A.C. McClurg, 1903, 334 p.

Keller, Allan. *Morgan's Raid.* Indianapolis: Bobbs-Merrill, 1961, 272 p.

Reid, Samuel Chester. *The Capture and Wonderful Escape of General John H. Morgan* as reported by Samuel C. Reid. Edited by Joseph J. Mathews. Atlanta: Emory University, 1947, 20 p.

Swiggett, Howard. *The Rebel Raiders: A Life of John Hunt Morgan.* Indianapolis: Bobbs-Merrill, 1934, 341 p.

John Mosby and Jeb Stuart

Daniels, Jonathan. *Mosby: Gray Ghost of the Confederacy.* Philadelphia: Lippincott, 1959, 122 p.

Jones, Virgil Carrington. *Ranger Mosby.* Chapel Hill: University of North Carolina Press, 1944, 347 p.

Mosby, John Singleton. *Mosby's War Reminiscences and Stuart's Cavalry Campaigns.* New York: Dodd, Mead, 1887, 264 p.

Thomason, John William. *Jeb Stuart.* New York: Scribner, 1934, 512 p.

William Quantrill

Barton, O.S. *Three Years with Quantrill: A True Story, told by his Scout John McCorkle.* New York: Buffalo-Head Press and J.F. Carr, 1966, 157 p.

Breihan, Carl W. *The Killer Legions of Quantrill.* Seattle: Hangman Press, 1971, 144 p.

Breihan, Carl W. *Quantrell and his Civil War Guerrillas.* New York: Promontory Press, 1959, 174 p.

Burch, John P. *Charles W. Quantrell: A True History of his Guerrilla Warfare on the Missouri and Kansas Border During the Civil War of 1861–1865 . . . as told by Captain Harrison Trow.* Vega, Texas: J.P. Burch, 1923, 266 p.

Edwards, John Newman. *Noted Guerrillas: Or, the Warfare of the Border, Being a History of the Lives and Adventures of Quantrell, Bill Anderson, George Todd, Dave Poole, Fletcher Taylor, Peyton Long, Oll Shepherd, Arch Clements, John Maupin, Tuck and Woot Hill, Wm. Gregg, Thomas Maupin, the James Brothers, the Younger Brothers, Arthur McCoy, and Numerous other well Known Guerrillas of the West.* Dayton, Ohio: Morningside Bookshop, 1976, 488 p. (facsimile of 1877 edition).

Spanish-American War

Azoy, Anastasio Carlos Mariano. *Signal 250! The Sea Fight off Santiago.* New York: D. McKay, 1964, 207 p.

Giddings, Howard Andrus. *Exploits of the Signal Corps in the War with Spain.* Kansas City, Mo.: Hudson-Kimberly, 1900, 126 p.

Halstead, Murat. *Full Official History of the War with Spain: Written over the Wires in the Discharge of Public Duty by the Highest Authorities of the Government, Heads of Departments and Bureaus . . . the Adjutant General, the Commanders of Fleets and Armies in Active Service, and the President of the United States . . .* Prepared by the War and Navy Departments. New Haven, Conn.: Butler and Alger, 1899, 794 p.

Roosevelt, Theodore, *President, U.S. The Rough Riders.* New York: Putnam, 1900, 300 p.

Young, James Rankin and **Moore, Joseph Hampton.** *Reminiscences and Thrilling Stories of the War by Returned Heroes, Containing Vivid Accounts of Personal Experiences by Officers and Men; Admiral Dewey's Report of the ... Battle of Manila; Graphic Account by Admiral Schley of the Naval Battle at Santiago ... to Which is added Admiral Cervera's Story of his Attempt to Escape from the Harbor of Santiago; Hobson's Vivid Account of the Sinking of the Merrimac ... Poems and Songs of the War, etc.* Philadelphia: National, 1899, 665 p.

South African War

De Wet, Christiaan Rudolf. *Three Years' War.* New York: Scribner, 1902, 448 p. (translation of *De strijd tusschen Boer en Brit).*

Farwell, Byron. *The Great Anglo-Boer War.* New York: Harper and Row, 1976, 495 p.

Griffith, Kenneth. *Thank God we Kept the Flag Flying: The Siege and Relief of Ladysmith, 1899–1900.* New York: Viking Press, 1974, 398 p.

Hammond, John Hays. *The Truth about the Jameson Raid* as related to Alleyne Ireland. Boston: Marshall Jones, 1918, 50 p.

Holt, Edgar. *The Boer War.* London: Putnam, 1958, 317 p.

Pakenham, Thomas. *The Boer War.* New York: Random House, 1979, 718 p.

Ralph, Julian. *An American with Lord Roberts.* New York: Frederick A. Stokes, 1901, 314 p.

Reitz, Deneys. *Commando: A Boer Journal of the Boer War.* New York: Praeger, 1970, 331 p.

Sampson, Victor and **Hamilton, Ian.** *Anti-Commando.* London: Faber and Faber, 1931, 220 p.

World War I
General

Bernstorff, Johann Heinrich Andreas Hermann Albrecht, graf von. *My Three Years in America.* London: Skeffington, 1920, 359 p.

Blankfort, Michael. *Behold the Fire: A Novel Based on Events that took Place Between 1914 and 1918 in London, Cairo, Constantinople, Jerusalem, and Some of the Villages of Palestine.* New York: New American Library, 1966, 397 p. (paperback).

Brown, Demetra Vaka. *In the Heart of German Intrigue.* Boston: Houghton Mifflin, 1918, 377 p. (London edition title: *Constantine, King and Traitor).*

Castex, Henri. *La "Grande Guerre" pour rien?* Presentation d'Abel Clarté. Paris: Roblot, 1974, 313 p.

Des Ombiaux, Maurice. *La Resistance de la Belgique envahie.* Paris: Bloud et Gay, 1916, 239 p.

Feuerlicht, Roberta Strauss. *The Desperate Act: The Assassination of Franz Ferdinand at Sarajevo.* New York: McGraw-Hill, 1968, 172 p.

Florence, Ronald. *Fritz: The Story of a Political Assassin.* New York: Dial Press, 1971, 337 p.

Gerard, James Watson. *Face to Face with Kaiserism* by the late ambassador to the German Imperial Court. New York: George H. Doran, 1918, 380 p.

Great Britain, Foreign Office. *Collected Diplomatic Documents Relating to the Outbreak of the European War.* London: H.M. Stationery Office, 1915, 561 p.

Hainsselin, Montague Thomas. *Naval Intelligence.* London: Hodder and Stoughton, 1918, 237 p.

Hall, William Reginald, *Sir* and **Peaslee, Amos J.** *Three Wars with Germany.* Edited by Joseph P. Sims. New York: Putnam, 1944, 309 p.

Hirschfeld, Magnus, ed. *The Sexual History of the World War.* New York: Panurge Press, 1934, 350 p.

Hoyt, Edwin Palmer. *The Army Without a Country.* New York: Macmillan, 1967, 243 p.

Johnson, Severance. *The Enemy Within: Hitherto Unpublished Details of the Great Conspiracy to Corrupt and Destroy France.* Translations by Edgard Léon. New York: James A. McCann, 1919, 297 p.

King, Jere Clemens, comp. *The First World War.* New York: Walker, 1972, 350 p.

Lewinsohn, Richard. *The Mystery Man of Europe, Sir Basil Zaharoff.* Philadelphia: Lippincott, 1929, 241 p.

Liddell Hart, Basil Henry. *The Real War, 1914–1918.* Boston: Little, Brown, 1930, 508 p.

March, Francis Andrew and **Beamish, Richard Joseph.** *History of the World War: An Authentic Narrative of the World's Greatest War.* Philadelphia: John C. Winston, 1919, 736 p.

Massart, Jean. *The Secret Press in Belgium.* Translated by Bernard Miall. New York: Dutton; London: T.F. Unwin, 1918, 96 p.

Millard, Oscar E. *Underground News: The Complete Story of the Secret Newspaper that Made War History.* New York: McBride, 1938, 287 p. (published in England under title *Uncensored*).

Muehlon, Wilhelm. *Dr. Muehlon's Diary: Notes Written Early in the War by the Ex-Director of Krupp's.* London: New York: Cassell, 1918, 247 p. (original: *Die verheerung Europas: Aufzeichnungen aus den ersten Kriegesmonaten.* Zürich: Orell Füszli, 1918).

Owen, Robert Latham. *The Russian Imperial Conspiracy, 1892–1914.* New York: A. and C. Boni, 1927, 212 p.

Pauli, Hertha Ernestine. *The Secret of Sarajevo: The Story of Franz Ferdinand and Sophie.* New York: Appleton-Century, 1965, 309 p.

Paxson, Frederic Logan. *America at War, 1917–1918.* Boston: n.p. 1939, 465 p. (first published as v. 2 of the author's *American Democracy and the World War*).

Schmidt, Charles, ed. *Les plans secrets de la politique allemande en Alsace-Lorraine (1915–1918).* Paris: Payot, 1922, 261 p. (paperback).

Scully, Charles Alison. *The Course of the Silver Greyhound.* New York: Putnam, 1936, 93 p.

Shotwell, James Thomson. *At the Paris Conference.* New York: Macmillan, 1937, 444 p.

Williamson, Alice Muriel Livingston. *What I Found out in the House of a German Prince* by an English-American Governess. New York: Frederick A. Stokes, 1915, 241 p.

War Cyclopedia: A Handbook for Ready Reference on the Great War. Edited by Frederic L. Paxson, Edward S. Corwin *et al.* Washington: U.S. GPO, 1918, 321 p.

Conduct of Military Operations

Alexander, Roy. *The Cruise of the Raider "Wolf."* New Haven: Yale University Press, 1939, 270 p.

Bott, Alan John. *Cavalry of the Clouds* by "Contact." Garden City, N.Y.: Doubleday, Page, 1918, 266 p. (first U.S. edition published under title *The Flying Ace;* English edition, *An Airman's Outings,* published by W. Blackwood).

Burdick, Charles Burton. *The Frustrated Raider: The Story of the German Cruiser Cormoran in World War I.* Carbondale: Southern Illinois University Press, 1979, 119 p.

Campbell, Gordon. *My Mystery Ships.* Garden City, N.Y.: Doubleday, Doran, 1929, 318 p.

Campbell, Gordon. *My Mystery Ships.* London: Hodder and Stoughton, 1928, 300 p.

Churchill, Winston Leonard Spencer, *Sir. The Unknown War: The Eastern Front.* Toronto: MacMillan Company of Canada, 1931, 396 p.

Dolbey, Robert Valentine. *Sketches of the East Africa Campaign.* London: J. Albemarle, 1918, 219 p.

Downes, Walter Douglas. *With the Nigerians in German East Africa.* London: Methuen, 1919, 352 p.

Gooch, John. *The Plans of War: the General Staff and British Military Strategy, c. 1900–1916.* London: Routledge and K. Paul, 1974, 348 p.

Griff, *pseud.* (A.S.G.). *Surrendered: Some Naval War Secrets.* Cross Deep, Twickenham, England: The Author, 1927, 246 p.

Herbert, Aubrey Nigel Henry Molyneux. *Mons, Anzac and Kut.* London: Hutchinson, 1930, 270 p.

Rutherford, Ward. *The Ally: The Russian Army in World War I.* London: Gordon and Cremonesi, 1977, 303 p. (paperback).

Sibley, J.R. *Tanganyikan Guerrilla: East African Campaign 1914–1918.* New York: Ballantine Books, 1971, 158 p.

Terraine, J.A. "The Great Confidence Trick." *Journal of the Royal United Service Institution,* v. CIII (February 1958), pp. 58–61.

Thomas, Lowell Jackson. *Raiders of the Deep.* Garden City, N.Y.: Doubleday, Doran, 1928, 363 p.

Toulmin, Harry Aubrey. *Air Service, American Expeditionary Force, 1918.* New York: D. Van Nostrand, 1927, 388 p.

Watt, Richard M. *Dare Call it Treason.* London: Chatto and Windus, 1964, 285 p.

Wynn, Wynn Elias. *Ambush.* London: Hutchinson, 1937, 256 p.

Biographies and Case Histories

Andrieu, Pierre. *Auf Horchposten vor Verdun, nach dem Bericht des Capitaine Henri Morin, erzählt von Pierre Andrieu.* Berlin: G. Stalling, 1939, 201 p.

Hoyt, Edwin Palmer. *The Phantom Raider.* New York: Crowell, 1969, 185 p. (Nikolaus P.R. Dohna-Schlodien).

Hoyt, Edwin Palmer. *Raider Wolf: The Voyage of Captain Nerger, 1916–1918.* New York: Pinnacle Books, 1977, 211 p. (Karl August Nerger).

Knightley, Phillip and **Simpson, Colin.** *The Secret Lives of Lawrence of Arabia.* New York: Bantam Books, 1971, 332 p. (Thomas E. Lawrence) (paperback).

Lawrence, Thomas Edward. *Revolt in the Desert.* New York: George H. Doran, 1927, 335 p.

Robertson, William Robert, Sir. *From Private to Field-Marshal.* London: Constable, 1921, 396 p.

Roskill, Stephen Wentworth. *Admiral of the Fleet Earl Beatty: The Last Naval Hero: An Intimate Biography.* New York: Atheneum, 1981, 430 p. (David Beatty).

Smithers, A.J. *Toby: A Real Life Ripping Yarn.* London; New York: Gordon and Cremonesi, 1978, 191 p.

Sykes, Christopher. *Wassmuss, "the German Lawrence."* London: Longmans, Green, 1936, 271 p.

Thomas, Lowell Jackson. *Count Luckner, the Sea Devil.* Garden City, N.Y.: Doubleday, Page, 1927, 308 p. (Felix Luckner).

Thomas, Lowell Jackson. *With Lawrence in Arabia.* Garden City, N.Y.: Garden City Publishing, 1924, 408 p. (Thomas E. Lawrence).

Wheatley, Dennis. *The Time has Come: The Memoirs of Dennis Wheatley. Volume 2: Officer and Temporary Gentleman, 1914–1919.* London: Hutchinson, 1978, 254 p.

Winstone, Harry Victor Frederick. *Captain Shakespear: A Portrait.* New York: Quartet Books, 1978, 236 p. (William Henry I. Shakespear).

Wintle, Alfred Daniel. *The Last Englishman: An Autobiography of Lieut.-Col. Alfred Daniel Wintle, M.C. (1st the Royal Dragoons).* London: Joseph, 1968, 288 p.

Russian Revolution
General

Ardamatskii, Vasilii Ivanovich. *Retribution.* Washington: U.S. Joint Publications Research Service, nos. 56005-1 and 56005-2, May 16, 1972, 2 v. (Translation from the Russian of Vozmezdie. Moscow: Molodaiia Gvardiia, 1968, 591 p.).

Budennyi, Semen Mikhailovich. *The Path of Valour.* Moscow: Progress Publishers, 1972, 433 p. (Translation of Proidennyi put').

Crankshaw, Edward. *The Shadow of the Winter Palace: Russia's Drift to Revolution, 1825–1917.* New York: Viking Press, 1976, 429 p.

Dvinov, Boris. L. *Ot legal'nosti k podpol'iu, 1921–1922.* Zapiski. Stanford, Calif.: Hoover Institution, 1968, 201 p.

Dzerzhinskii, Feliks Edmundovich. *Prison Diary and Letters.* Moscow: Foreign Languages Pub. House, 1959, 306 p. (translation of Dnevnik zakliuchennogo).

Figner, Vera Nikolaevna. *Mémoires d'une révolutionnaire.* Paris: Denoël/Gonthier, 1973, 334 p. (translation of Zapechatlennyi trud).

Futrell, Michael. *Northern Underground: Episodes of Russian Revolutionary Transport and Communications through Scandinavia and Finland, 1863–1917.* New York: Praeger, 1963, 240 p.

Krotov, Viacheslav Leonodovich. *Chonovtsy.* Moscow: Politizdat, 1974, 128 p.

Mackenzie, Frederick Arthur. *Russia Before Dawn.* London: T.F. Unwin, 1923, 288 p.

Malaparte, Curzio. *Coup d'Etat, The Technique of Revolution.* Translated by Sylvia Saunders. New York: Dutton, 1932, 251 p.

Mal'kov, Pavel Dmitrievich with **Sverdlov, Andrei IAkovlevich.** *Reminiscences of a Kremlin Commandant.* Translated from the Russian by V. Dutt. Moscow: Progress Publishers, [196?], 316 p.

Medvedev, Roi Aleksandrovich. *The October Revolution.* Translated by George Saunders. New York: Columbia University Press, 1979, 240 p.

Payne, Pierre Stephen Robert. *The Fortress.* New York: Simon and Schuster, 1967, 448 p.

Payne, Pierre Stephen Robert. *The Life and Death of Trotsky.* New York: McGraw-Hill, 1977, 498 p.

Petrov-Skilaletz, E., pseud. (Step, Eugene S.). *The Kronstadt Thesis for a Free Russian Government.* Translated by John F. O'Conor. New York: R. Speller, 1964, 134 p.

Porter, Cathy. *Alexandra Kollontai, a Biography: The Lonely Struggle of the Woman Who Defied Lenin.* New York: Dial Press, 1980, 553 p.

Prokof'ev, Vadim Aleksandrovich. *A v Rossii uzhe vesna: Povest' o V. Vorovskom.* Moscow: Politizdat, 1974, 463 p.

Prokof'ev, Vadim Aleksandrovich. *Vernye do kontsa: iskovtsy: dokumental'nyi rasskazy.* Moscow: Molodaia Gvardiia, 1977, 190 p.

Radziwill, Catherine, *Princess. The Firebrand of Bolshevism: The True Story of the Bolsheviki and the Forces that Directed them.* Boston: Small, Maynard, 1919, 293 p.

Ransome, Arthur. *Russia in 1919.* New York: B.W. Huebsch, 1919, 232 p. (U.S. edition of *Six weeks in Russia in 1919.* London: Allen and Unwin).

Revoliutsiia 1905-1907 godov: Dokumenty i materialy. Compiled by G.I. Vedernikova, IU. F. Mosev *et al.* Moscow: Politizdat, 1975, 405 p.

Saparov, Arif Vasil'evich. *The Game is Up.* Washington: U.S. Joint Publications Research Service, no. 55467, 17 March 1972, (translation of *Bitaia karta: khronika odnogo zagovora.* Leningrad: Leninizdat, 1967, 21 p.).

Serge, Victor. *Memoirs of a Revolutionary, 1901-1941.* Translated and edited by Peter Sedgwick. New York: Oxford University Press, 1963, 401 p.

Sisson, Edgar Grant. *One Hundred Red Days: A Personal Chronicle of the Bolshevik Revolution* by the special representative of President Wilson in Russia. New Haven: Yale University Press, 1931, 502 p.

Trotskii, Lev. *Terrorism and Communism: A Reply to Karl Kautsky . . . with France at a Turning Point.* Ann Arbor: University of Michigan Press, 1961, 191 p.

Ulam, Adam Bruno. *Russia's Failed Revolutions: From the Decembrists to the Dissidents.* New York: Basic Books, 1981, 453 p.

Woytinsky, Wladimir S. *Stormy Passage: A Personal History Through Two Russian Revolutions to Democracy and Freedom: 1905-1960.* New York: Vanguard Press, 1961, 550 p..

Early Revolutionary Movements

Avrich, Paul. *Russian Rebels, 1600-1800.* New York: Norton, 1976, 295 p.

Avrich, Paul, *comp. The Anarchists in the Russian Revolution.* Ithaca, N.Y.: Cornell University Press, 1973, 179 p.

Bobrovskaia, TSetsiliia Samoilovna Zelikson. *Twenty Years in Underground Russia: Memoirs of a Rank-and-File Bolshevik.* New York: International Publishers, 1934, 227 p. (translation of *Zapiski riadovogo podpol'shchika*).

Broido, Eva L'vovna. *Memoirs of a Revolutionary.* Translated from the Russian and edited by Vera Broido. New York: Oxford University Press, 1967, 150 p.

Broido, Vera. *Apostles into Terrorists: Women and the Revolutionary Movement in the Russia of Alexander II.* New York: Viking Press, 1977, 238 p.

Brower, Daniel R. *Training the Nihilists: Education and Radicalism in Tsarist Russia.* Ithaca, N.Y.: Cornell University Press, 1975, 248 p.

Field, Daniel. *Rebels in the Name of the Tsar.* Boston: Houghton Mifflin, 1976, 220 p.

Footman, David. *The Alexander Conspiracy: A Life of A.I. Zhelyabov.* LaSalle, Ill.: Open Court, 1974, 354 p. (previous editions published in London under title: *Red Prelude*).

Grosul, Vladislav IAkimovich. *Rossiiskie revoliutsionery v IUgo-Vostochnoi Evrope. (1859-1874 gg).* Kishinev: Shtiintsa, 1973, 539 p.

Ivanskii, Anatolii Ivanovich, *comp. Comet in the Night: The Story of Alexander Ulyanov's Heroic Life and Tragic Death as Told by his Contemporaries.* Translated from the Russian by Taras Kapustin. Edited by David Skvirsky. Moscow: Progress Publishers, 1968, 299 p. (translation of *Zhizn' kak fakel*).

Kropotkin, Petr Alekseevich, *Kniaz'. Memoirs of a Revolutionist.* Boston; New York: Houghton Mifflin, 1930, 502 p.

Lang, David Marshall. *The First Russian Radical: Alexander Radishchev, 1749-1802.* London: Allen and Unwin, 1959, 298 p.

Payne, Pierre Stephen Robert. *The Terrorists: The Story of the Forerunners of Stalin.* New York: Funk and Wagnalls, 1957, 361 p.

Prawdin, Michael, *pseud.* (Charol, Michael). *The Unmentionable Nechaev, a Key to Bolshevism.* New York: Roy, 1961, 198 p. (Sergei Gennadievich Nechaev).

Seth, Ronald. *The Russian Terrorists: The Story of the Narodniki.* London: Barrie and Rockliff, 1966, 303 p.

Stepniak, *pseud.* (Kravchinskii, Sergei Mikhailovich). *The Career of a Nihilist: A Novel.* New York: Harper, 1889, 320 p.

Stepniak, *pseud.* (Kravchinskii, Sergei Mikhailovich). *Russia under the Tzars.* Translated by William Westall. London: War and Downey, 1885, 2 v.

Stepniak, *pseud.* (Kravchinskii, Sergei Mikhailovich). *Underground Russia: Revolutionary Profiles and Sketches from Life.* Translated from the Italian. New York: Scribner, 1883, 272 p.

Ulam, Adam Bruno. *In the Name of the People: Prophets and Conspirators in Prerevolutionary Russia.* New York: Viking Press, 1977, 418 p.

Woodcock, George and **Avakumovic, Ivan.** *The Anarchist Prince: A Biographical Study of Peter Kropotkin.* New York: T.V. Boardman, 1950, 463 p.

Zetlin, Mikhail Osipovich. *The Decembrists.* Translated by George Panin. New York: International Universities Press, 1958, 439 p.

Overthrow of the Czar

Alexandrov, Victor. *The End of the Romanovs.* Translated by William Sutcliffe. Boston: Little, Brown, 1967, 256 p.

Brown, Douglas. *Doomsday 1917: The Destruction of Russia's Ruling Class.* New York: Putnam, 1976, 204 p.

Frankland, Noble. *Imperial Tragedy: Nicholas II, Last of the Tsars.* New York: Coward-McCann, 1961, 193 p.

Liepmann, Heinz. *The Mad Monk of Russia.* Translated from the German by Edward Fitzgerald. New York: Rolton House, 1964, 264 p.

Liepmann, Heinz. *Rasputin and the Fall of Imperial Russia.* Translated from the German by Edward Fitzgerald. New York: R.M. McBride, 1959, 264 p.

Null, Gary. *The Conspirator Who Saved the Romanovs.* Englewood Cliffs, N.J.: Prentice-Hall, 1971, 177 p. (Aron Simonovich).

Richards, Guy. *The Hunt for the Czar.* Garden City, N.Y.: Dell, 1971, 237 p. (paperback).

Richards, Guy. *Imperial Agent: The Goleniewski-Romanov Case.* New York: Devin-Adair, 1966, 284 p.

Summers, Anthony and **Mangold, Tom.** *The File on the Tsar.* New York: Harper and Row, 1976, 416 p.

Trewin, John Courtenay. *The House of Special Purpose: An Intimate Portrait of the Last Days of the Russian Imperial Family.* Compiled from the papers of their English Tutor, Charles Sydney Gibbes. New York: Stein and Day, 1975, 148 p.

Civil War and Allied Intervention

Azizbekova, Pista A.; Mnats'akanyan, Aramayis Navasardi et al. *Sovetskaia Rossiia i bor'ba za ustanovlenie i uprochenie vlasti Sovetov v Zakavkaz'e.* Baku: Azerneshr, 1969, 323 p.

Bochkareva, Mariia Leontievna Frolkova. *Yashka, My Life as Peasant, Officer and Exile, by Maria Botchkareva, Commander of the Russian Women's Battalion of Death, as Set Down by Isaac Don Levine.* New York: Frederick A. Stokes, 1919, 340 p.

Brinkley, George. A. *The Volunteer Army and Allied Intervention in South Russia, 1917-1921: A Study in the Politics and Diplomacy of the Russian Civil War.* Notre Dame, Ind.: University of Notre Dame Press, 1966, 446 p.

Duranty, Walter. *The Curious Lottery, and Other Tales of Russian Justice.* New York: Coward-McCann, 1929, 237 p. (Boris Savinkov).

Dushen'kin, Vasilii Vasil'evich. *Ural'skii reid.* Moscow: Oborongiz, 1973, 125 p.

Geroicheskoe podpol'e: V tylu denikinskoi armii: Vospominaniia. Compiled by O.N. Petrovskaia and A.M. Sedina. Moscow: Politizdat, 1976, 415 p.

Hodges, Phelps. *Britmis: A Great Adventure of the War; Being an Account of Allied Intervention in Siberia and of an Escape Across the Gobi to Peking.* London: J. Cape, 1931, 364 p.

Ivanov, Vsevolod Viacheslavovich. *Sobrania sochinenii. [Volume]1: Partizanskie povesti. Golubye peski. Vozvrashchenie Buddy.* Moscow: Khudozh. Lit., 1973, 624 p.

Kennedy, J.N. "The Anti-Bolshevik Movement in South Russia, 1917-1920." *Journal of the Royal United Service Institution,* v. LXVII (February-November 1922), pp. 600-621.

Kettle, Michael. *The Allies and the Russian Collapse, March 1917-March 1918.* London: Andre Deutsch, 1981, 287 p. (Russia and the Allies, 1917-1920; v 1).

Lazo, Sergei. *Sergei Lazo: Vospominaniia i dokumenty.* Compiled by G.E. Reikhberg, A.P. Shurygin *et al.* Moscow: Politizdat, 1974, 237 p.

Lehovich, Dimitry V. *White Against Red: The Life of General Anton Denikin.* New York: Norton, 1974, 556 p.

Maddox, Robert James. *The Unknown War with Russia: Wilson's Siberian Intervention.* San Rafael, Calif.: Presidio Press, 1977, 156 p.

Mitchell, David J. *1919: Red Mirage.* New York: Macmillan, 1970, 385 p.

Na boevom postu: sbornik: povest', rasskazy i ocherki. Compiled by A. Mironov. Minsk: Mastatskaia Literatura, 1974, 252 p.

Nikiforov, Petr Mikhailovich. *Zapiski prem'era DVR: pobeda leninskoi politiki v bor'be c interventsiei na Dal'nem Vostoke: 1917–1922 gg.* Moscow: Politizdat, 2d ed., 1974, 189 p.

Savinkov, Boris Viktorovich. *Delo Borisa Savinkova so stat'ei B. Savinkova: "pochemu IA priznal sovetskuiu vlast'."* Ann Arbor, Mich.; London: University Microfilms International, 1976, 160 p. (original published in Moscow: Gosudarstvennoe, 1924).

Savinkov, Boris Viktorovich. *Memoirs of a Terrorist.* Translated by Joseph Shaplen. New York: A. and C. Boni, 1931, 364 p.

Silverlight, John. *The Victors' Dilemma: Allied Intervention in the Russian Civil War.* New York: Weybright and Talley, 1970, 392 p.

Sokoloff, Boris. *The White Nights: Pages from a Russian Doctor's Notebook.* New York: Devin-Adair, 1956, 294 p.

Svidine, Nicolas. *Cossack Gold: The Secret of the White Army Treasure.* Translated from the French by Leonard Mayhew. Boston: Little, Brown, 1975, 188 p. (original: *Le secret de Nicolas Svidine*).

Ullman, Richard Henry. *Anglo-Soviet Relations, 1917–1921. Volume 1: Intervention and the War.* Princeton, N.J.: Princeton University Press, 1961, 360 p.

Vinokur, Boris Il'ich. *Chrezvychainoe poruchenie: Dokum. povest'.* Moscow: Politizdat, 1974, 207 p. (Leon Khristoforovich Popov) (fiction).

Wreden, Nicholas R. *The Unmaking of a Russian.* New York: Norton, 1935, 317 p.

Lenin and Stalin

Amba, Achmed. *I was Stalin's Bodyguard.* Translated by Richard and Clara Winston. London: F. Muller, 1952, 256 p. (original: *Ein Mensch sicht Stalin*).

Fishman, Jack and **Hutton, J. Bernard,** pseud. *The Private Life of Josif Stalin.* London: W.H. Allen, 1962, 214 p.

Grey, Ian. *Stalin, Man of History.* Garden City, N.Y.: Doubleday, 1979, 547 p.

Levine, Isaac Don. *Stalin's Great Secret.* New York: Coward-McCann, 1956, 126 p.

Malinin, Georgii Aleksandrovich. *Sviazhite nas s "Vavilonom!" (Iz istorii rasprostraneniia proizvedenii V.I. Lenina v Sarat. Gubernii).* Edited by V.B. Ostrovsk. Saratov: Privolzh. Kh. Izd-vo, 1973, 231 p.

Pearson, Michael. *The Sealed Train.* New York: Putnam, 1975, 320 p.

Smith, Edward Ellis. *The Young Stalin: The Early Years of an Elusive Revolutionary.* New York: Farrar, Straus and Giroux, 1967, 470 p.

Solzhenitsyn, Aleksandr Isaevich. *Lenin in Zurich: Chapters.* Translated by H.T. Willetts. New York: Farrar, Straus and Giroux, 1975, 309 p. (original: *Lenin v TSiurikhe*).

Trotskii, Lev. *Stalin: An Appraisal of the Man and his Influence.* Edited and translated from the Russian by Charles Malamuth. New York: Grosset and Dunlap, 1941, 516 p.

Tucker, Robert C. *Stalin as Revolutionary, 1879–1929: A Study in History and Personality.* New York: Norton, 1973, 519 p.

The Ulyanov Family. Edited by I.IA. Baranov. Moscow: Progress Publishers, 1968, 133 p. (Vladimir Il'ich Lenin).

Chinese Civil War

Barber, Noel. *The Fall of Shanghai.* New York: Coward, McCann and Geoghegan, 1979, 248 p.

Berkov, Robert. *Strong Man of China: The Story of Chiang Kai-shek.* Boston: Houghton Mifflin, 1938, 288 p.

Borisov, Oleg Borisovich. *The Soviet Union and the Manchurian Revolutionary Base: (1945-1949).* Translated from the Russian by David Fidlon. Moscow: Progress Publishers, 1977, 275 p. (original: *Sovetskii Soiuz i Man'chzhurskaia revoliutsionnia baza*).

Chiang Kai-shek. *Resistance and Reconstruction: Messages During China's Six Years of War, 1937-1943.* New York: Harper, 1943, 322 p.

Chih Hsia. *The Railway Guerrillas.* Peking: Foreign Languages Press, 1966, 604 p.

Crozier, Brian and **Chou, Eric.** *The Man who Lost China: The First Full Biography of Chiang Kai-shek.* New York: Scribner, 1976, 430 p.

Davis, Fei-ling. *Primitive Revolutionaries of China: A Study of Secret Societies in the Late Nineteenth Century.* Honolulu: University Press of Hawaii, 1977, 254 p. (translation of *Le società segrete in Cina, 1820-1911*).

De Jaegher, Raymond J. and **Kuhn, Irene Corbally.** *The Enemy Within: An Eyewitness Account of the Communist Conquest of China.* Garden City: N.Y.: Doubleday, 1952, 314 p.

Harrison, James P. *The Long March to Power: A History of the Chinese Communist Party, 1921-72.* New York: McMillan Press, 1972, 647 p.

Hu P'u-yü, comp. *A Brief History of the Chinese National Revolutionary Forces.* Translated by Wen Ha-hsiung. Taipei: Chung Wu, 1971, 286 p.

Jacobs, Daniel Norman. *Borodin, Stalin's Man in China.* Cambridge, Mass.: Harvard University Press, 1981, 369 p. (Mikhail Markovich Borodin).

Kahn, Ely Jacques. *The China Hands: America's Foreign Service Officers and What Befell Them.* New York: Viking Press, 1975, 337 p.

Kataoka, Tetsuya. *Resistance and Revolution in China: The Communists and the Second United Front.* Berkeley: University of California Press, 1974, 326 p.

Lindsay, Michael, *Baron Lindsay of Birker. The Unknown War: North China 1939-1945.* London: Bergstrom and Boyle Books, 1975, 112 p.

Loo Pin-fei. *It is Dark Underground.* New York: Putnam, 1946, 200 p.

Mao Tse-tung. *On Guerrilla Warfare.* Translated and with an introduction by Samuel B. Griffith. New York: Praeger, 1961, 123 p.

May, Gary. *China Scapegoat, the Diplomatic Ordeal of John Carter Vincent.* Washington: New Republic Books, 1979, 370 p.

Michael, Franz H. with **Chang Chung-li.** *The Taiping Rebellion: History and Documents. Volume 1: History.* Translations by Margery Anneberg et al. Seattle: University of Washington Press, 1966, 244 p.

Saga of Resistance to Japanese Invasion. Peking: Foreign Languages Press, 1959, 212 p. (translation of *K'ang Jih chan cheng ti ku shih*) (paperback).

Service, John S. *Lost Chance in China: The World War II Despatches of John S. Service.* Edited by Joseph W. Esherick. New York: Random House, 1974, 409 p.

Snow, Edgar. *Scorched Earth.* London: Gollancz, 1941, 188 p.

Sues, Ilona Ralf. *Shark's Fins and Millet.* Boston: Little, Brown, 1944, 331 p.

Tennien, Mark A. *Chungking Listening Post.* New York: Creative Age Press, 1945, 201 p.

The Unquenchable Spark. Peking: Foreign Languages Press, 1963, 152 p.

Vogel, Ezra F. *Canton Under Communism: Programs and Politics in a Provincial Capital, 1949-1968.* Cambridge: Harvard University Press, 1969, 448 p.

Wei Yü-hsiu Cheng and **Van Vorst, Bessie McGinnis.** *A Girl from China (Soumay Tcheng).* New York: Frederick A. Stokes, 1926, 249 p.

World War II
General

Calvocoressi, Peter and **Wint, Guy.** *Total War: Causes and Courses of the Second World War.* Harmondsworth, Middlesex, England: Penguin, 1979, 965 p. (paperback).

Deborin, Grigorii Abramovich. *Secrets of the Second World War.* Translated from the Russian by Vic Schnelerson. Moscow: Progress Publishers, 1971, 277 p. (translation of *Tainy vtoroi mirovoi voiny*).

Enser, A.G.S. *A Subject Bibliography of the Second World War: Books in English, 1939-1974.* London: Deutsch, 1977, 592 p.

Goralski, Robert. *World War II Almanac, 1931-1945: A Political and Military Record.* New York: Putnam, 1981, 486 p.

Hall, William Reginald, *Sir* and **Peaslee, Amos J.** *Three Wars with Germany.* Edited by Joseph P. Sims. New York: Putnam, 1944, 309 p.

Ienaga, Saburo. *The Pacific War: World War II and the Japanese, 1931-1945.* New York: Pantheon Books, 1978, 316 p. (paperback).

Mowat, R. C. *Ruin and Resurgence 1939-1965.* London: Blandford Press, 1966, 406 p.

Russell, Francis. *The Secret War.* Alexandria, Va.: Time-Life Books, 1981, 208 p.

The Russian Version of the Second World War: The History of the War as Taught to Soviet Schoolchildren. Edited by Graham Lyons. Hamden, Conn.: Archon Books, 1978, 142 p.

Economic Warfare

Ambruster, Howard Watson. *Treason's Peace: German Dyes and American Dupes.* New York: Beechhurst Press, 1947, 438 p.

Bruns, Werner. *La Guerre Economique en Chiffres.* Bruxelles: Maison Internationale d'Edition, 1941, 83 p.

Domke, Martin. *Trading with the Enemy in World War II.* New York: Central Book Co., 1943, 640 p.

Domke, Martin. *The Control of Alien Property.* Supplement to *Trading with the Enemy in World War II.* New York: Central Book Co., 1947, 334 p.

Draper, Alfred. *Operation Fish: The Race to Save Europe's Wealth, 1939-1945.* London: Cassell, 1979, 377 p.

Einzig, Paul. *Economic Warfare.* London: Macmillan, 1940, 151 p. (largely based on material from his *Economic Problems of the Next War,* published 1939).

Eton, Peter and **Leasor, James.** *Conspiracy of Silence.* London: Angus and Robertson, 1960, 239 p.

Glesinger, Egon. *Nazis in the Woodpile: Hitler's Plot for Essential Raw Material.* Indianapolis: Bobbs-Merrill, 1942, 262 p.

Moss, William Stanley. *Gold is Where You Hide it: What Happened to the Reichsbank Treasure?* London: A. Deutsch, 1956, 191 p.

Salmon, Patrick. "British Plans for Economic Warfare Against Germany 1937-1939: The Problem of Swedish Iron Ore." *Journal of Contemporary History,* v. 16, no. 1 (January 1981), pp. 53-71.

Walker, David Esdaile. *Adventure in Diamonds.* New York: Modern Literary Editions, 1955, 223 p. (paperback).

Woodward, Guy H. and **Woodward, Grace Steele.** *The Secret of Sherwood Forest: Oil Production in England During World War II.* Norman: University of Oklahoma Press, 1973, 266 p.

Diplomatic and Political Relations
General

Birse, Arthur Herbert. *Memoirs of an Interpreter.* New York: Coward-McCann, 1967, 254 p.

Carlgren, W. M. *Swedish Foreign Policy During the Second World War.* Translated by Arthur Spencer. New York: St. Martin's Press, 1977, 257 p.

Deakin, Frederick William Dampier. *The Brutal Friendship: Mussolini, Hitler, and the Fall of Italian Fascism.* New York: Harper and Row, 1962, 896 p.

Deane, John Russell. *The Strange Alliance: The Story of our Efforts at Wartime Cooperation with Russia.* New York: Viking Press, 1947, 344 p.

Dollmann, Eugen. *The Interpreter: Memoirs.* Translated from the German by J. Maxwell Brownjohn. London: Hutchinson, 1967, 352 p. (original: *Dolmetscher der Diktatoren).*

Friedländer, Saul. *Pius XII and the Third Reich: A Documentation.* Translated from the French and German by Charles Fullman. New York: Knopf, 1966, 238 p.

Gaulle, Charles de. *War Memoirs.* New York: Simon and Schuster, 1955-1960, 5 v.

Ismay, Hastings Lionel Ismay, *Baron. Memoirs.* London: Heinemann, 1960, 486 p.

Langer, William Leonard. *Our Vichy Gamble.* New York: Knopf, 1947, 412 p.

Launay, Jacques de. *Secret Diplomacy of World War II.* Translated by Eduard Nadier. New York: Simmons-Boardman, 1963, 175 p.

Marchal, Léon. *Vichy: Two Years of Deception.* Translated by Jean Davidson and Don Schwind. New York: Macmillan, 1943, 251 p.

Matt, Alphons. *Zwischen allen Fronten. Der Zweite Weltkrieg aus der Sicht des Büros Ha.* Frauenfeld; Stuttgart: Huber, 1969, 329 p.

Mee, Charles L. *Meeting at Potsdam.* New York: M. Evans, 1975, 370 p.

Newman, Bernard. *The Captured Archives: The Story of the Nazi-Soviet Documents.* London: Latimer House, 1948, 222 p.

Plehwe, Friedrich-Karl von. *The End of an Alliance: Rome's Defection from the Axis in 1943.* Translated from the German by Eric Mosbacher. London: Oxford University Press, 1971, 161 p. (original: *Schicksalsstunden in Rom*).

Root, Waverly Lewis. *The Secret History of the War.* New York: Scribner, 1945-1946, 3 v.

Svanidze, Budu. *My Uncle, Joseph Stalin.* Translated by Waverley Root. New York: Putnam, 1953, 235 p. (published in London in 1952 as *My Uncle Joe*) (disinformation, fictional).

Nazi Germany

Bernadotte af Wisborg, Folke, Greve. *The Curtain Falls: Last Days of the Third Reich.* Translated from the Swedish by Count Eric Lewenhaupt. New York: Knopf, 1945, 154 p. (also published as *The Fall of the Curtain.* London: Cassell).

Combs, George Hamilton. *Himmler ... Nazi Spider-man.* Philadelphia: David McKay, 1942, 64 p.

Frischauer, Willi. *Himmler, the Evil Genius of the Third Reich.* New York: Belmont Books, 1962, 221 p. (paperback).

Graber, G. S. *The Life and Times of Reinhard Heydrich.* New York: David McKay, 1980, 245 p.

Jordon, Max. *Beyond All Fronts, a Bystander's Notes on this Thirty Years.* Milwaukee: Bruce, 1944, 386 p.

King, Francis. *Satan and Swastika.* London: Granada, 1976, 288 p. (paperback).

Lang, Jochen von and **Sibyll, Claus.** *The Secretary: Martin Bormann, the Man who Manipulated Hitler.* Translated from the German by Christa Armstrong and Peter White. New York: Random House, 1979, 430 p.

Manvell, Roger and **Fraenkel, Heinrich.** *Himmler.* New York: Putnam, 1965, 285 p.

McGovern, James. *Martin Bormann.* New York: Morrow, 1968, 237 p.

Mosley, Leonard. *The Reich Marshal: A Biography of Hermann Goering.* New York: Dell, 1975, 476 p. (paperback).

Noakes, Jeremy and **Pridham, Geoffrey,** eds. *Documents on Nazism, 1919-1945.* New York: Viking Press, 1975, 704 p.

Speer, Albert. *Spandau, the Secret Diaries.* Translated from the German by Richard and Clara Winston. New York: Pocket Books, 1977, 514 p. (paperback).

Stevenson, William. *The Bormann Brotherhood.* New York: Harcourt, Brace, Jovanovich, 1973, 334 p.

Stevenson, William. *The Bormann Brotherhood.* New York: Bantam Books, 1974, 423 p. (paperback).

Wheeler-Bennett, John Wheeler. *The Nemesis of Power: The German Army in Politics, 1918-1945.* New York: St. Martin's Press, 1954, 829 p.

Wighton, Charles. *Heydrich, Hitler's Most Evil Henchman.* Philadelphia: Chilton, 1962, 288 p.

Williams, Wythe and **Parry, Albert.** *Riddle of the Reich.* New York: Prentice-Hall, 1941, 351 p.

Wulff, Wilhelm Theodor H. *Zodiac and Swastika: How Astrology Guided Hitler's Germany.* New York: Coward, McCann and Geoghegan, 1973, 192 p. (original: *Tierkreis und Hakenkreus*).

Wykes, Alan. *Heydrich.* New York: Ballantine Books, 1973, 158 p.

Wykes, Alan. *Himmler.* New York: Ballantine Books, 1972, 158 p.

Hitler

Bezymenskii, Lev Aleksandrovich. *The Death of Adolf Hitler: Unknown Documents from Soviet Archives.* New York: Harcourt, Brace and World, 1968, 114 p.

Boldt, Gerhard. *Hitler: The Last Ten Days.* Translated by Sandra Bance. New York: Coward, McCann and Geoghegan, 1973, 224 p. (original: *Die letzten Tage der Reichskanzlei*).

Davidson, Eugene. *The Making of Adolf Hitler.* London: MacDonald and Jane's, 1978, 408 p.

Germany, Wehrmacht, Oberkommando. *Hitler Directs his War: The Secret Records of his Daily Military Conferences.* Selected and annotated by Felix Gilbert, from the manuscript in the University of Pennsylvania Library. New York: Charter Books, 1950, 251 p.

Hanfstaengl, Ernst Franz Sedgwick. *Unheard Witness.* Philadelphia: Lippincott, 1957, 317 p. (U.S. edition of *Hitler: The Missing Years.* London: Eyre and Spottiswoode).

Henri, Ernst. *Hitler over Europe.* Translated by Michael Davidson. New York: Simon and Schuster, 1934, 294 p.

Infield, Glenn B. *Hitler's Secret Life: The Mysteries of the Eagle's Nest.* New York: Stein and Day, 1979, 317 p.

Langer, Walter Charles. *The Mind of Adolf Hitler: The Secret Wartime Report.* New York: Basic Books, 1972, 269 p.

Ludecke, Kurt Georg Wilhelm. *I Knew Hitler: The Story of a Nazi who Escaped the Blood Purge.* London: Jarrolds, 1938, 715 p.

Moore, Herbert and **Barrett, James W.** eds. *Who Killed Hitler? The Complete Story of How Death Came to Der Fuehrer and Eva Braun, Together with the First American Intelligence Report on the Mystery of Adolf Hitler's Death, as Developed by Private Intelligence, from Never Before Published Facts and Documents, at Variance with the Official British and Russian Intelligence Reports.* New York: Booktab Press, 1947, 176 p.

Musmanno, Michael Angelo. *Ten Days to Die.* Garden City, N.Y.: Doubleday, 1950, 276 p.

Schmidt, Paul. *Hitler's Interpreter.* Edited by R. H. C. Steed. New York: Macmillan, 1951, 286 p. (a translation of the second half of the author's German work entitled *Statist auf diplomatischer Bühne, 1923-45*).

Stone, Norman. *Hitler.* Boston: Little, Brown, 1980, 195 p.

Warlimont, Walter. *Inside Hitler's Headquarters, 1939-45.* Translated from the German by R. H. Barry. New York: Praeger, 1964, 658 p. (original: *Im Hauptquartier der deutschen Wehrmacht, 1939-45*).

Wiedemann, Fritz. *Der Mann, der Feldherr werden wolte: Erlebnisse und Erfahrungen des Vorgesetzten Hitlers im 1. Weltkrieg und seines späteren persönlichen Adjutanten.* Velbert: Blick and Bild Verlag für Politische Bildung, 1964, 270 p.

United Kingdom/United States

Action this Day: Working with Churchill. Memoirs by Lord Normanbrook ... *et al.* Edited by Sir John Wheeler-Bennett. London: Macmillan, 1968, 272 p.

Cadogan, Alexander, Sir. *The Diaries of Sir Alexander Cadogan, O.M., 1938-1945.* Edited by David Dilks. New York: Putnam, 1972, 881 p.

Hassett, William D. *Off the Record with F.D.R., 1942-1945.* London: Allen and Unwin, 1960, 366 p.

Hastings, Macdonald. *Passed as Censored: The War-Time Experiences of Macdonald Hastings.* London: Harrap, 1941, 160 p.

Leahy, William D. *I Was There: The Personal Story of the Chief of Staff to Presidents Roosevelt and Truman, Based on his Notes and Diaries Made at the Time.* New York: Whittlesey House, 1950, 527 p.

Reilly, Michael Francis. *Reilly of the White House, as told to William J. Slocum.* New York: Simon and Schuster, 1947, 248 p.

Roosevelt, Franklin Delano. *Roosevelt and Churchill: Their Secret Wartime Correspondence.* Edited by Francis L. Loewenheim, Harold D. Langley et al. New York: Dutton, 1975, 805 p.

Thompson, Reginald William. *Churchill and Morton: The Quest for Insight in the Correspondence of Major Sir Desmond Morton and the Author.* London: Hodder and Stoughton, 1976, 223 p.

Thompson, Walter Henry. *Assignment: Churchill.* New York: Farrar, Straus and Young, 1955, 309 p.

Thompson, Walter Henry. *I Was Churchill's Shadow.* London: C. Johnson, 1951, 200 p.

U.S. Bureau of the Budget. *The United States at War: Development and Administration of the War Program by the Federal Government. Prepared under the Auspices of the Committee of Records of War Administration by the War Records Section, Bureau of the Budget.* Washington: U.S. GPO, 1946, 555 p.

Wavell, Archibald Percival Wavell, *1st Earl of. Speaking Generally: Broadcasts, Orders and Addresses in Time of War (1939-43).* London: Macmillan, 1946, 165 p.

Consolidation of Political and Military Power
General

Alexandrov, Victor. *Journey Through Chaos.* New York: distributed by Crown, 1945, 437 p.

Berzins, Alfreds. *The Unpunished Crime.* New York: R. Speller, 1963, 314 p.

Butler, James Ramsay Montagu, *ed. Grand Strategy: Volume 1: Rearmament Policy* by N. H. Gibbs. London: H. M. Stationery Off., 1976, 859 p.

Churchill, Randolph Spencer. *Winston S. Churchill. Volume 5: The Prophet of Truth, 1922-1939* by Martin Gilbert. Boston: Houghton Mifflin, 1966.

Colvin, Ian Goodhope. *None so Blind: A British Diplomatic View of the Origins of World War II.* New York: Harcourt, Brace and World, 1965, 360 p. (U.S. edition of *Vansittart in Office.* London: V. Gollancz).

Colvin, Ian Goodhope. *Vansittart in Office: An Historical Survey of the Origins of the Second World War based on the Papers of Sir Robert Vansittart, Permanent Under-Secretary of State for Foreign Affairs, 1930-1938.* London: V. Gollancz, 1965, 360 p.

Cot, Pierre. *Triumph of Treason.* Translated by Sybille and Milton Crane. Chicago; New York: Ziff-Davis, 1944, 432 p.

Delzell, Charles F., *comp.* and *ed. Mediterranean Fascism, 1919-1945.* New York: Harper and Row, 1970, 364 p.

European Fascism. Edited by S. J. Woolf. New York: Random House, 1968, 387 p. (Reading University Studies on Contemporary Europe: Studies in Fascism, 1).

Finland, Ulkoasiainministeriö. *Finland Reveals her Secret Documents on Soviet Policy, March 1940-June 1941. The Attitude of the USSR to Finland after the Peace of Moscow.* New York: W. Funk, 1941, 109 p.

Fodor, Marcel William. *Plot and Counterplot in Central Europe: Conditions South of Hitler.* Boston: Houghton Mifflin, 1937, 317 p.

Germany, Auswärtiges Amt. *Nazi-Soviet Relations, 1939-1941: Documents from the Archives of the German Foreign Office.* Edited by Raymond James Sontag and James Stuart Beddie. Washington: U.S. GPO, 1948, 362 p.

Jackson, Ronald W. *China Clipper.* New York: Everest House, 1980, 224 p.

Jong, Louis de. *De geheime contacten met België, Frankrijk en Engeland in de neutraliteitsperiode, September 1939-Mei 1940.* Amsterdam: Noord-Hollandsche U.M., 1969, 17 p. (offprint from *Mededelingen Der Koninkljke Nederlandse Akademie van Wetenschappen.* Letterkunde, Nieuwe Reeks, Deel 32, no. 7, pp. 201-215).

Kimche, Jon. *The Unfought Battle.* New York: Stein and Day, 1968, 168 p.

Langdon-Davies, John. *Invasion in the Snow: A Study of Mechanized War.* Boston: Houghton Mifflin, 1941, 202 p. (U.S. edition of *Finland: The First Total War.* London: G. Routledge).

Lipski, Józef. *Diplomat in Berlin, 1933-1939.* Edited by Waclaw Jedrzejewicz. New York: Columbia University Press, 1968, 679 p.

Mosley, Leonard. *On Borrowed Time: How World War II Began.* New York: Random House, 1969, 509 p.

Nagy-Talavera, Nicholas M. *The Green Shirts and the Others: A History of Fascism in Hungary and Rumania.* Stanford, Calif.: Hoover Institution Press, Stanford University, 1970, 427 p. (based on the author's thesis, University of California).

Pol, Heinz. *Suicide of a Democracy.* Translated by Heinz and Ruth Norden. New York: Reynal and Hitchcock, 1940, 296 p.

Richardson, James O. *On the Treadmill to Pearl Harbor: The Memoirs of Admiral James O. Richardson as told to George C. Dyer.* Washington: Dept. of the Navy; U.S. GPO, 1973, 558 p.

Schechtman, Joseph B. *The Mufti and The Fuehrer: The Rise and Fall of Haj Amin el-Husseini.* New York: T. Yoseloff, 1965, 336 p.

Seldes, George. *Sawdust Caesar: the Untold History of Mussolini and Fascism.* 2d ed. New York: Harper, 1935, 459 p.

Shermer, David R. *Blackshirts: Fascism in Britain.* New York: Ballantine Books, 1971, 160 p.

Simone, André. *J'accuse! The Men Who Betrayed France.* New York: Dial Press, 1940, 354 p.

Taylor, Philip M. " 'If War Should Come:' Preparing the Fifth Army for Total War 1935-1939." *Journal of Contemporary History,* v. 16, no. 1 (January 1981), pp. 27-51.

Thompson, Laurence Victor. *The Greatest Treason: The Untold Story of Munich.* New York: Morrow, 1968, 298 p.

Tolstoy, Nikolai. *Stalin's Secret War.* London: Jonathan Cape, 1981, 463 p.

White, Leigh. *The Long Balkan Night.* New York: Scribner, 1944, 473 p.

Japan

Alcott, Carroll Duard. *My War in Japan.* New York: Holt, 1943, 368 p.

Bergamini, David. *Japan's Imperial Conspiracy.* New York: Simon and Schuster, 1972, 1364 p.

Brown, Arthur Judson. *The Mastery of the Far East: The Story of Korea's Transformation and Japan's Rise to Supremacy in the Orient.* New York: Scribner, 1919, 671 p.

Browne, Courtney. *Tojo: The Last Banzai.* New York: Holt, Rinehart and Winston, 1967, 260 p.

Butow, Robert Joseph Charles. *Tojo and the Coming of the War.* Princeton, N.J.: Princeton University Press, 1961, 584 p.

Byas, Hugh. *Government by Assassination.* London: Allen and Unwin, 1943, 369 p.

Byas, Hugh. *Government by Assassination.* New York: Knopf, 1942, 369 p.

Coox, Alvin D. *The Anatomy of a Small War: The Soviet-Japanese Struggle for Changkufeng-Khasan, 1938.* Westport, Conn.: Greenwood Press, 1977, 409 p. (Contributions in Military History; no. 13).

Ienaga, Saburo. *The Pacific War: World War II and the Japanese, 1931-1945.* New York: Pantheon Books, 1978, 316 p. (paperback).

Matsuo, Kinoaki. *How Japan Plans to Win.* A translation by Kolsoo K. Haan of the Japanese book, *The Three-Power Alliance and a United States-Japanese War.* Boston: Little, Brown, 1942, 323 p. (original: *Sankoku domei to Nichi-Beisen*).

Oakes, Virginia Armstrong. *White Man's Folly.* Boston: Houghton Mifflin, 1943, 415 p.

Tanaka, Giichi. *Japan's Dream of World Empire: The Tanaka Memorial.* Edited by Carl Crow. New York: Harper, 1942, 118 p. (translation of *T'ien-chung I-i shang Jih huang chih tsou chang.* Circulated in 1927 in Chinese. Purports to be a rough translation of a document presented to the Emperor of Japan on July 25, 1927, by Premier Tanaka, outlining the policy in Manchuria. It is considered by some authorities to be a complete hoax.)

Wheeler, Post. *Dragon in the Dust.* Hollywood, Calif.; New York: Marcel Rodd, 1946, 253 p.

Nazi Germany

Berndorff, Hans Rudolf. *General Zwischen Ost und West: Aus den Geheimnissen der Deutschen Republik.* Hamburg: Hoffmann und Campe, 1951, 320 p. (Kurt von Schleicher).

Blank, Aleksandr Solomonovich. *Iz istorii rannego Fashizhma v Germanii: Org., ideologiia, metody.* Moscow: Mysl', 1978, 208 p.

Cahen, Fritz Max. *Men Against Hitler.* Indianapolis: Bobbs-Merrill, 1939, 258 p.

Castellan, Georges. *Le rearmement clandestin du Reich, 1930-1935, vu par le 2^e Bureau de l'Etat-Major français.* Paris: Plon, 1954, 571 p.

Deighton, Len. *Blitzkrieg: From the Rise of Hitler to the Fall of Dunkirk.* New York: Knopf, 1980, 295 p.

DeMendelssohn, Peter. *Design for Aggression: The Inside Story of Hitler's War Plans.* New York: Harper, 1946, 270 p.

Diels, Rudolf. *Lucifer ante portas: zwischen Severing und Heydrich.* Stuttgart: Deutsche Verlags-Anstalt, 1950, 227 p. (paperback).

Gallo, Max. *The Night of Long Knives.* Translated from the French by Lily Emmet. New York: Harper and Row, 1972, 310 p.

Germany, Auswärtiges Amt. *Les archives secrètes de la Wilhelmstrasse-IX: Las annees de guerre—Livre II (11 Mai—22 Juni 1940).* Documents traduits de l'allemand par Michel Tournier. Paris: Plon, 1961, 425 p.

Gordon, Harold J. *Hitler and the Beer Hall Putsch.* Princeton, N.J.: Princeton University Press, 1972, 666 p.

Hoettl, Wilhelm. *The Secret Front: The Story of Nazi Political Espionage.* Translated from the German by R.H. Stevens. New York: Praeger, 1954, 327 p.

Irving, David John Cawdell. *The War Path: Hitler's Germany, 1933-1939.* New York: Viking Press, 1978, 301 p.

Jong, Louis de. *The German Fifth Column in the Second World War.* Chicago: University of Chicago Press, 1956, 308 p.

Koehler, Hansjürgen. *Inside Information.* London: Pallas, 1940, 269 p.

Lend, Evelyn. *The Underground Struggle in Germany. "News from Nowhere—," Excerpts from Underground Reports.* London: Fact Monograph, January 1938, 98 p.

Liang Hsi-huey. *The Berlin Police Force in the Weimar Republic.* Berkeley: University of California Press, 1970, 252 p.

Litten, Irmgard Wüst. *Beyond Tears.* New York: Alliance Book Corp., 1940, 325 p.

Maass, Walter B. *Assassination in Vienna.* New York: Scribner, 1972, 180 p.

Miller, Douglas Phillips. *Via Diplomatic Pouch.* New York: Didier, 1944, 248 p.

Papen, Franz von. *Memoirs.* Translated by Brian Connell. New York: Dutton, 1953, 634 p.

Pool, James and **Pool, Suzanne.** *Who Financed Hitler: The Secret Funding of Hitler's Rise to Power, 1919-1933.* New York: Dial Press, 1978, 535 p.

Pritchard, R. John. *Reichstag Fire: Ashes of Democracy.* New York: Ballantine Books, 1972, 159 p.

Rich, Norman. *Hitler's War Aims.* New York: Norton, 1974, 2 v.

Shirer, William Lawrence. *Berlin Diary: The Journal of a Foreign Correspondent 1934-1941.* Harmondsworth, England; New York: Penguin Books, 1979, 627 p.

Stahlenberg, Elisabeth von. *Nazi Lady: The Diaries of Elisabeth von Stahlenberg, 1933-1948.* London: Blond and Briggs, 1978, 254 p.

Steel, Johannes. *Escape to the Present.* New York: Farrar and Rinehart, 1937, 303 p. (autobiography).

Tobias, Fritz. *The Reichstag Fire.* New York: Putnam, 1964, 348 p.

Tobias, Fritz. *The Reichstag Fire: Legend and Truth.* London: Secker and Warburg, 1963, 348 p.

Tolstoy, Nikolai. *Night of the Long Knives.* New York: Ballantine Books, 1972, 159 p.

Vansittart, Robert Gilbert Vansittart, Baron. *Lessons of My Life.* New York: Knopf, 1943, 281 p.

World Committee for the Victims of German Fascism. *The Reichstag Fire Trial: The Second Brown Book of the Hitler Terror.* Based on material collected by the Committee ... with an introductory chapter...by Georgi Dimitrov. London: John Lane, Bodley Head, 1934, 362 p.

Young, Arthur Primrose. *The "X" Documents.* Edited by Sidney Aster. London: Deutsch, 1974, 253 p.

Spanish Civil War
General

Bolloten, Burnett. *The Grand Camouflage: The Spanish Civil War and Revolution, 1936-39.* New York: Praeger, 1961, 350 p.

Brome, Vincent. *The International Brigades: Spain, 1936-1939.* New York: Morrow, 1966, 317 p.

Broué, Pierre and **Témime, Emile.** *The Revolution and the Civil War in Spain.* Translated by Tony White. Cambridge, Mass.: M.I.T. Press, 1974, 413 p.

Carr, Raymond, ed. *The Republic and the Civil War in Spain.* London: Macmillan, 1973, 275 p.

Kurzman, Dan. *Miracle of November: Madrid's Epic Stand, 1936.* New York: Putnam, 1980, 352 p.

Landis, Arthur H. *The Abraham Lincoln Brigade.* New York: Citadel Press, 1967, 677 p.

Pérez López, Francisco. *Dark and Bloody Ground: A Guerrilla Diary of the Spanish Civil War.* Edited by Victor Guerrier. Boston: Little, Brown, 1972, 275 p. (translation of *El Mexicano*).

Phillips, Cecil Ernest Lucas. *The Spanish Pimpernel.* London: Heinemann, 1960, 264 p.

Plieseis, Sepp. *Partisan der Berge: Lebenskampf eines österreichischen Arbeiters.* Hrsg. von Julius Mader. Berlin: Deutscher Militärverlag, 1971, 316 p. (1946 ed. published under title: *Vom Ebro zum Dachstein*).

Rosenstone, Robert A. *Crusade of the Left: The Lincoln Battalion in the Spanish Civil War.* New York: Pegasus, 1969, 415 p.

Sovetskii Komitet Verteranov Voiny. *Pod snamenem Ispanskoi Respubliki, 1936-1939: vospominaniia sovetskikh dobrovol'tsev—uchastnikov natsional'no-revoliutsionnoi voinny v Ispanii.* Edited by Nikolai Nikolaevich Voronov, Ivan Mikhailovich Maiskii et al. Moscow: Nauka, 1965, 574 p.

Spain, Tribunal Supremo, Ministerio Fiscal. *The General Cause, the Red Domination in Spain, Preliminary Information Drawn up by the Ministry of Justice.* Madrid: A. Aguado, 1946, 392 p.

Thomas, Hugh. *The Spanish Civil War.* Rev. and enl. ed. New York: Harper and Row, 1977, 1115 p.

Tinker, Frank Glasgow. *Some Still Live.* New York: Funk and Wagnalls, 1938, 313 p.

Conduct of Military Operations

Blassingame, Wyatt. *The U.S. Frogmen of World War II.* New York: Random House, 1964, 171 p.

Bonciani, Carlo. *"F" Squadron.* Translated from the Italian by John Shillidy. London: J. M. Dent, 1947, 211 p. (fiction).

Brou, Willy Charles. *Combat Beneath the Sea.* Translated from the French by Edward Fitzgerald. New York: Crowell, 1957, 240 p.

Butler, Rupert. *Hand of Steel: The Enthralling True Story of the Commandos in World War II.* Feltham, Middlesex, England: Hamlyn Paperbacks, 1980, 261 p.

Cooper, Bryan. *The Buccaneers.* London: Macdonald, 1970, 160 p.

Craig, William. *The Fall of Japan.* New York: Dial Press, 1967, 368 p.

De Chair, Somerset Struben. *The Golden Carpet.* New York: Harcourt, Brace, 1945, 252 p.

Devlin, Gerard M. *Paratrooper!. The Saga of U.S. Army and Marine Parachute and Glider Combat Troops during World War II.* New York: St. Martin's Press, 1979, 717 p.

Flower, Desmond, and **Reeves, James,** eds. *The Taste of Courage: The War, 1939-1945.* New York: Harper, 1960, 1120 p.

Freeman, Roger Anthony. *B-17 Fortress at War.* London: Allan, 1977, 192 p.

Germany, Wehrmacht, Oberkommando. *Hitler Directs his War: The Secret Records of his Daily Military Conferences.* Selected and annotated by Felix Gilbert, from the manuscript in the University of Pennsylvania Library. New York: Charter Books, 1950, 251 p.

Gilman, J. D. and **Clive, John.** *KG 200: A Novel.* New York: Simon and Schuster, 1977, 317 p.

Gregory, Barry and **Batchelor, John.** *Airborne Warfare 1918-1945.* New York: Exeter Books, 1979, 128 p.

Impact, v. 1-3, no. 9 (April 1943—September/October 1945). New York: James Parton, 1980, (reprinted and bound).

Keitel, Wilhelm. *In the Service of the Reich.* Edited by Walter Görlitz. Translated by David Irving. New York: Stein and Day, 1979, 288 p. (originally published as *The Memoirs of Field-Marshal Keitel).*

Lee, Raymond Eliot. *The London Journal of General Raymond E. Lee, 1940-1941.* Edited by James Leutze. Boston: Little, Brown, 1971, 489 p.

Lewin, Ronald. *The Chief: Field Marshall Lord Wavell, Commander-in-Chief and Viceroy, 1939-1947.* New York: Farrar, Straus, Giroux, 1980, 282 p.

Look, comps. and eds. *My Favorite War Story.* New York; London: Whittlesey House and McGraw-Hill, 1945, 155 p.

Mrazek, James E. *Fighting Gliders of World War II.* London: Hale, 1977, 207 p.

The 100 Best True Stories of World War II. New York: W. H. Wise, 1945, 896 p.

Piekalkiewicz, Janusz. *The Cavalry of World War II.* New York: Stein and Day, 1980, 256 p. (translation of *Pferd und Reiter im II Weltkrieg).*

Sanderson, James Dean. *Behind Enemy Lines.* Princeton, N.J.: Van Nostrand, 1959, 322 p.

U. S. Military Academy, West Point, Dept. of Military Art and Engineering. *A Military History of World War II.* Edited by T. Dodson Stamps and Vincent J. Esposito. West Point: U.S. Military Academy, 1956, 2 v.

Updegraph, Charles L. *U.S. Marine Corps Special Units of World War II.* Washington: U.S. Marine Corps, Headquarters, Historical Division, 1977, 105 p.

Urquhart, Fred, ed. *Great True War Adventures.* London: Arco, 1957, 224 p.

Waldron, Thomas John and **Gleeson, James.** *The Frogmen: The Story of the Wartime Underwater Operators.* New York: Berkley, 1959, 173 p. (paperback).

Wilkinson, Burke. *By Sea and Stealth.* New York: Coward-McCann, 1956, 218 p.

China, Burma, India Theater

Adamson, Iain. *The Forgotten Men.* London: G. Bell, 1965, 195 p. (China).

Allen, Louis, *Sittang: The Last Battle: The End of the Japanese in Burma, July-August 1945.* New York: Ballantine Books, 1974, 264 p. (paperback).

Allied Forces, Southeast Asia Command. *Report to the Combined Chiefs of Staff by the Supreme Allied Commander, South-East Asia 1943-1945, Vice-Admiral the Earl Mountbatten of Burma.* London: H. M. Stationery Office, 1951, 280 p.

Barrett, David Dean. *Dixie Mission: The United States Army Observer Group in Yenan, 1944.* Berkeley: Center for Chinese Studies, University of California, 1970, 96 p. (China research monographs, no. 6).

Bidwell, Shelford. *The Chindit War: Stilwell, Wingate, and the Campaign in Burma, 1944.* London: Hodder and Stoughton, 1979, 304 p.

Blankfort, Michael. *The Big Yankee: The Life of Carlson of the Raiders.* Boston: Little, Brown, 1947, 380 p.

Bonham, Frank. *Burma Rifles: A Story of Merrill's Marauders.* New York: Berkley, 1965, 260 p. (paperback).

Burchett, Wilfred G. *Wingate's Phantom Army.* Bombay: Thacker, 1944, 233 p. (Burma).

Caldwell, Oliver J. *A Secret War: Americans in China, 1944-1945.* Carbondale: Southern Illinois University Press, 1973, 218 p. (paperback).

Callahan, Raymond. *Burma, 1942-1945.* Newark: University of Delaware Press, 1979, 190 p.

Clifford, Francis. *Desperate Journey.* London: Hodder and Stoughton, 1979, 192 p. (Burma).

Denny, John Howard. *Chindit Indiscretion.* London: C. Johnson, 1956, 256 p. (Burma).

Dorn, Frank. *Walkout: With Stilwell in Burma.* New York: Crowell, 1971, 258 p.

Eldridge, Fred. *Wrath in Burma: The Uncensored Story of General Stilwell and International Maneuvers in the Far East.* Garden City, N.Y.: Doubleday, 1946, 320 p. (Burma and China).

Fellowes-Gordon, Ian. *The Magic War: The Battle for North Burma.* New York: Scribner, 1972, 180 p. (1971 ed. has title: *The Battle for Haw Seng's Kingdom*).

Fergusson, Bernard. "Behind the Enemy's Lines in Burma." *Journal of the Royal United Service Institution,* v. XCI (February-November 1946), pp. 347-360.

Fergusson, Bernard. *Beyond the Chindwin, Being an Account of the Adventures of Number Five Column of the Wingate Expedition into Burma, 1943.* London: Collins, 1945, 255 p.

Fergusson, Bernard. *Return to Burma.* London: Collins, 1962, 256 p.

Halley, David. *With Wingate in Burma, Being the Story of the Adventures of Sergeant Tony Aubrey of the King's (Liverpool) Regiment During the 1943 Wingate Expedition into Burma.* Glasgow; London: W. Hodge, 1945, 189 p.

Hu P'u-yu. *A Brief History of Sino-Japanese War (1937-1945).* Taipei, Taiwan: Chung Wu, 1974, 358 p.

James, Richard Rhodes. *Chindit.* London: John Murray, 1980, 214 p. (Burma).

Jeffrey, William Frederick. *Sunbeams Like Swords.* London: Hodder and Stoughton, 1951, 175 p. (Burma).

Leasor, James. *Geheimkommando (Deutsche Schiffe im Indischen Ozean).* Vienna/Hamburg: Paul Zsolnay Verlag, 1978, 289 p. (India).

MacHorton, Ian with **Maule, Henry.** *Safer than a Known Way: One Man's Epic Struggle Against Japanese and Jungle.* London: Odhams Press, 1958, 224 p. (autobiographical) (Burma).

Miles, Milton E. with **Daniel, Hawthorne.** *A Different Kind of War: The Little-Known Story of the Combined Guerrilla Forces Created in China by the U.S. Navy and the Chinese during World War II.* Garden City, N.Y.: Doubleday, 1967, 629 p.

Morrison, Ian. *Grandfather Longlegs: The Life and Gallant Death of Major H. P. Seagrim.* London: Faber and Faber, 1947, 239 p. (Burma).

Mosley, Leonard. *Gideon Goes to War.* New York: Scribner, 1955, 256 p. (Orde Charles Wingate) (Burma).

Ogburn, Charlton. *The Marauders.* New York: Harper, 1959, 307 p. (Burma).

Peers, William R. and **Brelis, Dean.** *Behind the Burma Road, the Story of America's Most Successful Guerrilla Force.* Boston: Little, Brown, 1963, 246 p.

Rogers, Lindsay. *Guerrilla Surgeon.* Garden City, N.Y.: Doubleday, 1957, 280 p. (autobiographical) (Burma).

Rogers, Lindsay. *Guerrilla Surgeon.* London: Collins, 1957, 254 p. (autobiographical) (Burma).

Rolo, Charles James. *Wingate's Raiders: An Account of the Incredible Adventure that Raised the Curtain on the Battle for Burma.* London: Harrap, 1944, 199 p.

Seagrave, Gordon Stifler. *Burma Surgeon.* London: Gollancz, 1944, 159 p.

Seagrave, Gordon Stifler. *The Life of a Burma Surgeon.* New York: Ballantine Books, 1960, 224 p. (a compendium of material from the author's *Burma Surgeon* and *Burma Surgeon Returns,* including excerpts from his combat diary with an epilogue written in 1960).

Slim, William Slim, *1st Viscount. Defeat into Victory.* 2d ed. London: Cassell. 1972, 576 p. (Burma).

Smith, E. D. *Battle for Burma.* New York: Holmes and Meier, 1979, 190 p.

Stilwell, Joseph Warren. *The Stilwell Papers.* Arr. and edited by Theodore H. White. New York: W. Sloane Associates, 1948, 357 p. (China and Burma).

Stilwell, Joseph Warren. *The Stilwell Papers.* Arr. and edited by Theodore H. White. New York: Schocken Books, 1972, 357 p. (China and Burma) (paperback).

Stratton, Roy Olin. *The Army-Navy Game.* Falmouth, Mass.: Volta, 1977, 258 p. (China).

Stratton, Roy Olin. *SACO, the Rice Paddy Navy.* Pleasantville, N.Y.: C. S. Palmer, 1950, 408 p. (China).

Sykes, Christopher. *Orde Wingate.* London: Collins, 1959, 575 p. (Burma).

Tuchman, Barbara Wertheim. *Stilwell and the American Experience in China, 1911-45.* New York: Macmillan, 1971, 768 p.

U.S. War Department, General Staff. *Merrill's Marauders (February-May 1944),* ... Washington: Military Intelligence Division, U.S. War Dept., 1945, 117 p. (Burma).

Wilcox, W. A. *Chindit Column 76.* London: Longmans, Green, 1945, 137 p. (Burma).

EUROPEAN AND NORTH AFRICAN THEATERS
Allied Forces
General

Adleman, Robert H. and **Walton, George.** *The Devil's Brigade.* Philadelphia: Chilton Books, 1966, 259 p.

Dank, Milton. *The Glider Gang: An Eyewitness History of World War II Glider Combat.* Philadelphia: Lippincott, 1977, 273 p.

Gwynn-Browne, Arthur. *F.S.P., an N.C.O.'s Description of His and Others' First Six Months of War, January 1st-June 1st 1940.* London: Chatto and Windus, 1942, 159 p.

Hills, R.J.T. *Phantom was There.* London: E. Arnold, 1951, 344 p.

Lattre de Tassigny, Jean Joseph Marie Gabriel de. *The History of the French First Army.* Translated by Malcolm Barnes, with a Preface by General Eisenhower. London: Allen and Unwin, 1952, 532 p.

Rabinowitz, Louis Isaac. *Soldiers from Judaea: Palestinian Jewish Units in the Middle East, 1941-1943.* New York: American Zionist Emergency Council, 1945, 84 p.

Robertson, Terence. *The Ship with two Captains.* New York: Dutton, 1957, 256 p.

Schofield, Brian Betham. "The Defeat of the U-Boats During World War II." *Journal of Contemporary History,* v. 16, no. 1 (January 1981), pp. 119-129.

United Kingdom
Air and Airborne Troops

Brickhill, Paul. *The Dam Busters.* New York: Ballantine Books, 1955, 185 p. (paperback).

Gregory, Barry. *British Airborne Troops, 1940-45.* New York: Doubleday, 1975, 160 p.

Harrison, Derrick Inskip. *These Men are Dangerous: The Special Air Service at War.* 2d ed. London: Cassell, 1957, 240 p.

Hill, Robert. *The Great Coup.* London: Arlington Books, 1977, 208 p.

Newnham, Maurice. "Parachute Soldiers." *Journal of the Royal United Service Institution,* v. XCV (February-November 1950), pp. 589-592.

Saunders, Hilary Aidan St. George. *The Red Beret: The Story of the Parachute Regiment at War, 1940-1945.* London: M. Joseph, 1950, 336 p.

Seth, Ronald. *Lion and Blue Wings: The Story of the Glider Pilot Regiment, 1942-1945.* London: Gollancz, 1955, 245 p.

Commandos

Appleyard, John Ernest. *Geoffrey: Major John Geoffrey Appleyard, D.S.O., M.C. and BAR, M.A.: Being the Story of "Apple" of the Commandos and Special Air Service Regiment.* London: Blandford Press, 1946, 191 p.

Carter, Hodding. *The Commandos of World War II.* New York: Random House, 1966, 168 p. (juvenile literature).

Cook, Graeme. *Commandos in Action.* New York: Taplinger, 1974, 175 p.

Durnford-Slater, John. *Commando.* London: Kimber, 1953, 222 p.

Gilchrist, Donald. *Castle Commando.* Edinburgh: Oliver and Boyd, 1960, 146 p.

Great Britain, Combined Operations Command. *Combined Operations, 1940-1942.* London: H.M. Stationery Office, 1943, 144 p. (written by Hilary Aidan St. George Saunders).

Great Britain, Combined Operations Command. *Combined Operations: The Official Story of the Commandos.* New York: Macmillan, 1943, 155 p.

Holman, Gordon. *Commando Attack.* London: Hodder and Stoughton, 1942, 160 p.

Horan, H.E. "Combined Operations, 1939-1945." *Journal of the Royal United Service Institution,* v. XCVIII (February-November 1953), pp. 55-65.

Keyes, Elizabeth. *Geoffrey Keyes, V.C., M.C., Croix de Guerre, Royal Scots Greys, Lieut.-Colonel, 11th Scottish Commando.* London: G. Newnes, 1956, 278 p.

Ladd, J.D. *Commandos and Rangers of World War II.* New York: St. Martin's Press, 1978, 288 p.

McDougall, Murdoch C. *Swiftly They Struck: The Story of No. 4 Commando.* London: Odhams Press, 1954, 208 p.

Manders, Eric I.; Nihart, Brooke et al. "First Special Service Force, 1942-1943." *Military Collector and Historian,* v. XXI, no. 4 (Winter 1969), pp. 121-123.

Mills-Roberts, Derek. *Clash by Night: A Commando Chronicle.* London: Kimber, 1956, 204 p.

Saunders, Hilary Aidan St. George. *The Green Beret: The Story of the Commandos, 1940-1945.* London: M. Joseph, 1949, 362 p.

Strutton, Bill and **Pearson, Michael.** *The Beachhead Spies.* New York: Ace Books, 1958, 191 p. (paperback ed. of *The Secret Invaders.* London: Hodder and Stoughton, 1958, 286 p.).

U.S. War Department, General Staff. *British Commandos.* Washington: U.S. GPO, 1942 (reprinted by Paladin Press, Boulder, Colo., 1977).

Young, Peter. *Commando.* New York: Ballantine Books, 1969, 159 p.

Young, Peter. *Storm From the Sea.* London: Kimber, 1968, 221 p.

Naval and Amphibious Forces

Fergusson, Bernard. *The Watery Maze: The Story of Combined Operations.* New York: Holt, Rinehart and Winston, 1961, 445 p.

Hampshire, A. Cecil. *The Secret Navies.* London: Kimber, 1978, 272 p.

Hichens, Robert Peverell. *We Fought Them in Gunboats.* London: M. Joseph, 1944, 151 p.

Hughes-Hallett, J. "The Mounting of Raids." *Journal of the Royal United Service Institution,* v. XCV (February-November 1950), pp. 580-588.

Jullian, Marcel. *H.M.S. Fidelity.* New York: Norton, 1958, 223 p.

Maund, Loben Edward Harold. *Assault from the Sea.* London: Methuen, 1949, 311 p.

Morgan, E. V. St. J. "Sea Raiders in the 1939-45 War." *Journal of the Royal United Service Institution,* v. XCIV (February-November 1949), pp. 21-36.

Pugh, Marshall. *Frogman: Commander Crabb's Story.* New York: Scribner, 1956, 208 p.

Roskill, Stephen Wentworth. *White Ensign: The British Navy at War, 1939-1945.* Annapolis, Md.: U.S. Naval Institute, 1960, 480 p.

Slater, K.R.C. "The Arming of Our Maritime Reconnaissance Squadrons." *Journal of the Royal United Service Institution,* v. XCVI (February-November 1951), pp. 562-570.

Warren, Charles Esme Thornton and **Benson, James.** *The Midget Raiders: The Wartime Story of Human Torpedoes and Midget Submarines.* New York: W. Sloane Associates, 1954, 318 p. (London ed.: *Above Us the Waves*).

United States

Alexander, Frederick B., Jr. *The Operations of the "T" Force, 42d Infantry Division, from Würzburg, Germany, through Munich, Germany, 31 March - 15 May 1945.* n.p.: The Ground General School, October 1949, 24 p.

Allen, Robert Sharon. *Lucky Forward: The History of Patton's Third U.S. Army.* New York: Macfadden-Bartell, 1965, 321 p.

Altieri, James. *The Spearheaders.* New York: Popular Library, 1961, 271 p. (paperback).

Bailey, Thomas Andrew and **Ryan, Paul B.** *Hitler vs. Roosevelt: The Undeclared Naval War.* New York: Free Press, 1979, 303 p.

Butcher, Harry Cecil. *My Three Years with Eisenhower: The Personal Diary of Captain Harry C. Butcher, USNR, Naval Aide to General Eisenhower, 1942 to 1945.* New York: Simon and Schuster, 1946, 911 p.

Darby, William Orlando with **Baumer, William H.** *Darby's Rangers: We Led the Way.* San Rafael, Calif.: Presidio Press, 1980, 198 p.

Gavin, James Maurice. *On to Berlin: Battles of an Airborne Commander, 1943-1946.* New York: Viking Press, 1978, 336 p.

Glassman, Henry S. "Lead the Way, Rangers": A History of the Fifth Ranger Battalion. Washington: Ron Lane, 1980, 104 p. (paperback).

Infield, Glenn B. *The Poltava Affair: A Russian Warning—an American Tragedy.* New York: Macmillan, 1973, 265 p.

Ingersoll, Ralph McAllister. *Top Secret.* New York: Harcourt, Brace, 1946, 373 p.

Lane, Ronald L. *Rudder's Rangers.* Manassas, Va.: Ranger Associates, 1979, 191 p.

Sorvisto, Edwin M., comp. *2nd Ranger Bn.: Roughing it with Charlie.* Williamstown, N.J.: Antietam National Museum, [1978?], 75 p.

Weigley, Russell Frank. *Eisenhower's Lieutenants: The Campaign of France and Germany, 1944-1945.* Bloomington: Indiana University Press, 1981, 800 p.

Allied Operations: Campaigns and Battles
General

Alexander, Harold Rupert Leofric George Alexander, 1st Earl. *The Alexander Memoirs, 1940-1945.* Edited by John North. New York: McGraw Hill, 1962, 209 p.

Anders, Wladyslaw. *An Army in Exile: The Story of the Second Polish Corps.* London: Macmillan, 1949, 319 p. (operated with UK forces).

Baldwin, Hanson Weightman. *The Crucial Years, 1939-1941: The World at War.* New York: Harper and Row, 1976, 499 p.

Barker, Ralph. *The Blockade Busters.* New York: Norton, 1976, 224 p.

Bentwich, Norman De Mattos. *I Understand the Risks. The Story of the Refugees from Nazi Oppression Who Fought in the British Forces in the World War.* London: Gollancz, 1950, 192 p.

Bryant, Arthur. *The Turn of the Tide: A History of the War Years Based on the Diaries of Field-Marshal Lord Alanbrooke, Chief of the Imperial General Staff.* Garden City, N.Y.: Doubleday, 1957, 624 p.

Butler, James Ramsay Montagu, ed. *Grand Strategy. Volume 3. June 1941-August 1942.* Part I by J.M.A. Gwyer and Part II by J.R.M. Butler. London: H.M. Stationery Office, 1964, 783 p.

Chalfont, Arthur Gwynne Jones. *Baron, Montgomery of Alamein.* New York: Atheneum, 1976, 365 p.

De Guingand, Francis Wilfred, Sir. *Operation Victory.* London: Hodder and Stoughton, 1947, 488 p.

Devins, Joseph H. *The Vaagso Raid: The Commando Attack that Changed the Course of World War II.* Philadelphia: Chilton Book Co., 1968, 222 p.

Farran, Roy Alexander. *Operation Tombola.* London: Collins, 1960, 256 p.

Frankland, Noble. "The Dams Raid." *Journal of the Royal United Service Institution,* v. CIX (February-November 1964), pp. 127-130.

Grigg, John. *1943: The Victory that Never Was.* New York: Hill and Wang, 1980, 254 p.

Hackett, John Winthrop. *I was a Stranger.* Boston: Houghton Mifflin, 1978, 219 p.

Ironside, Edmund, Sir. *Time Unguarded: The Ironside Diaries, 1937-1940.* Edited by Roderick Macleod and Denis Kelly. New York: D. McKay, 1962, 434 p.

Macintyre, Donald G. F. W. *Narvik.* New York: Norton, 1960, 224 p.

McMillan, Richard. *Miracle Before Berlin.* London: Jarrolds, 1946, 160 p.

Michie, Allan Andrew. *Retreat to Victory.* Chicago: Alliance Book Corp., 1942, 492 p.

Olsen, Jack. *Aphrodite: Desperate Mission.* New York: Putnam, 1970, 328 p.

Orsborne, George Black. *Master of the Girl Pat.* Edited by Joe McCarthy. Garden City, N.Y.: Doubleday, 1949, 278 p.

Parkinson, Roger. *A Day's March Nearer Home: The War History from Alamein to VE Day Based on the War Cabinet Papers of 1942 to 1945.* New York: D. McKay, 1974, 551 p.

Pearse, Richard. *Three Years in the Levant.* London: Macmillan, 1949, 294 p.

Peniakoff, Vladimir. *Private Army.* London: Cape, 1950, 512 p. (U.S. edition: *Popski's Private Army*).

Piekalkiewicz, Janusz. *Schweiz 39-45: Krieg in einem neutralen Land.* Stuttgart: Motorbuch Verlag, 1979, 362 p.

Randall, Lewis Valentine. *Bridgehead to Victory: Plans for the Invasion of Europe.* Garden City, N.Y.: Doubleday, Doran, 1943, 183 p.

Smith, Douglas M. and **Carnes, Cecil.** *American Guerrilla Fighting Behind the Enemy Lines.* Indianapolis: Bobbs-Merrill, 1943, 316 p.

Sosabowski, Stanislaw. *Parachute General.* London: Kimber, 1961, 159 p. (paperback ed. of *Freely I Served*).

Tedder, Arthur William Tedder, *Baron. With Prejudice: The War Memoirs of Marshal of the Royal Air Force.* Boston: Little, Brown, 1966, 692 p.

Thompson, Reginald William. *Montgomery, the Field Marshal: The Campaign in North-West Europe, 1944-45.* New York: Scribner, 1969, 344 p.

Vintras, Roland Eugene. *The Portuguese Connection: The Secret History of the Azores Base.* London: Bachman and Turner, 1974, 183 p.

Zuckerman, Solly, *Sir. From Apes to Warlords.* New York: Harper and Row, 1978, 447 p. (autobiography of Churchill's Scientific Chief).

North Africa and Italy

Cowles, Virginia Spencer. *The Phantom Major: The Story of David Stirling and his Desert Command.* New York: Harper, 1958, 320 p.

Jewell, Norman Limburg Auchinleck. *Secret Mission Submarine...as told to Cecil Carnes.* Chicago: Ziff-Davis, 1944, 159 p.

Landsborough, Gordon. *Tobruk Commando.* New York: Avon, 1956, 188 p. (paperback).

L'Herminier, Jean. *Casablanca, 27 novembre 1942-13 septembre 1943.* London: Frederick Muller, 1953, 243 p.

Lewis, Norman. *Naples '44.* London: Collins, 1978, 206 p.

Owen, David Lloyd. *Providence Their Guide: A Personal Account of the Long Range Desert Group, 1940-45.* London: Harrap, 1980, 238 p.

Shaw, William Boyd Kennedy. *Long Range Desert Group: The Story of its Work in Libya, 1940-1943.* London: Collins, 1945, 256 p.

Swinson, Arthur. *The Raiders: Desert Strike Force.* New York: Ballantine Books, 1968, 160 p.

U.S. First Army. *Report of Operations, 20 October 1943 to 1 August 1944, under Command of Lt. Gen. Omar N. Bradley.* n.p.: U.S. First Army [1944?], 7 v.

U.S. First Army. *Report of Operations, 1 August 1944 to 22 February 1945, under Command of Gen. Courtney H. Hodges.* n.p.: U.S. First Army, [1945?], 174 p.

U.S. First Army. *Report of Operations, 23 February to 8 May 1945, Commanding General Courtney H. Hodges.* n.p.: U.S. First Army, [1945?], 2 v.

Westrate, Edwin Victor. *Forward Observer.* Philadelphia: Dutton, 1944, 179 p.

Western Front
Arnhem

Farrar-Hockley, Anthony. *Airborne Carpet: Operation Market Garden.* New York, Ballantine Books, 1969, 160 p. (paperback).

Hagen, Louis Edmund. *Arnhem Lift.* New York: Pinnacle Books, 1975, 128 p. (paperback).

Heaps, Leo. *The Evaders.* New York: Morrow, 1976, 245 p.

Piekalkiewicz, Janusz. *Arnhem 1944.* Translated by H.A. and A.J. Barker. New York: Scribner, 1977, 111 p.

Ryan, Cornelius. *A Bridge Too Far.* New York: Simon and Schuster, 1974, 670 p.

Battle of Britain

Deighton, Len. *Fighter: The True Story of the Battle of Britain.* New York: Knopf, 1978, 261 p.

Fleming, Peter. *Operation Sea Lion: The Projected Invasion of England in 1940: An Account of the German Preparations and the British Counter-Measures.* New York: Simon and Schuster, 1957, 323 p.

Longmate, Norman. *Air Raid: The Bombing of Coventry, 1940.* New York: D. McKay, 1978, 302 p.

Newman, Bernard. *They Saved London.* London: Laurie, 1952, 192 p.

Rawnsley, Cecil Frederick and **Wright, Robert.** *Night Fighter.* New York: Holt, 1957, 382 p.

France
General

Aron, Robert. *Histoire de la libération de la France, juin 1944-mai 1945.* Paris: A. Fayard, 1959, 779 p. (paperback).

Barber, Noël. *The Week France Fell: June 1940.* New York: Stein and Day, 1976, 321 p.

Cazaux, Yves. *Journal secret de la libération, 6 juin 1944-17 novembre 1944.* Paris: A. Michel, 1975, 351 p.

Harman, Nicholas. *Dunkirk: The Patriotic Myth.* New York: Simon and Schuster, 1980, 271 p.

Thornton, Willis. *The Liberation of Paris.* New York: Harcourt, Brace and World, 1962, 231 p.

Vaculik, Serge. *Air Commando.* Translated from the French by Edward Fitzgerald. London: Jarrolds, 1954, 303 p.

Dieppe

Austin, Alexander Berry. *We Landed at Dawn.* London: Gollancz, 1943, 127 p.

Leasor, James. *Green Beach.* New York: Morrow, 1975, 292 p.

Lepotier, Adolphe Auguste Marie. *Raiders from the Sea.* London: Kimber, 1954, 200 p. (English translation of *Raids sur mer: St. Nazaire, Dieppe*).

Maguire, Eric. *Dieppe, August 19.* London: Cape, 1963, 205 p.

Reyburn, Wallace. *Rehearsal for Invasion.* London: Harrap, 1943, 126 p. (paperback).

Reynolds, Quentin James. *Dress Rehearsal: The Story of Dieppe.* New York: Random House, 1943, 278 p.

Reynolds, Quentin James. *Raid at Dieppe.* New York: Avon Publications, n.d., 190 p. (paperback ed. of *Dress Rehearsal: The Story of Dieppe*).

Robertson, Terence. *Dieppe: The Shame and the Glory.* Boston: Little, Brown, 1962, 432 p.

Roskill, S. W. "The Dieppe Raid and the Question of German Foreknowledge." *Journal of the Royal United Service Institution,* v. CIX (February-November 1964), pp. 27-31.

Thompson, Reginald William. *At Whatever Cost: The Story of the Dieppe Raid.* New York: Coward-McCann, 1957, 215 p.

Thompson, Reginald William. *Dieppe at Dawn: The Story of the Dieppe Raid.* London: Hutchinson, 1956, 215 p.

Whitehead, William. *Echoes of Disaster: Dieppe, 1942.* Edited by Terence Macartney-Filgate. New York: St. Martin's Press, 1979, 191 p.

Normandy

Crookenden, Napier, *Sir. Dropzone Normandy: The Story of the American and British Airborne Assault on D Day 1944.* New York: Scribner, 1976, 304 p.

D-Day: The Normandy Invasion in Retrospect. Lawrence: University Press of Kansas, 1971, 254 p.

Morgan, Frederick Edgworth, *Sir. Overture to Overlord.* Garden City, New York: Doubleday, 1950, 302 p.

Perrault, Gilles. *The Secret of D-Day.* Translated from the French by Len Ortzen. Boston: Little, Brown, 1965, 249 p.

Stanford, Alfred Boller. *Force Mulberry: The Planning and Installation of the Artificial Harbor off U.S. Normandy Beaches in World War II.* New York: Morrow, 1951, 240 p.

Saint Nazaire

Horan, H.E. "Operation 'Chariot' ":The Raid on St. Nazaire, 27th-28th March, 1942. *Journal of the Royal United Service Institution,* v. CVI (February-November 1961), pp. 561-566.

Lepotier, Adolphe Auguste Marie. *Raiders from the Sea.* London: Kimber, 1954, 200 p.

Mason, David. *Raid on St. Nazaire.* New York: Ballantine Books, 1970, 157 p.

Phillips, Cecil Ernest Lucas. *The Greatest Raid of All.* Boston: Little, Brown, 1960, 270 p.

Axis Forces
General

Buss, Philip H. and **Mollo, Andrew.** *Hitler's Germanic Legions: An Illustrated History of the Western European Legions with the SS, 1941-1943.* London: Macdonald and Jane's, 1978, 144 p.

Deighton, Len. *Blitzkrieg: From the Rise of Hitler to the Fall of Dunkirk.* New York: Knopf, 1980, 295 p.

Keegan, John. *Waffen SS: The Asphalt Soldiers.* New York: Ballantine Books, 1970, 160 p. (paperback).

Lewin, Ronald. *The Life and Death of the Afrika Korps.* New York: Quadrangle, 1977, 207 p.

Liddell Hart, Basil Henry. *The German Generals Talk.* New York: Morrow, 1948, 308 p. (London ed.: *The Other Side of the Hill*).

Mabire, Jean and **Demaret, Pierre.** *La Brigade Frankreich.* Paris: Fayard, 1973, 460 p.

Die Nachhut. Heft no. 5, 15 Juni 1968. Munich: Arbeitsgemeinschaft Ehemaliger Abwehrangehoeriger (AGEA), 24 p.

Nobécourt, Jacques. *Hitler's Last Gamble: The Battle of the Bulge.* New Tower Pubs., [1980?], 303 p. (paperback).

O'Donnell, James Preston. *The Bunker: The History of the Reich Chancellery Group.* Boston: Houghton Mifflin, 1978, 399 p.

Operation Sea Lion. Edited by Richard Cox. San Rafael, Calif.: n.p., 1977, 190 p. (fiction).

Rommel, Erwin. *The Rommel Papers.* Edited by D. H. Liddell Hart. Translated by Paul Findlay. New York: Harcourt, Brace, 1953, 545 p.

Ruge, Friedrich. *Rommel in Normandy: Reminiscences.* Translated by Ursula R. Moessner. San Rafael, Calif.: Presidio Press, 1979, 266 p.

Schmidt, Paul Karl. *The Foxes of the Desert.* Translated from the German by Mervyn Savill. New York: Dutton, 1961, 370 p.

Sydnor, Charles W. *Soldiers of Destruction: The SS Death's Head Division, 1933-1945.* Princeton, N.J.: Princeton University Press, 1977, 371 p.

Air and Airborne Troops

Bekker, Cajus, *pseud.* (Berenbrok, Hans Dieter). *The Luftwaffe War Diaries.* Translated and edited by Frank Ziegler. Garden City, N.Y.: Doubleday, 1968, 399 p.

Edwards, Roger. *German Airborne Troops, 1936-1945.* Garden City: N.Y.: Doubleday, 1974, 160 p.

Hermann, Hauptmann, *pseud. The Luftwaffe, Its Rise and Fall.* New York: Putnam, 1943, 300 p.

Macksey, Kenneth John. *Kesselring: The Making of the Luftwaffe.* London: Batsford, 1978, 262 p.

Mason, Herbert Molloy. *The Rise of the Luftwaffe: Forging the Secret German Air Weapon, 1918-1940.* New York: Dial Press, 1973, 402 p.

Schliephake, Hanfried. *The Birth of the Luftwaffe.* Chicago: Regnery, 1971, 80 p.

Whiting, Charles. *Hunters from the Sky: The History of the German Parachute Regiment, 1940-1945.* London: Cooper, 1974, 209 p.

Naval and Amphibious Forces

Bekker, Cajus, *pseud.* (Berenbrok, Hans Dieter). *Einzelkämpfer auf See: die deutschen Torpedoreiter, Froschmänner und Sprengbootpiloten im zweiten Weltkrieg.* Oldenburg: G. Stalling, 1968, 210 p.

Bekker, Cajus, *pseud.* (Berenbrok, Hans Dieter). *Hitler's Naval War.* Garden City, N.Y.: Doubleday, 1974, 400 p.

Borghese, Iunio Valerio. *Se Devils.* Translated from the Italian by James Cleugh. Chicago: Regnery, 1954, 261 p. (Italian language ed.: *Decima flottiglia mas*).

Bragadin, Marc'Antonio. *The Italian Navy in World War II.* Translated by Gale Hoffman. Annapolis, Md.: U.S. Naval Institute, 1957, 380 p.

Cocchia, Aldo. *The Hunters and the Hunted: Adventures of Italian Naval Forces.* Translated by M. Gwyer. Annapolis, Md.: U.S. Naval Institute, 1958, 179 p.

Gallagher, Thomas Michael. *The X-craft Raid.* New York: Pinnacle Books, 1972, 186 p.

Hoyt, Edwin Palmer. *Raider 16.* New York: World Pub. Co., 1979, 255 p.

Hoyt, Edwin Palmer. *U-Boats Offshore: When Hitler Struck America.* New York: Stein and Day, 1978, 278 p.

Kennedy, Ludovic Henry Coverly. *Menace: The Life and Death of the Tirpitz.* London: Sidgwick and Jackson, 1979, 176 p.

Muggenthaler, August Karl. *German Raiders of World War II.* Englewood Cliffs, N.J.: Prentice-Hall, 1977, 308 p.

Potter, John Deane. *Fiasco: The Break-Out of the German Battleships.* New York: Stein and Day, 1970, 235 p.

Rohwer, Jürgen. *The Critical Convoy Battles of March 1943: The Battle for HX.229/SC122.* Translated by Derek Masters. Annapolis, Md.: Naval Institute Press, 1977, 256 p.

Schofield, Brian Betham. *The Attack on Taranto.* Annapolis, Md.: Naval Institute Press, 1973, 94 p.

Woodward, David. *The Secret Raiders: The Story of the German Armed Merchant Raiders in the Second World War.* New York: Norton, 1955, 288 p.

Woodward, David. *The Tirpitz: The Story, including the Destruction of the Scharnhorst, of the Campaigns Against the German Battleship.* New York: Norton, 1953, 223 p.

Otto Skorzeny, Commando

Foley, Charles. *Commando Extraordinary.* New York: Ballantine Books, 1955, 180 p.

Skorzeny, Otto. *Secret Missions: War Memoirs of the Most Dangerous Man in Europe.* Translated from the French by Jacques Le Clercq. New York: Dutton, 1950, 256 p.

Whiting, Charles. *Skorzeny.* New York: Ballantine Books, 1972, 159 p.

Soviet Units: Vlassov Movement

Bibliography on Vlassov Movement in World War II, 1941-1945. (Bibliographiia Osvoboditel'nogo dvizheniia narodov Rossii, 1941-1945). Compiled by Michael Schatoff. New York: All-Slavic Publishing House, 1961, 208 p.

Fischer, George. *Soviet Opposition to Stalin: A Case Study in World War II.* Cambridge: Harvard University Press, 1952, 230 p.

Steenberg, Sven. *Vlasov.* Translated from the German by Abe Farbstein. New York: Knopf, 1970, 230 p.

Strik-Strikfeldt, Wilfried. *Against Stalin and Hitler: Memoir of the Russian Liberation Movement, 1941-1945.* Translated from the German by David Footman. New York: John Day, 1973, 270 p.

Thorwald, Jürgen. *The Illusion: Soviet Soldiers in Hitler's Armies.* Translated from the German by Richard and Clara Winston. New York: Harcourt, Brace, Jovanovich, 1975, 342 p.

Eastern Front

Bezymenskii, Lev Aleksandrovich. *Ukroshchenie "Taifuna."* Moscow: Mosk. Rabochii, 1978, 224 p. (Battle of Moscow).

Blau, George E. *The German Campaign in Russia: Planning and Operations, 1940-1942.* Washington: Dept. of the Army, 1955, 187 p. (pamphlet no. 20-261a).

Caidin, Martin. *The Tigers are Burning.* New York: Hawthorn Books, 1974, 243 p. (Battle of Kursk, USSR).

Cecil, Robert. *Hitler's Decision to Invade Russia, 1941.* New York: David McKay, 1976, 192 p.

Combat in Russian Forests and Swamps: Historical Study. Washington: Dept. of the Army, 1951, 39 p. (pamphlet no. 20-231).

Costantini, Aimé. *L'Union Sovietique en Guerre (1941-1945) Tome 1: L'invasion.* Paris: Imprimerie Nationale, 1968, 282 p.

Drum, Karl. *Airpower and Russian Partisan Warfare.* New York: Arno Press, 1968, 63 p. (U.S. Air Force Historical Studies, no. 177).

Estonskii narod v velikoi otechestvennoi voine Sovetskogo Soiuza, 1941-1945: tom pervyi, Estonskii narod v bor'be za svobodu i nezavisimost' sovetskoi rodiny v 1941-1943 godakh. Tallin: EESTI Raamat, 1973, 615 p.

Gouré, Leon. *The Siege of Leningrad.* Stanford: Calif.: Stanford University Press, 1962, 363 p.

Jukić, Ilija. *The Fall of Yugoslavia.* Translated by Dorian Cooke. New York: Harcourt, Brace, Jovanovich, 1974, 315 p.

Kleinfeld, Gerald R. and **Tambs, Lewis A.** *Hitler's Spanish Legion: The Blue Division in Russia.* Carbondale: Southern Illinois University Press, 1979, 434 p.

Kozlov, Andrei Petrovich. *Trevozhnaia sluzhba.* Moscow: Voenizdat, 1973, 261 p.

Krylov, Ivan Nikititch, *pseud. Soviet Staff Officer.* Translated by Edward Fitzgerald. London: Falcon Press, 1951, 298 p.

La Maziere, Christian de. *The Captive Dreamer.* Translated by Francis Stuart. New York: Saturday Review Press, 1974, 271 p. (autobiographical).

Liberation Mission of the Soviet Armed Forces in the Second World War. Edited by A. A. Grechko, I.V. Parotkin *et al.* Translated from the Russian by David Fidlon. Moscow: Progress Publishers, 1975, 446 p. (original: *Osvoboditel'naia missiia Sovetskikh Vooruzhennykh Sil vo vtoroi mirovoi voine*).

Lucas, James Sidney. *War on the Eastern Front, 1941-1945: The German Soldier in Russia.* New York: Stein and Day, 1980, 1979, 214 p.

Maclean, Fitzroy. *Eastern Approaches.* London: J. Cape, 1949, 543 p.

Salisbury, Harrison Evans. *The 900 Days: The Siege of Leningrad:* New York: Harper and Row, 1969, 635 p.

Scriabine, Helene. *Siege and Survival: The Odyssey of a Leningrader.* Translated and edited by Norman Luxenburg. Carbondale: Southern Illinois University Press, 1971, 174 p. (translation of *Gody skitaniia*).

Seaton, Albert. *The Russo-German War, 1941-1945.* New York: Praeger, 1971, 628 p.

Sozhin, Grigorii Borisovich. *V kadre i za kadrom: zapiski telezhurnalista.* Murmansk: Murmanskoe Knizhnoe Izdatel'stvo, 1977, 175 p.

Thorwald, Jürgen. *Flight in the Winter: Russia Conquers, January to May 1945.* Edited and translated by Fred Wieck. New York: Pantheon, 1951, 318 p. (translation and condensation of *Es begann an der Weichsel* and *Das Ende an der Elbe*).

V boiakh za Karpaty. Compiled by B. S. Venkov. Uzhgorod: Karpati, 1975, 383 p.

Waffen SS in Russia: a Selection of German Wartime Photographs from the Bundesarchiv, Koblenz. Compiled by Bruce Quarrie. Cambridge, England: P. Stephens, 1980, 95 p.

Pacific Theater
General

Barbey, Daniel E. *MacArthur's Amphibious Navy: Seventh Amphibious Force Operations, 1943-1945.* Annapolis: U.S. Naval Institute, 1969, 375 p.

Callinan, Bernard J. *Independent Company: The 2/2 and 2/4 Australian Independent Companies in Portuguese Timor, 1941-1943.* London: Heinemann, 1953, 235 p.

Chambliss, William C. *Boomerang.* New York: Harcourt, Brace, 1944, 87 p. (fiction).

Connell, Brian. *Return of the Tiger.* Garden City: N.Y.: Doubleday, 1961, 282 p. (Operation Rimau).

Fraser, Ian. *Frogman V. C.* London: Angus and Robertson, 1957, 216 p.

Krueger, Walter. *From Down Under to Nippon: The Story of Sixth Army in World War II.* Washington: Zenger, 1979, 393 p.

Lord, Walter. *Incredible Victory.* New York: Harper and Row, 1967, 331 p. (Battle of Midway).

McKie, Ronald Cecil Hamlyn. *The Heroes.* New York: Harcourt, Brace, 1960, 307 p. (Operation Jaywick, Operation Rimau).

White, Osmar. *Green Armor.* New York: Norton, 1945, 288 p. (New Guinea and Solomon Islands).

Willoughby, Charles Andrew and **Chamberlain, John.** *MacArthur, 1941-1951.* New York: McGraw-Hill, 1954, 441 p.

Philippine Islands Campaign

Morison, Samuel Eliot. *History of United States Naval Operations in World War II. Volume XIII: The Liberation of the Philippines: Luzon, Mindanao, the Visayas, 1944-1945.* Boston: Little, Brown, 1959, 338 p.

St. John, Joseph F. *Leyte Calling* ... as told to Howard Handleman. New York: Vanguard Press, 1945, 220 p.

Steinberg, Rafael. *Return to the Philippines.* Alexandria, Va.: Time-Life Books, 1979, 208 p.

Underbrink, Robert L. *Destination Corregidor.* Annapolis, Md.: U.S. Naval Institute, 1971, 240 p.

Air Operations
General

Davis, Burke. *Get Yamamoto.* New York: Random House, 1969, 231 p.

Lawson, Ted W. *Thirty Seconds over Tokyo.* Edited by Robert Considine. New York: Random House, 1943, 221 p.

Thomas, Gordon and **Witts, Max Morgan.** *Enola Gay.* New York: Stein and Day, 1977, 327 p. (bombing of Hiroshima).

Kamikazes

Adams, Andrew, ed. *Born to Die: The Cherry Blossom Squadrons.* Translated by Nobuo Asahi and the Japan Tech. Co. Los Angeles: Ohara Publications, for the Hagoromo Society of Kamikaze Divine Thunder-bolt Corps Survivors, 1973, 221 p.

Barker, A. J. *Suicide Weapon.* New York: Ballantine Books, 1971, 160 p.

Inoguchi, Rikihei; Nakajima, Tadashi et al. *The Divine Wind: Japan's Kamikaze Force in World War II.* New York: Bantam Books, 1960, 220 p. (translation of *Kamikaze Tokubetsu Kogekitai*) (paperback).

Kuwahara, Yasuo and **Allred, Gordon T.** *Kamikaze.* New York: Ballantine Books, 1957, 187 p.

Millot, Bernard. *Divine Thunder: The Life and Death of the Kamikazes.* Translated by Lowell Bair. New York: McCall, 1970, 243 p. (translation of *L'épopée kamikazé*).

Nagatsuka, Ryuji. *I was a Kamikaze: The Knights of the Divine Wind.* Translated from the French by Nina Rootes. New York: Macmillan, 1974, 212 p. (original: *J'étais un kamikazé*).

Pearl Harbor Attack

Air Raid: Pearl Harbor!: Recollections of a Day of Infamy. Edited by Paul Stillwell. Annapolis, Md.: U.S. Naval Institute Press, 1981, 299 p.

Barker, A.J. *Pearl Harbor.* New York: Ballantine Books, 1971, 160 p. (paperback).

Lord, Walter. *Day of Infamy.* New York: Holt, 1957, 243 p.

Sakamaki, Kazuo. *I Attacked Pearl Harbor.* Translated by Toru Matsumoto. New York: Association Press, 1949, 133 p.

Submarine Operations

Blair, Clay. *Silent Victory: The U.S. Submarine War Against Japan.* Philadelphia: Lippincott, 1975, 1072 p.

Dissette, Edward and **Adamson, Hans Christian.** *Guerrilla Submarines: The Never-Before-Told True Story of the Secret Action that Changed the Course of the War in the Pacific.* New York: Ballantine Books, 1972, 238 p. (paperback).

Hashimoto, Mochitsura. *Sunk: The Story of the Japanese Submarine Fleet, 1941-1945.* Translated by E.H.M. Colegrave. New York: Holt, 1954, 276 p. (original: *I-go 58 kitoseri*).

Higgins, Edward T. with **Phillips, Dean.** *Webfooted Warriors: The Story of a "Frogman" in the Navy During World War II.* New York: Exposition Press, 1955, 172 p.

Sellwood, Arthur V. *Dynamite for Hire: The Story of Hein Fehler.* London: W. Laurie, 1956, 264 p. (German submarine operations).

Resistance Forces and Underground Movements
General

Dupuy, Trevor Nevitt. *The Military History of World War II. Volume 16: Asian and Axis Resistance Movements.* New York: F. Watts, 1965, 88 p. (juvenile literature).

Elliott-Bateman, Michael, ed. *The Fourth Dimension of Warfare. Volume I: Intelligence, Subversion, Resistance.* New York: Praeger, 1970, 181 p.

Gosset, Renee Pierre-. *Conspiracy in Algiers, 1942-1943.* Translated from the French by Nancy Hecksher. New York: The Nation, 1945, 248 p.

Haggerty, James Edward. *Guerrilla Padre in Mindanao.* New York: Longmans, Green, 1946, 257 p.

Harkins, Philip. *Blackburn's Headhunters.* New York: Norton, 1955, 326 p. (Philippines).

Heimler, Eugene, ed. *Resistance Against Tyranny: A Symposium.* New York: Praeger, 1967, 168 p.

Keats, John. *They Fought Alone.* Philadelphia: Lippincott, 1963, 425 p. (Philippines).

Miles, Milton E. *A Different Kind of War: The Little-Known Story of the Combined Guerrilla Forces Created in China by the U.S. Navy and the Chinese During World War II, as Prepared by Hawthorne Daniel from the Original Manuscript.* Garden City: N.Y.: Doubleday, 1967, 629 p.

Moine, André. *La déportation et la résistance en Afrique du Nord* (1939 - 1944). Paris: Editions Sociales, 1972, 319 p. (paperback).

Spencer, Louise Reid. *Guerrilla Wife.* Chicago: Peoples Book Club, 1945, 243 p. (Resistance in the Philippines).

Syrkin, Marie. *Blessed is the Match: The Story of Jewish Resistance.* Philadelphia: Jewish Publication Society of America; New York: Knopf, 1947, 361 p.

Willoughby, Charles Andrew, comp. *The Guerrilla Resistance Movement in the Philippines: 1941-1945.* New York: Vantage Press, 1972, 702 p.

Wise, William. *Secret Mission to the Philippines: The Story of the "Spyron" and the American-Filipino Guerrillas of World War II.* New York: Dutton, 1968, 160 p.

Wolfert, Ira. *American Guerrilla in the Philippines.* New York: Simon and Schuster, 1945, 301 p.

Europe
General

Army Times. *Heroes of the Resistance.* New York: Dodd, Mead, 1967, 133 p.

Belgium, Office Belge d'Information et de Documentation, London. *The Underground Press in Belgium.* London: Lincolns-Prager, 1944, 60 p.

Boolen, J. J. and **Does, Johannes Cornelius van der.** *Five Years of Occupation: The Resistance of the Dutch Against Hitler-Terrorism and Nazi-Robbery.* [n.p.] Printed on the Secret Press of D.A.V.I.D. [1945?], 122 p. (issued also under title: *Nederlands verzet tegen Hitler-terreur en Nazi-roof*).

Brome, Vincent. *Europe's Free Press: The Underground Newspapers of Occupied Lands Described as Far as the Censor Permits.* London: Feature Books, 1943, 127 p.

Brusselmans, Anne. *Rendez-Vous 127: The Diary of Madame Brusselmans, M.B.E., September 1940- September 1944.* Transcribed by Denis Hornsey. London: Benn, 1954, 172 p. (Belgium).

Duncan, Sylvia and **Duncan, Peter.** *Anne Brusselmans, M.B.E.* London: Benn, 1959, 207 p. (based on her diary).

Dupuy, Trevor Nevitt. *The Military History of World War II. Volume 15: European Resistance Movements.* New York: F. Watts, 1965, 88 p. (juvenile literature).

European Resistance Movements, 1939-1945. Oxford: Pergamon Press, 1964, 663 p. (proceedings of 2d International Conference on the History of Resistance Movements, Milan, 1961; reports in French and English).

Foot, Michael Richard Daniel. *Resistance: European Resistance to Nazism, 1940-1945.* New York: McGraw-Hill, 1977, 346 p.

Gerson, L. D., pseud. (Gern, Peter). *Schreieder und die Spione: der erste deutsche Bericht über das "England-Spiel."* Munich: Münchener Dom-Verlag, 1950, 61 p. (Netherlands).

Jong, Louis de. *Holland Fights the Nazis.* London: The Right Book Club, 1945, 138 p.

Jong, Louis de. *The Lion Rampant, the Story of Holland's Resistance to the Nazis.* Translated and adapted by Joseph W. F. Stoppelman. New York: Querido, 1945, 386 p.

Kuyck, Jacq. Th. *Partisanen-Vrouwen.* The Hague: De Pagter, [post 1945], 184 p.

Macksey, Kenneth John. *The Partisans of Europe in the Second World War.* New York: Stein and Day, 1975, 271 p.

Macksey, Kenneth John. *The Partisans of Europe in World War II.* London: Hart-David MacGibbon, 1975, 271 p.

Martens, Allard, *pseud.* with **Dunlop, Daphne.** *The Silent War: Glimpses of the Dutch Underground and Views on the Battle of Arnhem.* London: Hodder and Stoughton, 1961, 318 p.

Masaryk, Jan with **Paderewska-Wilkonska, Antonina** *et al. The Sixth Column: Inside the Nazi-Occupied Countries.* New York: Alliance Book Corp., 1942, 313 p.

Michel, Henri. *The Shadow War: European Resistance, 1939-1945.* Translated from the French by Richard Barry. New York: Harper and Row, 1972, 416 p. (original: *La guerre de l'ombre).*

Miller, Russell. *The Resistance.* Alexandria, Va.: Time-Life Books, 1979, 208 p.

Molden, Fritz. *Exploding Star: A Young Austrian Against Hitler.* London: Weidenfeld and Nicholson, 1978, 280 p. (Translation of *Fepolinski und Waschlapski auf dem berstenden Stern).*

Molodye antifashisty: Sbornik. Translated and compiled by V. Pekshev and S. Semanov. Moscow: Molo-daia Gvardaia, 1978, 238 p. (Europe).

Neave, Airey. *Little Cyclone.* London: Hodder and Stoughton, 1954, 189 p. (Belgium).

Orbaan, Albert. *Duel in the Shadows: True Accounts of Anti-Nazi Underground Warfare During World War II.* Garden City, N.Y.: Doubleday, 1965, 229 p. (Europe).

Pogibli za Avstriiu: Soprotivlenie Gitlerovskim okkupantam. Translated from the German by L. R. Leva-nevska. Moscow: Progress, 1974, 288 p. (original: Gestorben für Osterreich, Vienna, 1968).

Riess, Curt. *Underground Europe.* New York: Dial, 1942, 325 p.

Rigby, Françoise Labouverie. *In Defiance.* London: Elek, 1960, 224 p. (Belgium).

Seth, Ronald. *The Noble Saboteurs.* New York: Hawthorn, 1966, 188 p. (Reprint of *How the Resistance Worked,* 1961).

Seth, Ronald. *The Undaunted: The Story of Resistance in Western Europe.* London: F. Muller, 1956, 327 p.

Southon, Alfred with **Milroy, Vivian.** *Alpine Partisan.* London: Hammond and Co., 1957, 222 p. (Italy and France).

Suhl, Yuri, *ed.* and *tr. They Fought Back: The Story of the Jewish Resistance in Nazi Europe.* New York: Crown, 1967, 327 p.

Tilt, Notburga. *The Strongest Weapon.* Ilfracombe, England: Stockwell, 1972, 227 p. (Austria).

Van Woerdan, Peter. *In the Secret Place, a Story of the Dutch Underground.* Wheaton, Ill.: Van Kampen Press, 1954, 64 p.

Eastern Europe

Ainszstein, Reuben. *Jewish Resistance in Nazi-Occupied Eastern Europe: With a Historical Survey of the Jew as Fighter and Soldier in the Diaspora.* New York: Harper and Row, 1974, 970 p.

Bruce, George Ludgate. *The Warsaw Uprising, 1 August—2 October 1944.* London: Hart-Davis, 1972, 224 p.

Burgess, Alan. *Seven Men at Daybreak.* New York: Dutton, 1960, 231 p. (Czechoslovakia).

Dékán, István and **Kardos, Eva.** *Puti-dorogi: Vospominaniia.* Translated from the Hungarian by F. Oskol-kov. Moscow: Voenizdat, 1978, 479 p. (original: *Utak Es Osvények.)*

De Polnay, Peter. *Death and To-Morrow.* London: Secker and Warburg, 1942, 299 p. (Hungary).

Dolezal, Jiri and **Kren, Jan,** eds. *Die Kaempfende Tschechoslowakei (Dokumente ueber die Widerstands-bewegung des Tschechoslowakischen Volkes in der Jahren 1938-1945).* Prague: Verlag der Tschecho-slowakischen Akademie der Wissenschaften, 1964, 215 p.

Dzhurov, Dobri and **Dzhurova, Elena.** *Murgash: Vospominaniia.* Translated from the Bulgarian by J. Satarov and A. Koren'kov. Moscow: Voenizdat, 2d ed., 1974, 508 p.

Friedman, Philip, ed. *Martyrs and Fighters: The Epic of the Warsaw Ghetto.* New York: Lancer Books, 1954, 254 p. (paperback).

Garliński, Józef. *Fighting Auschwitz: The Resistance Movement in the Concentration Camp.* Greenwich, Conn.: Fawcett, 1975, 416 p. (an abridged translation of *Oświecim Walczacy,* first published in 1974).

Georgiev, Zdravko Velev. *Zapiski nachal'nika shtaba zony: vospominaniia.* Translated from the Bulgarian by I. M. Saburov. Moscow: Voenizdat, 1976. 186 p. (original: *Kogato Umirakhme).*

Goldstein, Bernard. *Five Years in the Warsaw Ghetto.* Translated and edited by Leonard Shatzkin. Garden City, N.Y.: Doubleday, 1961, 275 p. (paperback edition of *The Stars Bear Witness*).

Historia Militaris Polonica: History of the Polish Armed Forces. Edited by Witold Biegański, Piotr Stawecki et al. Warsaw: Ministry of Defence Publishing House, 1977, 413 p. (English paperback edition).

Ivanov, Miroslav. *The Assassination of Heydrich, 27 May 1942.* Translated from the French by Patrick O'Brian. London: Hart-Davis-MacGibbon, 1973, 292 p. (original: *L'attentat contre Heydrich, 27 mai 1942*).

Ivanov, Miroslov. *Target: Heydrich.* Translated from the French by Patrick O'Brian. New York: Macmillan, 1974, 292 p. (see above).

Jacobmeyer, Wolfgang. *Heimat und Exil; die Anfänge der polnischen Untergrundbewegung im Zweiten Weltkrieg.* [Hamburg]: Leibniz-Verlag, 1973, 369 p. (slight revision of the author's thesis, Ruhr-Universität Bochum, 1971).

Komorowski, Tadeusz. *The Secret Army.* New York: Macmillan, 1951, 407 p. (Poland).

Kulski, Julian Eugene. *Dying, We Live: The Personal Chronicle of a Young Freedom Fighter, Warsaw, 1939-1945.* New York: Holt, Rinehart and Winston, 1979, 304 p.

Nirenstein, Albert, ed. *A Tower From the Enemy: Contributions to a History of Jewish Resistance in Poland.* Translated from the Polish, Yiddish, and Hebrew by David Neiman; from the Italian by Mervyn Savill. New York: Orion Press, 1959, 372 p. (originally published in Italy as *Ricorda cosa ti ha fatto Amalek*).

Omiljanowicz, Aleksander. *Smysl zhizni: Sbornik rasskazov.* Translated from the Polish by P. K. Kostikov. Moscow: Voenizdat, 1973, 223 p. (original: *Sens zycia*).

Omiljanowicz, Aleksander. *V Tylu vraga.* Translated from the Polish by V. A. Glazov, P. K. Kostikov et al. Moscow: Voenizdat, 1975, 239 p.

Poland, Polskie Sily Zbrojne, Armia Krajowa. *The Unseen and Silent: Adventures From the Underground Movement Narrated by Paratroops of the Polish Home Army.* Translated from the Polish by George Iranek-Osmecki. New York: Sheed and Ward, 1954, 350 p. (original: *Drogi Cichociemnych*).

Shevtsov, Ivan Mikhailovich. *Nabat: Roman.* Moscow: Sovremennik, 1978, 652 p.

Sobibór, Martyrdom and Revolt: Documents and Testimonies. Presented by Miriam Novitch. New York: Holocaust Library, Schocken Books, 1980, 168 p.

Sosabowski, Stanislaw. *Parachute General.* London: Kimber, 1961, 159 p. (paperback ed. of *Freely I Served*)

Stenin, Afrikan Alekseevich. *"Ermak" na Morave.* Kiev: Politizdat Ukrainy, 1978, 247 p.

Stenin, Afrikan Alekseevich. *Liudi iz legend.* Moscow: Voenizdat, 1978, 223 p. (Czechoslovakia).

Stroop, Jüergen. *The Stroop Report: The Jewish Quarter of Warsaw Is No More!* Translated from the German by Sybil Milton. New York: Pantheon Books, 1979, 250 p. (original: *Es gibt keinen jüdischen Wohnbezirk in Warschau mehr*).

Stypulkowski, Zbigniew. *Invitation to Moscow.* New York: Walker, [1950?], 359 p. (Translation from the Polish of *W Zawrieusze Dziejoweij*).

Velev, Dincho. *Dolg i molodost'.* Translated from the Bulgarian by I.M. Saburov. Uzhgorod: Karpati, 1975, 383 p. (original: *Dulg i mladost*).

Walach, Stanislaw. *Partizanskie nochi: Dokum. povest'.* Translated from the Polish by M. Brukhnov. Moscow: Mol. Gvardiia, 1973, 207 p.

Wiener, Jan G. *The Assassination of Heydrich.* New York: Pyramid Books, 1971, 176 p. (paperback).

Zagórski, Waclaw. *Seventy Days.* Translated from the Polish by John Welsh. Maidstone, England: Mann, 1974, 266 p. (original: *Wicher Wolnosci*).

Zawodny, Janusz Kazimierz. *Nothing But Honour: The Story of the Warsaw Uprising, 1944.* Stanford, Calif.: Hoover Institution Press, 1978, 328 p. (Hoover Institution publication; 183).

Zolotar', Ivan Fedorovich. *Druz'ia poznaiutsia v bede: Dokum. povest'.* Moscow: Sov. Rossiia, 1973, 413 p. (Poland).

France

Aglion, Raoul. *The Fighting French.* New York: Holt, 1943, 315 p. (French edition: *L'épopée de la France combattante*).

Baudoin, Madeleine. *Histoire des groupes Francs (M.U.R.) des Bouches-du-Rhone, de septembre 1943 à la libération.* Paris: Presses Universitaires de France, 1962, 283 p.

Bidault, Georges. *Resistance: The Political Autobiography of Georges Bidault.* Translated from the French by Marianne Sinclair. New York: Praeger, 1967, 348 p. (original: *D'une résistance à l'autre*).

Bird, Michael J. *The Secret Battalion.* New York: Holt, Rinehart and Winston, 1964, 189 p.

Blumenson, Martin. *The Vildé Affair: Beginnings of the French Resistance.* Boston: Houghton Mifflin, 1977, 287 p.

Bonte, Florimond. *Les Antifascistes allemands dans la Résistance francaise.* Paris: Editions Sociales, 1969, 392 p. (paperback).

Braddon, Russell. *The White Mouse.* New York: Norton, 1957, 255 p. (U.S. edition of *Nancy Wake: The Story of a Very Brave Woman,* London: Cassell, 1956).

Chambard, Claude. *The Maquis: A History of the French Resistance Movement.* Translated by Elaine P. Halperin. Indianapolis: Bobbs-Merrill, 1976, 237 p.).

Choury, Maurice. *Tous bandits d'honneur! Résistance et libération de la Corse, juin 1940–octobre 1943.* Paris: Editions Sociales, 1958, 220 p. (paperback).

Collier, Richard. *Ten Thousand Eyes.* New York: Dutton, 1958, 320 p.

Dank, Milton. *The French Against the French: Collaboration and Resistance.* Philadelphia: Lippincott, 1974, 365 p.

Ehrlich, Blake. *Resistance: France 1940–1945.* New York: New American Library, [post 1965], 278 p. (paperback).

En souvenir de la visite à Washington des camarades de la Résistance Francaise aux anciens de l'O.S.S. June 1959, 40 p. (souvenir program).

Fernand-Laurent, Camille Jean. *Un peuple ressuscité.* [New York]: Brentano's, 1943, 278 p. (paperback).

Fourcade, Marie Madeleine. *Noah's Ark.* Translated from the French by Kenneth Morgan. New York: Dutton, 1974, 377 p. (Original: *L'Arche de Noël*).

Frenay, Henri. *L'énigme Jean Moulin.* Paris: R. Laffont, 1977, 307 p.

Frenay, Henri. *The Night Will End.* Translated from the French by Dan Hofstadter. New York: McGraw-Hill, 1976, 469 p.

Frenay, Henri. *La nuit finira.* Paris: R. Laffont, 1976, 607 p.

Frenay, Henri. *Volontaires de la nuit.* Paris: R. Laffont, 1975, 457 p.

Gillot, August and **Simone.** *Un couple dans la Résistance.* Paris: Editions Sociales, 1975, 334 p.

Guérard, Albert Joseph. *Maquisard, a Christmas Tale.* London: Longmans, Green, 1946, 186 p.

Guillain de Bénouville, Pierre. *The Unknown Warriors, a Personal Account of the French Resistance.* Translated from the French by Lawrence G. Blochman. New York: Simon and Schuster, 1949, 372 p.

[Jacques, *Capitaine***].** *Maquis victoires.* Mulhouse: Société Alsacienne d'Edition Alsatia, 1944, 135 p.

Kedward, Harry Roderick. *Resistance in Vichy France: A Study of Ideas and Motivation in the Southern Zone, 1940–1942.* Oxford: Oxford University Press, 1978, 311 p.

Kessel, Joseph. *L'armée des ombres, chronique de la résistance.* Edited by Jacques Schiffrin. New York: Pantheon Books, 1944, 261 p.

Kessel, Joseph. *Army of Shadows.* Translated from the French by Haakon Chevalier. New York: Knopf, 1944, 159 p.

Knight, Frida. *The French Resistance, 1940 to 1944.* London: Lawrence and Wishart, 1975, 242 p.

Leslie, Peter. *The Liberation of the Riviera: The Resistance to the Nazis in the South of France and the Story of Its Heroic Leader, Ange-Marie Miniconi.* New York: Wyndham Books, 1980, 254 p.

Liebling, Abbott Joseph and **Sheffer, Eugene Jay,** eds. *La république du silence, the Story of French Resistance.* New York: Harcourt, Brace, 1946, 534 p.

Marsden, Alexandrina. *Resistance Nurse.* London: Odhams Press, 1961, 208 p.

Michel, Henri. *Bibliographie critique de la Résistance.* [Paris]: Institut Pédagogique National, 1964, 223 p.

Michel, Henri. *Histoire de la Résistance (1940–1944).* Paris: Presses Universitaires de France, 1958, 127 p. (Que sais-je? no. 429).

Michel, Henri. *Histoire de la Résistance en France, 1940–1944.* Paris: Presses Universitaires de France, 1972, 127 p. (Que sais-je? no. 429).

Morize, André. *Resistance: France, 1940–1943.* Translated by Helen J. Huebener. [Boston]: Boston Chapter, France Forever, 1943, 92 p.

Mossu, René. *Les secrets d'une frontière.* Geneva: Edition du Milieu du Monde, 1946, 263 p. (Collection "Documents d'aujourd'hui," VIII; paperback).

Moulin, Jean. *Premier combat: journal posthume (Chartres 14-18 juin 1940).* [Paris]: Editions de Minuit, 1947, 169 p.

Noguères, Henri with **Degliame-Fouché, Marcel** (v. I–IV) and **Vigier, Jean-Louis** (v. I, II). *Histoire de la résistance en France de 1940 à 1945.* Paris: R. Laffont, 1967–1976, 4 v.

Ortzen, Len. *Famous Stories of the Resistance.* [London?]: A. Barker, 1979, 154 p.

Pacaut, René. *Maquis dans la plaine* ... 3ᵉ éd. revue et augmentée. Paris: le Hameau, 1974, 317 p.

Passy, Colonel, pseud. (Dewavrin, André). *Missions secrètes en France: novembre 1942—juin 1943).* Paris: Plon, 1951, 439 p. (paperback).

Passy, Colonel, pseud. (Dewavrin, André). *Souvenirs. Volume 1: 2ᵉ Bureau Londres.* Monte-Carlo: R. Solar, 1947, 237 p.

Pearson, Michael. *Tears of Glory: The Betrayal of Vercors 1944.* London: Macmillan, 1978, 254 p.

Perrault, Gilles. *La longue traque.* Paris: J. C. Lattès, 1975, 526 p. (paperback).

Rémy, pseud. (Renault-Roulier, Gilbert). *Comment meurt un réseau (fin 1943).* Monte-Carlo: R. Solar, 1947, 193 p. (v. 3 of his Mémoires d'un agent secret de la France libre; paperback).

Rémy, pseud. (Renault-Roulier, Gilbert). *Courage and Fear.* Translated from the French by Lancelot C. Sheppard. London: A. Barker, (1950), 320 p. (original: *Le livre du courage et de la peur,* v. 2 of his Mémoires d'un agent secret de la France libre).

Rémy, pseud. (Renault-Roulier, Gilbert). *Memoirs of a Secret Agent of Free France. Volume 1: The Silent Company, June 1940—June 1942.* Translated from the French by Lancelot C. Sheppard. New York: McGraw-Hill, 1948, 406 p.

Rémy, pseud. (Renault-Roulier, Gilbert). *La Résistance dans le Lyonnais: récits.* Neuilly-sur-Seine: Saint-Clair, 1975, 2 v.

Rémy, pseud. (Renault-Roulier, Gilbert). *La Résistance en Bretagne: récits.* Geneva: Editions Famot, 1974, 2 v.

Rochester, Devereaux. *Full Moon to France.* New York: Harper and Row, 1977, 261 p.

Sanguedolce, Joseph. *Résistance: de Saint-Etienne à Dachau.* Paris: Editions Sociales, 1973, 174 p. (paperback).

Schips, Martin. *Partisanen auf zum Sturm: Tatsachenroman aus dem Kampf der Franzoesischen Patrioten.* Zurich: Gotthard Verlag, 1944, 216 p.

Schoenbrun, David. *Soldiers of the Night: The Story of the French Resistance.* New York: Dutton, 1980, 512 p.

Tillon, Charles. *Les F.T.P., témoignage pour servir à l'histoire de la Résistance.* Paris: R. Julliard, 1967, 386 p.

Vercors, pseud. (Bruller, Jean). *The Battle of Silence.* Translated from the French by Rita Barisse. New York: Holt, Rinehart and Winston, 1968, 286 p. (original: *La Bataille du silence, souvenirs de minuit,* Paris: Presses de la Cité, 1967) (fiction).

Vomécourt, Philippe de. *An Army of Amateurs.* Garden City, N.Y.: Doubleday, 1961, 307 p. (U.S. edition of *Who Lived to See the Day.* London: Hutchinson).

Wynne, Barry. *The Empty Coffin: The Story of Alain Romans.* London: Souvenir Press, 1959, 196 p.

Germany

Andreas-Friedrich, Ruth. *Berlin Underground, 1938-1945.* Translated by Barrows Mussey. New York: Holt, 1947, 312 p.

Bartz, Karl. *The Downfall of the German Secret Service.* Translated from the German by Edward Fitzgerald. London: W. Kimber, 1956, 202 p.

Deutsch, Harold Charles. *The Conspiracy Against Hitler in the Twilight War.* Minneapolis: University of Minnesota Press, 1968, 394 p.

Dulles, Allen Welsh. *Germany's Underground.* New York: Macmillan, 1947, 207 p.

Forman, James D. *Code Name Valkyrie: Count von Stauffenberg and the Plot to Kill Hitler.* New York: S. G. Phillips, 1973, 256 p.

Galante, Pierre with **Silianoff, Eugène.** *Operation Valkyrie: the German Generals' Plot Against Hitler.* Translated from the French by Mark Howson and Cary Ryan. New York: Harper and Row, 1981, 274 p. (original: *Hitler est-il mort?* Paris: Plon, 1981).

Gallin, Mary Alice. *German Resistance to Hitler: Ethical and Religious Factors.* Washington: Catholic University of America Press, 1969, 259 p.

Germans Against Hitler, July 20, 1944. Compiled by Erich Zimmermann and Hans-Adolf Jacobsen; translated from the German by Allan and Lieselotte Yahraes. Bonn: Press and Information Office of the Federal Government of Germany, 1960, 328 p. (paperback).

Gisevius, Hans Bernd. *To the Bitter End.* Translated from the German by Richard and Clara Winston. Boston: Houghton Mifflin, 1947, 632 p.

Gollwitzer, Helmut; Kuhn, Käthe et al., eds. *Du hast mich heimgesucht bei Nacht: Abschiedsbriefe und Aufzeichnungen des Widerstandes 1933-1945.* Munich: C. Kaiser, 1954, 320 p.

Gollwitzer, Helmut; Kuhn, Käthe et al., eds. *Dying We Live: The Final Messages and Records of the Resistance.* Translated from the German by Reinhard C. Kuhn. New York: Pantheon, 1956, 285 p.

Graham, James. *The Conspirators.* New York: Award Books, 1968, 224 p. (paperback edition of *The Sword and the Umbrella,* 1964).

Hellwig, Joachim and **Oley, Hans.** *Der 20. Juli 1944 und der Fall Heusinger.* Berlin: Verlag der Nation, 1959, 1 v. (unpaged).

Helmreich, Ernst Christian. *The German Churches Under Hitler: Background, Struggle, and Epilogue.* Detroit: Wayne State University Press, 1979, 616 p.

Herwarth von Bittenfeld, Hans-Heinrich with **Starr, S. Frederick.** *Against Two Evils: Memoirs of a Diplomat-Soldier During The Third Reich.* New York: Rawson, Wade, 1981, 318 p.

Hoffmann, Peter. *The History of the German Resistance, 1933-1945.* Translated from the German by Richard Barry. Cambridge, Mass.: M.I.T. Press, 1977, 847 p. (original: *Widerstand, Staatsstreich, Attentat*).

Hoffmann, Peter. *Hitler's Personal Security.* London: Macmillan, 1979, 321 p.

Jansen, Jon B. and **Weyl, Stefan,** pseuds. *The Silent War: The Underground Movement in Germany.* Translated by Anna Caples. Philadelphia: Lippincott, 1943, 356 p.

Kernmayr, Erich. *Verrat an Deutschland: Spione und Saboteure gegen das eigene Vaterland.* Göttinger: K. W. Schütz, 1965, 318 p.

Kirst, Hans Hellmut. *The Affairs of the Generals.* Translated from the German by J. Maxwell Brownjohn. New York: Coward, McCann and Geoghegan, 1979, 253 p. (original: *Generalsaffaeren*) (fiction).

Kolosov, L. and **Petrov, N.** "Immortality of Those Who Have Fallen." Washington: U.S. Joint Publications Research Service, March 21, 1972, 34 p. (translation No. 55490 of serial article from *Izvestiya,* Moscow, October 8-10, 1969).

Kramarz, Joachim. *Stauffenberg, the Architect of the Famous July 20th Conspiracy to Assassinate Hitler.* Translated from the German by R. H. Barry. New York: Macmillan, 1967, 255 p. (original: *Claus Graf Stauffenberg*).

Löwenstein-Wertheim-Freudenberg, Hubertus, Prinz zu. *What Was the German Resistance Movement?* Bad Godesberg: Grafes, 1965, 64 p.

Manvell, Roger and **Fraenkel, Heinrich.** *The Canaris Conspiracy: The Secret Resistance to Hitler in the German Army.* New York: Pinnacle Books, 1969, 316 p. (paperback).

Manvell, Roger. *The Conspirators: 20th July 1944.* New York: Ballantine Books, 1971, 160 p. (Politics in Action, no. 1) (paperback).

Mason, Hebert Molloy. *To Kill the Devil: The Attempts on the Life of Adolph Hitler.* New York: Norton, 1978, 280 p.

Neuhaus, Wolfgang. *Ego Nazivali Ivanom Ivanovichem.* Moscow: Voenizdat, 1970, 328 p. (translation of *Kampf gegen "Sternlauf": der Weg des deutschen Partisanen Fritz Schmenkel,* Berlin: Deutscher Militärverlag, 1968) (fiction)

Pechel, Rudolf. *Deutscher Widerstand.* Erlenbach-Zürich: E. Rentsch, 1947, 343 p.

Prittie, Terence Cornelius Farmer. *Germans Against Hitler.* Boston: Little, Brown, 1964, 291 p.

Reynolds, Nicholas. *Treason Was No Crime: Ludwig Beck, Chief of the German General Staff.* London: Kimber, 1976, 317 p.

Roon, Ger van. *German Resistance to Hitler: Count von Moltke and the Kreisau Circle.* London: Van Nostrand Reinhold, 1971, 400 p. (translation of *Neuordnung im Widerstand: Der Kreisauer Kreis innerhalb der deutschen Widerstandsbewegung.* Munich: R. Oldenbourg, 1967).

Rothfels, Hans. *The German Opposition to Hitler: An Assessment.* Translated from the German by Lawrence Wilson. London: O. Wolff, 1961, 166 p.

Schlabrendorff, Fabian von. *The Secret War Against Hitler.* Translated by Hilda Simon. New York: Pitman, 1965, 438 p. (includes material from his *Offiziere gegen Hitler,* 1946).

Schmitthenner, Walter and **Buchheim, Hans,** eds. *Der deutsche Widerstand gegen Hitler: Vier historisch-kritische Studien von Hermann Graml.* Cologne: Kiepenheuer and Witsch, 1966, 287 p.

Schramm, Wilhelm, *Ritter von. Conspiracy Among Generals.* Translated and edited by R.T. Clark. New York: Scribner, 1956, 215 p. (translation of *Der 20 Juli in Paris*).

Strassner, Peter. *Verräter: das Nationalkomitee "Freies Deutschland"—Keimzelle der sogenannten DDR.* Siegburg-Niederpleis, Austria: Ring-Verlag Helmut Cramer, 1963, 452 p.

Sykes, Christopher. *Tormented Loyalty: The Story of a German Aristocrat Who Defied Hitler.* New York: Harper and Row, 1969. 477 p. (reprint of *Troubled Loyalty*, London, 1968).

Tomin, Valentin Romanovich and **Grabowski, Stefan.** *Die Helden der Berliner Illegalität: Reportage* über den gemeinsamen Kampf deutscher und sowjetischer Anti-faschisten. Translated from the Russian by Gerhart Hass. Berlin: Dietz, 1967, 174 p. (original: *Po sledam geroev berlinskogo podpol'ia*).

West, Paul. *The Very Rich Hours of Count von Stauffenberg.* New York: Harper and Row, 1980, 365 p.

Whiting, Charles. *Hitler's Werewolves: The Story of the Nazi Resistance Movement, 1944-1945.* New York: Bantam Books, 1973, 208 p. (paperback).

Young, Arthur Primrose. *The "X" Documents.* Edited by Sidney Aster. London: Deutsch, 1974, 253 p.

Zeller, Eberhard. *The Flame of Freedom: the German Struggle Against Hitler.* Translated from the 4th German edition by R. P. Heller and D. R. Masters. Coral Gables, Fla.: University of Miami Press, 1969, 471 p. (original: *Geist der Freiheit*).

Mediterranean

Amery, Julian. *Sons of the Eagle, a Study in Guerilla War.* London: Macmillan, 1948, 354 p. (Albania).

Bailey, Ronald H. *Partisans and Guerrillas.* Alexandria, Va.: Time-Life Books, 1978, 208 p. (Balkan Peninsula).

Battaglia, Roberto. *The Story of the Italian Resistance.* Translated and edited by P. D. Cummins. London: Odhams, 1957, 287 p. (original: *Storia della resistenza italiana*).

Casson, Stanley. *Greece Against the Axis.* Washington: American Council on Public Affairs, 1943, 150 p.

Condit, D. M. *Case Study in Guerrilla War: Greece During World War II.* Washington: American University, Special Warfare Research Division, 1961, 338 p.

Corpo volontari della Libertà. *La Resistenza italiana.* Milano, 1947, unpaged.

Downes, Donald C. *The Easter Dinner.* New York: Pocket Books, 1961, 234 p. (paperback, fiction about Italian resistance).

Eudes, Dominique. *The Kapetanios: Partisans and Civil War in Greece, 1943-1949.* Translated from the French by John Howe. New York: Monthly Review Press, 1972, 381 p.

Farran, Roy Alexander. *Operation Tombola.* London: Collins, 1960, 256 p. (Italy).

Gallagher, J. P. *Scarlet Pimpernel of the Vatican.* New York: Coward-McCann, 1967, 184 p.

Galleni, Mauro. *Sovetskie partizany v Ital'ianskom dvizhenii soprotivleniia.* Translated from the Italian and edited by E. A. Brobsk. Moscow: Progress, 1970, 223 p. (original: *I partigiani sovietici nella Resistenza italiana*, Rome: Editori Riuniti, 1967).

Hood, Stuart Clink. *Pebbles From My Skull.* London: Hutchinson, 1963, 153 p. (Italy).

Jecchinis, Chris. *Beyond Olympus: The Thrilling Story of the "Train-Busters" in Nazi-Occupied Greece.* London: Harrap, 1960, 218 p.

Kédros, André. *La résistance grecque, 1940–1944.* Paris: R. Laffont, 1966, 543 p.

Meneghello, Luigi. *The Outlaws.* Translated by Raleigh Trevelyan. New York: Harcourt, Brace and World, 1967, 272 p. (translation and revision of *I piccoli maestri*).

Pesce, Giovanni. *And No Quarter: An Italian Partisan in World War II: Memoirs of Giovanni Pescoe.* Translated by Frederick M. Shaine. Athens: Ohio University Press, 1972, 269 p. (translation of *Senza tregua*).

Reid, Francis. *I Was in Noah's Ark.* London: Chambers, 1957, 143 p. (Greece).

Rosengarten, Frank. *The Italian Anti-Fascist Press (1919–1945): From the Legal Opposition Press to the Underground Newspapers of World War II.* Cleveland Press of Case Western Reserve University, 1968, 263 p.

Saraphes, Stephanos G. *ELAS: Greek Resistance Army.* London: Merlin Press, 1980, 556 p. (translation of *Ho ELAS*).

Symmachos, *pseud. Greece Fights On.* London: L. Drummond, 1943, 143 p.

Wason, Elizabeth. *Miracles in Hellas: The Greeks Fight On.* New York: Macmillan, 1943, 263 p.

Whittle, Peter. One Afternoon at Mezzegra. Englewood Cliffs, N.J.: Prentice-Hall, 1969, 195 p.

Windsor, John. *The Mouth of the Wolf.* Sidney, B.C.: Gray's 1967, 223 p. (Italy).

Wingate, John. *Never So Proud; Crete: May, 1941, the Battle and Evacuation.* New York: Meredith Press, 1967, 233 p. (fiction).

Woodhouse, Christopher Montague. *One Omen.* London: Hutchinson, 1950, 208 p. (fiction about Greek resistance).

Zotos, Stephanos. *Greece: The Struggle for Freedom.* New York: Crowell, 1967, 194 p.

Scandinavia

Andenaes, Johannes; Riste, Olav *et al. Norway and the Second World War.* Oslo: Tanum, 1966, 167 p.

Astrup, Helen and **Jacot, B. L.** *Oslo Intrigue.* New York: McGraw-Hill, 1954, 237 p. (U.S. edition of *Night Has a Thousand Eyes,* London: Macdonald, 1953).

Baden-Powell, Dorothy. *Pimpernel Gold: How Norway Foiled the Nazis.* New York: St. Martin's Press, 1978, 207 p.

Broch, Theodor. *The Mountains Wait.* London: M. Joseph, 1943, 192 p. (Norway) (autobiography).

Drummond, John Dorman. *But for These Men: (How Eleven Commandos Saved Western Civilization).* New York: Award Books, 1965, 219 p. (paperback) (Norway).

Hansson, Per. *The Greatest Gamble.* Translated by Maurice Michael. New York: Modern Literary Editions, 1967, 224 p. (Norway; translation of *Det storste spillet*) (paperback).

Haukelid, Knut Anders. *Attack on Telemark.* New York: Ballantine Books, 1974, 160 p. (paperback of *Skis Against the Atom.* London: W. Kimber).

Hovelsen, Leif. *Out of the Evil Night.* Translated from the Norwegian by John Morrison. London: Blandford Press, 1959, 160 p. (original: *All verden venter*).

Howarth, David Armine. *Across to Norway.* New York: Sloane, 1952, 286 p. (U.S. edition of *The Shetland Bus,* London).

Howarth, David Armine. *We Die Alone.* New York: Macmillan, 1955, 231 p. (Norway).

Höye, Bjarne and **Ager, Trygve, M.** *The Fight of the Norwegian Church Against Nazism.* New York: Macmillan, 1943, 180 p.

Klefos, Brede. *They Came in the Night: Wartime Experiences of a Norwegian American.* New York: Crown, 1959, 206 p.

Lampe, David. *The Savage Canary: The Story of Resistance in Denmark.* London: Cassell, 1957, 236 p.

Manus, Max with **Giles, Dorothy.** *9 Lives Before Thirty.* Garden City, N.Y.: Doubleday, 1947, 328 p. (Norway).

Muus, Flemming Brunn. *The Spark and the Flame.* Translated from the Danish and edited by Varinka Muus and J. F. Burke. London: Museum Press, 1956, 172 p. (original: *Ingen taender et lys*).

Norway Does Not Yield: The Story of the First Year. New York: American Friends of German Freedom, 1941, 64 p.

Olsen, Oluf Reed. *Two Eggs on my Plate.* Translated from the Norwegian by F. H. Lyon. Chicago: Rand McNally, 1953, 365 p. (original: *Vi kommer igjen and Contact*).

Riste, Olav and **Nökleby, Berit.** *Norway 1940-45: The Resistance Movement.* Oslo: Tanum, 1970, 92 p.

Sonsteby, Gunnar Fridtjof Thurmann. *Report From No. 24.* Prepared from a translation from the Norwegian by Maurice Michael. New York: L. Stuart, 1965, 192 p.

Thomas, John Oram. *The Giant-Killers: The Story of the Danish Resistance Movement, 1940-1945.* London: M. Joseph, 1975, 320 p.

Worm-Müller, Jacob Stenerson. *Norway Revolts Against the Nazis.* London: L. Drummond, 1941, 152 p.

Yugoslavia

Adamic, Louis. *The Eagle and the Roots.* Garden City, N.Y.: Doubleday, 1952, 531 p.

Committee For A Fair Trial for Gen. Draza Mihailovich, Commission of Inquiry. *Patriot or Traitor: The Case of General Mihailovich: Proceedings and Report.* . . . Stanford, Calif.: Hoover Institution Press, 1978, 499 p. (Hoover Institution publication; 191).

Davidson, Basil. *Partisan Picture.* Bedford, England: Bedford Books, 1946, 351 p.

Deakin, Frederick William, *The Embattled Mountain.* London: Oxford University Press, 1971, 284 p.

Dedijer, Vladimir. *Tito.* New York: Simon and Schuster, 1953, 443 p.

Dedijer, Vladimir. *With Tito Through the War: Partisan Diary, 1941-1944.* London: Hamilton, 1951, 403 p. (an abridged translation, by Alec Brown, of the author's *Dnevnik*).

Dilas, Milovan. *Wartime.* Translated by Michael B. Petrovich. New York: Harcourt, Brace, Jovanovich, 1977, 470 p.

Donlagic, Ahmet; Atanackovic, Zarko et al. *Yugoslavia in the Second World War.* Translated by Lovett F. Edwards. Belgrade: (Medunarodna Stampa—Interpress), 1967, 245 p. (original: *Jugoslavija u drugom svetskom ratu*).

Hehn, Paul N. *The German Struggle Against Yugoslav Guerrillas in World War II: German Counter-Insurgency in Yugoslavia, 1941-1943.* Boulder, Colo.: East European Quarterly; New York: Columbia University Press, 1979, 153 p. (East European monograph; no. 57).

Huot, Louis. *Guns for Tito.* New York: L. B. Fischer, 1945, 273 p.

Maclean, Fitzroy. *Disputed Barricade: The Life and Times of Josip Broz-Tito, Marshal of Jugoslavia.* London: J. Cape, 1957, 480 p.

Maclean, Fitzroy. *The Heretic: The Life and Times of Josip Broz-Tito.* New York: Harper, 1957, 436 p.

Maclean, Fitzroy. *Tito, a Pictorial Biography.* New York: McGraw-Hill, 1980, 127 p. (paperback).

Maclean, Fitzroy. *Tito: The Man Who Defied Hitler and Stalin.* New York: Ballantine Books, 1957, 424 p.

Milazzo, Matteo J. *The Chetnik Movement and the Yugoslav Resistance.* Baltimore: Johns Hopkins University Press, 1975, 208 p.

Mitchell, Ruth. *The Serbs Choose War.* Garden City, N.Y.: Doubleday, Doran, 1943, 265 p.

Padev, Michael. *Marshal Tito.* London: F. Muller, 1944. 129 p.

Petrovic, Svetislav Sveta. *Free Yugoslavia Calling.* Translated and edited by Joseph Ciszek Peters. New York: Greystone Press, 1941, 356 p.

Roberts, Walter R. *Tito, Mihailovic, and the Allies, 1941-1945.* New Brunswick, N.J.: Rutgers University Press, 1973, 406 p.

Rootham, Jasper. *Miss Fire: The Chronicle of a British Mission to Mihailovich, 1943-1944.* London: Chatto and Windus, 1946, 224 p.

Strutton, Bill. *Island of Terrible Friends.* New York: Norton, 1962, 192 p.

Tomasevich, Jozo. *The Chetniks.* Stanford, Calif.: Stanford University Press, 1975, 508 p

Vrgovich, Stevan. *Partizanskimi tropami.* Translated by M. D. Kovalev. Moscow: Voenizdat, 1977, 142 p.

USSR

Adamovich, Aliaksandr Mikhailavich. *Khatynskaia povest'.* Moscow: Voenizdat, 1973, 206 p.

Anoshkin, Ivan. *Kompas pakazvae na zakhad.* Minsk: Mastatskaia Literatura, 1976, 208 p.

Armstrong, John Alexander, ed. *Soviet Partisans in World War II.* Madison: University of Wisconsin Press, 1964, 792 p.

Asmolov, Aleksei Nikitovich. *Front v tylu vermakhta.* Moscow: Politizdat, 1977, 320 p.

Avengers: Reminiscences of Soviet Members of the Resistance Movement. Translated from the Russian by David Skvirsky. Moscow: Progress, 1965, 278 p. (original: *O chem ne govorilos' v svodkakh*).

Bakraze, Davit'. *Karpatskii reid.* Moscow: DOSAAF, 1968, 160 p.

Beliavets, Vlas Fedorovich. *Donetskie mstiteli: Zap. partizana.* Kiev: Politizdat Ukrainy, 1978, 223 p.

Bezman, Efim Savel'evich. *Chasovye partizanskogo efira.* Leningrad: Lenizdat, 1976, 155 p.

Bezman, Efim Savel'evich and **Stromilov, Nikolai N.** *Chasovye partizanskogo efira.* Leningrad: Lenizdat, 1976, 155 p.

Blizniuk, Semen and **Sykhan, Iurii.** *Operatsiia "Tereblia": Ocherki.* Uzhgorod: Karpati, 1978, 304 p.

Bor'ba latyshskogo naroda v gody Velikoi Otechestvennoi voiny. Edited by A. Drizulis. Riga: Zinatne, 1970, 931 p.

Braiko, Petr Evseevich and **Kalinenko, Oksana Semenovna.** *Vnimanie, Kovpak!* Moscow: DOSAAF, 2d ed., 1975, 481 p. (fiction).

Briantsev, Georgii Mikhailovich. *Konets osinogo gnezda.* **Medvedev, Dmitrii Nikolaevich.** *Eto bylo pod Rovno.* Moscow: Det-Lit, 1968, 559 p. (fiction).

Bychkov, Lev Nikolaevich. *Partizanskoe dvizhenie v gody Velikoi Otechestvennoi voiny, 1941-1945: Kratkii ocherk.* Moscow: Mysl', 1965, 453 p.

Cooper, Matthew. *The Nazi War Against Soviet Partisans, 1941-1944.* New York: Stein and Day, 1979, 217 p.

Cooper, Matthew. *The Phantom War: The German Struggle Against Soviet Partisans, 1941-1944.* London: Macdonald and Janes, 1979, 219 p.

Dewitt, Kurt. *The Role of the Partisans in Soviet Intelligence.* Maxwell Air Force Base, Alabama: Air Research and Development Command, Human Resources Research Institute, January 1954, 52 p.

Didyk, Praskov'ia Gerasimovna. *B Tylu vraga: Povest'.* Kishinev: Kartia Moldoveniaske, 1973, 300 p.

Dixon, Cecil Aubrey and **Heilbrunn, Otto.** *Communist Guerilla Warfare.* New York: Praeger, 1954 and 1962, 229 p.

Endzheiak, Vladimir Ivanovich and **Kuznetsov, Anatolii Petrovich.** *Osobaia partizansko-diversionnaia.* Kiev: Politizdat Ukrainy, 1977, 204 p.

Fadeev, Aleksandr Aleksandrovich. *The Young Guard: A Novel.* Translated from the Russian by Violet Dutt. Moscow: Progress, 1973. 2 v.

Fedorov, Aleksei Fedorovich. *The Underground R. C. Carries on.* Translation edited by L. Stoklitsky. Moscow: Foreign Languages Pub. House, 1949-1950, 2 v.

Galkin, Lev. *Temnaia nochka-den' partizanskii.* 2d ed. Khar'kov: Prapor, 1973, 264 p.

Gofman, Genrikh Borisovich. *Chernyi general; Dvoe nad okeanom: Povesti.* Moscow: Sov. Pisatel', 1977, 413 p.

Gorchakov, Ovidii Aleksandrovich. *Lebedinaia pesnia: Dokum. povest'.* Moscow: Voenizdat, 1968, 228 p.

Grani otvagi i stoikosti. Edited by A. I. Usov. Syktyvkar: Komi Knizhnoe Izd-vo., 1975, 216 p.

Gridnev, Viktor Mikhailovich. *Bor'ba krest'ianstva okkupirovannykh oblastei RSFSR protiv nemetsko-fashistskoi okkupatsionnoi politiki: 1941-1944.* Moscow: Nauka, 1976, 231 p.

Gubskii, Nikolai Fedorovich. *Nezabyvaemoe.* Minsk: Belarus', 1976, 157 p.

Howell, Edgar M. *The Soviet Partisan Movement, 1941-1944.* [Washington]: Dept. of the Army, 1956, 217 p.

IAkovenko, Vladimir Kirillovich. *Partizanskoe mezhdurech'e.* Moscow: Politizdat, 1976, 284 p.

Ignatov, Petr Karpovich. *Zapiski partizana.* Moscow: Mosk. Rabochii, 1973, 695 p.

Isakov, Ivan Ivanovich. *Groza nad Oredezhem.* Leningrad: Lenizdat, 1975, 229 p.

Karov, D. *Partizanskoe dvizhenie v SSSR v 1941-1945 gg.* Munich, 1954. (series: Institut po izucheniiu istorii i kul'tury SSSR. Issledovaniia i materialy, Ser. 1, no. 11; summaries in English, German and French).

Klimov, Ivan Frolovich and **Grakov, Nikita Ermolaevich.** *Partizany Vileishchiny.* [Minsk: Belarus', 1967], 361 p.

Klokov, Vsevolod Ivanovych. *Vsenarodnaia bor'ba v tylu nemetsko-fashistskikh okkupantov na Ukraine, 1941-1944: Istoriogr. ocherk.* Kiev: Nauk. Dumka, 1978, 123 p.

Kolmsee, Peter. *Der Partisanenkampf in der Sowjetunion: Über Charakter, Inhalt und Formen des Partisanenkampfes in der UdSSR, 1941-1944.* Berlin: Deutscher Militärverlag, 1963, 132 p. (Militärhistorische Studien, 6)

Komunistychnaia Partyia Belarusi. *Podpol'nye partiinye organy Kompartii Belorussii v gody Velikoi Otechestvennoi voiny (1941-1944): Kratkie svedeniia ob organizatsii, strukture i sostave.* Minsk: Belarus', 1975, 270 p.

Kostin, S. and **IAkushev, Lavrentii Trofimovich.** *Sled "Komety": Dokum. povest'.* Moscow: DOSAAF, 1978, 176 p.

Kostiukovskii, Boris Aleksandrovich. *Nit' Ariadny: Dokym.-khudozh. povest'.* Moscow: Mol. Gvardiia, 1975, 317 p.

Kovpak, Sydir Artemovych. *Our Partisan Course.* Translated from the Russian by Ernst and Mira Lesser. London: Hutchinson, 1947, 126 p.

Krivitsky, Alexander and **Krainov, Pavel.** *Tales of the Bryansk Woods.* Translated from the Russian by D. L. Fromberg. Moscow: Foreign Languages Pub. House, 1944, 120 p.

Krutikov, Ivan Ivanovich. *V prifrontovykh lesakh: zapiski partizana.* Leningrad: Lenizdat, 1965, 318 p.

Kugai, Pëtr Trofimovich and **Kalinichev, S.** *U "Volch'ego logova."* Translated from the Ukrainian. Moscow: Molodaia Gvardiia, 1977, 272 p.

Kuprin, Georgii Semenovich. *Sovest' zovet: zapiski komissara.* Moscow: Sov. Rossiia, 1978, 288 p.

Kuzin, Il'ia Nikolaevich. *Notes of a Guerilla Fighter.* Moscow: Foreign Languages Pub. House, 1942, 63 p. (translation of *Zapiski partizana*).

Liudi legend. Edited by L. Toropov. Moscow: Polit. Lit-ry, 1965-75, v. 1-3, 5 (of a 5 v. set).

Liventsev, Viktor Il'ich. *Partizanskii krai: Literaturnaia zapis' Rygora Nekhaia.* Minsk: BSSR, 1956, 383 p.; Minsk: Belarus', 1969, 400 p.

Lobanok, Vladimir Eliseevich. *Partizany prinimaiut boi: Lit. zapis' M. B. Taratkevicha.* Moscow: Politizdat, 1972, 304 p.

Logunova, Tat'iana Afanas'evna. *Partiinoe podpol'e i partizanskoe dvizhenie v zapadnyky i tsentral'nykh oblastiakh RSFSR: Iiul' 1941-1943 gg.* Moscow: Mosk. Universiteta, 1973, 226 p.

Lukashov, Mikhail Trofimovich. *Po tylam vraga.* Kiev: Politizdat Ukrainy, 1974, 262 p.

Machul'skii, Roman Naumovich. *Bechnyi ogon': partisanskie zapiski.* Minsk: Belarus', 1978, 445 p.

Mialo, Ivan Ivanovich. *Vernost': Roman.* Moscow: Sov. Pisatel', 1969, 340 p.

Miniailo, Viktor Oleksandrovych. *Krov' moego syna: roman.* Translated from the Ukrainian by V. Doronin and E. TSvetkov. Moscow: Sov. Pisatel', 1974, 341 p.

Moskvin, Nikolai Ivanovich. *Partizanskimi tropami.* Moscow: DOSAAF, 1971, 415 p.

Na rubezhakh shakhterskogo kraia. Compiled by D. F. Akul'shin. Donetsk: Donbas, 1975, 140 p.

Navumenka, Ivan IAkaulevich. *Sorok tretii: roman.* Translated from the Belorussian by Mikhail Gorbachev. Moscow: Sov. Pisatel', 1976, 368 p.

Novikau, Ivan Hryhor'evich. *Litsom k opasnosti: [Dokum. povest'].* Translated from the Belorussian by M. Gorbachev. Minsk: Mastatskaia Lit., 1974, 255 p.

Pavlov, IAkov Savel'evich *Komissar Bymazhkov.* Minsk: Belarus', 1978, 221 p.

Petrov, IUrii Pavlovich. *Partizanskoe dvizhenie v Leningradskoi oblasti: 1941-1944.* Leningrad: Lenizdat, 1973, 451 p.

Plotnikov, Ivan Fedorovich. *Deciat' tysiach geroev.* Moscow: Nauka, 1967, 216 p.

Pronin, Alexander. *Guerrilla Warfare in the German-Occupied Soviet Territories 1941-1944.* Ann Arbor, Mich.: University Microfilms, 1976, 268 p. (Photocopy of Ph.D. Thesis, Georgetown University, 1965).

Redelis, Valdis. *Partisanenkrieg: Entstehung und Bekämpfung der Partisanen- und Untergrundbewegung im Mittelabshnitt der Ostfront, 1941 bis 1943.* Heidelberg: K. Vowinckel, 1958, 152 p. (Series: Die Wehrmacht im Kampf, v. 17).

Rozy na snegu: Rasskazy o geroiakh nezrimogo fronta. Compiled by N. I. Kondrashova and N. V. Masolov. Leningrad: Lenizdat, 1973, 352 p.

Sergeev, Valentin Mikhailovich. *Krasnaia lenta.* Moscow: Politizdat, 1975, 205 p.

Shvedova, Irina Fedorovna. *Liza Chaikina.* Moscow: Politizdat, 1976, 80 p. (fiction).

Snaipery: Sbornik. Compiled by E. Nikiforov and G. Evstigneev. Moscow: Molodaia Gvardiia, 1976, 160 p.

Sovetskie partizany: Iz istorii partizanskogo dvizheniia v gody Velikoi Otechestvennoi voiny. Edited by V. E. Bystrov. Moscow: Polit. Lit-ry, 1961, 830 p.

Titkov, Ivan Filippovich. *Brigada "Zhelezniak".* Minsk: Belarus', 1976, 269 p.

TSkitishvili, Karlo Varlamovich. *Zakavkaz'e v partizanskoi voine, 1941-1945 gg.* Tiflis: TSK KP Gruzii, 1973, 302 p.

V prinemanskikh lesakh: Vospomenaniia partizan i podpol'shchikov. Compiled by B. P. Verkhos', V. A. Nedel'ko et al. Minsk: Belarus', 1975, 319 p.

Vagner, David. *Rytsari bez strakha: Dokum. povest'.* Translated from the German by A. Kydriavtsev. Alma Ata: Zhazushy, 1977, 80 p.

Vaupshasov, Stanislav Alekseevich. *Partizanskaia khronika.* 2d ed. Minsk: Belarus', 1971, 399 p.

Vergasov, Il'ia Zakharovich. *Geroicheskie byli iz zhizni Krymskikh partisan.* Moscow: Detskaia Literatura, 1975, 63 p.

Vergasov, Il'ia Zakharovich. *Ostanetsia s toboiu navsegda...: Roman.* Moscow: Sov. Pisatel', 1977, 302 p.

Veselov, Il'ia Ivanovich. *V tylu vraga: [Dokum. povest'].* Perm': Permskoe Knizhnoe Izd-vo, 1975, 184 p.

Volovich, Konstantin Nikolaevich. *Zhar dalekikh kostrov: zapiski komandira partizanskogo polka.* Leningrad: Lenizdat, 1974, 188 p.

Zakharov, Ivan Kuz'mich. *Voina v kraiu ozer.* Minsk, Belarus', 1973, 319 p.

Zbanats'kyi, IUrii Oliferovych. *My—ne iz legendy.* Translated from the Ukrainian by Anatolii Tonkel'. Moscow: Voenizdat, 1978, 522 p.

Zharikov, Andrei Dmitrievich. *IUnye partizany.* Moscow: Prosseshchenie, 1974, 128 p.

Zhilianin, IAkim Aleksandrovich; Pozniakov, I. et al. *Bez linii fronta.* Minsk: Belarus', 1975, 317 p.

Zhunin, Sergei Georgievich. *Ot Dnepra do Buga.* Minsk: Belarus', 1974, 252 p.

Znamena Pobedy: Stat'i, ocherki, korrespondentsii, pis'ma: sbornik. Edited by A. I. Lukovets ... et al. Moscow: Pravda, 1975, 2 v.

Algerian Revolution

Bidault, Georges. *Resistance: The Political Autobiography of Georges Bidault.* Translated from the French by Marianne Sinclair. New York: Praeger, 1967, 348 p. (original: D'une *résistance à l'autre*).

Bocca, Geoffrey. *The Secret Army.* Englewood Cliffs, N.J.: Prentice-Hall, 1968, 268 p.

Courrière, Yves. *Les feux du deésespoir: la fin d'un empire.* Paris: Fayard, 1971, 794 p. (paperback).

Courrière, Yves. *Les Fils de la Toussaint.* Paris: Fayard, 1968, 450 p. (paperback).

Courrière, Yves. *L'heure des colonels.* Paris: Fayard, 1970, 730 p. (paperback).

Courrière, Yves. *Le Temps des léopards.* Paris: Fayard, 1969, 697 p. (paperback).

Hamon, Hervé and **Rotman, Patrick.** *Les Porteurs de valises: la résistance française à la guerre d'Algérie.* Paris: A. Michel, 1979, 434 p.

Heggoy, Alf Andrew. *Insurgency and Counterinsurgency in Algeria.* Bloomington: Indiana University Press, 1972, 327 p.

Henissart, Paul. *Wolves in the City: The Death of French Algeria.* London: Hart-Davis, 1971, 508 p.

Horne, Alistair. *A Savage War of Peace: Algeria, 1954-1962.* New York: Viking Press, 1977, 604 p.

Hutchinson, Martha Crenshaw. *Revolutionary Terrorism: The FLN in Algeria, 1954-1962.* Stanford, Calif.: Hoover Institution Press, Stanford University, 1978, 178 p.

Jacquin, Henri. *La guerre secrète en Algérie.* Paris: O. Orban, 1977, 320 p.

Joesten, Joachim. *The Red Hand: The Sinister Account of the Terrorist Arm of the French Right-Wing "Ultras"—in Algeria and on the Continent.* London: Abelard-Schuman, 1962, 200 p.

Morland; Barangé et al. *Histoire de l'Organisation de l'armeé secrète.* Paris: R. Julliard, 1964, 605 p.

Mouton, Claude. *La Contrerévolution en Algérie.* Vouillé, France: Diffusion de la Pensée Française, 1972, 675 p. (paperback).

Servan-Schreiber, Jean Jacques. *Lieutenant in Algeria.* Translated from the French by Ronald Matthews. New York: Knopf, 1957, 231 p.

Talbott, John E. *The War Without a Name: France in Algeria, 1954-1962.* New York: Knopf and Random House, 1980, 305 p.

Trinquier, Roger. *La guerra moderna y la lucha contra las guerrillas.* Barcelona: Editorial Herder, 1965, 187 p. (Spanish edition of: *La guerre moderne.* Paris: La Table Ronde, 1961, 196 p.).

Trinquier, Roger. *Modern Warfare: A French View of Counterinsurgency.* Translated from the French by Daniel Lee. New York: Praeger, 1964, 115 p.

Arab-Israeli Conflicts

General

Ari'el, Dan. *Explosion.* Tel-Aviv: Olive Books of Israel, 1972, 192 p.

Barber, Rowland. *The Midnighters: A Documentary Novel Based on the Memoirs of Martin Allen Ribakoff.* New York: Bantam Books, 1972, 304 p. (paperback).

Eytan, Steve. *Das Auge Davids: Israels Geheimdienst in Aktion.* Translated from the French by Ingrid Kollpacher. Vienna-Munich-Zürich: Verlag Fritz Molden, 1971, 224 p.

Frank, Gerold. *The Deed.* New York: Simon and Schuster, 1963, 317 p.

Glubb, John Bagot, Sir. *War in the Desert, an R.A.F. Frontier Campaign.* New York: Norton, 1961, 352 p.

Golan, Aviezer. *Operation Susannah, as told by Marcelle Ninio ... et al.* Translated from the Hebrew by Peretz Kidron. New York: Harper and Row, 1978, 383 p.

Harkabi, Yehoshafat. *Arab Strategies and Israel's Response.* New York: Free Press, 1977, 194 p.

Kagan, Binyamin. *The Secret Battle for Israel.* Translated from the French by Patsy Southgate. Cleveland: World Pub., 1966, 299 p.

Katz, Shmuel. *Days of Fire.* Garden City, N.Y.: Doubleday, 1968, 317 p.

Lilienthal, Alfred M. *The Zionist Connection: What Price Peace?* New York: Dodd, Mead, 1978, 372 p.

O'Ballance, Edgar. *The Electronic War in the Middle East, 1968-70.* Hamden, Conn.: Shoe String Press, 1974, 148 p.

Reisman, William Michael. *The Art of the Possible: Diplomatic Alternatives in the Middle East.* Princeton, N.J.: Princeton University Press, 1970, 161 p.

Safran, Nadav. *Israel, the Embattled Ally.* Cambridge: Harvard University Press, 1978, 633 p.

St. John, Robert. *The Boss: The Story of Gamal Abdel Nasser.* New York: McGraw-Hill, 1960, 325 p.

Sevela, Efraim. *Farewell, Israel!* Translated from the Russian by Edmund Browne. South Bend, Ind.: Gateway Editions, 1977, 295 p.

British Mandate/Palestine

Avriel, Ehud. *Open the Gates! A Personal Story of "Illegal" Immigration to Israel.* New York: Atheneum, 1975, 369 p.

Begin, Menachem. *The Revolt.* Tel-Aviv: Hadar Pub., 1964, 386 p. (translation of *ha-Mered*).

Crum, Bartley Cavanaugh. *Behind the Silken Curtain: A Personal Account of Anglo-American Diplomacy in Palestine and the Middle East.* New York: Simon and Schuster, 1947, 297 p.

Eliot, George Fielding. *Hate, Hope and High Explosives: A Report on the Middle East.* Indianapolis: Bobbs-Merrill, 1948, 284 p.

Fergusson, Bernard, Sir. *The Trumpet in the Hall, 1930-1958.* London: Collins, 1971, 286 p.

Katz, Doris Kaplan. *The Lady was a Terrorist, During Israel's War of Liberation.* New York: Shiloni Pub., 1953, 192 p.

Sherf, Zeev. *Three Days.* Translated by Julian Louis Meltzer from the Hebrew. Garden City: N.Y.: Doubleday, 1962, 298 p.

Wilson, Evan M. *Decision on Palestine: How the U.S. Came to Recognize Israel.* Stanford, Calif.: Hoover Institution Press, Stanford University, 1979, 244 p.

Israeli Forces

Allon, Yigal. *Shield of David: The Story of Israel's Armed Forces.* New York: Random House, 1970, 272 p.

Avneri, Aryeh. *Sabra Commandos.* Tel-Aviv: Olive Books of Israel, 1972, 176 p.

Luttwak, Edward and **Horowitz, Dan.** *The Israeli Army.* New York: Harper and Row, 1975, 461 p.

Rubenstein, Murray and **Goldman, Richard.** *Shield of David: An Illustrated History of the Israeli Air Force.* Englewood Cliffs, N.J.: Prentice-Hall, 1978, 223 p.

Schiff, Zeev. *A History of the Israeli Army (1870-1974).* Translated and edited by Raphael Rothstein. New York: Simon and Schuster, 1974, 338 p.

Stevenson, William. *Zanek! A Chronicle of the Israeli Air Force.* New York: Viking Press, 1971, 344 p.

Terrorists and Guerrillas

Al-Rayyis, Riyad Najib and **Nahas, Dunia.** *Guerrillas for Palestine.* London: Croom Helm, 1976, 155 p.

Clarke, Thurston. *By Blood and Fire: The Attack on the King David Hotel.* London: Hutchinson, 1981, 347 p.

Cohen, Geulah. *Woman of Violence: Memoirs of a Young Terrorist, 1943-1948.* Translated from the Hebrew by Hillel Halkin. New York: Holt, Rinehart and Winston, 1966, 275 p. (Lohame Herut Yisrael).

Dobson, Christopher. *Black September: Its Short, Violent History.* New York: Macmillan, 1974, 179 p.

Katz, Doris Kaplan. *The Lady was a Terrorist, During Israel's War of Liberation.* New York: Shiloni Pub., 1953, 192 p. (Irgun Zvai Leumi).

Mardor, Meir. *Strictly Illegal.* Translated by H. A. G. Shmuckley. London: R. Hale, 1957, 239 p.

O'Ballance, Edgar. *Language of Violence: The Blood Politics of Terrorism.* San Rafael, Calif.: Presidio Press, 1979, 365 p.

O'Neill, Bard E. *Revolutionary Warfare in the Middle East: The Israelis vs. the Fedayeen.* Boulder, Colo.: Paladin Press, 1974, 140 p.

Pryce-Jones, David. *The Face of Defeat: Palestinian Refugees and Guerrillas.* New York: Holt, Rinehart and Winston, 1972, 179 p.

Schiff, Zeev and **Rothstein, Raphael.** *Fedayeen: Guerillas Against Israel.* New York: McKay, 1972, 246 p.

Slater, Leonard. *The Pledge.* New York: Simon and Schuster, 1970, 350 p.

Zionist Organization of America. *Hagana: A History of Jewish Resistance.* New York: Zionist Organization of America, Education Department, 1946, 16 p.

Wars
1948-1973

Adan, Avraham. *On the Banks of the Suez: An Israeli General's Personal Account of the Yom Kippur War.* San Rafael, Calif.: Presidio Press, 1980, 479 p. (Israel-Arab War, 1973).

Bell, J. Bowyer. *Terror Out of Zion: Irgun Zvai Leumi, and the Palestine Underground, 1929-1949.* New York: St. Martin's Press, 1977, 374 p. (Israel-Arab War, 1948-1949).

Haykal, Muhammad Hasanayn. *The Road to Ramadan.* New York: Quadrangle, 1975, 285 p. (Israel-Arab War, 1973).

Herzog, Chaim. *The War of Atonement, October, 1973.* Boston: Little, Brown, 1975, 300 p.

Pearson, Anthony. *Conspiracy of Silence: The Attack on the U.S.S. Liberty.* London: Quartet Books, 1978, 179 p. (Israel-Arab War, October 1973).

Pryce-Jones, David. *The Face of Defeat: Palestinian Refugees and Guerrillas.* New York: Holt, Rinehart and Winston, 1972, 179 p. (Israel-Arab War, 1967-)

Young, Peter. *Bedouin Command: With the Arab Legion, 1953-1956.* London: Kimber, 1956, 203 p.

Entebbe Airport Raid

Ben Porat, Yesha'yahu; Haber, Eitan *et al. Entebbe Rescue.* Translated by Louis Williams. New York: Dell Publishing, 1977, 346 p.

Hastings, Max. *Yoni: Hero of Entebbe.* New York: Dial Press/J. Wade, 1979, 248 p.

Stevenson, William. *90 Minutes at Entebbe, with Material by Uri Dan.* New York: Bantam Books, 1976, 216 p. (paperback).

Biographies and Case Histories

Carpozi, George, Jr. *A Man of Peace: Anwar Sadat.* New York: Manor Books, 1977, 243 p. (paperback).

Eban, Abba Solomon. *Abba Eban: An Autobiography.* New York: Random House, 1977, 628 p.

Greenfield, Richard Pierce and **Greenfield, Irving A.** *The Life Story of Menachem Begin.* New York: Manor Books, 1977, 242 p. (paperback).

Haber, Eithan. *Menachem Begin: The Legend and the Man.* Translated by Louis Williams. New York: Delacorte Press, 1978, 321 p.

Kiernan, Thomas. *Arafat: The Man and the Myth.* New York: Norton, 1976, 281 p.

Kollek, Teddy and **Kollek, Amos.** *For Jerusalem: A Life.* New York: Random House, 1978, 269 p.

Lau-Lavie, Naftali. *Moshe Dayan. A Biography.* London: Vallentine, Mitchell, 1968, 223 p.

Litvinoff, Barnet. *Weizmann: Last of the Patriarchs.* New York: Putnam, 1976, 288 p.

Pritzke, Herbert. *Bedouin Doctor: The Adventures of a German in the Middle East.* Translated from the German by Richard Graves. London: Weidenfeld and Nicolson, 1957, 257 p.

Rabin, Yitzhak. *The Rabin Memoirs.* Boston: Little, Brown, 1979, 344 p.

Shavit, Maty. *On the Wings of Eagles: The Story of Arik Sharon, Commander of the Israel Paratroopers.* Tel-Aviv: Olive Books, 1972, 160 p. (English ed. of *Arik min ha-tsanhanim*).

Weizman, Ezer. *On Eagle's Wings: The Personal Story of the Leading Commander of the Israeli Air Force.* New York: Macmillan, 1976, 302 p.

Korean War

Gardella, Lawrence. *Sing a Song to Jenny Next: The Incredible True Account of a Secret U.S. Raid into China.* New York: Dutton, 1981, 246 p.

Heinl, Robert Debs, Jr. *Victory at High Tide: The Inchon-Seoul Campaign.* Philadelphia: Lippincott, 1968, 315 p.

Willoughby, Charles Andrew and **Chamberlain, John.** *MacArthur, 1941-1951.* New York: McGraw-Hill, 1954, 441 p.

Vietnam and Southeast Asian Conflicts

Bain, Chester Arthur. *Vietnam: The Roots of Conflict.* Englewood Cliffs, N.J.: Prentice-Hall, 1967, 184 p.

Braestrup, Peter. *Big Story: How the American Press and Television Reported and Interpreted the Crisis of Tet 1968 in Vietnam and Washington.* Garden City, N.Y.: Anchor Press/Doubleday, 1978, 2 v. (paperback).

Burchett, Wilfred G. *The Furtive War: The United States in Vietnam and Laos.* New York: International Publishers, 1963, 224 p.

Burchett, Wilfred G. *Vietnam: Inside Story of the Guerilla War.* New York: International Publishers, 1965, 253 p.

Buttinger, Joseph. *Vietnam: A Dragon Embattled.* New York: Praeger, 1967, 2 v.

Chomsky, Noam and **Herman, Edward S.** *After the Cataclysm: Postwar Indochina and the Reconstruction of Imperial Ideology.* Boston: South End Press, 1979, 392 p. (paperback).

Cooper, Chester L. *The Lost Crusade: America in Vietnam.* New York: Dodd, Mead, 1970, 559 p.

Corson, William R. *The Betrayal.* New York: Norton, 1968. 317 p.

David, Heather. *Operation: Rescue—the First Complete Account of the Daring Drop into North Vietnam to Rescue American Prisoners of War.* New York: Pinnacle Books, 1971, 190 p. (paperback).

Duncan, Donald. *The New Legions.* New York: Random House, 1967, 275 p.

Elford, George Robert. *Devil's Guard.* New York: Delacorte Press, 1971, 297 p.

Fall, Bernard B. *Viet-Nam Witness, 1953-66.* New York: Praeger, 1966, 363 p.

Fenn, Charles. *Ho Chi Minh: A Biographical Introduction.* New York: Scribner, 1973, 144 p.

Gettleman, Marvin E., ed. *Vietnam: History, Documents, and Opinions on a Major World Crisis.* Greenwich, Conn.: Fawcett Publications, 1965, 448 p. (paperback).

Kahin, George McTurnan and **Lewis, John W.** *The United States in Vietnam.* New York: Dial Press, 1967, 465 p.

Kelly, Francis John. *U.S. Army Special Forces, 1961-1971.* Washington: U.S. GPO, 1973, 227 p. (paperback).

Lewy, Guenter. *America in Vietnam.* New York: Oxford University Press, 1978, 540 p.

Mallin, Jay. *Terror in Viet Nam.* Princeton, N.J.: Van Nostrand, 1966, 114 p.

Moore, Robin. *The Green Berets.* New York: Crown Publishers, 1965, 341 p. (fiction).

Nguyen-cao-Ky. *Twenty Years and Twenty Days.* New York: Stein and Day, 1976, 239 p.

O'Daniel, Larry J. *Missing in Action: Trail of Deceit.* New Rochelle, N.Y.: Arlington House, 1979, 304 p.

Paillat, Claude. *Dossier secret de l'Indochine.* Paris: Presses de la Cité, 1964, 407 p.

Patti, Archimedes, L.A. *Why Viet Nam? Prelude to America's Albatross.* Berkeley: University of California Press, 1980, 612 p.

Peers, William R. *The My Lai Inquiry,* New York: Norton, 1979, 306 p.

The Pentagon Papers: As Published by the New York Times, Based on Investigative Reporting by Neil Sheehan. Written by Neil Sheehan et al. Articles and Documents edited by Gerald Gold, Allan M. Siegal et al. New York: Bantam Books, 1971, 677 p.

Pike, Douglas Eugene. *The Viet-Cong Strategy of Terror.* Saigon: U.S. Mission Vietnam, 1970, 126 p.

Radvanyi, Janos. *Delusion and Reality: Gambits, Hoaxes, and Diplomatic One-Upmanship in Vietnam.* South Bend, Ind.: Gateway Editions, 1978, 295 p.

Raskin, Marcus G. and **Fall, Bernard B.,** eds. *The Viet-Nam Reader: Articles and Documents on American Foreign Policy and the Viet-Nam Crisis.* New York: Vintage Books, 1965, 415 p.

Riesen, René. *Jungle Mission.* Translated by James Oliver. New York: Crowell, 1957, 204 p.

Rogers, Bernard William. *Cedar Falls—Junction City: A Turning Point.* Washington: U.S. GPO, 1974, 172 p.

Schemmer, Benjamin F. *The Raid.* New York: Harper and Row, 1976, 326 p.

Shaplen, Robert. *The Lost Revolution: The U.S. in Vietnam, 1946-1966.* Rev. ed. New York: Harper and Row, 1966, 406 p. (paperback).

Sharp, Ulysses S. Grant. *Strategy for Defeat: Vietnam in Retrospect.* San Rafael, Calif.: Presidio Press, 1978, 324 p.

Shawcross, William. *Sideshow: Kissinger, Nixon, and the Destruction of Cambodia,* New York: Simon and Schuster, 1979, 467 p.

Starobin, Joseph Robert. *Eyewitness in Indo-China,* New York: Cameron and Kahn, 1954, 187 p. (paperback).

Trager, Frank N. *Why Viet Nam?* New York: Praeger, 1966, 238 p.

Trinquier, Roger. *La Guerra Moderna Y La Lucha Contra las Guerrillas.* Barcelona: Editorial Herder, 1965, 187 p. (Spanish ed. of *La Guerre Moderne.* Paris, 1961).

Trinquier, Roger. *Modern Warfare: A French View of Counterinsurgency.* Translated from the French by Daniel Lee. New York: Praeger, 1964, 115 p.

Weller, Jac. *Fire and Movement: Bargain-Basement Warfare in the Far East.* New York: Crowell, 1967, 268 p.

Winters, Frank. *"Vietnam Pearl Harbor."* Saga, December 1968, p. 14+.

XIII. WEAPONS
General

Baldwin, Ralph Belknap. *The Deadly Fuze: The Secret Weapons of World War II.* San Rafael, Calif.: Presidio Press, 1980, 332 p.

Bar-Zohar, Michel. *The Hunt for German Scientists.* New York: Avon Books, 1970, 223 p. (paperback).

Bergier, Jacques. *Secret Weapons—Secret Agents.* London: Hurst and Blackett, 1956, 184 p.

Brockway, Fenner and **Mullally, Frederic.** *Death Pays a Dividend.* London: Gollancz, 1945, 158 p.

Canan, James W. *The Superwarriors: The Fantastic World of Pentagon Superweapons,* New York: Weybright and Talley, 1975, 375 p.

Clark, Ronald William. *The Rise of the Boffins.* London: Phoenix House, 1962, 268 p.

Farago, Ladislas. *The Tenth Fleet.* New York: Paperback Library, 1962, 319 p.

Ford, Brian J. *Allied Secret Weapons: The War of Science.* New York: Ballantine Books, 1971, 160 p. (paperback).

Grand Pre, Donn R. *Confessions of an Arms Peddler.* Lincoln, Va.: Chosen Books, 1979, 202 p.

Great Britain. *Guide to Search for Means of Secret Graphic Communication or Sabotage.* London: H.B.M. Government, June 1944, 10 p.

Great Britain, The War Office. *Counter-Sabotage.* London: The War Office, June 1943, 24 p.

Haarer, Alec Ernest. *A Cold-blooded Business.* London: Staples Press, 1958, 208 p.

Hartley, Arthur Bamford. *Unexploded Bomb: A History of Bomb Disposal,* New York: Norton, 1959, 272 p.

Hogg, Ian V. and **King, J.B.** *German and Allied Secret Weapons of World War II.* Edited by Bernard Fitzsimons. Secaucus, N.J.: Chartwell Books, 1976, 127 p.

Hogg, Ian V. *German Secret Weapons of World War II.* London: Arms and Armour Press, 1970, 80 p.

Homze, Edward L. *Arming the Luftwaffe: The Reich Air Ministry and the German Aircraft Industry.* Lincoln: University of Nebraska Press, 1976, 296 p.

Howe, Russell Warren. *Weapons: The International Game of Arms, Money, and Diplomacy.* Garden City, N.Y.: Doubleday, 1980, 798 p.

Infield, Glenn B. *Disaster at Bari,* New York: Ace Books, 1973, 368 p. (paperback).

Jordan, George Racey and **Stokes, Richard L.** *From Major Jordan's Diaries,* New York: Harcourt, Brace, 1952, 284 p.

Kemp, Norman. *The Devices of War.* London: W. Laurie, 1956, 232 p.

Koch, R. W. *The FP-45 Liberator Pistol, 1942-1945.* Long Beach, Calif.: Research, 1976, 116 p.

Lasby, Clarence G. *Project Paperclip: German Scientists and the Cold War.* New York: Atheneum, 1971, 338 p.

Lester, Richard. "Construction of Confederate Ironclad Rams in Great Britain." *Military Collector and Historian.* v. 26, no. 2 (Summer 1974), pp. 72-80.

Liepmann, Heinz. *Poison in the Air.* Translated from the German by Eden and Cedar Paul. Philadelphia: Lippincott, 1937, 308 p.

Low, Archibald Montgomery. *Mine and Countermine.* New York: Sheridan House, 1940, 224 p.

Macrae, Robert Stuart. *Winston Churchill's Toyshop.* Kineton, England: Roundwood Press, 1971, 228 p.

Miller, John Anderson. *Men and Volts at War: The Story of General Electric in World War II.* London: Whittlesey House, 1947, 272 p.

Morpurgo, J. E. *Barnes Wallis: A Biography.* Harlow, England: Longman, 1972, 400 p.

Pawle, Gerald. *Secret Weapons of World War II.* New York: Ballantine Books, 1967, 351 p. (paperback edition of *The Secret War, 1939-45.* London, 1956).

Perry, Geoffrey E. "Russian Hunter-Killer Satellite Experiments." *Military Review,* October 1978, pp. 1-8.

Powell, Edward Alexander. *The Army behind the Army.* New York: Scribner, 1919, 470 p.

Richardson, Cordell. *Uranium Trail East.* London: Bachman and Turner, 1977, 144 p.

Rudel, Hans Ulrich. *Stuka Pilot.* Translated from the German by Lynton Hudson. New York: Bantam Books, 1979, 290 p. (paperback).

Sampson, Anthony. *The Arms Bazaar. From Lebanon to Lockheed,* New York: Bantam Books, 1978, 401 p. (paperback).

Shutt, James A. and **Thatcher, Joseph.** "The Courtenay Coal Torpedo." *Military Collector and Historian,* v. XI, no. 1 (Spring 1959), pp. 7-8.

Stagg, James Martin. *Forecast for Overlord, June 6, 1944.* New York: Norton, 1971, 128 p.

Streetly, Martin. *Confound and Destroy: 100 Group and the Bomber Support Campaign.* London: Mcdonald and Jane's Publishers, 1978, 279 p.

Uhl, Michael and **Ensign, Tod.** *GI Guinea Pigs: How the Pentagon Exposed our Troops to Dangers More Deadly than War: Agent Orange and Atomic Radiation.* New York: Playboy Press, 1980, 256 p.

U.S. Army Air Forces. *The Attack on Crete and Notes on the German XI Air Corps.* n.p.: Director of Intelligence Services, U.S. Army Air Forces, September 1942, 96 p.

U.S. War Department. *Basic Field Manual: Military Intelligence: Identification of United States Armored Vehicles.* Washington, U.S. GPO, 1943, 53 p. (FM30-40).

Weart, Spencer R. *Scientists in Power.* Cambridge: Harvard University Press, 1979, 343 p.

Missiles/Rockets

Collier, Basil. *The Battle of the V-Weapons, 1944-45.* London: Hodder and Stoughton, 1964, 191 p.

Dornberger, Walter. *V-2.* Translated by James Cleugh and Geoffrey Halliday. New York: Viking Press, 1958, 281 p.

Ford, Brian J. *German Secret Weapons: Blueprint for Mars.* New York: Ballantine Books, 1969, 160 p.

Garlinski, Jozef. *Hitler's Last Weapons: The Underground War Against the V1 and V2.* London: J. Friedmann, 1978, 244 p.

Green, William. *Rocket Fighter.* New York: Ballantine Books, 1971, 159 p. (paperback).

Huzel, Dieter K. *Peenemünde to Canaveral.* Englewood Cliffs, N.J.: Prentice-Hall, 1962, 247 p. (autobiographical).

Irving, David John Cawdell. *The Mare's Nest.* Boston: Little, Brown, 1965, 320 p.

McGovern, James. *Crossbow and Overcast.* New York: Morrow, 1964, 279 p.

Mader, Julius. *Geheimnis von Huntsville. Die wahre Karriere des Raketenbarons Wernher von Braun.* 3., verb. Aufl. Berlin: Deutscher Militärverlag, 1965, 427 p.

Orlov, Aleksandr Semenovich. *Sekretnoe oruzhie tret'ego reikha.* Moscow: Nauka, 1975, 159 p.

Pocock, Rowland F. *German Guided Missiles of the Second World War.* New York: Arco Pub., 1967, 120 p.

Nuclear Weapons

Amrine, Michael. *The Great Decision: The Secret History of the Atomic Bomb.* New York: Putnam, 1959, 251 p.

Amrine, Michael. *Secret: A Novel.* Boston: Houghton Mifflin, 1950, 311 p.

Biew, A.M. *Kapitsa: The Story of the British-Trained Scientist who Invented the Russian Hydrogen Bomb.* Translated from the German by James Cleugh. London: F. Muller, 1956, 288 p.

Blumberg, Stanley A. and **Owens, Gwinn.** *Energy and Conflict: The Life and Times of Edward Teller.* New York: Putnam, 1976, 492 p.

Dean, Gordon E. *Report on the Atom: What You Should Know About the Atomic Energy Program of the United States.* New York: Knopf, 1953, 321 p.

Evans, Medford. *The Secret War for the A-Bomb.* Chicago: Regnery, 1953, 302 p.

Feis, Herbert. *Japan Subdued: The Atomic Bomb and the End of the War in the Pacific.* Princeton, N.J.: Princeton University Press, 1961, 199 p.

Goudsmit, Samuel Abraham. *Alsos.* New York: H. Schuman, 1947, 259 p.

Groueff, Stéphane. *Manhattan Project: The Untold Story of the Making of the Atomic Bomb.* Boston: Little, Brown, 1967, 372 p.

Herken, Gregg. *The Winning Weapon: The Atomic Bomb in the Cold War, 1945–1950.* New York: Knopf, 1980, 425 p.

Irving, David John Cawdell. *The Virus House.* London: Kimber, 1967, 288 p.

Knebel, Fletcher and **Bailey, Charles W., II.** *No High Ground.* New York: Harper, 1960, 272 p.

Kunetka, James W. *City of Fire: Los Alamos and the Birth of the Atomic Age, 1943–1945.* Englewood Cliffs, N.J.: Prentice-Hall, 1978, 234 p.

Lamont, Lansing. *Day of Trinity.* New York: Atheneum, 1965, 333 p.

Laurence, William Leonard. *Dawn Over Zero: The Story of the Atomic Bomb.* 2d ed. enl. New York: Knopf, 1946, 289 p.

Laurence, William Leonard. *The Hell Bomb.* New York: Knopf, 1951, 198 p.

Morland, Howard. *The Secret that Exploded.* New York: Random House, 1981, 288 p.

Pash, Boris T. *The Alsos Mission.* New York: Universal Publishing and Distributing Corp., 1970, 256 p. (paperback).

Purcell, John Francis. *The Best-Kept Secret: The Story of the Atomic Bomb.* New York: Vanguard Press, 1963, 188 p.

The Secret History of the Atomic Bomb. Edited by Anthony Cave Brown and Charles B. MacDonald. New York: Dial Press, 1977, 582 p.

Sherwin, Martin J. *A World Destroyed: The Atomic Bomb and the Grand Alliance.* New York: Vintage Books, 1977, 327 p.

Stout, Wesley Winans. *Secret.* Detroit: Chrysler Corp., 1947, 67 p.

Radar and Electronics

Addison, E.B. "The Radio War." *Journal of the Royal United Service Institution,* v. XCII (February–November 1947), pp. 29–42.

Dickson, Paul. *The Electronic Battlefield.* Bloomington: Indiana University Press, 1976, 244 p.

Jones, Reginald Victor. "Lord Cherwell's Judgment in World War II." *Journal of the Royal United Service Institution,* v. CVIII (February 1963), pp. 321–327.

Millar, George Reid. *The Bruneval Raid: Flashpoint of the Radar War.* Garden City, N.Y.: Doubleday, 1974, 221 p.

Palii, Aleksandr Ignat'evich. *Radioelektronnaia bor'ba.* Moscow: Voenizdat, 1974, 271 p.

Price, Alfred. *Instruments of Darkness.* London: Kimber, 1967, 254 p.

Watson-Watt, Robert Alexander, *Sir. Three Steps to Victory: A Personal Account by Radar's Greatest Pioneer.* London: Odhams Press, 1957, 480 p.

INDEX

I. AUTHORS, EDITORS, AND COMPILERS

II. TITLES

III. SOURCES

Allied Forces 3, 63, 165
American Heritage 29, 31, 32, 33, 38, 86, 105, 110, 133, 136, 137, 143, 146, 147, 148, 149
American Historical Review 20, 143, 144
Center for National Security Studies 9, 94
Foreign Affairs 3, 10, 12, 50, 94, 132
Foreign Policy 8, 10, 12, 95, 98, 116, 117, 131
Germany, Federal Republic of. Official Government Documents 45, 63, 84, 121, 180
Germany, Wehrmacht 127, 160, 164
Great Britain, Official Government Documents 19, 22, 30, 36, 50, 66, 86, 92, 151, 167, 190
Infantry Journal 6, 28, 29
International Security 54, 55, 57, 110
Journal of Contemporary History 7, 27, 28, 51, 133, 158, 161, 166
Journal of the Royal United Service Institution 2, 27, 29, 49, 54, 80, 114, 115, 123, 124, 125, 126,
     129, 130, 133, 139, 140, 152, 155, 165, 166, 167, 168, 170, 171, 192
Military Collector and Historian 15, 99, 149, 167, 191
Military Review 9, 11, 20, 191
National Strategy Information Center 6, 9, 54, 55, 80
New York Historical Society 143, 144, 145, 146
Penthouse 12, 18, 76, 79, 91
The Reader's Digest 24, 52, 110
Strategic Review 55, 80, 94
USSR, Official Government Documents 6, 47, 49, 66, 70, 72, 74, 75, 125, 163, 184
U.S. Air Force 92, 138, 172
U.S. Army 12, 23, 28, 30, 51, 54, 72, 77, 92, 139, 172, 184
U.S. Central Intelligence Agency 13, 20, 57, 89, 96
U.S. Congress, House 19, 57, 78, 81, 83, 87, 88, 91, 94, 104, 105, 109, 125
U.S. Congress, Senate 10, 19, 39, 46, 54, 78, 81, 86, 87, 90, 95, 96, 101, 102, 104, 132
U.S. Joint Publications Research Service 2, 5, 6, 18, 26, 38, 39, 45, 46, 52, 71, 80, 83, 85, 89, 90,
     120, 134, 153, 154, 180
U.S. Library of Congress 70, 78, 90, 147
U.S. Marine Corps 81, 92, 130
U.S. Navy 12, 51, 131, 149, 150
U.S. Office of Strategic Services 13, 90, 92
U.S. War Department 13, 25, 30, 48, 88, 92, 106, 139, 150, 166, 167, 191
Wall Street Journal 45, 76, 78, 135
Washington Post 19, 49, 56, 96